BHAKTI BEYOND THE FOREST

BHAKTI BEYOND THE FOREST

Current Research on Early Modern Literatures in North India, 2003-2009

Papers Presented at the Tenth International Bhakti Conference: Early Modern Literatures in North India held at Sapientia, Hungarian University of Transylvania, Miercurea Ciuc, Romania between 22-24 July 2009

Edited by

IMRE BANGHA

MANOHAR
2013

First published 2013

ISBN 978-81-7304-982-8

Published by
Ajay Kumar Jain *for*
Manohar Publishers & Distributors
4753/23 Ansari Road, Daryaganj,
New Delhi 110 002

Printed at
Salasar Imaging Systems
Delhi 110 035

Contents

Preface

The *Tenth International Bhakti Conference: Early Modern Literatures in North India* took place at Sapientia – Hungarian University of Transylvania, in Miercurea Ciuc, Romania between 22 and 24 July 2009. Keeping in line with its tradition it aimed to investigate from a diversity of perspectives how bhakti in general contributed to the formation of early modern literary culture in north India. Without prioritising Hindu ways the papers examined literatures in their social, economic, and political settings, especially those that flourished from 1500 to 1800 CE. in north India. Not more than a decade ago this conference, running under various shorter or longer names, was the only regular international forum to discuss academic achievements on the field of vernacular or devotional literature in early modern India and is still the sole regular venue for the exchange of ideas among scholars of early vernacular India from North America, Western Europe, India, Japan and East Central Europe. It has also been a tradition that the contributors represent all active generations of scholars.

This volume publishes eighteen papers organised into four sections focussing on community formation, social embeddedness, ideology and forms of expression. The individual papers present current research on Hindu, Jain and syncretistic Hindu-Muslim traditions from between the fifteenth and the eighteenth centuries often tracing the antecedents of a certain phenomenon to earlier developments or examining their afterlives. The papers engage with one or several Hindi, Sanskrit, Marathi and Gujarati texts and study their material in the light of a variety of disciplines including theology, linguistics, social history and musicology. In the appendix Winand Callewaert gives an updated list of corrections in *The Millennium Kabīr Vāṇī*, one of the most important volumes to appear about Kabīr.

In the opening article J.S. Hawley investigates how the four teaching traditions or sects that gained acceptance at the court of Savāī Jaisingh were claimed to have been spawned in the south of India and at a certain point transplanted through continuing lineages into the religious life of north India. Recent research by Monika Horstmann showed how this notion had been deployed not just in some abstract sense but as a feature of royal policy, shaping decisions about patronage and legitimacy that had effects in the real world. In his presentation Hawley supplemented Professor Horstmann's exposition by reviewing various ways in which the *catuḥsampradāya* idea came to figure in sectarian sources from Nābhādās and Anantadās onward through the mid-eighteenth century—and, in particular, its complicated and sometimes conflictual relationship to other fourfold formulations: four *vyūha*s, four *akhāḍā*s, four directions, four *pothī*s, and perhaps, in the background, four Vedic *saṁhitā*s.

As part of his ongoing research Dalpat Rajpurohit examines how the Dādūpanth developed its huge devotional anthologies called *Sarvāṅgī.* His research is concerned with tracing the tradition of compiling anthologies and the significance of the Dādūpanth within the *bhakti* movement. He presented a study of the *Sarvāṅgī* tradition, especially the *Sarvāṅgī* of Dādū's first-generation disciple Rajjabdās, the debate about its time of compilation (*c.*1595-1604?), and its content in comparison with the *Sarvāṅgī* of Dādū's third-generation disciple Gopāldās (*c.*1627). The *Dādūpanth* became a centre of heightened literary activity during the last decade of the sixteenth century and at the beginning of the seventeenth century. Sources composed around 1595 indicate that theme-based compilations gained importance in the Dādūpanth at this time. Thus on the one hand, the Dādūpanth anticipates almost all the traditions of anthologies and hagiographies such as the *bhaktamāl* and *parchaī* literature, and on the other it initiated traditions of theme-based anthologies like those of the *Sarvāṅgī* and *Pañcvāṇī*.

James P. Hare traced transmission and reception of Nābhādās's *Bhaktamāl* in manuscript form during the eighteenth and early nineteenth centuries. This late sixteenth-or early-seventeenth century collection of hagiographies praises the qualities of over nine hundred saints and thereby sets the boundaries of a devotional community that far exceeds the 'Rāmānandī' sectarian context in which its author wrote. Inclusivity is among the most conspicuous features of the *Bhaktamāl*. This text gives central importance to the *bhakta*s themselves. The first major commentary on the *Bhaktamāl*, Priyādās's *Bhaktirasabodhinī*, interprets the text from a more clearly defined sectarian perspective. Priyādās's work, completed in 1712, presents a conception of the Vaishnava community that differs sharply from Nābhādās's outlook. He shifts the focus from the devotees to God and emphasizes the importance of the sect or religious order, increases the role of royal patrons and grants spiritual importance to caste. Through the *Bhaktamāl* and its most influential commentary, we witness a debate over the boundaries of a religious community.

In the next article Galina Rousseva-Sokolova compares two versions of Gokulnāth's *Caurāsī vaiṣṇavan kī vārtā*, 'The Lives of the Eighty-four Vaishnavas', the main hagiographical collection of the Puṣṭimārga sect. Its apparent linguistic simplicity and semantic straightforwardness have contributed to its broad popularity. Today it is available in two main printed versions. Discrepancies between both traditions go beyond the scale of verbosity or the editing of repetitive passages and add up to altogether distinct types of construction of the figure of the saint.

Yoshifumi Mizuno presents the various Sanskrit and vernacular incarnations of the story of Candrahāsa, with the famous motive of the letter of death that orders the murder of its bearer, which was even used by Shakespeare. The story of this legendary Vaishnava devotee was particularly popular and has been documented throughout India for a millennium in various languages and mediums, including the *Bhaktamāl* of Nābhādās.

Teiji Sakata writes about how in the eastern part of the Hindi belt Shiva and Parvati have been perceived to assist young couples in their marriage as testified in early Avadhi narratives and in more modern folk songs. Sakata argues that in the context of marriage this child-bearing divine couple has been ubiquitous, transcending sectarian and religious boundaries.

Françoise Mallison's paper examines the attitude towards wealth in the Religious Literature of Medieval Gujarat. In a region with a substantial commercial community, religious groups also had to face the question of wealth. Its complexities are treated in various genres and various religions in Gujarat, such as the *Sudāmāsāra* by the fifteenth-century poet Soma, Ismaili hagiographic tales (especially those concerning Pīr Śams) and hymns dealing with the practice and the theory of the *dasondh* tax. Wealth is ever present, whether as wealth one owes to God's grace as a proof of His blessing or as wealth one has to get rid of in order to earn His favour.

Monika Horstmann and Anand Mishra examines the opinions on the importance of ritual by comparing two contemporaneous approaches by leaders of freshly established Vaishnava sampradayas, namely those in the *Bhaktihaṃsa* and the *Bhaktihetunirṇaya* of Viṭṭhalanātha and in the *Bhaktisaṁdarbha* of Jīva Gosvāmī representing the Vallabhans and the Gauḍīyas of the northern type, respectively. The two religious authorities are informed by different traditions but share their reliance on the *Bhāgavata Purāṇa.* The difference between the two is that 'the Puṣṭimārgīya position has God accord unconditional grace which anticipates all human acts of *bhakti*, whereas the Gauḍīya position ascribes to the *satsaṅg* the power to coerce Bhagavān to give his grace.'

Maya Burger presents Jayatrām's Hindi work on Yoga, the *Jogpradīpakā* (1718), composed in the centre of Krishna devotion, Vrindavan. The author is, however, a Rama-bhakta and his hatha-yoga is imbued with a vision of yoga as leading to the eternal contemplation on Sītārāma (Siyārām). The paper examines Jayatrām's particular view of bhakti and the intricate relationship he establishes between hatha-yoga and bhakti In view of the modern vernacular idioms of yoga in India and indeed worldwide, this study documents the transition from the Sanskrit of the few to a wider public.

Basing her research primarily on Bhartṛhari and Kabīr, Florina Dobre-Brat from Bucharest discusses the development of deified speech from the impersonal to the personal. It was Bhartṛhari who after Vedic antecedents established the Brahman Word Principle (*brahman-śabda-tattva*) that manifests itself as the world. About a thousand years after Bhartṛhari, through the mediation of Nāth yogic tenets, some of Bhartṛhari's concepts became one of the central ideas of Kabīr's poetry. Kabīr's *sabad* is almost impossible to be grasped by any of our faculties but, nevertheless, is the only way to salvation.

Kiyokazu Okita in his paper 'From Ontology to Aesthetics: A Bengal Vaishnava Interpretation of an Upanishadic Passage "So 'ham"' discussed that while other schools of Vedanta interpret this phrase from an ontological perspective, Baladeva Vidyābhūṣaṇa, a Bengal Vaishnava Vedantist of the eighteenth century offered an aesthetic interpretation based on his examination of the *Gopālatāpanyupaniṣad* in his commentary on the *Vedānta-sūtra*s called the *Govinda-bhāṣya*.

An other paper on Bengal Vaishnavism by Rita Jeney discusses the usage of Krishna's names by Jīva Gosvāmī in his Sanskrit *Harināmāmṛta-vyākaraṇa*. Jīva Gosvāmī wrote his grammatical rules in sutras in a way that in addition to the grammatical they also have a theological meaning. The title of the work *The Nectarian Grammar of Hari's Names* or *Immortality with Sanskrit Grammar* reflects the double purpose of the work. The recitation of the rules leads to devotional advancement since Krishna's names are used as grammatical terms. The paper gives a typological analysis of the more than hundred grammatical terms that include Krishna's names. The terminology is original with different levels of coherence with the grammatical phenomena and with the interconnection of its elements.

John E. Cort presents Bhakti in performance among north Indian Digambar Jains. The author demonstrates that bhakti has been central to Jain practice and doctrine for two millennia. The seventeenth through nineteenth centuries witnessed a vibrant intellectual, devotional and cultural flourishing among the Digambar Jains of North India. In cities throughout the region laymen gathered in circles known as *maṇḍalī*s (circles), *goṣṭhī*s (symposia), *śailī*s (poetic lineages) and, in a term that seems to have been specific to Jaipur, *sahelī*s (friends). A study of the contemporary performance of these hymns as part of individual worship at home and in the temple, as well as their performance in weekly devotional gatherings by classically trained *sahelī*s from the late-nineteenth through the twentieth century, indicates that the hymns are divided into two main genres, the devotional hymns (*bhajan*s) and the spiritual hymns (*adhyātma pad*s).

Imre Bangha's paper on Kabīr's prosody refutes the widespread belief that the uneducated Kabīr did not care much about poetic metre. Taking into consideration syncopation and making minor emendations and excisions often suggested by other early manuscripts, most of Kabīr's stanzas can be reconstructed as being written in one or another variety of the *caupāī* or in the *sār* metre. Theṣe two forms account for 85 per cent of the poems in the *Millennium Kabīr Vāṇī*. By excising hypermetrical words one can systematically reconstruct more concise, more powerful poems, which later performers amplified by exclamations, explanatory pronouns, phrases and names of God. As poems became more and more detached from their original environment of performance, explanatory amplifications helped their understanding or their appropriation.

Indira Y. Junghare's essay examines in the context of a north American centre of Hindu worship how the language of devotion transcends diverse linguistic structures. The languages of the worship related to the Hindu-Muslim saint Saibaba from Shirdi, Marathi and partially Hindi, are not only present in the liturgical worship but also as inspiring decoration of the temple and as general religious terminology embedded into English. The paper presents how the phonetics, morphology, syntax and semantics of the Marathi *ārtī*s becomes simplified through inculturation in Minnesota.

Florence Pasche Guignard in her paper surveys the terminology of 'body' in Mīrābāī's *Padāvalī* with reference to female ornaments and cosmetics as a particular way to express devotion. The songs attributed to the Rajasthani poetess contain ample references to adornment, where ornaments can be referred to as obstacles on the spiritual path but can also take on a more positive meaning as symbols of anticipation of union. This positive attitude seems to be less marked in poetry attributed to male authors.

Hiroko Nagasaki's essay presents the similarities and differences between the Hindi *mātric chand*s, forms inherited from Apabhramsha and analysed through Sanskrit prosodic rules, and the Perso-Arabic moraic metre. Already Jagannathprasad Bhanu pointed out some parallelism between early Hindi and Urdu moraic metres showing that some of the *chand*s used by Tulsīdās, such as the *gītikā, harigītikā*, etc., overlap with Persian patterns used by early Sufis. The author shows that many other early forms, including *dohā*, can be analysed in a similar way.

Takako Tanaka in her paper discusses the fundamental principles to realize the most elaborated and highly artistic performance in *samāj-gāyan* as the means of bhakti. The word *śṛṅkhlā* literally means 'chain', that is, 'a series of links or rings connected or fitted into one another' and this definition provides a fitting image for the structure of *samāj-gāyan*. Even though the use of *śṛṅkhlā* by Bhatt performers was seen only in its textual and liturgical aspect, the singing form consisted of a series of connected musical and textual units that reminds one of the *śṛṅkhlā* of music. A chain-like structure in both musical and textual terms can be observed as a sequence of lines and stanzas, slow and fast sections, main singer *mukhiyā* and secondary singer *jhelā* alterations. On a higher level, it is a sequence of verses corresponding to the sequence of Krishna's *līlā*. *Śṛṅkhlā* denotes all the combinations of the texts, the divine sports and the musical factors sung in each *samāj* ritual.

IMRE BANGHA

Notes on the Transliteration and the Dates

Indian terms that are familiar in English and can be found in the *Oxford English Dictionary* as well as modern Indian names are normally spelt in English. This means that terms and names such as bhakta, hatha-yoga, samadhi, sampradaya, raga, Krishna, Shiva, etc., are treated as English words. Other technical terms, titles of works and quoted passages are italicized and spelt as in the original language with diacritics. Pre-nineteenth-century Indian proper names, including names of sects and institutions, are transliterated with diacritics. They will be capitalized but not italicized. When otherwise anglicized Indic terms are part of a longer phrase or are used in a non-English sense (e.g. *rāga* in the sense of 'passion' or 'attachment'), they will be italicized and provided with diacritics. In this way the same word depending on its context may appear in different forms. The reader will find the word sampradaya in a general sense, Nimbāditya Sampradāy as a proper name and *catuḥ* or *cār sampradāy(a)* as part of an Indic phrase.

The transliteration for terms in Hindi, Urdu and Sanskrit follows those of the dictionaries of McGregor, Platts and Monier-Williams respectively with a few deviations from their systems. Whenever possible, *anusvāra*s are spelt out as homorganic nasals. In other cases the *anusvāra* sign is transliterated by an *ṁ* not with a subscript but with a superscript dot evoking the Devanagari form of the *anusvāra*. A vocalic *r̥* is marked with a subscript circlet instead of a dot. Monier-Williams' *sh* is changed into *ṣ* with a subscript dot while Platts' *sh* will be an *ś*. In this way subscript dots more consistently stand for retroflex sounds. When *anusvāra*s stand for nasalization and not for homorganic nasals, such as in final position in non-Sanskritic words or before nasals in manuscripts, they are marked as nasalization. If a word is current in the same context both in Sanskrit and Hindi, then a Sanskritic transliteration is preferred over the Hindi one. In the transliteration of Hindi and Urdu words the indistinct final sound will be spelt as *a* after clusters of consonants with the exception of nasal-plosive clusters, such as *panth*, *aṅg*, etc. If the same phenomenon happens in the middle of long words, the *a* may be spelt out, as has become a tradition in words like Anantadās or *Aṅgabandhu*. In a few other Sanskritic words, such as *pradīpakā*, this *a* is also retained. When old Hindi poetry is cited, the modern silent *a* is always transliterated since it has a metrical value and is still pronounced in recitation. When, however, individual words or short phrases are quoted from poetry, this *a* is treated as in regular Hindi words.

Dates in the book, if not indicated otherwise, refer to the Common Era. The Vikram Era or other dating of manuscripts and works are indicated only occasionally. The Common Era years are achieved by subtracting 57 years from the *Vikram Saṁvat*, if no Indic month is specified in it.

CONSTRUCTING BHAKTI COMMUNITIES

CHAPTER 1

The Four Sampradayas—and Other Foursomes[1]

JOHN STRATTON HAWLEY

One of the main purposes of the idea of 'the bhakti movement' is to show how the striking innovations that made their appearance in the bhakti landscape of north India around the sixteenth century were actually continuous with earlier religious formations further south. A principal feature of this narrative, one that makes its appearance in countless textbooks and monographs, is the concept of the four teaching traditions—the *catuḥ* or *cār sampradāy*(*a*). Its purpose is to show how the theological and initiatory lineages established by Rāmānuja, Nimbārka, Madhva, and Viṣṇusvāmī from about the eleventh century onwards in south India travelled north some centuries afterwards and set up shop in a new way. When this genealogy is exposited with maximum clarity, we learn that each of these southern orders had an anchorage in primordial time—Śrī, Sanakādi (Sanaka et al.), Brahma and Rudra—and that their more recent expressions, all northern, were shaped by another set of four religious leaders: respectively, Rāmānand, Keśav Kāśmīrī Bhaṭṭ, Caitanya and Vallabhācārya.

This is one of the great ideas in the historiography of Indian religion and, like the gods themselves, part of its greatness is measured by the fact that it floats some distance above the ground. As far as I have been able to determine, there is no evidence that any south Indian observer of the shape of Vaishnava religion ever perceived these four traditions as a group until very recent times. Rather, these bedrock formations, these four great pillars, seem to have been added to the edifice they are said to support rather late—a figment of the north Indian imagination.

But whose north Indian imagination? One major location is obviously Rāmānandī: the idea of the four sampradayas occurs both in the undated *Pīpā Parcaī* of Anantadās (his *parcaī* of Nāmdev dates to 1588) and in the *Bhaktamāl* of Nābhādās (*c.* 1600). Another possible source is Gauḍīya: the *Gauragaṇoddeśadīpikā* of Kavikarṇapūra, for which we have 1544 or, more persuasively, 1576 as possible dates. The *Gauragaṇoddeśadīpikā* argues that the Caitanya tradition can be traced back to that of the Madhvites. A third *sāmpradāyik* tradition that may early have been involved in putting forward this idea is that of the Vallabhites. Here, the document to be reckoned with is the *Sampradāyapradīpa* of Dvivedī Gadākhya, more commonly known as Gadādhara Bhaṭṭa, who says that he writes this 'Lamp of the Sects' (or does he really mean just one sect?) from Vrindavan in 1553 (vs 1610). For symmetry and full representation, it would be good if there were also a Nimbārkī source that might go back to the sixteenth century, but I know of none. We do find several other texts sometimes claimed as pertaining to this generative moment—the Caitanyite *Sampradāyabodhinī* of Manohardās, the Rāmānandī *Rāmapaṭala* and the Vallabhite *Sakalācāryamatasaṅgraha*—but they all appear to have been written later on.[2] At least one of these, the *Sampradāyabodhinī*, was composed, understandably enough, during the period when the Kachvāhā court of Jai Singh II attempted to use this four-sampradaya rubric as the basis for actual state policy. This is the moment that Monika Horstmann has exposited so brilliantly in her recent *magnum opus*, *Der Zusammenhalt der Welt*.[3] Others on the list may also not be as early as their dates proclaim.

In another essay, I have had a chance to explore one important aspect of the four-sampradaya idea—its eagerness to claim a past that was deep in a specifically southern way.[4] Here, instead, I will focus not on the sampradaya aspect of the four-sampradaya idea but on its fourness. In an Indian setting, it seems obvious that the number four gestures at something stable, permanent and complete, and that is certainly a major facet of the beauty of the concept of the four sampradayas. But we must remember that the power of such an ideal is actually generated by a world in which things are decidedly unstable, impermanent and incomplete. Let us, therefore, consider how several early representations of the four-sampradaya paradigm make this point about contingency themselves, revealing the uneven turf on which they stand precisely at the moment when they implicitly deny it. We will conclude by trying to imagine what other 'foursomes' may have stood in the background as the four-sampradaya idea was formed, giving weight and value to this new conception of four-square historical perfection as it emerged in the course of the sixteenth century.

The Partialness and Partiality of the Four Sampradayas

As we have seen, most early articulations of this paradigm originate from within the boundaries of the paradigm itself—one of the communities implied therein—but for one early statement of the four-sampradaya idea, this is not so. This makes it an attractive place from which to begin our survey. The text in question is the famous *Dabistān-i Mazāhib* (School of Religions), written in the middle of the seventeenth century by Mūbad Śāh (a.k.a. Saiyid Ẓu'lfiqār al-Ḥusainī), an adherent of the Āzar Kaivānī branch of the Zoroastrian Parsi community.[5] A substantial proportion of this Persian digest of 'world religions' was dedicated to giving an account of the religious life of the Hindus, so Mūbad Śāh devoted a chapter to groups he called Vaishnavas and Vairāgīs, these categories corresponding roughly to the distinction between laypersons and renunciants. It sounds like a clear and well-balanced approach but, in fact, Mūbad Śāh displays a certain degree of taxonomic discomfort as he pursues it. He notes that while the Vairāgīs 'profess to be Vaishnavas', they actually draw their membership from 'whoever among the Hindus, Muselmans, or others, wishes'.[6] We will see how this bears upon our theme.

Mūbad Śāh uses the rubric of the four sampradayas to give structure to his descriptive accounts of both Vaishnavas and Vairāgīs. In fact, he uses it in such a way that it bridges the two. Although he does not mention the term itself (*cār sampardā*) until the beginning of his discussion of the Vairāgīs,[7] he makes it clear that he understands this list of 'four classes' to pertain as well to the Vaishnava communities he has already sketched—'as before said', to use his own words.[8] This fulcrum-like moment is actually the only time Mūbad Śāh provides a list as such (the four sequential nouns given in Column 2 below), but it corresponds tolerably well to what he has already explained about the Vaishnavas in a more discursive way (drawn together in Column 1):

[Vaishnavas]	*[Vairāgīs]*
Madhu acārī	*Rāmānuja*
Rāmānandī	*Nimānuja*
Harbayāntī	*Mādhoācārac*
Rādhā-balabī	*Rādhā-balabī.*[9]

It is likely that the term Mūbad Śāh heard as Harbayāntī actually designated the Nimbārkīs and that the name Nimānuja refers to the same group.[10] One can understand how a verbal report might have produced these 'deformities', especially if the interlocutor was not himself a member of the Nimbārka or Nimbāditya Sampradāy. The disparity between Rāmānand and Rāmānuja in the terminology of self-designation used by the Rāmānand Sampradāy is a familiar one but it is intriguing that Mūbad Śāh's source(s) seem to have conflated the Vallabhite community with that of the Rādhāvallabhīs. Mūbad is interested in the fact that members of this sect do not observe the *ekādaśī* fast as other Vaishnavas do, and 'deliver their wives to the disposition of their preceptors and masters, and hold this praiseworthy'.[11] The former fits the theology of Hit Harivaṁś and the Rādhāvallabhī community but the latter sounds like a reference to a feature of Vallabhite practice that became the butt of severe criticism two centuries later in the so-called Maharaja Libel Case of 1861.

The list of conversation partners that Mūbad Śāh gives at the end of his section on the Vairāgīs suggests that at least some of his information came from an interview with a Rāmānandī Vairāgī called Nārāin Dās that took place in Lahore in 1642 (AH 1052).[12] He also reports as relevant three conversations he had in Gujarat in 1640,[13] but the fact that these were with members of the Pirānā community and that they are reported at the very end of the section on Vairāgīs, where the four-sampradaya frame is no longer explicitly in play, suggests that these informants were probably not among the sources for what Mūbad Śāh tells us about the four sampradayas themselves. His Rāmānandī informant, by contrast, seems just right for this role. And given the great interest in the Madhvite community that became manifest among Caitanyite theologians at the time of the disputations surrounding Savāī Jai Singh, one is impressed by the relatively ample theological detail Mūbad Śāh is able to supply about the Madhvites more than half a century earlier. It far exceeds anything he has to say about the Nimbārkīs or (Rādhā)Vallabhites, where we find a paucity that matches his unsure grasp on their names.

Thus, at the same time that Mūbad Śāh is endeavouring to make the four sampradayas work as his overarching framework, he also gives us hints that he commands only a partial view of the whole. It is a tribute to his ethnographic honesty that he does not try to convince us of more than he knows, stretching the canopy of the four sampradayas over more than it was intended to cover. His conversation with a Rāmānandī makes it natural for him to move on from his listing of the four sampradayas into an exposition of Kabīr, but he doesn't stop there. Kabīr brings Nāmdev to mind,[14] and from there he quickly moves on—via Parrah Kaivān, an important figure in his own Āzar Kaivānī community—to other Vairāgīs associated with the Pirānā Khojās of Gujarat, whom he had visited in 1640.

So by the time Mūbad Śāh has finished with the Vairāgīs and is ready to move on to the Cārvākas—an astonishing leap, and one that shows how unapologetically he navigated between oral and written sources—he has revealed the appealing range of the four-sampradaya concept and at the same time displayed its limitations. If his informant(s) used this idea as a way to relate laypeople to ascetics, he is evidently glad to follow suit. But he also seems to recognize that the four-sampradaya rubric doesn't entirely capture the full range of what might come in under the heading of Vairāgīs; and he notes the limitations of the latter concept, too, since it leans more specifically toward Vaishnavism (he notes the doctrine of the avatars) than would be indicated by the full range of self-identified 'Vairāgīs' whom he surveys.[15] He stops short of asserting independent sectarian identities for Kabīrpanthīs, Pirānā Satpanthīs[16] and the Punjabi devotees of Nāmdev, focusing on individual exemplary Vairāgīs (we might say Sants), but it is striking that he allows himself to stray well beyond whatever boundaries might be implied by the idea of the four sampradayas. Given this and his occasional caveats along the way, it seems plausible that we should read this narrative sequence not simply as run-on prose but as something more artful in its desire not to be overly constrained by the categories he specifically employs.

Yet we may be giving Mūbad Śāh too much credit. Fuzzy borders of this kind are nothing new in the discourse of the four sampradayas. We also encounter them in each of the sixteenth-century sources we now proceed to review. The first of these comes from the Rāmānandī writer, Anantadās. In one way, on account of his sectarian location, Anantadās seems to write from 'inside' the four sampradayas, yet in another way he allies himself with a broader tradition, one that is not disciplined by *guru-śiṣya* relations. Anantadās appeals to the four-sampradaya motif only once in his writings—at the end of his *parcaī* on Pīpā and his wife Sītā, which is the longest of the *parcaī*s that have come down to us under his name. This may be significant. Shorter *parcaī*s can end as they will, it seems, but in this more comprehensive piece of hagiographical writing, Anantadās seems to have felt the need for a similarly more comprehensive conclusion. Toward the end of the thirty-fifth and final chapter, he says (in the edition of Winand Callewaert)

cāri saṁpradā bhītari āvai; so bhagatā̃ hari kai mani bhā̃vai.
sadā kulīna kahāvai soī; mukati nahi tau agati na hoī.

People who come within the four teaching traditions—
such bhaktas are pleasing to Hari.
They'll always be accounted as of good family,
finding release, or at least not being lost.[17]

Here, as in the *Dabistān*, an appreciation of the broader context is important to understanding Anantadās's perspective on the four sampradayas. After this *caupāī* he gives us three *caupāī*s that concern his own lineage (35.26-28); soon afterwards, as if his package has now been suitably wrapped, he is done (35.29-32). Even more significant is the passage that precedes our four-sampradaya verse, for Anantadās begins to gesture in the direction of closure already in verse 11, immediately after he has completed his narrative of Pīpā *per se*. At that point he introduces a framework that also has four parts to it—the four directions. Having explained at length how Pīpā's sphere of bhakti influence extends as far west as Dvārakā (7.12-12.14; 35.1-10), he now mentions bhaktas associated with the east (Kabīr and Raidās), south (Nāmdev) and north (Dhanā, 35.12-13). These are followed by a larger tally of bhaktas who have no specific association with the points of the compass, making a total of sixteen in all (35.12-17), and a passage (35.18-24) that expands the lens even further, to an indeterminate number of other bhaktas (*jan*) who people the Kali domain (*kali paisār*, v. 18).

Thus we see that for Anantadās the four-sampradaya rubric takes its place in a larger landscape that is structured by another foursome (the directions), a four-squared listing (the sixteen bhaktas[18]), and much more. Against this background it becomes clear that in this narrative formulation, at least, the four sampradayas serve only as a way for Anantadās to introduce his own lineage. Otherwise, he has no concern about what the *sāmpradāyik* standing of a bhakta might be, and he makes a fair amount of room for an element of indeterminacy in his reporting, emphasizing the fact that his knowledge has its limits (*kali paisāra bhaye jaṁna jete; aura na jā̃naū̃ hū̃hĩge kete*, 35.18). This is the overwhelming and somewhat amorphous bhakti ambience that made it easy for subsequent interpreters to head for a word like *āndolan* or movement in describing the whole.

We find a rather different deployment of the motif of the four sampradayas in Nābhādās's *Bhaktamāl*. It is notable both for its important contribution to shaping the overall text and at the same time for the fact that, as in Anantadās's *Pīpā Parcaī*, it does not entirely command the terrain that surrounds it. This time, perhaps, the partial range of the four-sampradaya concept is understandable, for Nābhādās takes us back over the broad sweep of world history in a way that Anantadās does not. How could the four sampradayas pertain to epochs that preceded the Kaliyuga, where they do not belong? Yet because of that very fact—the clear Kaliyuga delimitation of the four-sampradaya rubric—it is all the more striking that Nābhā makes an effort to link this concept to the praise formula with which he began his exposition of bhaktas who have peopled the world from the start. This was praise offered to the twenty-four embodied forms through which the Lord has historically 'played' (*līlā*) in the world, beginning with the ten avatars of Vishnu (*chappay* [hereinafter §] 5). Nābhā recalls these twenty-four after many *chappay*s in which no mention is made of them, and does so precisely at the point when he commences his narrative of the Kaliyuga. By means of this linkage and in the text itself, he makes it clear that the force that these twenty-four avatars once exerted is now supplanted by that of the founders (*gurumukh*) of the four sampradayas (§27), whom he is about to list individually. Before doing so, however, he makes this general point:

> *caubīsa prathama hari bapu dhare tyaũ caturvyūha kaliyuga pragaṭa.*

> Earlier Hari took on twenty-four bodies—
> so, in this Kali age, four formations.[19]

Vijay Pinch has written persuasively about what happens next, arguing that a main part of Nābhā's purpose, after announcing the four-sampradaya idea, is actually to mute its force so as to introduce a considerably less restrictive interpretation of the field in which bhakti operates. Pinch sees this implicitly Brahmanical formula as implying a well-defined lineage of celibate renunciants, while Nābhādās himself, by contrast, was probably not, strictly speaking, a sadhu but a bhakta in a more general sense.[20] I am not sure I can follow Pinch all the way down this road, but it is clear that Nābhā's own sense of the term sampradaya allows him to gloss it not only with a good Sanskrit term like *mārga* but also with the Persian *jamāt*. The phrase he uses is *śrī acāraj jāmāt*

(§33). The broader point Pinch makes is absolutely correct: the four-sampradaya motif serves well as a suturing device for the overall narrative but does not determine its particulars. Though Nābhādās gives it a more elaborate exposition than Anantadās or, for that matter, Mūbad Śāh, and brings to bear the high Pāñcarātra language of *vyūha*, he lets his narrative widen to embrace not only the initiation-bestowing Rāmānuja but the four *mahant*s who are remembered as having shared Rāmānuja's own initiation (*gurubandhu*, §31). In a phrase that may make us recall Anantadās, he compares them to the elephants that anchor the world's four compass points (*diggaj*), for they lend stability to 'the land of bhakti' (*bhakti bhūmi*, §31).

Like Anantadās and Mūbad Śāh, in their different ways, Nābhā displays little anxiety about the fact that the *sāmpradāyik* rubric only covers a certain amount of the terrain laid out under the general heading of the Kaliyuga. His treatment of Caitanya is a case in point. Caitanya appears later in the *Bhaktamāl* but when he does, Nābhādās suggests no link between him and the four sampradayas. Rather, he pairs the great ecstatic with Nityānanda, allowing the two of them to bask in their own light as beacons to Bengal (*gauḍades*, *pūrba mahī*), reformers in the face of hypocrisy (*pākhaṇḍ*).[21] Unlike the cosmopolitan four-sampradaya formulation, this is a regional narrative, and we also find regional groupings elsewhere in Nābhā's text.

Looking back over what we have seen so far, we begin to wonder whether, narratively speaking, a certain amount of untamed turf is necessary to display the gloriously trimmed order of the four sampradayas, just as a fairway scarcely counts as a proper fairway unless it is surrounded by a good bit of rough. Nothing in the notion of the four sampradayas *per se* requires this; in fact, its four-part shape suggests a certain universal coverage instead. Yet the way Mūbad Śāh, Anantadās and Nābhādās have used this motif in practice suggests that it may have been felt to work best where there was still more turf to be described but not absorbed. Anantadās has made us aware, however, that it was not always a simple contrast between a four-square order and whatever undifferentiated matter remained. Additional four-part schemes could be brought to bear in the cause of making sense of some of the terrain that lay beyond the four sampradayas. Our next example will display that pattern even more clearly. Here, a certain amount of rough persists, but our author constructs a whole new nine-hole course alongside the first—or rather, needless to say, a four-hole course, the better to suit the part.

The author of whom I am speaking is the Dādūpanthī Rāghavdās, who composed his massive *Bhaktamāl* either in 1660 or in the second decade of the eighteenth century (to be specific, in either 1713 or 1720).[22] Like his predecessors, Rāghavdās foregrounds the four-sampradaya scheme, and like Nābhādās he depicts it as providing the key to religious order in the Kaliyuga.[23] Some rough persists—and no wonder, considering that Rāghavdās is working with a much larger field of Kaliyuga data than any of his predecessors. Agar Chand Nahta, who prepared the edition of Rāghavdās's *Bhaktamāl* published by the Rajasthan Oriental Research Institute, makes rather a point of this by designating two sections of the work as being general in nature (*samudāī*),[24] and Rāghavdās himself gestures in this direction by using the phrases *sant sakal* and *sādh sakal*.[25]

Yet what is fascinating about Rāghavdās is that he doesn't stop there. Not only does he make room for separate lists of *saṁnyāsī*s and *nāth*s as part of the bhakti repertoire of the Kali age,[26] but he also takes the four-part scheme of religious order that he has already introduced and uses it to generate another. Rāghavdās calls this new quartet the *cār panth*, distinguishing it explicitly from its parent or pair by saying that it is *nirguṇ* in nature, whereas the four sampradayas had been of the opposite sort—*saguṇ*. Like Nābhādās and Mūbad Śāh in their different ways, Rāghavdās creates an analogy between the householder and celibate formations by designating them with a single scheme and a single name: he calls the leaders of both quartets *mahant*s. Borrowing a formulation that we meet in the *Bhaktamāl* of Nābhādās, he says that just as the *mahant*s of the four sampradayas were *vyūha*s to the present age—flanks of a single divine presence in the old Pāñcarātra military metaphor—so have the four *nirguṇ mahant*s also become manifest, presumably at a later stage.[27] Either the listeners are being asked to recall his own earlier passage about the four sampradayas in a structural way (though that is now many *caupāīs* past), or they are being asked to perceive a temporal relationship between the earlier *saguṇī* (or as he says, *triguṇī*) *ācārya*s and the *nirguṇī mahant*s who have followed them in more recent times.[28]

Either way—and they are not mutually exclusive—this is an arresting formulation. On the one hand, it echoes the technique Nābhā had used to introduce the four sampradayas, but, on the other, it achieves something new: it brings the language of *panth*s alongside that of sampradayas. What are these *panth*s? To use Rāghavdās's own words, they are *nānak kabīr dādū jagan*, with the fourth of these terms designating the Nirañjanī Panth.[29] As Rāghavdās is a Dādūpanthī, his special purpose is, understandably, to create a rubric that will allow for a substantial exposition of the bhaktas he sees as being encompassed by the Dādūpanth. He allots 69 *caupāī*s to this task, more than he gives to the other three *panth*s taken together. Yet it is striking that he keeps Dādū in the third position rather than advancing him to the first, as you might think he would. Is it because this formula did not originate in Dādūpanthī usage, or perhaps because it was intended to refer to a sense of chronology that remembers Nānak and Kabīr as having preceded Dādū? Could it even be that the prestige of the *Granth Sāhib* as a classifying text—or its wide availability—was such that Rāghavdās accepted its order of things, placing Nānak (for Sikhs, the many Nānaks) first, and allowing Kabīr to appear as pre-eminent among the *bhagat*s? Of course, for Rāghavdās the *guru/bhagat* distinction disappears, but it is noteworthy that the order remains.

If we favour an early eighteenth-century date for Rāghavdās's *Bhaktamāl*, then it accords with several other signs that certain groups of Dādūpanthīs, especially the Uttarādhās with their Punjabi connections, were beginning to interact with and pattern themselves after the Sikhs.[30] The trend continued into the nineteenth century. Do we have something new and distinctive here or can we fit Rāghavdās comfortably in the lineage of the other authors we have studied so far? Whatever one decides, it is apparent that the rhetoric of the four sampradayas, as we meet it in Rāmānandī writings, is no longer entirely determinative of the way the concept will be understood and contextualized beyond the Rāmānandī pale.

Among Dādūpanthīs, one can see this not only in Rāghavdās but in the compositions of his contemporary, Sundardās. Sundardās was the *panth*'s best known literary figure in Rāghavdās's time, and it happens that he also refers to the *cār sampradāy*, although he does not use that phrase explicitly. We meet this reference in one of Sundardās's *savaiyā*s and there too, as in Rāghavdās, we sense that the four sampradayas were a well-accepted feature of the religious landscape.[31] As in Rāghavdās, they receive an apparently neutral treatment, as if from somewhat outside the ranks—and yet, not in an entirely uncritical way. Adopting a familiar ploy, Sundardās makes the point that to be a true exponent of one of these communities, one must live up to the real meaning of the names they bear, suggesting that this is not always the case in practice,

rāmānandī hoi tau tū̃ tucchānanda tyāga kari
rāma nāma bhaji rāmānanda hī kaū̃ dhyāiye;
nimbādatī hoi tau tū̃ kāmanā kaṭuka tyāgi
amṛta kau pāna kari adhika aghāiye;
madhvācārī hoi tau tū̃ madhura mata kaū̃ bicāri
madhura madhura dhuni hṛdai madhva gāiye;
biṣṇusvāmī hoi tau tū̃ byāpaka biṣṇu kaū̃ jā̃ni
sundara biṣṇu kaū̃ bhaji biṣṇu maĩ samāiye.

Are you a Rāmānandī—someone who joys in Rām?
Then leave the joys of baser things,
Sing the name of Rām,
And keep the joys of Rām in your mind.
Are you a Nimbārkī—from a *nīm* tree he saw the sun?
Then leave behind your bitter lusts
And drink of immortality.
Let that satisfy your thirst.
Are you a Madhvācārī—your guru, the apostle of sweetness?
Then let your thoughts be sweet ones.
In your heart sing only sounds
Where sweetness, sweetness reigns.

Are you a Viṣṇusvāmī—having Vishnu as master?
Then know there's nowhere Vishnu is not.
Sing to Vishnu, Sundar says—
In Vishnu be contained, be content.

While Rāghavdās makes it clear that he is a close reader of Nābhādās, suggesting that he may be indebted to Nābhā for the way in which he understands the concept of the four sampradayas, here we seem to have moved somewhat further away. The question then arises as to whether there may be yet other locales and institutional settings where the Rāmānandīs did not provide the only pipeline to the four-sampradaya paradigm. I would, therefore, like to present a final example of the theme we have been pursuing—the idea that each usage of the four-sampradaya theme conceals a particular perspective that belies the seemingly even-handed catholicity of the rubric itself. As we have seen, even the placid-sounding Sundardās turns out to have his own point of view and one with a little edge to it.

The text I have in mind is the *Sampradāyapradīpa*, which announces that it was written by a Dvivedī called Gada—or, more familiarly, Gadādhara Bhaṭṭa—in vs 1610 (CE 1553). As with Rāghavdās, however, this date is somewhat problematic. The *Sampradāyapradīpa* may indeed be a sixteenth-century text, as its date proclaims, but there is also the possibility that it should be more closely aligned with Rāghavdās's own period and identified as a pre-dated product of the second half of the seventeenth century. It is at this time that the oldest clearly dated manuscript copies begin to appear.[32]

The *Sampradāyapradīpa* is a Sanskrit treatise (note the shift in medium) that is considerably shorter than the *Bhaktamāl* of Rāghavdās, but no less whole-heartedly devoted to the task of expositing a worldview framed by the idea of the four sampradayas. Gadādhara plays with that notion in each of the three internal chapters that provide the main substance of this five-chapter composition. Yet he too compromises the taxonomical tidiness that the four-sampradaya idea seems intended to provide. He modifies it in such a way that the Caitanyite community emerges as a sub-sampradaya in the lineage of Viṣṇusvāmī; he adds in

the sixteenth century would be an appropriation of an earlier effort on the part of Vallabhites themselves, even if it ended up not being as consistent, exclusive or forceful as these Vallabhites might have wished.[34] To follow our hypothesis about the Vallabhite-Caitanyite rivalry, perhaps the Puṣṭimārgīs felt the need to claim this connection even in the face of Vallabha's own somewhat derogatory comments about Viṣṇusvāmī (*Subodhinī* 3.32.37) on account of the fact that their position of power in relation to the Kachvāhā/Mughal state was considerably less secure than that of the Gauḍīyas in the sixteenth century itself. Or, to read all this—including the *Sampradāyapradīpa*—as a later development, perhaps the Vallabhites were trying to make mincemeat of certain Gauḍīya claims to a past that involved the Madhva Sampradāya. But however one reads the *Sampradāyapradīpa*—whether as a sixteenth-century document or as one that was composed toward the end of the seventeenth century when its manuscripts first mention the dates of their being copied, it is clear that its articulation of the idea of the four sampradayas carries an element of fuzziness that reminds us of other usages that we have encountered. It is not the same sense of fuzziness or partiality, certainly, but it belongs to the same conceptual family.

The Four Sampradayas and Other Foursomes

If the boundaries built into and around the idea of the four sampradayas are indeed so fuzzy (perhaps inevitably so), why did it make sense to articulate this doctrine of four teaching traditions in the first place? Why not some completely different rubric, perhaps an elaboration or recasting of the three-acharya (or, alternately, three *bhāṣyakāra*) idea that actually does seem to have been a familiar part of southern thinking: Śaṅkara, Rāmānuja and Madhva?[35] In concluding, I would like to return to the metaphor of golf and speculate about what other 'foursomes' may already have been out there on the course, laying out the terms that caused this new conception to make its way onto the great fairway of Indian intellectual life in the way that it did—as a foursome. As anyone who has ever played the game can attest, other foursomes can often be almost as important to one's sense of well-being as the members of one's own God-given constellation. As the idea of the *cār sampradāy* was first shaped and later developed and modified, what other meanings of 'fourness' was it intended to absorb, qualify or reject? Let me briefly name four possibilities and then return to put a little flesh on the bones of each. They are:

(1) the kind of firm, foundational 'fourness' that characterizes the golden age of the Satyayuga
(2) the four Vedic Saṁhitās and the lineages of Brahmins who were charged with their upkeep and articulation, together with other attempts to mimic or displace the model they represented
(3) the idea of the four directions, both in a general sense and in regard to the way this motif had been used to structure pre-existing monastic communities
(4) the general idea of order to which the number four makes an appeal, yet with a specific correlate: the use of this number to box in Kabīr and all that he stood for.

The Satyayuga

One of the interesting features of the discourse that surrounds the *cār sampradāy* formulation as we meet it in Anantadās, Nābhādās, and Rāghavdās is that the Kaliyuga is not explicitly separated out as the fourth world-age. Considering our theme, you might think it would be. Instead, however, the Kaliyuga is depicted not so much as the latest example of how time follows a path of ever-worsening degeneracy but as a contrast to a more generalized, less striated prior age when things were substantially different—a time when one did not need the special protections provided by the four sampradayas to be able to survive. We have seen this pattern in a kernel form in Anantadās's *Pīpā Parcaī*, with his mention of the purity, dignity or stability that is conferred by belonging to one of the four sampradayas as against anything available in the past. We meet the motif in a more developed form in Rāghavdās. It is present in Nābhādās, too, via the connection between the 24 avatars and the four *vyūhas*.[36]

became determinative in the Vijayanagara state, and concludes that the system of the four *āmnāyas* (sacred traditions) probably crystallized in the late sixteenth or early seventeenth century.[42]

Given the pattern of interchange and rivalry that existed between Shaivas and Vaishnavas, both in south India and further north, this specific trajectory is worth pondering, but perhaps the more powerful fact is that there was a rather widespread idea that ascetic formations might take a four-part shape, as if to mimic the four-directional quarters. One finds it among the Jains, in the Shaiva *akhāḍā*s, and in the Udāsī *akhāḍā*s and *dhūnī*s, with their proximity to the Sikhs.[43] The notable thing about the idea of the four sampradayas, in this regard, is that it was not always confined to renunciant usage even in its earliest formulation, if we consider that the *Sampradāyapradīpa* may qualify for that award.[44] And until well into the seventeenth century, if not the early eighteenth, we lack a clear sense that the rubric of the four sampradayas was thought of either conceptually or organizationally as an answer to the strength of the Shaiva ascetic orders.[45]

Boxing in Kabīr

Finally, it is worth considering whether there was a generally felt need for a clearly visible—and clearly Vaishnava—model to control and, if possible, reorient the powerful network of associations that was growing up around the figure of Kabīr. Here we see a 'Vedic' reaction to the phenomenon of Kabīr and all that he stood for—Islamic, pseudo-Islamic or otherwise subaltern. Thus, he had to be Brahminized in the thinking of the Rāmānand Sampradāy. In fact, one way of thinking about the origins of the sampradaya itself is to consider it as more or less coterminous with this process of Brahminization. The existence of a 'Hindi' Rāmānand as against a 'Sanskrit' Rāmānanda, as shown so elegantly by Purushottam Agrawal, importantly modifies but does not essentially challenge this understanding of what happened in actual history.[46]

In a related but different way, the Dādūpanth, with its lower-class origins and its record of open participation by Muslims extending back to the guru himself, had to be excluded from the *cār sampradāy* formulation as it emerged in Rāmānandī writings. That formulation drew a clear line between Kabīr, whose prestige (and perhaps institutional force) it claimed, and Dādū, whom it did not—perhaps as an expression of a close rivalry between Rāmānandīs and Dādūpanthīs 'on the ground' in and around Amer. The Sikhs, too, were silently excluded by Anantadās and Nābhādās, though Rāghavdās tried his best to find a way to include them—this in response, no doubt, to connections that were not just conceptual but real, especially in the real world of Sant militias. All this suggests that it may not just have been the desire of certain powerful Rāmānandīs to be associated with 'Vedic' lineages that caused the retrospective disciplining of Kabīr within Rāmānand's Brahmanical cell. It may have been the protean power of Kabīr, the Kabīrpanthīs and all those who recited the poetry that circulated in and around Kabīr's name that made this adjustment necessary after the fact.

If one gazes upon the wonderful murals of 'Medieval Saints' that line the upper walls of the Hindi Bhavan in Shantiniketan, one can still see the results, as one can in the written works of its patron, Hazariprasad Dvivedi.[47] Here, Kabīr emerges as a major conduit in the transmission of bhakti from south India to the north. He appears as a major figure in the fresco that lines the southern wall of the Hindi Bhavan and his influence spreads around the corner into the long Banarasi scene that moves northwards, along the western wall. Rāmānand can be seen on the south wall too. He stands very near the figure of Rāmānuja, who is at its centre, seeming to facilitate this south-to-north transfer by passing it on to Kabīr, just as Nābhādās had said. Yet, as we have seen, there is nothing to suggest that the institution of the four sampradayas actually developed in the south and moved north. On the contrary, its appeal to the old—and to the geographic representation of that 'old' in the south—points to its distinctive newness as a sixteenth-century idea that grew up in the north. Similarly, if you visit the Four-Sampradaya Ashram in Vrindavan, you find yourself in a place whose origins stretch back scarcely more than a hundred years. Here too, an aroma of newness swirls around this notion of time immemorial.

13. Shea and Troyer, *Dabistan*, p. 196.
14. Shea and Troyer evidently misconstrued 'Nāmdev' as 'the name Dayu' (ibid., *Dabistan*, p. 192), as Joel Lee points out (New York, 14 June 2009)
15. Ibid., pp. 195-6.
16. The fact that Mūbad Śāh drew attention to this latter grouping already in the middle of the seventeenth century opens the way forward to the sort of turf that Dominique-Sila Khan and others have been exploring in much more recent times—often without the benefit of detailed historical evidence. On this particular triad, see D.-S. Khan, *Conversions and Shifting Identities: Ramdev Pir and the Ismailis of Rajasthan,* Delhi and Paris: Manohar and Centre de Sciences Humaines, 1997, pp. 250-8; on the limits of her evidence, see pp. 39-40.
17. *Pīpā parcaī* 35.25 in W.M. Callewaert and S. Sharma, *The Hagiographies of Anantadās: The Bhakti Poets of North India*, Richmond: Curzon, 2000, p. 276, but the translation is my own.
18. These include, in addition to Pīpā, Kabīr and Raidās (east), Nāmdev (south), Dhanā (north) and the following bhaktas who are mentioned without directional referents: Bīthal, Sen, Aṅgad, Bhuvan, Mādhavdās Jagannāthī, Trilocan, Mīrābāī, Raṅkā and Baṅkā, and Caturbhuj and his wife. Anantadās himself invokes the number sixteen as he comes to the end of the list (35.17).
19. N. Jha, *Bhaktamāl: pāṭhānuśīlan evaṁ vivecan*, Patna: Anupam Prakāśan, 1978, §27, part 2, p. 10. The symbol § refers to the *chappay*s and *dohā*s that structure the *Bhaktamāl.*
20. W.R. Pinch, 'History, Devotion and the Search for Nabhadas of Galta', in *Invoking the Past: The Uses of History in South Asia*, ed. Daud Ali, Delhi: Oxford University Press, 1999, pp. 383-99, especially pp. 388, 396-9. I have used the term 'Brahmanical' but Pinch does not. He speaks of 'an orthoprax Ramanandi order' (p. 379) and characterizes the four-sampradaya idea as comprising, in Nābhādās's writing, 'four orthodox religious perspectives descending from Viṣṇu' (p. 381), and contrasts all of this to the shudras, untouchables, women and so forth, who constituted the 'ragtag band' Nābhādās favoured (p. 380).
21. Jha, *Bhaktamāl* §71, part 2, p. 26.
22. Difficulties in interpreting the date contained in the text (*saṁvat satrahai sai satrahotarā*) have led to considerable discussion among scholars. There are three possibilities—vs 1717, 1770 and 1777 (corresponding to CE 1660, 1713, and 1720). Dalpat Rajpurohit has highlighted some of the main arguments that can be marshalled for the first of these options in n. 10 of his essay for this volume. To his list must be added the important fact that only the 30 June 1660 date correlates with the day of the week (Saturday) and lunar timing (*śukla pakṣa* 3, *āsāḍh*) that appear as part of Rāghavdās's colophon, as given in the oldest manuscript at our disposal

(scribed in CE 1804), the one that serves as the basis for the edition by A. Nahta, *Rāghavdāskṛt bhaktamāl: caturdāskṛt ṭīkā sahit*, Jodhpur: Rājasthān Prācyavidyā Pratiṣṭhān, 1965. Monika Horstmann deserves credit for pointing this out: M. Horstmann, 'The Flow of Grace: Food and Feast in the Hagiography and History of the Dadupanth', *Zeitschrift der Deutschen Morgenländischen Gesellschaft*, vol. 150, no. 2, 2000, p. 515, n. 9. There is, however, a major unsolved puzzle if we opt for the 1660 date. As Winand Callewaert observes, Rāghavdās mentions Guru Harkiśan among Guru Nānak's successors (Nahta, *Bhaktamāl*, p. 176). Guru Harkiśan did not take the throne until October 1661. With regard to the two eighteenth-century dates, it may perhaps be regarded as odd that Rāghavdās does not go on to list all ten of the Sikh gurus since the last did not die until 1708. Other aspects of the text—e.g. the firm decision to regard Caitanya and the Gauḍīyas as members of the Mādhva Sampradāya—seem to me to fit more comfortably with an eighteenth-century dating than the seventeenth-century possibility, but the calendrical alignment to which Monika Horstmann has drawn attention is hard to gainsay. On the other hand, however, Callewaert's arguments as to the plausibility of the date VS 1777 on strictly linguistic grounds are worth considering. With regard to all this, see W.M. Callewaert, 'Bhagatmāls and Parcaīs in Rajasthan', in *According to Tradition: Hagiographical Writing in India*, ed. Winand M. Callewaert and Rupert Snell, Wiesbaden: Harrassowitz, 1994, p. 96; Callewaert and Sharma, *The Hagiographies of Anantadās*, pp. 28-9. In my mind, at least, the issue is not yet entirely solved.

23. Nahta, *Bhaktamāl* §115.3-4, p. 48.
24. Ibid., pp. 18, 21.
25. Ibid., §290, p. 142.
26. This important point has been noticed by M. Horstmann, 'Dādūpanthī Anthologies of the Eighteenth and Nineteenth Centuries', in *Bhakti in Current Research 2000-2003: Proceedings of the Ninth International Conference on Early Devotional Literature in New Indo-Aryan Languages, Heidelberg, 23-26 July 2003*, ed. Monika Horstmann, New Delhi: Manohar, 2006, p. 169; and emphasized in a different context by P. Burchett, 'Kacchwaha Influence on Bhakti Religious Formations in Mughal India: Politics, Patronage, and Literature in Galta, Vrindaban and Beyond, *c.* 1500-1650' unpublished essay, Columbia University, 2008, pp. 19, 22-3.
27. Rāghavdās displays his debt to Nābhādās on a number of other occasions as well, from the title on down. He mimics Nābhā in the general design of his work, following him, for instance, in addressing himself to the general structure of the universe (in Rāghavdās's case, *saptadvīp*, *navakhaṇḍ*, *vedadvīp*, §§ 111-13; Nābhādās §§ 235) just before introducing the Kaliyuga and the four sampradayas (§§ 114-15). Similarly, at a level of greater detail, he frequently plays off Nābhā's language in fashioning his own approach to

1991, pp. 43-4. The fact that a four-sampradaya motif also appears in Shaiva usage is a different matter. From what I understand on the basis of Clark, *The Daśanāmī Saṁnyāsīs*, pp. 121-2, these are subsidiary to the four-*maṭhāmnāya* classification and do not have an independent conceptual life of their own.

46. P. Agrawal, 'In Search of Ramanand: The Guru of Kabir and Others', in *Ancient to Modern: Religion, Power, and Community in India*, ed. Ishita Banerjee-Dube and Saurabh Dube, Delhi: Oxford University Press, 2009. See also, online, the version in *Pratilipi* (March 2009).
47. J. Chakrabarti, R.S. Kumar and A.K. Nag, *The Santiniketan Murals,* Calcutta: Seagull Books, 1995, plates 34-45.
48. *Hinduism Today*, July-September 2008, p. 44.

BIBLIOGRAPHY

Agrawal, P., 'In Search of Ramanand: The Guru of Kabir and Others', in *Ancient to Modern: Religion, Power and Community in India*, ed. Ishita Banerjee-Dube and Saurabh Dube, Delhi: Oxford University Press, 2009, pp. 135-70.

Askari, S.H., 'Dabistan-i-Mazahib and Diwani-Mubad', in *Indo-Iranian Studies presented for the Golden Jubilee of the Pahlavi Dynasty of Iran*, ed. F. Mujtabai, Delhi: Indo-Iran Society, 1977, pp. 85-104.

Bansal, N.C., *Caitanya sampradāy: siddhānt aur sāhitya*, Agra: Vinod Pustak Mandir, 1980.

Behl, A., 'Pages from the Book of Religions: Comparing Self and Other in Mughal India', in *Notes from a Mandala: Essays in Honor of Wendy Doniger*, ed. L. Patton and D. Haberman, Newark: University of Delaware Press, 2010, pp. 113-49.

Bhatt, G.H., 'A Further Note on Vishṇusvāmī and Vallabhāchārya', in *Proceedings and Transactions of the Eighth All-India Oriental Conference, December 1935*, Bangalore: Government Press, 1937, pp. 322-31.

——, 'Vishṇusvāmī and Vallabhāchārya', in *Proceedings and Transactions of the Seventh All-India Oriental Conference, December 1933*, Baroda: Oriental Institute, 1935, pp. 449-58.

Burchett, P., 'Kacchwaha Influence on Bhakti Religious Formations in Mughal India: Politics, Patronage, and Literature in Galta, Vrindaban and Beyond, *c*. 1500-1650', New York: Columbia University, 2008.

Burton, A., 'Temples, Texts, and Taxes: The Bhagavad-gita and the Politico-Religious Identity of the Caitanya Sect', PhD dissertation, Australian National University, 2000.

Callewaert, W.M., 'Bhagatmāls and Parcaīs in Rajasthan', in *According to Tradition: Hagiographical Writing in India*, ed. W.M. Callewaert and R. Snell, Wiesbaden: Harrassowitz, 1994.

Callewaert, W.M. and S. Sharma, *The Hagiographies of Anantadās: The Bhakti Poets of North India*, Richmond: Curzon, 2000.

Chakrabarti, J., R.S. Kumar and A.K. Nag, *The Santiniketan Murals*, Calcutta: Seagull Books, 1995.

Clark, M., *The Daśanāmī Saṁnyāsīs: The Integration of Ascetic Lineages into an Order*, Leiden: E.J. Brill, 2006.

Digby, S. 'Some Asian Wanderers in Seventeenth Century India: An Examination of Sources in Persian', *Studies in History*, vol. 9, no. 2, 1993, pp. 247-64.

Elkman, S.M., *Jīva Gosvāmin's Tattvasandarbha: A Study on the Philosophical and Sectarian Development of the Gauḍīya Vaiṣṇava Movement*, Delhi: Motilal Banarsidass, 1986.

Halbfass, W., *Philology and Confrontation: Paul Hacker on Traditional and Modern Vedānta*, Albany, NY: State University of New York Press, 1995.

Hawley, J.S., 'The Four Sampradayas: Ordering the Religious Past in Mughal North India', *South Asian History and Culture,* vol. 2, no. 2, 2011, pp. 160-83.

Horstmann, M., 'Dādūpanthī Anthologies of the Eighteenth and Nineteenth Centuries', in *Bhakti in Current Research 2000-2003: Proceedings of the Ninth International Conference on Early Devotional Literature in New Indo-Aryan Languages, Heidelberg, 23-26 July 2003*, ed. M. Horstmann, Delhi: Manohar, 2006, pp. 163-78.

——, *Der Zusammenhalt der Welt: Religiöse Herrschaftslegitimation und Religionspolitik Mahārājā Savāī Jaisinghs (1700-1743)*, Wiesbaden: Harrassowitz Verlag, 2009.

——, 'The Flow of Grace: Food and Feast in the Hagiography and History of the Dadupanth', *Zeitschrift der Deutschen Morgenländischen Gesellschaft*, vol. 150, no. 2, 2000, pp. 513-80.

Jha, N., *Bhaktamāl: pāṭhānuśīlan evaṁ vivecan*, Patna: Anupam Prakāśan, 1978.

Khan, D.-S., *Conversions and Shifting Identities: Ramdev Pir and the Ismailis of Rajasthan*, Delhi and Paris: Manohar and Centre de Sciences Humaines, 1997.

Mann, G.S., *The Goindval Pothis*, Cambridge, MA: Harvard University Press, 1996.

——, *The Making of Sikh Scripture*, New York: Oxford University Press, 2001.

Minkowski, C., 'Nilakaṇṭha Caturdhara and the Genre of Mantrarahasyaprakāśikā', paper presented at the Second International Vedic Workshop, Kyoto, 1999.

Mishra, R.C., ed. *Sundar-granthāvalī*, Delhi: Kitābghar, 1992.

Nahta, A., *Rāghavdāskṛt bhaktamāl: caturdāskṛt ṭīkā sahit, Rājasthān purātan granthamālā* 78, Jodhpur: Rājasthān Prācyavidyā Pratiṣṭhān, 1965.

Pinch, W.R., 'History, Devotion and the Search for Nabhadas of Galta', in *Invoking the Past: The Uses of History in South Asia*, ed. D. Ali, New Delhi: Oxford University Press, 1999.

Shastri, K., ed., *Sampradāyapradīpa: Sampradāy pradīp kā bhāvānuvād*, Kankaroli: Vidyā-Vibhāg [1935?].

Shastri, S.S.S., ed., *The Śivādvaita of Śrīkaṇṭha*, Madras: University of Madras, 1930.

Shea, D. and A. Troyer, *The Dabistan, or, School of Manners*, 3 vols., Paris and London: Oriental Translation Fund of Great Britain and Ireland, 1843.

Thiel-Horstmann, M., 'Warrior Ascetics in 18th Century Rajasthan and the Religious Polity of Jai Singh II', in *Bhakti in Current Research 1982-1985: Proceedings of the Third International Conference on Devotional Literature in New Indo-Aryan Languages*, ed. M.K. Gautam and G.H. Schokker, Lucknow and Leiden: Indo-European Publishers, 1991.

CHAPTER 2

Thematic Groupings of Bhakti Poetry: The Dādūpanth and *Sarvāṅgī* Literature[1]

Dalpat Rajpurohit

In the summer of 2009, I was sitting at the Dādū temple in Naraina on a hot afternoon. A Dādūpanthī householder from Jaipur happened to walk up to the steps of the temple with his harmonium. He sang three songs. One was attributed to Dādū, the second to Kabīr and the third to Sūrdās. The singer performed these songs on the steps of the temple understood to be the epicentre of the Dādūpanth. Not only was he singing *bhajan*s attributed to Dādū but also to Kabīr and to the Krishna-devotee Sūr as well. His selection is similar to what we see in the *Sarvāṅgī*s belonging to the Dādūpanthī anthological tradition, aiming to collect *Sant-vāṇī,* the songs of the early modern poet-saints of India, thematically. The *Sarvāṅgī* tradition is a group of texts which unite a diverse array of bhakti poets irrespective of their sectarian affiliation by arranging their poetry according to the various themes of bhakti literature.

The *Sarvāṅgī* tradition begins with the *Sarvāṅgī* of Rajab, one of the primary disciples of the sixteenth-century Sant Dādū. This literary tradition became popular among the disciples of Dādū in the seventeenth century, and especially flourished in modern-day Rajasthan and the Punjab.

The classification of songs into sections called *aṅg*s, became important in the Dādūpanth in its *Sarvāṅgī* and *Pañc-vāṇī* traditions. The *aṅg*-type classification was also significant in some other early anthologies like the *Aṅgabandhū* (compiled before the death of Dādū in 1603 [?]) and the *Guṇ gañj-nāmā* of the Dādūpanthī Jagannāthdās. Together these anthologies set a structural ideal for the compilation of the sayings of the Sants, a model that continued to be followed in Hindi literature until the twentieth century.[2]

At present, two *Sarvāṅgī*s are available in print; the first is the *Sarvāṅgī* composed by Rajab, which has been published three times. It was edited first by Shahabuddin Iraqi,[3] a historian of Aligarh Muslim University, then by Dharmapal Simhal of Panjab University, Chandigarh,[4] and recently by the independent scholar, Brajendra Kumar Simhal.[5] The CE 1714 manuscripts of Rajab's *Sarvāṅgī* contain verses of 88 Sants.[6] The CE 1756 manuscript which Dharmapal Simhal used for his edition has the sayings of 137 identified Sants and also includes the *Guṇ gañj-nāmā* of Jagannāthdās. The editions of Rajab's *Sarvāṅgī* present the different traditions of the circulations of the *Sarvāṅgī* manuscripts that are preserved in Rajasthan, Punjab and Banaras.[7] Winand Callewaert has also conducted a detailed study of Rajab's *Sarvāṅgī*. His edition, however, does not have the full text but contains only the *sākhī*s of Rajab along with their English translation.[8]

The second *Sarvāṅgī* that has been published was composed by Gopāldās in CE 1627. Gopāldās was a grand disciple (*potā-śiṣya*) of Dādū and the *Sarvāṅgī* composed by him has also been edited by Callewaert.[9] This *Sarvāṅgī* is particularly significant as it presents the poems of 137 Sants and, unlike Rajab's *Sarvāṅgī*, it has no issues with its date of compilation. A comparison of these two *Sarvāṅgī*s provides glimpses into the literarisation of the sayings of bhakti Sants within the Dādūpanth.

The *Sarvāṅgī* tradition contains a variety of songs of popular as well as lesser-known Sants. Manuscripts of the *Sarvāṅgī* of Rajab, as well as other anthologies grouped into *aṅg*s such as the *Sarvāṅgī granth* of Harīdās (CE 1695), *Sarvāṅg-sār kā sabad* by Santdās (in a manuscript from the nineteenth century) and the *Sarvāṅg-sār* by Rāmcaraṇ and Navalrām, are preserved in the various centres of the Rajasthan Oriental Research Institute.

Rajab and the *aṅg* Type Classification in the Dādūpanthī Anthologies

In the *Sarvāṅgī*, the verses (both *pads* and *sākhīs*) of Sants are grouped into *aṅgs*. This process of dividing *Sant-vāṇīs* into *aṅgs* is a common practice among the modern publications of the songs of Sants. The *sākhīs* are always grouped according to their theme and the *pads* (verses) are grouped according to their Raga. This classification is true of almost all the collections of anthologies compiled in the early modern period and their subsequent editions in the twentieth century. But a question which remains is when was this tradition first established? Who first compiled these *aṅg*-based anthologies and why? How have the so-called *nirguṇ* and *saguṇ* poets been categorized in the earliest-known anthologies? All these questions are important and warrant further research.

The study of the *Sarvāṅgī* literature is important for multiple reasons. First, it is necessary for a complete study of the sayings of Sants. Second, it is helpful to study the transmission of bhakti poetry in this particular anthological tradition in the time-span of almost a hundred years in the seventeenth century to study the practice of compiling the *Sant-vāṇī* in *aṅgs* and Ragas (rhythm), and to study the legends, religious and sectarian beliefs in the Sant community of this period. This essay will present a brief overview describing the origin and development of the *Sarvāṅgī* literary traditions in their various aspects, along with the sectarian development of the Dādūpanth. Let us first examine the *Sarvāṅgī* of Rajab, which holds great importance for our current research of bhakti as it presents a large and early corpus of songs by early modern poet-saints.

The *Sarvāṅgī* of Rajab is a text of the songs of the holy men famous around *c.* 1600, whose songs, legends and repertoire were orally received by Rajab. Callewaert identified 88 Sants who are believed to have lived between the twelfth century and the seventeenth century. The text narrates hagiographical and autobiographical episodes from the lives of various holy men. The *Sarvāṅgī* tradition, especially that of the *Sarvāṅgī* of Rajab, is an important source for studying the phenomenon of compiling anthologies during the early modern period as it appears to be the very first text in which the *Vāṇī*s of such a high number of Sants are grouped according to their *aṅg*s.

For Rajab, his *Sarvāṅgī* was a text of great spiritual importance as is shown in the very beginning of the text in the *Astuti kau aṅg* or the section of prayer. The 'section of prayer' is the first section among the 144 sections in the text. The grouping of poetry into the 'section of prayer' means that all the verses grouped in this section have a common theme, prayer (*Astuti*). This *aṅg* may have the verses of so many different Sants but because they all sing about a common section, 'prayer', they are all grouped in this section. Rajab groups the poetry of Rāmānand, Nāmdev, Kabīr, Pīpā, Raidās, Dhanā, Dādū, Sūrdās, Tulsīdās and many other Sants. Sectarian and non-sectarian are grouped together in the same *aṅg* due to their shared theme.

Rajab begins his *Sarvāṅgī* with 'the section of prayer' (*Astuti kau aṅg*). Praise for the guru (personal/impersonal) in the anthologies of this time is very common. Almost all the Dādūpanthī anthologies begin with the *Guru kau aṅg* (section of guru). However, what is particularly interesting in the *Sarvāṅgī* of Rajab is that this *Sarvāṅgī* begins with 'the section of prayer' in which Rajab praises *the Sarvāṅgī itself* as a text of spiritual importance containing the words of holy men.

śrabaṅgī su sugandha argajā chappana bhoga lagāi;
yahu parimala parasāda prāṇapati mihamā̃ kahi na jāi.[10]

From the *Sarvāṅgī* comes a fragrance of perfume and the offering of fifty-six foods,
This is a pure offering to the lord of the soul whose glory cannot be told.

A few couplets of this kind occur at the beginning of this *Sarvāṅgī,* which demonstrate that it had an important place in the bhakti community at the time of Rajab (around 1600). At the time of the compilation of this *Sarvāṅgī*, there were not too many anthologies of this kind. In fact, it is possible that it was the very first anthological text of its kind in the tradition of bhakti literature.

The *Sarvāṅgī* of Rajab has greatly influenced the disciples of Dādū as can be seen in Rāghavdās's *Bhaktamāl*, the 'Garland of Devotees'. In his *Bhaktamāl*, Rāghavdās specifies that Rajab, the composer of a *Sarvāṅgī*, was the foremost disciple of Dādū. He praises Rajab, stating,

> *śrabaṅgī tata kathyau, kābi sarba hī kī lyāyau;*[11]
>
> He recited the *Sarvāṅgī* and brought the poetry of all.

The above line illustrates two things: the first is that Rajab's *Sarvāṅgī* was honoured by the early generations of Dādū's disciples in the Dādūpanth and the second is that this anthology must have been compiled prior to the *Bhaktamāl* of Rāghavdās.[12] Rāghavdās's *Bhaktamāl* is a major hagiographical source for the study of the bhakti traditions around the seventeenth century. Singing the *Sarvāṅgī* had great importance at the time of Rāghavdās, who was a fifth generation disciple of Dādū. His *Bhaktamāl* has the largest numbers of bhaktas of any in the *Bhaktamāl* tradition.

Along with Dādūpanthī hagiographical texts like the *Bhaktamāl* of Rāghavdās, the *Sarvāṅgī* of Rajab and later anthologies in the *Sarvāṅgī* tradition shed light on important aspects of early modern devotion, such as the question of the distinction between *nirguṇ* and *saguṇ* bhakti. The art of composing legends and compiling anthologies of songs sung by the Sants around 1600 can also serve as points of departure for a further study of bhakti sensibility and of textual circulation.

Early twentieth-century Indian scholars of bhakti such as Hazariprasad Dvivedi, Kshitimohan Sen and Parashuram Chaturvedi gave a prominent place to Rajab's *Sarvāṅgī* in the study of bhakti.[13] Sen and Chaturvedi presumed that Rajab started compiling his anthologies, such as the *Aṅgabandhu* (a collection of Dādū's poems), at least ten years before the writing of the *Ādi Granth* (1604).[14] The *aṅg*-type grouping, as in the *Aṅgabandhu*, is followed in the *Sarvaṅgī*. However, these scholars also made it clear that the *Sarvāṅgī* was an anthology of the *nirguṇ* school of bhakti. As the complete text of Rajab's *Sarvāṅgī* was not published until CE 1985, early scholars could not provide any authentic proof to establish its date of compilation. Therefore, the *Ādi Granth* has long remained the primary authentic source of the songs of the Sants. Regardless of the debate over its time of compilation, Rajab's *Sarvāṅgī* is particularly important as it contains a larger amount of *pad*s of many poet-saints such as Rāmānand, Gorakhnāth, Bakhnā, Hardās, Bājīd, Mahmūd, Śekh Bahāvadī, etc., than does the *Ādi Granth*.

Let us take a brief account of the earliest compilations of the *Sant-vāṇī*. The earliest discovered and published collection of the songs of the Sants is the *Mohan pothī*, also called the *Goindvāl pothī*s (1570-2).[15] In this collection, the verses are grouped according to their Ragas, as in the Fatehpur anthology (1582).[16] This is an indication that the technique of compilation using the Raga order predates the use of the *aṅg* ordering of poems. Furthermore, compilations in the Raga order are more closely linked with the singing of the *Sant-vāṇī*. The need for distributing the *Sant-vāṇī* into thematic sections comes later, when a new singing tradition began in which members of the Sant community compiled and sang verses from a variety of Sants under specific themes. It is true that the *Guru Granth* does not structure the songs in this way as its compilers kept adding more sayings (of mostly their own Guru tradition with a few other of poet-saints) in the Raga structure. Rajab while presenting songs of a larger community of poet-saints outside his sect, proposed a new organizational scheme. The songs were first thematically organized and then organized by Raga within each theme. In his *Sarvāṅgī*, the highest number of verses are attributed to Kabīr and not to Dādū. This model of thematic groupings became more prominent and can be seen in the editions of Kabīr and Raidās's poetry.

Simultaneously, around the last decade of the sixteenth century when Dādūpanthī devotees started to compile the sayings of the Sants, they first grouped the *pad*s of their guru into the *aṅg* order. According to tradition, the first Dādūpanthī collection is the *Aṅgabandhū*, which is said to have been compiled by Rajab possibly before the death of Dādū in 1603.[17] It has not been established beyond doubt as to which disciple grouped the poetry of Dādū into thematic sections and it is true that the earliest extant manuscript of the *Aṅgabandhū* dates only from 1828.[18] Nevertheless, the fact that the *Dādū-vāṇī* which is used for the *akhaṇḍ-pāṭh* at Naraina is classified into the very same *aṅg*s as the *Aṅgabandhū,* may hint at the early origin of the *Aṅgabandhū.*

The *Aṅgabandhū* is grouped into 37 *aṅg*s in which most of the *aṅg*s clearly match those of Rajab's *Sarvāṅgī* and the *Rajab-vāṇī.* According to P.D. Barthwal, the *Aṅgabandhū* is the best collection of Dādū's poetry.[19] The renowned scholar of Sant literature, Parashuram Chaturvedi, called the *Aṅgabandhū* 'the ideal of its kind of anthologies'.[20] The earliest manuscript of the *Dādū-vāṇī* (in which we find 37 *aṅg*s) is the CE 1653 manuscript. It served as the basis of the Nāgarīpracāriṇī Sabhā edition of the *Dādū granthāvalī* by Parashuram Chaturvedi.

It is clear from the above that the practice of classifying the *Sant-vāṇī* thematically postdates the Raga-based anthologies. Rajab himself grouped his own *Vāṇī* into 193 *aṅg*s.[21] Thus, the emergence of the *Sarvāṅgī* tradition around 1600 provided the pattern of compilation by *aṅg* for other works as well.

The Dates of the *Sarvāṅgī* Anthologies

The following part of the paper briefly surveys the individual anthologies of the *Sarvāṅgī* tradition, and discusses their time of compilation, their structures and the motivations of the various Sant-compilers in the light of the development of this tradition.

According to Rāghavdās's *Bhaktamāl*, Rajab was Dādū's favourite among his 52 main disciples. In fact, Jangopāl's *Dādūjanma-līlā-parcaī* (*c.* CE 1620) suggests that Rajab was with Dādū at the time of his death,

> *dayāladāsa aru rajaba āyau gavana samai darśana tini pāyau.*[22]
>
> Dayāldās and Rajab also came to see Dādū at his death.

Rajab's *Sarvāṅgī* is the oldest extant *Sarvāṅgī*. Its compiler was an extraordinary editor since he rarely repeated a *sākhī* or *pad* in different *aṅgs*. Rajab's *Sarvāṅgī* includes works by 88-117 identified poets distributed into 144-9 *aṅgs*. The *Sarvāṅgī* was an ongoing literary tradition and the compilers who came after Rajab continued to add sayings of other Sants into it. As can be seen from printed editions, the earliest dated manuscript (Iraqi 1985, Callewaert 1978) had 86-8 poet-saints while the 1756 manuscript from Punjab edited by Dharmapal Simhal contains the songs of 137 Sants distributed into 144 *aṅgs*. Brajendra Kumar Simhal's recent edition contains 149 *aṅgs* and the work of 117 Sants.

The *Sarvāṅgī* tradition was equally famous in Punjab. Interestingly, Simhal also consulted a manuscript of a *Sarvāṅgī* written in the Gurmukhī script by a follower of Sikhism.[23] This Punjabi manuscript begins with the praise of Nānak, the first guru in the Sikh tradition.

The Punjabi version is comprises verses of Dādū and Rajab, which shows that the compiler of this *Sarvāṅgī* was familiar with the *Sarvāṅgī* of Rajab and tried to impose his own *Guru* tradition on it. The fact that the Devanāgarī manuscript of Rajab's *Sarvāṅgī* from Punjab, which Simhal cites, contains only thirteen verses by Nānak suggests that the Dādūpanth and Sikhism were in some sort of competition as regards the production of texts in the seventeenth century.

Around 1600, the Dādūpanth emerges as a sect with increased literary activity. In addition to its *Sarvāṅgī* and *Pañc-vāṇī* collections, the *Guṇ gañj-nāmās* attributed to Jagannāthdās and to Bājīd established a third tradition. All these anthologies followed the model of grouping songs into different *aṅgs*.

Thematic compilation was given great importance in the very early period of the formation of the Dādūpanth. In his *Sarvāṅgī*, Rajab attempted to anthologize all Sant songs that were famous in his times. This is also suggested by Rāghavdās in his *Bhaktamāl*: He says that Rajab recited the *Sarvāṅgī* and brought the poetry of all into it (*sarbāṅgī tata kathyau, kābi sarba hī kī lyāyo*).[24] Rajab included more Sants and more verses than the compiler of the *Ādi Granth*. The *Sarvāṅgī* features not only the verses of popular Sants like Rāmānand, Kabīr, Nāmdev, Raidās, Dādū, Sūrdās, Tulsīdās, Nānak and Nāths (such as Gorakhnāth and Charpatnāth), but also some other lesser-known yet significant Sants like Bakhnā and Bājīd. He did not restrict the language of the *pad*s to the various forms of the vernacular but also included Sanskrit and Persian compositions.

As noted, the year of the compilation of Rajab's *Sarvāṅgī* is widely debated. However, most twentieth-century scholars hold that the Sikhs and the Nirañjanīs emulated Rajab in including the *Vāṇī*s of Sants from outside their *panth* into their anthologies,[25] and, therefore, Rajab's *Sarvāṅgī* must predate these traditions.

Barthwal described a CE 1603 manuscript of the *Sarvāṅgī*, which is said to be preserved in the *Nāgarīpracāriṇī Sabhā* in Banaras as manuscript 1409. There is no physical evidence of Barthwal's claim as no one has been able to locate the manuscript after him. The contents he describes exactly match the *Sarvāṅgī* of Rajab published later.[26]

In an older work, Callewaert had noted ten different versions of Rajab's *Sarvāṅgī*. The earliest (CE 1714) served as a basis for Callewaert's edition.[27] Yet in a later work, Callewaert stated that he had consulted the 'original' manuscript of Rajab's *Sarvāṅgī* dating possibly to CE 1620.[28] The earliest source which mentions Rajab's *Sarvāṅgī* is the *Bhaktamāl* of Rāghavdās. This work, in all probability, was compiled in 1660, about sixty years after the probable year of the compilation of Rajab's *Sarvāṅgī*.

Criteria to determine the date of the *Sarvāṅgī* should include, but not be limited to, the following questions: when did the poet-saints whose *pad*s became part of the *Sarvāṅgī* live? How was the work of a particular Sant incorporated into it? What determined the inclusion of a poem into it? How does the development of the *Sarvāṅgī* tradition relate to the development of the Dādūpanth?

Rāghavdās's *Bhaktamāl* is the principal *Bhaktamāl* of the Dādūpanth. There are two other smaller *Bhaktamāl*s compiled by Jaggā and Caindās in the Dādūpanth, but these two sources do not mention the *Sarvāṅgī* of Rajab. Among the early historians of Hindi literature, Shivsingh Sengar, in his *Śivsiṁh Saroj* (1833), provides no information concerning Rajab except for two couplets.[29] The Mishra brothers in their *Miśrabandhu Vinod* (1913) give 1643 as the year of the compilation of Rajab's *Sarvāṅgī* but do not offer any proof for this assertion.[30] Rajab does not receive any place in the *History of Hindi Literature* (1929) by Ramchand Shukla. Shukla's history established the literary canon of Hindi literature, which has largely remained unchallenged for almost a century.

Purohit Harinarayan, Sharma's article entitled 'Mahātmā Rajjabjī' (1935) became the basis for the subsequent understanding of Rajab. In this article, Sharma indicates a long period from CE 1595 to 1668 as the time of the compilation of Rajab's *Sarvāṅgī* and the *Rajab-vāṇī*. He writes that Rajab was so close to Dādū that after the latter's death in 1603, Rajab closed his eyes so that he would not see anybody else. He used to open his eyes only to write the *Sant-vāṇī*.[31]

Several others such as Dharmapal Simhal, the editor of Rajab's *Sarvāṅgī*, believes that the *Sarvāṅgī* is not an individual anthology but a long tradition begun by Rajab. Later, he argues, other songs were added to the original *Sarvāṅgī*. The *Sarvāṅgī* edited by Simhal is based on a later manuscript dated 1756. The higher number of authors and verses in his *Sarvāṅgī* than in the edition by Shahabuddin Iraqi must have prompted him to develop the notion that the *Sarvāṅgī* was an ongoing literary tradition. Iraqi claimed 1673 to be the year of compilation but did not give any argument to support this.[32]

Callewaert regards the time of compilation of Rajab's *Sarvāṅgī* to be *c*. 1620.[33] His argument is based on the legends related to the poet-saint Nāmdev, whose life was chronicled by Anantadās, a Rāmānandī, in *c*. 1588. Callewaert reasons that the legends in Anantadās' hagiographies of Sants like Nāmdev should match those told by Rajab if both lived at the same time. As he finds a major difference between the approaches of Anantadās and Rajab, Callewaert argues that Rajab's *Sarvāṅgī* must be later than Anantadās' compositions.[34]

Callewaert writes that Anantadās, in his *Nāmdev parcaī*, relates magical stories, crediting Nāmdev with many miraculous deeds. For example, Nāmdev rotates a temple so that it faces a different direction. He also reanimates a bullock. According to Callewaert, these legends became Brahmanized at a later stage and a cow took the place of the bullock. In his *Sarvāṅgī*, Rajab also relates the legends surrounding the life of Nāmdev and tells the story of how he reanimated a cow. Thus, Callewaert concludes that Rajab's *Sarvāṅgī* came later when the Brahminization of these legends had already occurred.

Anantadās *Parcaī*, however, tells both versions: that Nāmdev both re-animated a bullock and a cow,

kalajugi prathama nāmade bhayau; kaisau apane basi kari liyau.
dūdha pivai ra devaḷa pheriyau; pātsāhi saṅga jhagarau niberiyau.
tana mana pārabrahma ku arapiyau; gāi jivai hāthī darapyau.
sūkhī seja jalā̃ maī āni; rājā parjā sabahi jāni.
apane hāthi chāni hari chāi; svāna rūpa dhari roti ṣāi.
balada jivāi ru ratha calāyau; nāmei kahyau tahā̃ hari āyau.[35]

The first bhakta who lived in the Kali age was Nāmdev,
he had God in his hands.
He gave God milk, made the temple turn around,
and settled the quarrel with the Sultan.
He surrendered mind and body to the ultimate Brahman,
reanimated a cow and scared an elephant.
He pulled out, dry, a bed from a river,
the king and all the people were witnesses.
With his own hands Hari repaired the roof of his hut,
and took the form of a dog to eat the bread offered by Nāmdev.
Nāmdev reanimated a bullock and made a cart to move again.
Hari appeared anywhere on the instruction of Nāmdev.[36]

Anantadās' *Parcaī* indicates that both accounts (the reanimation of a cow and that of an ox), were very popular in Sant communities. Rajab's *Sarvāṅgī*, therefore, does not include a so-called Brahmanized version of the miracle but narrates one out of the two pre-existing stories. Contrary to what Callewaert has asserted the *Nāmdev parcaī* itself dispels the notion that Rajab drew on a later, Brahmanized oral tradition. Instead, it demonstrates that Anantadās and Rajab both narrate the same legends. As far as the 'Brahmanized' legends about Nāmdev are concerned, Harirām Vyās who flourished before Anantadās and Rajab was singing the same legends about Nāmdev in Vrindaban.[37] There are some other *pads* of Dādū's first-generation disciples such as by Bājīd in Gopāldās' *Sarvāṅgī*[38] whose legends are very similar to those attributed to Anantadās. The legends related to the lives of Nāmdev and Kabīr in the hagiographical verses of Dādūpanthī poet-saints such as Bājīd, Bakhnā and Rajab are very similar to those of the hagiographies sung by Anantadās in his *parcaīs*, which indicates that these poet-saints were drawing from the same oral lore.[39]

The most noteworthy element, however, is also related to the time of the compilation of Rajab's *Sarvāṅgī*. This *Sarvāṅgī* does not contain any of the *pad*s of Sundardās, known in the Dādūpanth as 'Sundardās Chote' or Sundardās the younger, even though it was well known at the time in the Dādūpanth and beyond that he was the most learned of all the Sants. Besides it is also said that Sundardās was very close to Rajab. According to Purohit Harinārāyan Sharma, in 1607 (vs 1663), on the first *Phālgun melā*, Sundardās came to Naraina when he was eleven, and after that, he, Rajab, Jagjīvandās and some other Dādūpanthīs went to Kashi. While there, Rajab and Sundardās spent a great deal of time together; Sundardās often used to go to Sanganer to meet Rajab and when he later heard about the death of Rajab, he was deeply grieved. Eventually, he also died in Sanganer in 1689 (vs 1746).[40]

Yet, despite his supposedly close ties to Rajab, none of Sundardās' verses were included into Rajab's *Sarvāṅgī*. The most apparent reason for this is that Sundardās, traditionally said to have been born in 1596, was very young when Rajab prepared his anthology. The view that Rajab's *Sarvāṅgī* was compiled before the death of Dādū was proposed and supported by Barthwal and Kshitimohan Sen, according to whom Rajab anthologized the sayings of his guru, Dādū, in *aṅg* order at least ten years before the compilation of the *Guru Granth Sāhib* in 1604.[41]

A second *Sarvāṅgī* was compiled in 1627 by Dādū's third-generation disciple, *potā-śiṣya*, Gopāldās, which, in modern scholarship, came to light much later than Rajab's. It was Callewaert who discovered this manuscript in Jaipur and published it in 1993.[42] This anthology is particularly important because it bears a date. The colophon dates it to 1627 (vs 1684). As the date appears to be genuine, there is no debate about this *Sarvāṅgī*'s time of compilation.

In his *Sarvāṅgī*, Gopāldās collected the poems of about 138 poet-saints. He included the compositions of the so-called *nirguṇ* Sants such as Dādū, Kabīr, Pīpā, Senā, Nāmdev, Ravidās, Nānak, Bājīd and Bakhnā, as well as the poems of Gorakhnāth, Bhartṛhari, Rāmānand, Sūrdās and other poet-saints famous in his time. Therefore, the significance of this anthology is not just that it has a more accurate date of compilation, but that it provides some information on the ever-increasing canon of songs used by the saint community in the first half of the seventeenth century.

A Comparison of the Two Sarvāṅgīs

What is the reason behind the structural differences in Rajab's and Gopāldās's *Sarvāṅgīs*? If we consider the time of compilation of Rajab's *Sarvāṅgī* to be before the death of Dādū, then the two *Sarvāṅgīs* must have a time difference of approximately twenty-five to thirty years. During these years, a major historical event altered the Dādūpanth.

Rāghavdās, in his *Bhaktamāl*, writes that Garībdās, Dādū's son, was the first abbot at the Dādūpanthī centre in Naraina.[43] After the death of Dādū in 1603, his disciples were institutionalized as a sect, which is called the Dādūpanth today. Dādū had started making disciples in his lifetime and he had a large group of them around him when he died. Naraina, where Dādū lived before his death, and Bhairāṇā, where he died, became sacred places for the Dādūpanth. These developments in the Dādūpanth influenced the next generation of Dādū's disciples.

In Rajab's *Sarvāṅgī*, Kabīr appears as the most abundantly represented poet with about 159 poems, whereas in Gopāldās's anthology, Dādū appears as the biggest poet with 403 verses. There is also a difference in the positioning of the various *aṅg*s in the two *Sarvāṅgīs*, even though the number of the Ragas is similar in both.

Gopāldās' *Sarvāṅgī* commences with the praise of Dādū in the *Gurudev kau aṅg* (the section of the guru), whereas Rajab's *Sarvāṅgī* begins with the *Astuti kau aṅg* (the section of prayer), in which Rajab praises not only the guru but also his text, the

Sarvāṅgī. Following the *Astuti kau aṅg*, the second *aṅg* is the encounter with the guru, *Bheṇṭ kau aṅg* (the section of meeting), followed by the *Guru kau aṅg*. Almost all Dādūpanthī anthologies begin with the phrase *Dādū namaḥ nirañjana* (Dādū bows to the Untainted One) and Rajab's *Sarvāṅgī* is no exception. Praise of the guru is the primary characteristic of the poetry of *nirguṇ* devotion. However, in the *Sarvāṅgī* of Rajab, the placement of the *Astuti kau aṅg* is unique. For Rajab, praising his *Sarvāṇgī* was no less than worshipping an idol. Verses worshipping the *Sarvāṅgī* itself as a unique text and the *Astuti kau aṅg* are not present in the *Sarvāṅgī* of Gopāldās.

Sūrdās and the *Karuṇā/Bīnati* Poems in Rajab and Gopāldās's *Sarvāṅgī*

Interestingly the Sant community is perceived differently in the *Sarvāṅgī*s and in the *Pañc-vāṇīs*. The *Pañc-vāṇī* collections comprise the works of five Sants: Dādū, Kabīr, Nāmdev, Raidās and Hardās, all so-called *nirguṇ* bhaktas. However, the five Sants with the greatest number of compositions in the two *Sarvāṅgī*s include Sūrdās as well. Modern histories present Sūrdās as one of the *saguṇ* bhaktas *par excellence* but, for Rajab, the sensibility of some of Sūr's *pad*s match the other so-called *nirguṇ* bhaktas and their *pad*s are grouped into the same *aṅg*s.

The five major poets of Rajab's *Sarvāṅgī* are Dādū, Kabīr, Nāmdev, Sūrdās and Raidās. In the two *Sarvāṅgī*s, Sūr's *vinay* poetry appears frequently, especially in the *Karuṇā binati kau aṅg* (the section of compassion and petition) in Rajab and in *Bharosa binati kau aṅg* (the section of trust and petition) in Gopāldās. The *Karuṇā binati kau aṅg* in Rajab's *Sarvāṅgī* is one of the largest *aṅg*s, and contains the highest number of *pad*s of Sūr along with those of Kabīr, Raidās, Dādū, Bājīd, Nāmdev, Tursī and Rajab.[44] Sixteen of the 50 *pad*s attributed to Sūr in Rajab's *Sarvāṅgī* are found in this *aṅg*. In Gopāldās's *Sarvāṅgī*, the *Bharosā binati kau aṅg* contains the highest number of the *pad*s of Sūr.

Various characters and symbols of Sūr's *vinay* (or *karuṇā bīnati/bharosa binati*) poems that the *Sarvāṅgī*s contain are also familiar to Dādū's disciples and often figure in their own poetry. For example, Krishna's compassion (*karuṇā*) for Draupadī and the Pāṇḍavas is also sung by the Dādūpanthīs. There are quite a few *pad*s attributed to the Dādūpanthīs which not only share Sūr's approach but also have a similar vocabulary. These *pad*s demonstrate that Sūrdās must have been very popular among the Dādūpanthīs. Rajab's *Sarvāṅgī* includes not only Sūr but also a *pad* from the *Vinaypatrikā* of Tulsīdās.[45] Where should we then place the *Sarvāṅgī* tradition in the history and historiography of the bhakti movement? The inclusion of the poems of *saguṇī*s alongside those of the *nirguṇī*s supports John S. Hawley's notion that in these earlier anthologies, the categorization of *nirguṇ* and *saguṇ* was not as distinct and firm as it became later.[46] This means that the legends that are retold in the *Sarvāṅgī* were grounded in the religious beliefs of the people of that period and these beliefs were not categorized as either *nirguṇ* or *saguṇ*.

Interestingly, in the *Bamek saṁhitā kau aṅg* (Section of intelligence) of Rajab's *Sarvāṅgī*, we find a *pad* signed as Sūrdās which was later attributed to Kabīr:[47]

apanapaũ āpahi bisariyaũ.
jaise svāna kāñca mandira maĩ, bhrami bhrami bhũki maryau;
jaise kesari ujhaki kūpa maĩ pratibimba dekha pariyau;
jiũ gaja phaṭaka saila ari ura ḍāri danta aṛāi pariyau;
markaṭa mūnthi chāḍi na dīnī ghari ghari bāri phiryau;
sūradāsa nalini kau suvanā, kahi kaune pakariyau.[48]

The self forgets itself
as a frantic dog in a glass temple
  barks himself to death;
as a lion, seeing a form in the well
  leaps on the image;
as a rutting elephant sticks his tusk
  in a crystal boulder;
the monkey has his fistful of sweets
  and won't let go, so;
  from house to house he gibbers;
Kabīr says, parrot-on-a-pole
  Who has caught you?[49]

This *pad* made an interesting journey. In order to trace its textual history, I tried to locate it in other seventeenth-century anthologies. I could not find it in Gopāldās' *Sarvāṅgī*. However, it occurred as a *pad* of Sūrdās again in another *Sarvāṅgī* anthology of 1696, a manuscript of which is preserved at the Rajasthan Oriental Research Institute in Jodhpur (numbered as 34235). According to the colophon, it was written in 1696. This can be considered the third *Sarvāṅgī* in the tradition. While this *pad* is in the *Rāmkalī* Raga in Rajab's *Sarvāṅgī*, it is in the *Sāraṅg* Raga in the Rajasthan Oriental Research Institute manuscript. The fact that the same *pad* is under two different Ragas in the two *Sarvāṅgī*s indicates that it was famous in two different oral traditions. We can also infer that Rajab's attribution of this *pad* to Sūr was not a mistake but the poem was perceived as a song of Sūrdās in the seventeenth century.

The absence of this *pad* from *The Millennium Kabīr Vāṇī* shows that it was initially not attributed to Kabīr.[50] Early historians of Hindi literature also attributed this *pad* to Sūrdās and, as late as the nineteenth century, Shivsingh Sengar, in his *Śivsingh Saroj*, introduced Sūrdās with only two of his *pad*s, one of which was the very same one.[51] But for some twentieth-century Hindi scholars of bhakti, it is a *pad* by Kabīr. In the *Bījak of Kabīr* and in Hazari Prasad Dvivedi's *Kabīr*, this same *pad* is presented as one of Kabīr.[52] The imagery in this *pad* is similar to that of Kabīr's *pad*s but attributing it to Kabīr is a product of dividing the bhakti poets into *nirguṇ* and *saguṇ* bhaktas. For Rajab, Sūr and Kabīr had same themes in many of their verses, therefore both of them could be grouped together. This explains the twentieth-century tendency to assign authorship to poems based on preconceived notions about the thematic sensibilities of certain poets. For example, Shivsingh Sengar, in his nineteenth-century account of Hindi literature attributed the aforementioned *pad* to Sūr. Then, in the twentieth-century it was attributed to Kabīr by Hazari Prasad Dvivedi.

Many verses in the *Sarvāṅgī*s provide invaluable information on the lives of the various Sants of India. An example of this can be found in Rajab's *Sarvāṅgī* in a section called *Granth sādh mahimā* composed in Sanskrit. Rajab writes about different castes and clans of the Sants, including the Nāths.

In both *Sarvāṅgīs*, we find many verses with historical and hagiographic references. These anthologies contain *pads*, which, recalling the legends of devotees, describe Sants of the Dādūpanth and those from other communities. In these verses, the Sants sing about themselves, about other poets and sects, and evoke legends of their contemporaries and earlier poets.

The *Sarvāṅgī* of Haridās

As has been mentioned, the anthology of 1696, preserved at the Rajasthan Oriental Research Institute, Jodhpur, and numbered as 34235, is from the same anthological tradition and is explicitly called *Sarvāṅgī* by the scribe of the manuscript. This *Sarvāṅgī* has 129 *aṅgs* and presents *pads* in 23 Ragas. The colophon dates it to 1696 (vs 1753) and states that it was copied by Haridās in the village called Bagaṛdehrā. Haridās, who describes himself as a disciple of Śyāmdās, the disciple of Kalyāṇdās, may also be the compiler of the text. The structure of this manuscript follows the basic pattern of the two *Sarvāṅgīs* that it chronologically succeeds. Although this *Sarvāṅgī* is a copy of Rajab's text, at many places from others it differs, so much that it should be considered the third extant *Sarvāṅgī* of the Dādūpanth. Haridās is in the disciple tradition of Rajab and his *Sarvāṅgī* copies the *aṅgs* of Rajab's *Sarvāṅgī*. This *Sarvāṅgī* is important to examine the development of the *Sarvāṅgī* tradition, the inclusion and exclusion of the Sants, as well as their increasing and decreasing verses, as it was possibly compiled almost hundred years after the proposed date of Rajab's *Sarvāṅgī*.

Conclusion

The theme-based model for grouping the diverse array of bhakti poets that was introduced by the Dādūpanth, was a great contribution to bhakti literature. Therefore, even though it was a Dādūpanthī textual tradition, its importance expands beyond sectarian boundaries. The *Sarvāṅgīs* illustrate a characteristic feature of the Dādūpanth: that the community was not only in dialogue with other bhakti communities in its geographical area but also gave a textual foundation to the poems of Sants from different sects. The *Sarvāṅgīs* show that the content of an individual poem was given great importance. Therefore, grouping poetry into *aṅgs* became the basis of this tradition and the affiliation of the Sants to varied schools did not bear much importance for the *Sarvāṅgīkārs*, the compilers of the *Sarvāṅgīs*. While many communities would follow their example, it appears that the Dādūpanthī anthologies may be the earliest instances of thematically anthologized bhakti poetry.

NOTES

1. Most of the research for this paper was done for my M.Phil. thesis (2005-7) at JNU, Delhi. I am thankful to Prof. Purusottam Agrawāl and Prof. Jack Hawley for their advice, suggestions and very helpful comments. I would like to thank Tyler Williams, Prof. Allison Busch, Patton Burchett and Christine Karwoski for their comments and criticism on earlier drafts of this paper.
2. H.P. Dvivedi, *Hindī sāhitya: udbhav aur vikās*, New Delhi: Rājkamal Prakāśan, 2003, p. 78 and P. Chaturvedi, *Uttarī bhārat kī sant paramparā*, 2nd edn., Allahabad: Bhāratī Bhandār, 1964, p. 507.
3. S. Iraqi, ed., *Rajjabdās kī sarvāṅgī*, Aligarh: Granthāyan, 1985.
4. D. Simhal, ed., *Sarvāṅgī: guṇ gañj-nāmā sahit*, Jalandhar: Deepak Publishers, 1990.
5. B.K. Simhal, ed., *Rajjab kī sarbaṅgī*, Raygarh: Brajmohan Sā̃vaṛiyā, 2010.
6. This is, however, not the earliest manuscript. Brajendra Kumar Simhal consulted a handwritten book from 1707 for his edition.
7. Iraqi presents his version as based on the two earliest manuscripts of Rajab's *Sarvāṅgī*. One is from the Nāgarīpracāriṇī Sabhā (NPS) Library, Varanasi. No. 1394 (dated as vs 1771/CE 1714) and the other is from The Dādū Mahāvidyālaya in Jaipur, Bastā No. 3 (vs 1819/CE 1762). Dr. Simhal's version is based on a manuscript dating from vs 1813/CE 1756, which was copied at the village of Ghirācaũ (District Sangrur, Punjab) and is now at the Central State Library in Patiala (Punjab).
8. W.M. Callewaert, 'The Sarvāṅgī of the Dādūpanthī Rajab', revised doctoral dissertation, Departement Oriëntalistiek, Katholieke Universiteit, 1978.
9. W.M. Callewaert, ed., *The Sarvāṅgī of Gopāldās: A 17th Century Anthology of Bhakti Literature*, Delhi: Manohar, 1993.
10. Iraqi, ed., *Rajjabdās kī sarvāṅgī*, p. 102. Similar couplets occur throughout the text.
11. A. Nahta, *Rāghavdāskṛt bhaktamāl: caturdāskṛt ṭīkā sahit*, Jodhpur: Rājasthān Prācyavidyā Pratiṣṭhān, 1965, p. 187.

12. Rāghavdās's *Bhaktamāl* has been dated by modern scholars to 1660, 1713 or CE 1720. The reason for this debate is the couplet Rāghavdās gives in the colophon of his *Bhaktamāl*: *saṁvata satraha sai satraha ūtarā, śukla pakṣa śanivāra; tithi tritiyā āṣaḍha kī, rāgho kiyau bicāra.* (Nahta, *Bhaktamāl*, p. 246). Both editors of this *Bhaktamāl* translate *satraha sai satraha ūtarā* as VS 1717 (CE 1660). D.N. Lorenzen, 'The Kabir-panth and Social Protest', in *The Sants: Studies in a Devotional Tradition of India*, ed. Karine Schomer and W.H. McLeod, Delhi: Motilal Banarsidass, 1987 p. 288 and Chaturvedi, *Uttarī bhārat kī sant paramparā*, p. 514 also support the translation of 1660 (VS 1717). Without going too much into this debate, I would like to suggest that when Jangopāl, a disciple of Dādu, in his *Dādū janma līlā parcaī* (*c.* 1610 to 1620), signs *solahasai ikautara (ika+utara)* as Dādū's year of birth, he also means VS 1601. Therefore, *satraha sai satrahautara (satraha + utara)* is presumably VS 1717. See also Hawley, n. 22 in this volume.
13. Dvivedi, *Hindī sāhitya: udbhav aur vikās*, p. 95, K. Sen, *Medieval Mysticism of India*, London: Luzac and Co., 1935, p. 111; Chaturvedi, *Uttarī bhārat kī sant paramparā*, p. 507,
14. Sen, *Medieval Mysticism of India*, p. 104; Chaturvedi, *Uttarī bhārat kī sant paramparā*, p. 507.
15. G.S. Mann, *The Goindval Pothis*, Cambridge, MA: Harvard University Press, 1996.
16. G.N. Bahura and K.E. Bryant, *The Padas of Sūrdās,* Jaipur: Sawai Mansingh II Museum, 1982.
17. The idea that it was Rajab who first grouped Dādū's *Vāṇī* into *aṅgs* has been proposed by two noted scholars of Sant literature, Hazari Prasad Dvivedi in his *Hindī sāhitya kī bhūmikā* and Parashuram Chaturvedi in his *Uttarī bhārat kī sant paramparā*, Iraqi, ed., *Rajjabdās kī sarvāṅgī* (p. 53) and other Dādūpanthī scholars also support this notion. See, for example, R.C. Mishra, *Sant rajab alī,* Delhi: Sant Sāhitya Sansthān, 2002, p. 27 or N. Pandey, *Sant rajjab,* Varanasi: Viśvavidyālay Prakāśan, 2004, p. 69.
18. C.P. Tripathi, ed., *Śrī svāmī dādūdayāl kī vāṇī*, Ajmer: Vaidik Mantrālaya, 1907. (This collection is based on the manuscripts of the *Aṅgabandhū*)
19. P. Barthwal, *Traditions of Indian Mysticism Based upon the Nirguna School of Hindi Poetry*, Delhi: Heritage, 1978, p. 282.
20. Chaturvedi, *Uttarī bhārat kī sant paramparā*, p. 507.
21. P. Narayandas, ed., *Śrī rajjab bānī*, Ajmer: Narayansingh Shekhavat, 1967.
22. W.M. Callewaert, *The Hindī Biography of Dādū Dayāl*, Delhi: Motilal Banarsidass, 1988, chapter 15: 22 p. 122. (The translation given here is by Callewaert.)
23. Simhal, ed., *Sarvāṅgī: guṇ gañj-nāmā sahit*, p. 27.
24. Nahta, *Bhaktamāl*, p. 187.
25. P. Chaturvedi, ed., *Bhaktikāl (nirguṇ bhakti), Hindī sāhitya kā bṛhat itihās*, 4, Varanasi: Nāgarīpracāriṇī Sabhā, 1968, p. 198.

26. P.D. Barthwal, ed., *Rāmānanda kī hindī racnāyẽ*, Varanasi: Nāgarīpracāriṇī Sabhā, 1955, p. 1. The most noteworthy point is that Barthwal did consult this manuscript as he categorically mentions a *pad* of Rāmānand in the '*tīrath taskar aṅg*', which can be found in the same *aṅg* of the *Sarvāṅgī* of Rajab (Iraqi, ed., *Rajjabdās kī sarvāṅgī*, pp. 490-1).
27. Callewaert, 'The Sarvāṅgī of the Dādūpanthī Rajab', p. 81.
28. W.M. Callewaert, 'Padas of Guru Nānak in Rajasthani Manuscripts', in *Bhakti in Current Research 2000-2003: Procedings of the Ninth International Conference on Early Devotional Literature in New Indo-Aryan Languages, Heidelberg, 23-26 July 2003*, ed. Monika Horstmann, Delhi: Manohar, 2006, p. 51.
29. T.N. Dikshit, ed., *Śivsiṁh saroj*, Lucknow: Tejkumar Press, 1966, p. 292.
30. G. Mishra, S. Mishra and S. Mishra, *Miśrabandhu-vinod, athavā hindī-sāhitya kā itihāsa tathā kavi-kīrttana*, 3 vols., Khandava & Prayag: Hindī Granth Prasārak Maṇḍalī, 1913, vol. 2, p. 475.
31. P.H. Sharma, ed., *Sundar granthāvalī*, Calcutta: Rajasthan Research Society, 1936, vol. 1, p. 59.
32. Iraqi, ed., *Rajjabdās kī sarvāṅgī*, p. 55.
33. Callewaert, 'Padas of Guru Nānak in Rajasthani Manuscripts', p. 51.
34. Callewaert, 'The Sarvāṅgī of the Dādūpanthī Rajab', p. 74.
35. W.M. Callewaert and S. Sharma, *The Hagiographies of Anantadās: The Bhakti Poets of North India*, Richmond: Curzon, 2000, p. 39.
36. Ibid., pp. 32-3.
37. H.R.M. Pauwels, *In Praise of Holy Men: Hagiographic Poems by and about Harirām Vyās*, Groningen: Egbert Forsten, 2002, p. 93.
38. Callewaert, ed., *The Sarvāṅgī of Gopāldās*, p. 183. On this page, there are a few *sākhī*s referring to some legends such as *sākhī* 85 about Kabīr and a *pad* by Bājīd at the end.
39. In her article on the Dādūpanthī anthologies, Monika Horstmann suggested that the Dādūpanth was possibly a writing community from the beginning and Dādū himself arranged for his sayings to be written down. See M. Horstmann, 'Dādūpanthī Anthologies of the Eighteenth and Nineteenth Centuries', in *Bhakti in Current Research 2000-2003*, ed. Horstmann, Delhi: Manohar, 2006, pp. 163-77.
40. Sharma, ed., *Sundar granthāvalī*, pp. 57-61.
41. Sen, *Medieval Mysticism of India*, p. 104.
42. Callewaert, ed., *The Sarvāṅgī of Gopāldās*.
43. Nahta, *Bhaktamāl*, p. 183.
44. See Iraqi, ed., *Rajjabdās kī sarvāṅgī*, p. 223 (*aṅg* 39) and *aṅg* 78 of Gopāldās's *Sarvāṅgī*.
45. See *Vibhacār bardāi kau aṅg* in Iraqi, ed., *Rajjabdās kī sarvāṅgī*, p. 593.
46. J. S. Hawley, 'The Sant in Sur Das', in *The Sants: Studies in a Devotional Tradition of India*, ed. W.H. McLeod and Karine Schomer, Berkeley &

Delhi: Berkeley Religious Studies Series & Motilal Banarsidass, 1987, pp. 191-211.

47. It is missing from the earliest Kabīr-manuscripts as published in W.M. Callewaert, S. Sharma and D. Taillieu, *The Millennium Kabīr Vāṇī: A Collection of Pads*, Delhi: Manohar, 2000. It is, however, included with some variation as *śabd* 76 in S. Singh, ed., *Kabīr Bījak*, Allahabad: Nilābh Prakāśan, 1972, pp. 136-7 and as *pad* 209 in H.P. Dvivedi, ed., *Kabīr*, 9th edn., Delhi: Rājkamal Prakāśan, 2002, p. 261.
48. Iraqi, ed., *Rajjabdās kī sarvāṅgī*, p. 419.
49. The translation is adapted from the one published in L.B. Hess and S. Singh, *The Bijak of Kabir*, 1st Indian edn., Delhi: Motilal Banarsidass, 1986, p. 67.
50. Callewaert, Sharma and Taillieu, *The Millennium Kabīr Vāṇī*. (This collection of *Kabīr-Vāṇī* is based on dated manuscripts from the sixteenth and seventeenth centuries.)
51. Dikshit, ed., *Śivsiṁh saroj*, p. 320.
52. *Pad* 209 in Dvivedi, ed., *Kabīr*, p. 261 and Hess and Singh, *The Bijak of Kabir*, p. 67.

BIBLIOGRAPHY

Bahura, G.N. and K.E. Bryant, *The Padas of Sūrdās*, Jaipur: Sawai Mansingh II Museum, 1982.

Barthwal, P.D., *Traditions of Indian Mysticism Based upon the Nirguna School of Hindi Poetry*, Delhi: Heritage, 1978.

——, ed., *Rāmānanda kī hindī racnāyẽ*, Varanasi: Nāgarīpracāriṇī Sabhā, 1955.

Callewaert, W.M., *The Hindī Biography of Dādū Dayāl*, Delhi: Motilal Banarsidass, 1988.

——, 'Padas of Guru Nānak in Rajasthani Manuscripts', in *Bhakti in Current Research 2000-2003: Procedings of the Ninth International Conference on Early Devotional Literature in New Indo-Aryan Languages, Heidelberg, 23-26 July 2003*, ed. M. Horstmann, Delhi: Manohar, 2006, pp. 49-114.

——, 'The Sarvāṅgī of the Dādūpanthī Rajab', revised doctoral dissertation, Departement Oriëntalistiek, Katholieke Universiteit, 1978.

——, ed., *The Sarvāṅgī of Gopāldās: A 17th Century Anthology of Bhakti Literature*, Delhi: Manohar, 1993.

Callewaert, W.M., and S. Sharma, *The Hagiographies of Anantadās: The Bhakti Poets of North India*, Richmond: Curzon, 2000.

Callewaert, W.M., S. Sharma and D. Taillieu, *The Millennium Kabīr Vāṇī: A Collection of Pads*, Delhi: Manohar, 2000.

Chaturvedi, P., *Uttarī bhārat kī sant paramparā*, 2nd edn., Allahabad: Bhāratī Bhandār, 1964.

——, ed., *Bhaktikāl (nirguṇ bhakti), Hindī sāhitya kā bṛhat itihās*, 4, Varanasi: Nāgarīpracāriṇī Sabhā, 1968.

Dikshit, T.N., ed., *Śivsiṁh saroj*, Lucknow: Tejkumar Press, 1966.
Dvivedi, H.P., *Hindī sāhitya: udbhav aur vikās*, Delhi: Rājkamal Prakāśan, 2003.
——, ed., *Kabīr*, 9th edn, Delhi: Rājkamal Prakāśan, 2002.
Hawley, J.S., 'The Sant in Sur Das', in *The Sants: Studies in a Devotional Tradition of India*, ed. W.H. McLeod and K. Schomer, *Berkeley Religious Studies*, Berkeley & Delhi: Berkeley Religious Studies Series & Motilal Banarsidass, 1987, pp. 191-211.
Hess, L.B. and S. Singh, *The Bijak of Kabir*, 1st Indian edn, Delhi: Motilal Banarsidass, 1986.
Horstmann, M., 'Dādūpanthī Anthologies of the Eighteenth and Nineteenth Centuries', in *Bhakti in Current Research 2000-2003*, ed. Horstmann, Delhi: Manohar, 2006, pp. 163-78.
Iraqi, S., ed., *Rajjabdās kī sarvāṅgī*, Aligarh: Granthāyan, 1985.
Lorenzen, D.N., 'The Kabir-panth and Social Protest', in *The Sants: Studies in a Devotional Tradition of India*, ed. Schomer and McLeod, Delhi: Motilal Banarsidass, 1987, pp. 281-303.
Mann, G.S., *The Goindval Pothis*, Cambridge, MA: Harvard University Press, 1996.
Mishra, G., S. Mishra and S. Mishra, *Miśrabandhu-vinod, athavā hindī-sāhitya kā itihāsa tathā kavi-kīrttana,* 3 vols, Khandava & Prayag: Hindī Granth Prasārak Maṇḍalī, 1913.
Mishra, R.C., *Sant rajab alī*, Delhi: Sant Sāhitya Sansthān, 2002.
Nahta, A., *Rāghavdāskṛt bhaktamāl: caturdāskṛt ṭīkā sahit, Rājasthān purātan granthamālā* 78, Jodhpur: Rājasthān Prācyavidyā Pratiṣṭhān, 1965.
Narayandas, P., ed., *Śrī rajjab bānī*, Ajmer: Narayansingh Shekhavat, [1967].
Pandey, N., *Sant rajjab*, Varanasi: Viśvavidyālay Prakāśan, 2004.
Pauwels, H.R.M., *In Praise of Holy Men: Hagiographic Poems by and about Harirām Vyās, Groningen Oriental Studies*, v 18, Groningen: Egbert Forsten, 2002.
Sen, K., *Medieval Mysticism of India*, London: Luzac and Co., 1935.
Sharma, P.H., ed., *Sundar granthāvalī*, Calcutta: Rajasthan Research Society, 1936.
Singh, S., ed., *Kabīr Bījak*, Allahabad: Nilābh Prakāśan, 1972.
Simhal, B.K., ed., *Rajjab kī sarbaṅgī*, Raygarh: Brajmohan Sāvaṛiyā, 2010.
Simhal, D., ed., *Sarvāṅgī: guṇ gañj-nāmā sahit*, Jalandhar: Deepak Publishers, 1990.
Tripathi, C.P., ed., *Śrī svāmī dādūdayāl kī vāṇī*, Ajmer: Vaidik Mantrālaya, 1907.

CHAPTER 3

Nābhādās' *Bhaktamāl* and Manuscript Culture[1]

JAMES P. HARE

Introduction

Nābhādās composed his *Bhaktamāl* in the late sixteenth or early seventeenth century. This collection of hagiographies, the title of which could be translated as 'The Garland of Devotees', praises hundreds of saints and thereby sets the boundaries of a devotional community that far exceeds the Rāmānandī sectarian context in which its author wrote. Inclusiveness is among the most conspicuous features of Nābhādās' text. The bhaktas whom Nābhādās praises include various manifestations and avatars of God, poets who sang praises to God in a number of languages, and devotees who worshipped God according to several different paths. They include men and women, and people from all social strata. They come from throughout South Asia and from the near present as well as from the mythological past. Nābhādās gives central importance to the devotees themselves. For him, bhakti is the only proper basis for human society. He rejects caste, kingship, and even family in favour of a community joining human society and the divine in bhakti.[2]

Within about a century of its composition, the *Bhaktamāl* became the site of a debate over the boundaries of a religious community defined by bhakti. Priyādās' *Bhaktirasabodhinī*,

'The Awakening of the Essence of Bhakti', interprets the *Bhaktamāl* from a more clearly-defined sectarian perspective. Priyādās, a Gauṛīy Vaishnava, completed his text in Vrindavan in CE 1712. In his commentary, he selectively explains and extrapolates Nābhādās' verses. Priyādās presents a conception of the Vaishnava community that differs sharply from Nābhādās' outlook. He accepts Nābhādās' frame even as he modifies its logic. He shifts Nābhādās' focus from the devotees to God and emphasizes the importance of the sampradaya. He increases the role of royal patrons and grants spiritual importance to caste. Through the *Bhaktamāl* and its most influential commentary, we witness a debate over the boundaries of this religious community. The tension between Nābhādās and Priyādās can, in hindsight, be viewed as a debate over the boundaries and composition of what would later come to be called Hinduism. In the colonial context of the nineteenth century, this debate would becomc more prominent and well-defined, but many of the ingredients were already present during the seventeenth and early eighteenth centuries.[3]

This essay considers the transmission and reception of Nābhādās' *Bhaktamāl* during the eighteenth and early nineteenth centuries. I begin by offering a summary of existing *Bhaktamāl* manuscripts. This overview permits several observations: the *Bhaktamāl* was a popular text with a wide geographical reach. Its appeal was broad and not limited to one or two sampradayas. Priyādās serves as the central figure in this tradition; the entire *Bhaktamāl* tradition flows through him. I conclude by exploring some of the implications of these observations.

Sources

Several scholars have considered some of the many *Bhaktamāl* manuscripts found in India and abroad. Ram Das Gupta[4] and Gilbert Pollet,[5] in their dissertations, each reviewed the *Bhaktamāl* and *Bhaktirasabodhinī* manuscripts available in England.[6] The most recent and complete account of these manuscripts is found in Pollet's *Eight Manuscripts of the Hindī Bhaktamāla in England*.[7] Pollet and Gupta were working with the manuscripts available in Britain, which only represent a sliver of the *Bhaktamāl*'s manuscript tradition. In this respect at least, their work has been superseded by Narendra Jha's.[8] As part of the effort of composing his critical edition of Nābhādās' *mūl* text, Jha surveys numerous manuscripts of the *Bhaktamāl* both with and without a commentary. He notes that the *Bhaktamāl* was an extremely popular text and that hundreds of *Bhaktamāl* manuscripts exist in north India. Many of these manuscripts are housed in sectarian institutes and are unavailable to research scholars.[9] Jha managed to see about 50 manuscripts. The oldest of these, dated 1642, is located in Jodhpur's Rajasthan Oriental Research Institute (RORI). A slightly more recent study of the *Bhaktamāl* tradition is Kailash Chandra Sharma's *Bhaktamāl aur hindī kāvya mẽ uskī paramparā* (The *Bhaktamāl* and its Tradition in Hindi Poetry).[10] There are 12 commentaries and translations among Sharma's sources, including the *Bhaktirasabodhinī*. Of these, five are commentaries on Nābhādās' and Priyādās' texts dating to the mid-nineteenth century or earlier.

My own archival research focused on key sites in the *Bhaktamāl* tradition. As Jha notes, the *Bhaktamāl* was an extremely popular text, and its popularity was widespread. It seems that every archive contains multiple copies of this text. In order to limit a potentially endless search for manuscripts, I decided to confine my search to several sites associated with the transmission of the *Bhaktamāl*: Jaipur, Vrindavan, Kolkata, and Avadh. Nābhādās was associated with the Galta monastery near present-day Jaipur. Priyādās wrote his commentary in Vrindavan. The first printed *Bhaktamāl* was produced under the auspices of the College of Fort William in Calcutta, present-day Kolkata. 'Sitaramsharan' Bhagavan Prasad 'Rupkala' compiled the 'standard' edition of the *Bhaktamāl* in Ayodhya, which Naval Kishore published in Lucknow.[11] I also searched for manuscripts in archives in Jodhpur and Allahabad due to their significant collections. My focus was not by any means exclusive and these sites were not equally productive. Jodhpur and Allahabad, in particular, host important archives for this project while Kolkata and Lucknow did not prove particularly fruitful.

Manuscripts

Jha usefully divides *Bhaktamāl* manuscripts into three categories: the first type contains only the *mūl* text; the second type contains the *mūl* text alongside Priyādās' commentary; the third type contains the *mūl* text, Priyādās' commentary, and an *upaṭīkā* or *vyākhyā* sub-commentary by a third individual. Priyādās is the *Bhaktamāl*'s earliest-known commentator, and all subsequent commentators have taken the combined text of Priyādās and Nābhādās as their subject.

I am aware of 11 manuscripts of Nābhādās' *mūl* text that do not include Priyādās' commentary or reflect its influence. Jha describes six of these manuscripts. One of them is found in the Sarveśvar Kāryālay of the Nimbārka Śodh Saṁsthān in Vrindavan. Jha estimates the date of this *Bhaktamāl* manuscript to be around 1713, and the scribe seems to have been a member of the Nimbārka Sampradāy from the Braj region. The RORI in Udaipur houses a single manuscript of the *Bhaktamāl* without a commentary, dated 1667. The RORI in Jodhpur houses four manuscripts of the *Bhaktamāl* without a commentary. One is dated 1705; another is undated but was probably copied in 1667 or 1668. A relatively recent manuscript carries the date 1832. This archive houses the oldest-known *Bhaktamāl,* completed in 1642. In addition to these six, Jha notes that the 1909 Khoj Report of the Nāgarīpracāriṇī Sabhā lists a single manuscript of the *Bhaktamāl* without a commentary, dated to 1713, and located in the royal library of Neemrana, Rajasthan.[12] In addition to those listed by Jha, the RORI in Jodhpur houses another manuscript of the *Bhaktamāl* without a commentary. This manuscript is incomplete and damaged. It was copied in Bikaner in 1723. The Vrindavan Research Institute also houses three *Bhaktamāl*s without commentary. Each of these manuscripts, however, is undated, unsigned, and incomplete.

Unlike manuscripts that only include Nābhādās' *mūl* text, those that contain Priyādās' commentary are plentiful. Hundreds of these manuscripts exist and are found throughout India, particularly in the north. Jha managed to examine about 50 manuscripts. All but six of these include Priyādās' commentary. These can be found at the Benares Sanskrit University, the Hindī Sāhitya Sammelan in Allahabad, the Nāgarīpracāriṇī Sabhā in Varanasi; the Hit Āśram and the Nimbārka Śodh Saṁsthān in Vrindavan; the Bihār Rāṣṭrabhāṣā Pariṣad in Patna; and the RORI branches in Jaipur, Jodhpur and Udaipur.[13] I have located additional manuscripts in the RORI in Jaipur and Jodhpur, as well as in the Allahabad Museum and the Vrindavan Research Institute. Pollet describes eight manuscripts of the *Bhaktamāl* along with the *Bhaktirasabodhinī* kept in the United Kingdom. These manuscripts are found in the India Office Library and the British Museum Library—now both part of the British Library—as well as in the Bodleian Library.[14] The identities of most of the scribes who copied these manuscripts are unknown, but the sectarian affiliation of several of them can be identified, including Rādhāvallabhī, Kabīrpanthī, Rāmānujī, and Rāmsnehī.

The third category of manuscripts includes Nābhādās' *mūl* text, Priyādās' commentary, and a sub-commentary by another author. These sub-commentators include Bālakrām, Vaiṣṇavdās, Lāldās, Sevāhitdās, and Hulāsdās. Several sub-commentaries have also been written by unknown authors. Bālakrām's *Bhaktamāl kī bhaktadām guṇacitraṇī ṭīkā* expands upon the *Bhaktamāl* by elucidating the lives of nearly every bhakta in the *Bhaktamāl*, including those merely mentioned by Nābhādās and those ignored by Priyādās.[15] Vaiṣṇavdās' *Bhaktamāl dṛṣṭānt* is a commentary on the combined texts of Nābhādās and Priyādās, like every *Bhaktamāl* commentary I have seen. Vaiṣṇavdās follows the order of the *Bhaktirasabodhinī*, and he comments on nearly every bhakta. He does not sharply distinguish between the *Bhaktamāl* and the *Bhaktirasabodhinī* but groups them under a single sub-heading.[16] Lāldās' *Bhaktamāl saṭippaṇ* is another commentary on both Nābhādās and Priyādās. It is a verse composition in Hindi and Sanskrit. Lāldās seeks to clarify the meaning of the original texts and then presents these authoritative texts for proof and context. The *Bhaktamāl saṭippaṇ* does not illuminate the lives of the bhaktas but, rather, praises their personalities.[17] Sevāhitdās' *Bhaktamāl kī vacanakā ṭīkā* is a Braj Bhasha prose commentary on the combined text of Nābhādās and Priyādās, located in the Śrī

Rādhāvallabh Mandir in Banswara, Rajasthan. Sevāhitdās wrote this commentary in 1855 in Dungarpur (Giripur), Rajasthan, in prose commentary with the introduction and conclusion in verse. Sevāhitdās comments on all verses of the *Bhaktamāl*, even those ignored in the *Bhaktirasabodhinī*. He narrates many episodes from the lives of bhaktas that are not found in the Priyādās commentary.[18] Hulāsdās, too, commented on the texts of Nābhādās and Priyādās. His sub-commentary expands upon the text in extensive, analytical prose. This manuscript includes several stanzas that are not found elsewhere, along with a commentary on these verses. Jha speculates that Hulāsdās composed these verses himself.[19] Not all sub-commentaries on the *Bhaktamāl* and *Bhaktirasabodhinī* have an identified author. A manuscript in the Nāgarīpracāriṇī Sabhā, copied by a scribe named Lakṣmaṇdās in 1787, includes an anonymous verse commentary. Jha is dismissive of this text as containing only supernatural stories.[20] The Rajasthan Oriental Research Institute in Jodhpur, the Vrindavan Research Institute and the Allahabad Museum each house manuscripts with sub-commentaries by unknown authors.

Popularity and Regional Diffusion

This overview of *Bhaktamāl* manuscripts permits several observations: the *Bhaktamāl* was a popular text during the eighteenth and early nineteenth centuries. Its reputation was not local but is evident across north India. Its popularity was not restricted to one or two sampradayas; rather, several saw the *Bhaktamāl* as an important work, and Priyādās plays a crucial role in the transmission of the *Bhaktamāl* tradition. I expand on each of these observations below, beginning with the *Bhaktamāl*'s widespread popularity.

The popularity of the *Bhaktamāl* is evident in the number of manuscripts that survive. The preceding section refers to approximately 100 manuscripts that I have either seen or that are described in the secondary literature. This represents only a fraction of the total number of preserved manuscripts. As noted above, Jha, in 1978, reports that hundreds of *Bhaktamāl* manuscripts exist throughout India but complains that many of these manuscripts are unavailable to researchers. Many more are most probably in private hands or are lost or destroyed.

This popularity is not limited to any particular locality. Today, these manuscripts can be found in archives across north India as well as in England. Very few of these manuscripts report where they were copied, and in most cases, the archives have not recorded their origin. What little evidence there is indicates a wide distribution across north India, including Rajasthan, Braj, present-day Haryana, Uttar Pradesh and Bihar.

The *Bhaktamāl* had a wide circulation prior to the arrival of print in north India. Such a diffusion should not be entirely surprising. Edward C. Dimock, Jr., and Tony K. Stewart describe manuscripts of Kṛṣṇadās Kavirāj's *Caitanya Caritāmṛta* as spreading across a wide geographical area with remarkable consistency. The holiness of the text for Gauṛīy Vaishnavas as well as the structure of the text itself made this consistency possible. Dimock and Stewart characterize the early scribal copies of the text as mass-produced and compare its power to unite a diverse community with the role attributed to the press by Benedict Anderson in defining the imagined community of the nation.[21] In the case of such a text, it is unsurprising that the consistency of print editions would largely continue to be maintained by a vigilant community.[22] A detailed treatment of textual drift in the *Bhaktamāl*'s manuscript tradition is beyond the scope of this study, but it is clear that the *Bhaktamāl* was not constrained in the same manner as the *Caitanya Caritāmṛta*. Nābhādās' text does not provide the same checks against interpolation as Kṛṣṇadās Kavirāj's, and the *Bhaktamāl* does not play the same role as the *Caitanya Caritāmṛta* for a single sampradaya. Indeed, as we will see below, the *Bhaktamāl* has been claimed by a variety of sampradayas.

The wide distribution of manuscripts in pre-colonial South Asia is not unusual. Sheldon Pollock argues that South Asian literary culture deliberately rejected the technology of printing. He coins the term 'script-mercantilism' to discuss the robust world of preprint publishing in South Asia. Citing a variety of examples, Pollock argues that this was a literary culture 'for which an entirely adequate and appropriate technology had been developed and maintained for centuries'. For Pollock, script-mercantilism has had a greater impact than print-capitalism in India.[23] The technology of print may not have represented as sharp a break in South Asia as in Europe. However, the case in Europe may not be as clear as is commonly believed.[24]

Through which channels did the *Bhaktamāl* achieve this geographical diffusion? Two possibilities seem likely: sectarian structures and royal courts. In either of these cases, which are by no means mutually exclusive, diffusion would have happened through a literary culture that combined manuscripts and performance. The allusive style of the *Bhaktamāl* suggests that it would be an ideal text for recitation and exposition by a *kathāvācak*, and Priyādās himself is described in legend as a *Bhaktamāl* reciter. It seems clear that by the nineteenth century, at any rate, there was a tradition of *Bhaktamāl* recitation.[25] *Kathāvācak*s were not necessarily embedded in *sāmpradāyik* contexts, but these expository traditions considered alongside sectarian commentaries, discussed below, indicate that the *Bhaktamāl* may have spread primarily through *sāmpradāyik* transmission.

While such avenues of transmission seem likely, royal courts offer another possibility. Allison Busch has highlighted the role of Mughal imperial and sub-imperial courts in patronizing Braj Bhāṣā literature, particularly in the *rīti* mode.[26] Could the *Bhaktamāl* have been recited and copied in a courtly context? Nābhādās celebrates kings who are generous to bhaktas, and Priyādās praises royal patrons to an even greater degree. Priyādās also demonstrates an astute awareness of the Mughal context, for example, by portraying Akbar as a wise patron of bhakti.

The archival evidence does not, unfortunately, allow us to trace the institutional channels of the *Bhaktamāl*'s diffusion with any confidence. A close and systematic examination of *Bhaktamāl* manuscripts may reveal some insights, but such a study is beyond the scope of this essay. Certainly, copies of the *Bhaktamāl* have found their way into both sectarian and royal archives, but their paths into these archives have not been recorded.

During the eighteenth century, the *Bhaktamāl* was a popular text over much of north India. It was by no means the only text to achieve such a distribution. Indeed, such a capacity has been identified as characteristic of pre-colonial South Asian literary cultures. The avenues by which the *Bhaktamāl* achieved this popularity are unclear, but both sectarian formations and royal courts may have played a role.

Sectarian Diffusion

This geographical diversity is matched by a diversity in terms of sampradaya. The *Bhaktamāl* and *Bhaktirasabodhinī* are Rāmānandī and Gauṛīy compositions, respectively. In addition to these two communities, the Rādhāvallabhīs, Nimbārkīs, Rāmasnehīs, Dādūpanthīs and Kabīrpanthīs all copied, commented on, or composed texts modelled on the *Bhaktamāl*. Again, the evidence here is limited since most manuscripts do not record the *sāmpradāyik* affiliation or even the name of the scribe. It is tempting to see the *Bhaktamāl*'s sectarian diffusion as the enactment of Nābhādās' vision of a supra-sectarian bhakti community, but the narrowly sectarian concerns of some of these texts complicate such an understanding.

The *Bhaktamāl* has largely remained within a Vaishnava context, but its appeal to Kabīrpanthīs and Dādūpanthīs challenges an understanding of the *Bhaktamāl* as a strictly Vaishnava text. The Kabīrpanth can be understood as Vaishnava only in the broadest possible sense. Their Kabīr, who is known through the *Bījak*, does refer to Rām, but only to mean God in general, not the avatar of Vishnu and husband of Sita. He completely ignores Krishna, at least as a deity worthy of veneration.[27] Similarly, the Dādūpanth focuses its devotion on the guru and generally conceives of God in a *nirguṇ* manner.[28] The *Bhaktamāl* tradition spanned the divide between the Vaishnava sampradayas and *sant panth*s, suggesting, perhaps, that this distinction was not as strong as earlier understood.[29]

Sāmpradāyik affiliation does not automatically lead to an obviously sectarian agenda. The commentaries described by Kailash Chandra Sharma generally match the *Bhaktamāl* in terms of expansiveness and inclusiveness. Bālakrām, Vaiṣṇavdās, and Lāldās all partake of the *Bhaktamāl*'s ecumenical flavour. Sharma notes, in particular, that Sevāhitdās, despite his Rādhāvallabhī affiliation, betrays no sectarian bias.[30] Nābhādās' vision of a broad community united by bhakti seems alive and well in the manuscript tradition. Clearly, such a vision had an appeal beyond his particular sampradaya. Nābhādās was not alone in imagining this community.

While Nābhādās may have succeeded in planting the seeds of a united bhakti community, this vision did not remain unchallenged, even within the *Bhaktamāl* literary tradition. In Vṛndāvandās' *Bhaktanāmāvalī* or *Vaiṣṇav-vandanā*, we can see the *Bhaktamāl* tradition bridging boundaries of language while becoming narrowly sectarian. This work is fully bilingual. It was composed in Braj Bhasha, apparently for the benefit of the Vaishnava community of Vrindavan, and translated into Bengali. This *Bhaktanāmāvalī* praises some 70 bhaktas. It contains 156 stanzas and was composed in about 1757. This *Bhaktanāmāvalī* is a firmly sectarian work. It begins by praising Caitanya Mahāprabhu and his descendants. It lacks the expansiveness and non-sectarian feel of Nābhādās' *Bhaktamāl* or even Priyādās' *Bhaktirasabodhinī*. Vṛndāvandās praises only Gauṛīy bhaktas and individuals associated with Caitanya during his life such as his parents and guru.[31] While Priyādās also praises Caitanya in his opening verse, he does not limit his praise to Gauṛīy figures or even focus on these bhaktas in particular.[32] The main force of the *Bhaktamāl* tradition may be to transcend sectarian divisions, but even such an inclusive vision is vulnerable to particularistic appropriation.

Should such a narrowly sectarian vision be considered part of the *Bhaktamāl* tradition at all? True, the *Bhaktanāmāvalī* praises a set of saints and has a generic relation to Nābhādās' text, but the *Bhaktamāl*'s uniqueness lies, in part, in its inclusiveness. Nābhādās did not simply compose a collection of hagiographies;

he crafted a *mālā* which presents a unified vision. Does a text which limits itself to celebrating a particular sampradaya still fall within the bounds of the *Bhaktamāl* tradition? Perhaps, or perhaps not, but it does not take such a radical transformation to bring the *Bhaktamāl* in line with sectarian concerns. One technique to modify the boundaries of Nābhādās' *mālā* would be to add or substract stanzas. Jha finds both of these phenomena in the manuscripts he collected for his critical edition.[33] A closer analysis of these manuscripts may reveal whether these excisions and interpolations reflect particular concerns.

There is a level on which it seems that Nābhādās' vision was triumphant: through its charisma the *Bhaktamāl* imagined into being a new kind of community that spanned the boundaries of diverse sampradayas. On another level, however, it seems like the *Bhaktamāl* simply provides a new platform from which various sampradayas may launch their polemics. Both of these positions have much truth in them. The *Bhaktamāl* offers a powerful vision of an expansive devotional community. It also, from at least the time of its first commentary, provides a location for debates about the nature of this community. These debates constitute the *Bhaktamāl* tradition. Nābhādās' vision is powerful in itself, but his text has always served as a not-quite-blank slate for different conceptions of the community of bhaktas.

The Role of Priyādās

Within this tradition, however, the central figure may not even be Nābhādās. The crucial role played by Priyādās in the *Bhaktamāl* tradition cannot be underestimated. Of the hundred or so texts surveyed above, all but seven include his commentary and only one of these manuscripts was written after CE 1723. Priyādās is the only individual to comment directly on Nābhādās' *mūl* text on its own. All known subsequent commentators take the combined text of the *Bhaktamāl* and the *Bhaktirasabodhinī* as the object of their analysis. The *Bhaktamāl* tradition seems to unanimously endorse Priyādās' claim that his commentary is indistinguishable from the *mūl* text. The entire stream of *Bhaktamāl* tradition flows through

Priyādās, and he seems to be largely responsible for the popularity of this text.

Priyādās deliberately sought to blur the boundary between his words and those of Nābhādās. Claiming a direct connection to Nābhādās, he asserts that the latter speaks through him and that not even a connoisseur can distinguish between their texts. Despite this claim of equivalence, Priyādās does not simply expand upon Nābhādās' message but modifies it in several significant ways. Scholars have often repeated this traditional understanding. The shadow cast by Priyādās is long. The failure to distinguish between the perspectives of Nābhādās and Priyādās has resulted in what Heidi Pauwels, following M.A. Bernstein, calls 'backshadowing'.[34] Nābhādās stands in multiple shadows. The first is cast by the eighteenth-century Priyādās, the second by twentieth-century scholars. In many ways, Nābhādās can be seen as an example of a successful community builder, initiating a tradition that would become central to the nineteenth-century consolidation of modern Hinduism, but it is precisely this success that may occlude our attempts at understanding Nābhādās on his own terms.

Priyādās succeeded in establishing himself as the central figure in the *Bhaktamāl* tradition. He makes no secret of the fact that he wishes those who hear his words to conflate them with those of Nābhādās. Such a conflation helps to obscure Nābhādās' vision behind that of Priyādās'. By writing a commentary on the *Bhaktamāl*, Priyādās has placed his own stamp firmly on this tradition.

Conclusion

Nābhādās began the *Bhaktamāl* tradition, but Priyādās' commentary may be the more influential text. In almost telegraphic verse, Nābhādās imagined a new kind of devotional community. Priyādās endorsed Nābhādās' vision but redefined the nature of the bhakti which bound this community together. He claimed that his commentary was as authoritative as the words of Nābhādās, and subsequent tradition universally seems to accept this claim.

Nābhādās' vision of a supra-sectarian religious community seems to have been realized at least in part in the adoption of his *mālā* across north India and by a number of sampradayas.

By the nineteenth century, this manuscript tradition was well-established, and the arrival of print did not bring about a sudden transformation. Early print editions seem to be a straightforward continuation of the manuscript tradition; they even look like manuscripts. These editions increased the quantity of texts available, but there does not seem to be much in the way of qualitative change in the texts themselves. Indian publishers eventually brought out editions of the text with exegeses and with what would now be recognized as the standard apparatus of printed books, bringing the *Bhaktamāl* into new contexts, but this transformation was gradual. British scholar-administrators also published selections from the *Bhaktamāl* and drew on this text in their research. They found it to be a practical guide to the religious communities of north India. Partly in response to these and other Orientalist representations of Hindu society, Bharatendu Harishchandra and his contemporaries articulated an understanding of modern Hinduism that recapitulated Nābhādās' imagined devotional community.[35]

By the first decade of the twentieth century, a sense of fixity emerged in this tradition. Bhagvan Prasad 'Rupkala' and George Abraham Grierson, separated by the racial and national divides of the British Empire but united by a shared sense of devotional religiosity, created compelling exegetical commentaries that enabled new readerships to engage with the *Bhaktamāl*. Rupkala, much like a twentieth-century Priyādās, attempted to bring order to a relatively chaotic terrain. He created an edition of the *Bhaktamāl* which would come to be recognized as standard, accompanied by a commentary which incorporated multiple interpretations without explicitly adjudicating between them. Such an approach could be read as an endorsement of a broadly inclusive Hinduism, which contains room for a variety of doctrinal opinions. Grierson began the first English language commentary on the *Bhaktamāl* in a series of articles in the *Journal of the Royal Asiatic Society*. These articles served as an endorsement of Rupkala's edition and commentary while advancing an agenda of sympathy and love across the internal boundaries of the empire.[36]

The devotional community imagined by Nābhādās and his successors is an important predecessor for modern Hinduism. The *Bhaktamāl* tradition is a single literary and religious thread spanning the colonial divide. Through close attention to this thread, we can gain a more complete understanding of the continuities and disruptions around this transition as well as of other continuities and disruptions unrelated to this divide.

NOTES

1. I express my gratitude to the participants in the Tenth International Bhakti Conference in Mircurea Ciuc, Romania, where I presented an earlier version of this paper. Thanks are also due to Jack Hawley and Rachel McDermott who read and provided helpful feedback on an earlier draft. A more detailed version of this essay may be found as chapter four of my doctoral dissertation, J.P. Hare, 'Garland of Devotees: Nābhādās, Bhaktamāl and Modern Hinduism', doctoral dissertation, Columbia University, 2011.
2. For more on Nābhādās and his *Bhaktamāl*, see V. Pinch, 'History, Devotion and the Search for Nābhādās of Galta', in *Invoking the Past: The Uses of History in South Asia*, ed. Daud Ali, Delhi: Oxford University Press, 1999. See also chapter two of my dissertation.
3. For a more detailed consideration of Priyādās' *Bhaktirasabodhinī* and the tensions between it and the *Bhaktamāl*, see J.P. Hare, 'A Contested Community: Priyādās and the Re-imagining of Nābhādās's Bhaktamāl', *Sikh Formations: Religion, Culture, Theory*, vol. 3, no. 2, 2007, pp. 185-98.
4. R.D. Gupta, 'Studies in the Bhaktirasa-bodhinī of Priyā Dāsa', unpublished Ph.D. dissertation, University of London, 1967.
5. G. Pollet, 'Studies in the Bhakta Mâla of Nâbhâ Dâsa', unpublished Ph.D. dissertation, University of London, 1963.
6. Pollet and Gupta consider the *Bhaktamāl* and the *Bhaktirasabodhinī*, respectively, but the manuscripts described by them include both Nābhādās' *mūl* text along with Priyādās' commentary.
7. G. Pollet, 'Eight Manuscripts of the Hindī Bhaktamāla in England', *Orientalia Lovaniensia Periodica*, vol. 1, 1970, pp. 203-22.
8. N. Jha, *Bhaktamāl: pāṭhānuśīlan evaṁ vivecan*, Patna: Anupam Prakāśan, 1978.
9. Jha complains that due to 'arrogance, lack of generosity, or sectarian rivalry', many manuscripts are unavailable to researchers. Jha, *Bhaktamāl*, vol. 1, p. 181.

10. K.C. Sharma, *Bhaktamāl aur hindī kāvya mẽ uskī paraṁparā*, Rohtak: Manthan Publishing, 1983.
11. My dissertation explores each of these topics in detail. See chapter two for more on Nābhādās, chapter three for Priyādās, chapter five for early print editions of the *Bhaktamāl* and chapter six for Rupkala.
12. Jha, *Bhaktamāl*, pp. 200-13.
13. Ibid., pp. 181-96.
14. Pollet, 'Eight Manuscripts', pp. 203-4.
15. Sharma, *Bhaktamāl*, pp. 125-7.
16. Ibid., pp. 127-9.
17. Ibid., pp. 131-2.
18. Ibid., pp. 133-5.
19. Jha, *Bhaktamāl*, vol. 1, pp. 185-7.
20. Ibid., pp. 188-9.
21. B. Anderson, *Imagined Communities: Reflection on the Origin and Spread of Nationalism*, London: Verso, 1983; E.C. Dimock and T.K. Stewart, *Caitanya Caritāmṛta of Kṛṣṇadāsa Kavirāja: A Translation and Commentary*, Cambridge, Mass: Dept. of Sanskrit and Indian Studies, Harvard University, 1999, p. 53.
22. Dimock and Stewart, *Caitanya Caritāmṛta*, p. 57.
23. S. Pollock, 'Literary Culture and Manuscript Culture in Precolonial India', in *Literary Cultures and the Material Book*, ed. Simon Eliot, Andrew Nash and Ian Willison, London: British Library, 2007, pp. 85-91.
24. See chapter five of my dissertation.
25. R.D. Gupta, 'Priyā Dās, Author of the Bhaktirasabodhinī', *Bulletin of the School of Oriental and African Studies*, vol. 32, no. 1, 1969, pp. 67-8.
26. A. Busch, 'The Anxiety of Innovation: The Practice of Literary Science in the Hindi/Riti Tradition', *Comparative Studies of South Asia, Africa, and the Middle East*, vol. 24, no. 2, 2004, pp. 45-59.
27. J.S. Hawley, 'The Received Kabir: Beginnings to Bly', in *Three Bhakti Voices*, ed. John Stratton Hawley, Delhi: Oxford University Press, 2006, pp. 269-70; For more on the Kabīrpanth and the *Bījak* of Kabīr, see L.B. Hess and S. Singh, *The Bijak of Kabir*, 1st Indian edn, Delhi: Motilal Banarsidass, 1986.
28. On the mixing of *nirguṇī* and *saguṇī bhajans* in early Dādūpanthī anthologies, see Dalpat Rajpurohit's article in this volume.
29. For a suggestion that the *nirguṇ/saguṇ* distinction is anachronistic when applied to early modern north Indian bhakti literature, see J.S. Hawley, 'The Nirguṇ/Saguṇ Distinction', in *Three Bhakti Voices*, Delhi: Oxford University Press, 2005, pp. 70-86. An exploration of how this distinction developed in the literary historiography of north India is T. Williams, '"Nirgun" and "Sagun" in the Discourse of Literary Historiography' paper presented at the Tenth International Bhakti Conference: Early Modern

Literatures in North India, Sapientia-Hungarian University of Transylvania, Miercurea Ciuc, Romania, 2009.
30. Sharma, *Bhaktamāl*, pp. 124-35.
31. Ibid., pp. 124-5.
32. For an exploration of Priyādās' treatment of Gauṛīy bhaktas, see P. Lutgendorf, 'Kṛṣṇa Caitanya and His Companions as Presented in the Bhaktamāla of Nābhā Jī and the Bhaktirasabodhinī of Priyā Dāsa', M.A. thesis, University of Chicago, 1981.
33. Jha, *Bhaktamāl*, pp. 181-251.
34. H. Pauwels, 'Hagiography and Community Formation: The Case of a Lost Community of Sixteenth-Century Vrindavan', *Journal of Hindu Studies*, vol. 3, no. 1, 2010, p. 4.
35. See chapter five of my dissertation.
36. See chapter six of my dissertation.

BIBLIOGRAPHY

Anderson, B., *Imagined Communities: Reflection on the Origin and Spread of Nationalism*, London: Verso, 1983.

Busch, A., 'The Anxiety of Innovation: The Practice of Literary Science in the Hindi/Riti Tradition', *Comparative Studies of South Asia, Africa, and the Middle East,* vol. 24, no. 2, 2004, pp. 45-59.

Dimock, E.C., and T.K. Stewart, *Caitanya Caritāmṛta of Kṛṣṇadāsa Kavirāja: A Translation and Commentary*, Cambridge, Mass: Dept. of Sanskrit and Indian Studies, Harvard University, 1999.

Gupta, R.D., 'Priyā Dās, Author of the Bhaktirasabodhinī', *Bulletin of the School of Oriental and African Studies,* vol. 32, no. 1, 1969, pp. 57-70.

——, 'Studies in the Bhaktirasa-bodhinī of Priyā Dāsa', unpublished Ph.D. dissertation, University of London, 1967.

Hare, J.P., 'A Contested Community: Priyādās and the Re-imagining of Nābhādās's Bhaktamāl', *Sikh Formations: Religion, Culture, Theory,* vol. 3, no. 2, 2007, pp. 185-98.

——, 'Garland of Devotees: Nābhādās' Bhaktamāl and Modern Hinduism', doctoral dissertation, Columbia University, 2011.

Hawley, J.S., 'The Nirguṇ/Saguṇ Distinction', in *Three Bhakti Voices*, Delhi: Oxford University Press, 2005, pp. 70-86.

——, 'The Received Kabir: Beginnings to Bly', in *Three Bhakti Voices*, ed. J.S. Hawley, Delhi: Oxford University Press, 2006, pp. 267-78.

Hess, L.B., and S. Singh, *The Bijak of Kabir*, 1st Indian edn, Delhi: Motilal Banarsidass, 1986.

Jha, N., *Bhaktamāl: pāṭhānuśīlan evaṁ vivecan*, Patna: Anupam Prakāśan, 1978.

Lutgendorf, P., 'Kṛṣṇa Caitanya and His Companions as Presented in the Bhaktamāla of Nābhā Jī and the Bhaktirasabodhinī of Priyā Dāsa', M.A. thesis, University of Chicago, 1981.

Pauwels, H., 'Hagiography and Community Formation: The Case of a Lost Community of Sixteenth-Century Vrindavan', *Journal of Hindu Studies,* vol. 3, no. 1, 2010, pp. 53-90.

Pinch, V., 'History, Devotion and the Search for Nābhādās of Galta', in *Invoking the Past: The Uses of History in South Asia*, ed. D. Ali, *SOAS Studies on South Asia: Understandings and Perspectives*, Delhi: Oxford University Press, 1999, pp. 367-99.

Pollet, G., 'Eight Manuscripts of the Hindī Bhaktamāla in England', *Orientalia Lovaniensia Periodica,* vol. 1, 1970, pp. 203-22.

——, 'Studies in the Bhakta Mâla of Nâbhâ Dâsa', unpublished Ph.D. dissertation, University of London, 1963.

Pollock, S., 'Literary Culture and Manuscript Culture in Precolonial India', in *Literary Cultures and the Material Book*, ed. S. Eliot, A. Nash and I. Willison, *British Library Studies in the History of the Book*, London: British Library, 2007, pp. 77-94.

Sharma, K.C., *Bhaktamāl aur hindī kāvya mẽ uskī paraṁparā*, Rohtak: Manthan Publishing, 1983.

Williams, T., '"Nirgun" and "Sagun" in the Discourse of Literary Historiography', paper presented at the Tenth International Bhakti Conference: Early Modern Literatures in North India, Sapientia-Hungarian University of Transylvania, Miercurea Ciuc, Romania, 2009.

CHAPTER 4

Sainthood Revisited: Two Printed Versions of the *Lives of the Eighty-four Vaishnavas* by Gokulnāth

GALINA ROUSSEVA-SOKOLOVA

The *Lives of the Eighty-four Vaishnavas* (*Caurāsī vaiṣṇavan kī vārtā*, henceforward *CVV*) is a seventeenth-century text relating the biographies of the disciples of Vallabhācārya, founder of the Puṣṭimārga ('the path of grace', also known as Vallabh Sampradāy), one of the most important sects of north Indian Krishna bhakti.

While the founding theological treatises of the sect were predictably written by Vallabha in Sanskrit, the lives of the saints were compiled in Brajbhasha prose. They were presumably composed by Gokulnāth (1552-1641), Vallabhācārya's grandson and the fourth son of Viṭṭhalnāth, Vallabha's successor as leader of the sect. So if Vallabha's writings represent, in a way, the theological core of the doctrine, its esoteric essence, which was presented in a prestigious but hardly accessible language for a layman, Gokulnāth developed its exoteric aspect in a language close to what was spoken in everyday life.[1] This was in the spirit of the bhakti ideology itself, according to which the path to salvation through love is open to everybody, regardless of caste, sex or education.

Gokulnāth's collection of stories represents a sort of practical guide for the application of the methods of the Puṣṭimārga. Those stories were transmitted orally in the beginning. It is still unclear exactly by whom and when they were put in writing. According to one version, a disciple called Kṛṣṇa Bhaṭṭ did it.[2] According to another, Gokulnāth himself supervised the editing, which was actually done by Harirāy (1590-1715), his grand nephew.[3]

When the text of the hagiographies was finally written down, it developed into several recensions and exists in at least two printed versions today. One of them consists of the texts of the stories without any commentary. It was most probably first published in 1883 in Mathura and, according to Hariharnath Tandan, has had six later editions from Mathura, Baroda and Mumbai, of which he does not systematically give dates.[4] There is, however, a more popular modern version, which includes the commentary of Harirāy called *Bhāv-prakāś*—'enlightening of the feeling'. The standard edition of this version is that of Dvarikadas Parikh from 1948, reprinted several times. According to the editor, it is based on a manuscript dating from 1695. Today, this version is the most widely-disseminated one among the Vaishnavas.

In an article published in 1994, Richard Barz presented these two versions, calling the shorter one *Caurāsī bārttā*, based on the title of its first printed edition of Mathura (1883). The one I will be referring to in this article, however, is generally called *CVV* and dates from 1928. It is listed as 'number 3' in Hariharnath Tandan's history of the *Vārtā*s' publications.[5]

As has been mentioned, the main difference between the two versions is the presence of the commentary by Harirāy in the longer one. According to traditional explanation, the need for a commentary appeared in certain passages where the behaviour of the Vaishnavas might otherwise have seemed strange or even immoral. Moreover, Harirāy supplies information about the lives of the saints before their initiation by Vallabhācārya. This version is known as *Tīn janma kī līlā vālī*, 'with elucidation of the *līlā* of the three lives'. The 'three lives' here mean the life of the saint before the initiation, his life thereafter and his life as a female companion of Krishna in his eternal realm, the *golok*. In a way, Harirāy personifies the voice of Vallabhācārya here, unveiling the true meaning of otherwise uncomplicated events and contextualizing them in the spirit of the Puṣṭimārga.

The *vārtā*s are particularly interesting for a scholar of Indian religion since they are peripheral to rather than being part of the Sanskrit theological core of the Puṣṭimārga. They are theology in the flesh: they transpose abstract principles into a narration where the actors (both human and divine) do and say things. For the devotees, they function as an interface between the sect and the society at large. As a literary product, they are a typical example of the 'story with a message' genre.[6] They share with their European analogues a certain type of narrative simplicity, realism and an important didactic aspect. As the 'roman à thèse' typically does, they give the audience interpretative keys to reality, the combination of which constitutes the ideological framework of the sect. This interpretative level is, obviously, much more explicit and developed in the *Tīn janma* version than in the shorter one, though it is not entirely absent from the latter. The *vārtā*s also possess an important pragmatic aspect: they contain implicit injunctions on how a true bhakta should think and act. Finally, they are interesting to us because they seek to convey a certain image of the sect in the competitive religious landscape of seventeenth-century India and, in doing so, indirectly reflect the society they functioned in.

The purpose of this paper is to bring the versions together and see what a parallel reading can yield concerning the way the *vārtā*s function. Such a reading can also shed light on how they evolved since the shorter version obviously precedes the longer one. This is not an easy task, primarily due to the size of the texts: 368 pages for the shorter and 571 densely printed pages for the longer. Within them, every *vārtā* is a separate narrative unit and within each *vārtā*, every *prasaṅg* (episode) also stands for itself. I shall first deal with the differences in style between the texts, and then discuss the accretions and occasional omissions of the *Tīn janma kī līlā vālī* text. Henceforward, I shall refer to the latter for convenience as the *Tīn janma kī līlā* version, as opposed to the *CVV* version.

Style

The differences between the two versions of the *vārtās* are clearly more than the incorporation of a commentary. The *Tīn janma kī līlā* retells the same episodes but words them differently. As straightforward and unsophisticated as its style may be, the *CVV* is even more conversational. This impression is furthered by the fact that there is no punctuation at all in the 1928 publication. Instead of full stops, there are abundant conjunctions and words functioning as conjunctions like *aur*, *ab*, *tab*, *pāche*, *tāte* and *so*, resulting in the fact that a whole chapter can read as an endless single sentence. As a matter of fact, the *CVV* text is the closest thing to an uncut transcript with the typical amorphous quality of improvised oral exposition. The *Tīn janma kī līlā* is more structured and concise. Hariharnath Tandan and Richard Barz have analysed the style of samples of both texts. The conclusion of Barz is that the *CVV*, though supposedly shorter, is definitely the more verbose of the two.

Accretions

The most obvious accretion to the text of the *CVV* is the commentary of Harirāy. It is omnipresent, occasionally cutting a *prasaṅg* right after the first sentence and running, at times, for pages. It is not a simple addition to the main text; it modifies its whole perspective and the way it is perceived. How does this happen?

Clarifying the Doctrine

First of all, Harirāy's text represents a sort of Frequently Asked Questions compendium for the followers of the sect. It answers concerns of a technical/ritual nature as in *prasaṅg* 5 of the *vārtā* of Dāmodardās Harsānī, the first of the eighty-four. Here is the translation:

That day was the commemorative day of the death (*śrāddha*) of Dāmodardās' father. Then came Śrī Gusāīṁ-jī (Viṭṭhalnāth, Vallabhācārya's youngest son and successor) and performed the ceremony. Then Dāmodardās went (to the temple) for the *utthāpan darśan*. Śrī Gusāīṁ-jī then asked Dāmodardās: 'Give me my fee (*dakṣiṇā*) for the *śrāddha*!' Dāmodardās said: 'I shall tell you something that will serve as your fee.' And he recited and interpreted a verse from the *Siddhāntarahasya*. Then Śrī Gusāīṁ-jī said: 'Tell me more!', but Dāmodardās said 'I have considered only so much (for a fee)' and Śrī Gusāīṁ-jī remained silent. Later, Dāmodardās told him everything about the *mārga*, the commentary *Subodhinī* of the *Bhāgavata-purāṇa*. He commented and disclosed the secret of Śrī Vallabhācārya-jī's books before Śrī Gusāīṁ-jī .

From then, Śrī Gusāīṁ-jī didn't let Dāmodardās bow in front of him. He did it because he thought in his mind: 'Śrī Vallabhācārya-jī is always present in the heart of Dāmodardās. He shouldn't have to bow to anybody.' So he didn't let him. And he did not let him take *caraṇāmṛt* from him.

Then Śrī Vallabhācārya appeared in front of Dāmodardās and told him to always take *caraṇāmṛt* from Śrī Gusāīṁ-jī . So, in the morning, Dāmodardās went to Śrī Gusāīṁ-jī and asked for *caraṇāmṛt*. Śrī Gusāīṁ-jī refused. But Dāmodardās told him that it was an order from Śrī Vallabhācārya. Then Śrī Gusāīṁ-jī let him have *caraṇāmṛt*.

Bhāv-prakāś: The purpose of the *śrāddha* is the following: the father of Dāmodardās is saved since he is among the bhaktas. Thus in the *maryādāmārga* (the path of 'ordinary devotion' based on following prescriptions and performing rituals to which Puṣṭimārga is considered superior), the Man-lion told Prahlād that twenty-one generations of bhaktas shall be saved. (Furthermore) Dāmodardās is a *puṣṭimārgīya*. How could there be a doubt that Dāmodardās' father would be saved? But to be part of the Puṣṭimārga there has to be a connection established with it. Śrī Gusāīṁ-jī established it by performing the *śrāddha* ceremony. . . .

Then another doubt arises: Dāmodardās had the *śrāddha* performed. His father's connection with the Puṣṭimārga was established. But the other bhaktas didn't. So how about their fathers? That's why among the *divine souls*,[7] Dāmodardās is the most prominent (*adhidaivik*). Through the connection that was established for his father, all the fathers, of the bhaktas were connected to the Puṣṭimārga.[8]

This is a typical example of how the commentary works. Here, it deals with 'salvation technicalities'. Bhakti may be the ideology of the day but traditional concerns about salvation and the well-being of the forefathers remain. The Puṣṭimārga cannot afford to leave these concerns unanswered. The commentary fulfils this task by reassuring the audience about the 'soteriological capacity' of bhakti, on the one hand, and by establishing a sort of ritual 'wiring', through which the benefits of direct communication with Vallabhācārya's lineage can reach each and every (present and future) bhakta.

Dāmodardās is not an average bhakta; he is the first among equals. The *vārtā* says that when Vallabhācārya decided to retire, both his sons were too young and so he entrusted the sacred knowledge of the sect to Dāmodardās, together with the charge to transmit it in due time. This privileged relationship is further illustrated by the following episode that is only present in the *Tīn janma kī līlā*. One day when Vallabha was sleeping in his lap, Dāmodardās chased away Srīnāth-jī himself with the words 'Don't come near, you will wake up Mahāprabhu-jī!' And later he asked the famous rhetorical question: '*Dān baṛo ke dātā baṛo*?', meaning that the 'gift', *dān* (of Krishna bhakti) goes where the 'giver', *dātā*, (Vallabhācārya) sends it and, therefore, it is the giver who is more valuable for humans. We can put our finger on another editorial choice here: a tendency to further underline, throughout the commentary, the absolute prominence of Vallabhācārya and Viṭṭhalnāth, their essential identity with divinity, and their unique and absolutely necessary role as go-betweens. When the two texts are seen in parallel, both the commentary and the rewording of the *vārtā* in the *Tīn janma kī līlā* version point in that direction.

The same goes for the topic of the preservation of the purity of the *mārga*. For instance, Mīrābāī is mentioned twice in the *vārtā*s: once in the *vārtā* of Rāmdās and once in that of Kr̥ṣṇadās *adhikārī*. Each time she is described as a wealthy bhakta, a bestower of valuable gifts. However, the donations she eagerly offers to the followers of Vallabhācārya are turned down, while representatives of other *mārga*s queue for them in vain. The *Tīn janma kī līlā* version makes this point with even more determination than the *CVV*, both through the commentary and the nuanced editing of the main text.

Building Hierarchies

While the importance of the leader of the sect is a theme that is already infused into the stories of the *CVV*, the *Bhāv-prakāś* commentary adds an entirely new dimension by building additional hierarchies among the bhaktas through their identification with a specific *gopī* in the eternal *līlā* of *golok*. In the beginning of each *vārtā*, the personal details of the bhaktas are meticulously given: their name, sex, caste, social status and age. This goes to exemplify the basic tenet of bhakti, according to which divine grace is available to everybody. The *Bhāv-prakāś* adds another, subtler hierarchy. In *golok*, the *gopī*s surround the divine couple in concentric circles. There are the ones who are in direct contact with them. Candrāvalī, incarnated as Viṭṭhalnāth, is the most prominent among them. Then there are other circles of *gopī*s catering to the needs of the first circle. The identification of the saints in the commentary in the beginning of the *vārtā* positions them in terms of their proximity to the divine couple and, thus, defines their level of sainthood, predicting the importance of what is about to follow for the community.

Offering Alternative Motivations

From the perspective of the narrative, the commentary of Harirāy gives an additional dimension to the development of the plot by changing, or rather supplementing, the motivational engine behind it. When the events do not fit the ideology or in other words, when good bhaktas behave badly, the commentary steps in by explaining their behaviour with interference from above: with events, developing on a different plane of reality. In *golok*, where nothing much happens by definition, there are still tales of jealousy, frustration and curses which get resolved on earth.

Transmotivation, according to Gérard Genette, is one of the major semantic transformations at work in hypertextuality.[9] When a text is reworking an older text, it can transform it by either assigning a cause to an event where none is specified, by concealing the original motivation of an act, or by substituting it with another, which is a combination of the first two methods. Justifying the developments of a well-known narrative with events from previous lives has been a very common procedure throughout the history of Indian literature. What we have here is only a slight variation of the original formula: instead of former lives, the setting is another plane of reality.

The *golok* events are present only in the *Bhāv-prakāś*; the *CVV* never speaks of the eternal *līlā*. It does, however, speak of an invisible plane of reality—that is, invisible to some. In a great number of episodes, Śrīnāth, the lord of the Govardhan temple, steps in as an actor and his intervention is the main focus of the narrative. His presence can be visible or invisible to the other characters like the *vārtā*, cited above, where Dāmodardās Harsānī stops the approaching deity from waking up his master, or the *vārtā* of the poor brahman widow,[10] offering *chapati* to the icon in her home altar, unaware that Krishna himself is sitting next to her, gulping down the simple meal ravenously. In the last case, the story gets revealed through the accidental presence of Vallabhācārya who sees what remains invisible to others and gives an edifying account for the benefit of the bhaktas.

Another fascinating example is the *vārtā* of Rāmdās, a brahman from Mewar, who served as a priest in Mīrābāī's home:

> One day Rāmdās went to Mīrābāī's house. He sang a few *pads* by Vallabhācārya to the Ṭhākur of Mīrābāī. Then Mīrābāī said: 'Sing some *viṣṇupad* for Śrī Ṭhākur-jī (now)!' At that moment Rāmdās got angry: 'You, immoral woman, are these (*pads*) your master's? That's it, I shall never see your face again!' And he left, taking all of his family with him. Mīrābāī pleaded a lot with him. She offered him money, but he took nothing. He went to live in another village with his family. Such a vessel of grace was Rāmdās. So absorbed in his Lord that he never saw Mīrābāī again.
>
> *Bhāv-prakāś*: Here is what this *vārtā* exemplifies: First, never go to followers of another *mārga*. And if you go, do not talk to them about your *mārga*. Do not sing the *kirtan* of your *mārga*, otherwise it incurs suffering. . . . In this way you have to remain hidden when you travel through the country. When Rāmdās sang the *kirtan* of Śrī Vallabhācārya,

Śrī Govardhandhar (Krishna) thought: 'In doing so he shall reveal the *mārga*!' So he made Mīrābāī say: 'Sing that too for Śrī Ṭhākur-jī!' Then Rāmdās understood everything. He thought: 'What have I done? Śrī Govardhandhar had to go into all this trouble because of me! From now on I shall not even drink water from this village. . . .'[11]

This short *vārtā* is exemplary in many respects. First, it illustrates the editorial choices of the *Tīn janma kī līlā* version: compared to the *CVV*, the embarrassing fact that Rāmdās was at the service of Mīrābāī, earning his living from her, is belittled and barely mentioned. Then, it is a good example of how the interpretation changes the story without really changing it on the level of events. Third, the sudden enlightenment of Rāmdās, his faculty of seeing through appearances, is also a typical demarcation line that the *vārtās* (especially in the *Tīn janma kī līlā* version) draw between different degrees of sainthood.

Only the greatest bhaktas are able to see reality in all of its multiple layers, including the *golok* dimension. Practically only Vallabhācārya and Viṭṭhalnāth are shown to be in this category. Other devotees are still capable of seeing the invisible level, that is, seeing the living god behind temple images and interacting with him. Dāmodardās Harsānī and all the *aṣṭachāp* poets fall into this category. Lesser followers, such as the poor brahman widow, get the benefits of their candidly pure devotion, without a clue of the true nature of reality or the subtle combination of unearthly factors at play.

This superimposition of motivational drives onto the main plot is particularly conspicuous in the case of ambiguous figures like Kṛṣṇadās Adhikārī.[12] Kṛṣṇadās was a shudra and a celebrated poet among the *aṣṭachāp*. He was also appointed manager to the Śrīnāth temple and is praised in the *vārtā* for cleverly driving the officiating Bengali brahmans out of the temple. At the same time, he had a fondness for female devotees (including a prostitute) and he also got involved in the controversy over the succession of Vallabhācārya by taking the side of the descendants of Gopīnāth, Vallabha's eldest son and Viṭṭhalnāth's brother. As a result, he banned Viṭṭhalnāth for several months from the temple.

In this complicated case of Kṛṣṇadās, the commentary goes on and on, page after page. Layer upon layer of interpretations accumulate, cocooning the *vārtā*, until the initial motive for the quarrel (as well as that of the final reconciliation) between Kṛṣṇadās and Viṭṭhalnāth is completely obscured. It is as if a simple melody was being reworked to be played by an orchestra: the conductor of the orchestra reads the full score with all the melodies played by the different instruments in parallel. The harmony between the scores of the different instruments is as important as the separate tunes being played. Similarly the *Tīn janma kī līlā* version invites the audience to follow the story not only as a horizontal sequence of events but also as a multi-layered whole, where every layer is synchronized with the others in order to ensure a plausible 'vertical' motivation to the main narrative sequence.

Omissions

While the *Tīn janma kī līlā* is obviously a longer text than the *CVV*, the number of *vārtā*s it contains, according to the table of contents, is smaller. Despite its title and the significance attached to the number eighty-four, the *CVV* contains ninety-two *vārtā*s. Each of them is present in the *Tīn janma kī līlā* version. The only difference is that the editor grouped bhaktas with family relations or with friendship under the same number, thus judiciously bringing the total down to eighty-four.

While the number of saints appears smaller, the number of episodes included in each *vārtā* is definitely higher. Here, again, the differences between the versions are complex. Many separate episodes have been regrouped or placed elsewhere. Where completely new episodes appear in the *Tīn janma kī līlā* version, these could mostly be called 'miracle' episodes, involving divine interventions. Such is the case with the *vārtā* of Sūrdās.

Occasionally though, the *Tīn janma kī līlā* version may skip some details. In the same *vārtā* of Sūrdās, for instance, the *CVV* presents the episode relating the poet's first meeting with Vallabhācārya thus:

> ... *Sūrdās-jī svāmī hai āp sevak karte sūrdās-jī bhagavadīya hai gān bahut āchau karte tāte bāhut log sūrdās-jīke sevak bhae hute...*
>
> ... Sūrdās-jī was a master, he had followers (*sevak*) himself, he was a holy man and sang so well and many people had become his followers....

This passage was omitted in the *Tīn janma kī līlā* version where it is just mentioned that one *sevak* of Sūrdās (in this context, it could mean 'servant' and not necessarily 'follower') spotted Vallabhācārya and his party, and went to inform Sūrdās about their arrival. In this case, one can suspect that the purpose of editing was not for mere conciseness of style. Obviously, the *Tīn janma* editor(s) were uncomfortable with the fact of the popularity of Sūrdās prior to his meeting with Vallabhācārya.

The *vārtā*s of the 84 Vaishnavas in both its versions, just like the *vārtā*s of the 252 Vaishnavas supposedly initiated by Viṭṭhalnāth, and included in a later collection, are puzzling objects of research. They are difficult to encompass within a single study: there are too many of them and the reader can sometimes feel overwhelmed by their volubility. Actually, their sheer number invites the application of statistical methods. Although they are not to be trusted as a accurate source of historical information, they reveal to the curious reader a fascinating motley gathering of people and stories, charmingly depicted in a deliberately simple style. Those stories reflect indirectly the society they were composed in and a system of values that certainly does not belong exclusively to any single sect.

NOTES

1. On the history, versions and authorship of the *CVV*, see R.K. Barz, 'The Caurāsī vaiṣṇavan kī vārtā and the Hagiography of the Puṣṭimārga', in *According to Tradition: Hagiographical Writing in India*, ed. W.M. Callewaert and R. Snell, Wiesbaden: Harrassowitz Verlag, 1994, pp. 45-62; H. Tandan, *Vartā-sāhitya: ek bṛhat adhyayan*, Aligarh: Bhārat Prakāśan Mandir, 1961. On the sect of Vallabhācārya, see R.K. Barz, *The Bhakti Sect of Vallabhācārya*, Faridabad: Thomson Press (India) Limited, 1976; P. Bennett, *The Path of Grace: Social Organization and Temple Worship in a*

Vaishnava Sect, Delhi: Hindustan Publishing Corporation, 1993; P. Mital, *Braj ke dharma-sampradāyoṁ kā itihās*, Delhi: National Publishing House, 1968, pp. 212-302.

2. Tandan, *Vartā-sāhitya*, p. 125.
3. Barz, 'The Caurāsī vaiṣṇavan kī vārtā', pp. 46-7.
4. Tandan, *Vartā-sāhitya*, p. 105.
5. *Caurāsī vaiṣṇavan kī vārtā*, Mumbai: Lakṣmī Veṅkateśvar Press, 1928. I should mention here that I did not use a physical copy of the book but a scanned version available at the Digital Library of India site (http://www.new.dli.ernet.in), which, though rather user-unfriendly at times, is a unique tool for anyone interested in old Indian printed materials.
6. For a semiotic analysis of the genre, see S.R. Suleiman, *Authoritarian Fictions: The Ideological Novel as a Literary Genre*, Princeton: Princeton University Press, 1992. During the discussion of the paper at the conference, Monika Horstmann and Françoise Mallison objected to the term 'propaganda literature' that I used in the initial version of this paper, pointing out that hagiographies are usually read among followers of the sect and not used as a tool for proselytizing. Hence, I will refrain from using it, although my understanding of 'propaganda' is more inclusive and has an important 'motivational' aspect addressed to the supporters of the corresponding ideology. My own experience of the flourishing 'agitation and propaganda' cultural production during the years of the communist regime in Bulgaria is that the greater part of it aimed to boost the morale of the citizens locally. The conversion of the rest of the world came after this.
7. *Daivī jīv*, a soul with potential for salvation in the doctrine of Vallabhācārya. See also Barz, *The Bhakti Sect of Vallabhācārya*, pp. 70-2.
8. D. Parikh, ed., *Caurāsī vaiṣṇavan kī vārtā: tīn janma kī līlā bhāvanā vālī*, Mathura: Śrī Govardhan Granthamālā Kāryālaya, 1970, pp. 9-10. All the translations included in this paper are based on this edition. Differences from the *CVV* version (beside the *Bhāv-prakāś*) are noted in the discussion.
9. G. Genette, *Literature in the Second Degree*, Lincoln: University of Nebraska Press, 1997, p. 324. Genette defines hypertextuality as 'any relation uniting a text B (. . .) to an earlier text A (. . .) upon which it is grafted in a manner that is not that of a commentary' (p. 5). While Genette's categories are elaborated on the basis of the European literary experience the concept of hypertextuality can prove helpful in enlightening the Indian landscape as well (see, for instance, P. Benoît, 'Rewriting Valmiki: Krittibasa Ramayana as a Hypertext', in *Narrative Strategies: Essays on South Asian Literature and Film*, ed. V. Dalmia and T. Damsteegt, Leiden: Research School CNWS, 1998, pp. 3-18.
10. *Vārtā* 49 in the *CVV*, 42 in the *Tīn janma kī līlā* version, where the brahman widow becomes a kshatriya one.
11. *Vārtā* 54 in the *CVV*, 47 in the *Tīn janma kī līlā* version.

12. In both versions this is the last *vārtā*. For a translation, see Barz, *The Bhakti Sect of Vallabhācārya*, pp. 207-56. See also R.K. Barz, 'Kṛṣṇadās Adhikārī: An Irascible Devotee's Approach to the Divine', in *Bhakti Studies*, ed. G. Bailey and I.K. Watson, Delhi: Sterling Press, 1992, pp. 23650.

BIBLIOGRAPHY

Barz, R.K., *The Bhakti Sect of Vallabhācārya*, Faridabad: Thomson Press (India) Limited, 1976.

——, 'The Caurāsī vaiṣṇavan kī vārtā and the Hagiography of the Puṣṭimārga', in *According to Tradition: Hagiographical Writing in India*, ed. W.M. Callewaert and R. Snell, Wiesbaden: Harrassowitz Verlag, 1994, pp. 45-62.

——, 'Kṛṣṇadās Adhikārī: An Irascible Devotte's Approach to the Divine', in *Bhakti Studies*, ed. G. Bailey and I.K. Watson, Delhi: Sterling Press, 1992, pp. 236-50.

Bennett, P., *The Path of Grace: Social Organization and Temple Worship in a Vaishnava Sect*, Delhi: Hindustan Publishing Corporation, 1993.

Benoît, P., 'Rewriting Valmiki: Krittibasa Ramayana as a Hypertext', in *Narrative Strategies: Essays on South Asian Literature and Film*, ed. V. Dalmia and T. Damsteegt, Leiden: Research School CNWS, 1998, pp. 3-18.

Caurāsī vaiṣṇavan kī vārtā, Mumbai: Lakṣmī Veṅkateśvar Press, 1928.

Genette, G., *Literature in the Second Degree*, Lincoln: University of Nebraska Press, 1997.

Mital, P., *Braj ke dharma-sampradāyoṁ kā itihās*, Delhi: National Publishing House, 1968.

Parikh, D., ed. *Caurāsī vaiṣṇavan kī vārtā: tīn janma kī līlā bhāvanā vālī*, Mathura: Śrī Govardhan Granthamālā Kāryālaya, 1970.

Suleiman, S.R., *Authoritarian Fictions: The Ideological Novel as a Literary Genre*, Princeton: Princeton University Press, 1992.

Tandan, H., *Vartā-sāhitya: ek bṛhat adhyayan*, Aligarh: Bhārat Prakāśan Mandir, 1961.

CHAPTER 5

On and Around the Story of Candrahāsa: The Transmission of a Tale and Bhakti

YOSHIFUMI MIZUNO

Candrahāsa is a fictitious Vaishnava devotee mentioned in Nābhādās' *Bhaktamāl* whose story has been documented throughout India for a millennium in various languages and mediums. The tale of this devotee was, above all, a popular tool to propagate Vaishnava bhakti but it also appeared in other contexts. The narrative is made up of various plots that can be traced not only in India but also in the Middle East and in Europe, including Shakespeare's *Hamlet*.

The earliest version of the Candrahāsa story is found in the Sanskrit *Jaimini-bhārata*,[1] also called the *Jaiminīyāśvamedha*, a retelling of the Aśvamedhika-parvan of the *Mahābhārata*.[2] The *Jaimini-bhārata* was composed in the eleventh or twelfth century.[3] Here, the story, extending from the second half of verse 21 in Chapter L to the end of Chapter LVIII, is described in relative length in 616 verses,[4] mostly in *śloka*.[5] In this first documented version, the narrative already appears with a superimposed layer of Vaishnavism.[6]

Outline of the Story of Candrahāsa in the *Jaimini-bhārata*

The frame story of the *Jaimini-bhārata* is narrated by Jaimini. As for the story of Candrahāsa, Jaimini induces Nārada to tell Arjuna the story after the manner of the *Mahābhārata*. Following a German scholar, J. Schick's edition it may be outlined as follows:

(L) The baby son of the king of Medhavi in Kerala loses his parents during an attack by a neighbouring nation. An old nursemaid adopts him, takes him to another country, Kauntalaka, raising him there until he is three years old. Two years later, the five-year-old orphan joins a banquet meant for Brahmanas organised by Dhṛṣṭabuddhi, the minister of Kauntalaka. During this event, a Brahmana predicts that the orphan will become the successor of Dhṛṣṭabuddhi even though the latter has a son. The evil-minded minister wishes to kill the boy and hires men to murder him. However, the killers fail because of the youngster's devotion towards the *śālagrāma* stone. Hence, they cut off the congenitally deformed sixth finger of his left foot and show it to Dhṛṣṭabuddhi as evidence of their feigned success.

(LI) A feudal lord, Kulinda, finds the wounded boy in a forest and carries him to his residence in Candanāvatī. Kulinda and his wife intend to raise him as their own son; they name him as Candrahāsa, or one with beautiful fair face laughing at even the moon, upon consulting an astrologer. Candrahāsa, who is very pious, constantly chants the name of Hari, a practice that angers his teacher. He is immersed in Vishnu bhakti even after studying all the Vedas.

(LII) Candrahāsa grows up to be a brave sixteen-year-old and Kulinda on his return from a victorious campaign transfers his feudal lordship to him. During his enthronement ceremony, Candrahāsa declares that he will govern the country according to the principles of devotion to Vishnu. His reign promotes the welfare and prosperity of the nation and its people. One day, some of Candrahāsa's attendants pay tribute to the suzerain in Kauntalaka, but refuse to partake of the meals offered by the minister Dhṛṣṭabuddhi since they are fasting on the day of *ekādaśī*, in accordance with the precepts of Vishnu bhaktas. Dhṛṣṭabuddhi becomes enraged at their behaviour and decides to carry out a reconnaissance of Candanāvatī. During his visit, while conversing with the lord of Candanāvatī, Dhṛṣṭabuddhi realises that Candrahāsa is, in fact, the orphan boy who has supposedly been murdered. Consequently, he plans his murder once again, out of fear of the original prophecy.

(LIII) Dhṛṣṭabuddhi asks Candrahāsa to deliver a sealed letter to his son, Madana, without breaking the seal. The message in the letter is that the bearer should be poisoned. The delivery takes place in the spring, when nature is resplendent. Dhṛṣṭabuddhi's daughter and the princess

Campakamālinī and their girl companions are near the palace, plucking flowers in a field and bathing in a pond.

(LIV) Dhṛṣṭabuddhi's daughter happens to notice Candrahāsa who, under the protection of Vishnu, is sleeping near the shore of the pond; she almost instantly falls in love with him. She notices the letter addressed to her brother, Madana, in Candrahāsa's bosom. Picking it up, she breaks the seal and reads the words therein: 'Give poison to the bearer of this letter immediately'. She rewrites it adding 'yā' just after the word poison (*viṣa*); the revised word (*viṣayā*) is actually her name. Candrahāsa, who is fast asleep, takes no notice of what she does. Later, he delivers the letter to Madana.

(LV) Reading the letter's message, Madana immediately holds a wedding ceremony for his sister, Viṣayā, and Candrahāsa. The citizens of Kauntalaka are overjoyed and he is bestowed with various forms of wealth.

(LVI) Meanwhile, in Candanāvatī, Dhṛṣṭabuddhi, who does not know what has actually happened, blames Kulinda and his people without reason and unjustly tortures them. On hearing the actual tidings from a herald, Dhṛṣṭabuddhi realises that his attempt to murder Candrahāsa has again failed.

(LVII) At his residence, Dhṛṣṭabuddhi, incorrigibly plans the murder of Candrahāsa for the third time. He orders a few humble servants to hide at the shrine of the Goddess Candikā and kill anyone who comes there during the evening. Dhṛṣṭabuddhi then urges Candrahāsa to visit the shrine alone and, following family tradition, to seek the blessings of the goddess for his auspicious marriage. Meanwhile, the king of Kauntalaka has a premonition of death; he consults a court priest about his successor. The king, who has decided to abdicate in favour of Candrahāsa, sends an attendant, Madana, to find the Vishnu bhakta Candrahāsa, as soon as possible. Thus, Madana arrives at Candrahāsa's residence just as the latter is preparing to leave for the shrine. Madana asks him not to visit the shrine and to go to the palace instead. Madana visits the shrine in place of Candrahāsa and is consequently killed by the murderers hired by his own father.

(LVIII) When Dhṛṣṭabuddhi learns of this tragic incident, he immediately rushes to the shrine only to find his son's corpse. In a fit of agony, he kills himself. On hearing these tidings, Candrahāsa, who has already been crowned king and who is married to princess Campakamālinī in fair bigamy, arrives at the shrine and offers pieces of his flesh as a sacrifice to the Goddess Candikā. He is just about to sacrifice his life when the goddess herself appears before him, pleased by his devotion. She restores both Dhṛṣṭabuddhi and Madana to life. Subsequently, Dhṛṣṭabuddhi becomes a changed man and all live in prosperity. Thus, the greatness of the *śālagrāma* stone is evinced.

In another version introduced by J.T. Wheeler[7] with an English summary, the setting is not Kerala but the Dekkan, none of the characters but Chandrahāsa, Madan and Viṣayā (in the vernacularized form Bikya)[8] share the names of Schick's Jaimini version, and no episode of *ekādaśī* or *śālagrāma* appears. A saint called Gālava, whose name is only mentioned two or three times in Schick's version, plays an important role here. Although the outline is fairly similar to that of Schick's version, the underlying theme is of miraculous omens and not of devotion. The divergences indicate that the story of Candrahāsa had been floating in various streams of transmission.

Vernacular Versions

Set in Kerala in its popular version, Candrahāsa story was widely known in medieval and modern south India and several vernacular versions have been preserved. Among them, a Kannada version, included in the *Jaimini-bhārata* of Lakṣmīśa (1520-?),[9] is considered to be the most famous.[10] Even the *Amar Chitra Katha* series based the English adaptation of the story on this version.[11]

As has been shown by William Smith, the *Jaimini-bhārata* has also been adapted into eastern Indian vernaculars, crediting its entertainment value for its popularity in Assamese, Bengali and Oriya.[12] The name of Candrahāsa is also mentioned in Nābhādās' Hindi *Bhaktamāl* and Priyādās, in his *Bhaktirasabodhinī* (1712) commentary, provides the condensed story. Furthermore, some altered versions can also be observed in Hindi drama, as well as in the oral lore of various languages.[13] Although the history of transmission is not clear, it can be said that the story of Candrahāsa was present across India in forms independent of the *Jaimini-bhārata*.

On referring to the motif, indexes of folktales edited by scholars in worldwide folkloric study,[14] we can find that numerous folktales share motifs, if not specific details, with the story of Candrahāsa.

Analysis of the Plot

In order to compare its various versions and similar tales, it is best to divide the Candrahāsa story into several plots with a particular motif in each. Here, I am bringing together the findings of earlier studies not only from Indian literature but also from comparative literature and global folklore.

Plot A: an (learned priest's) unpleasant prophecy (that an unknown orphan will succeed to one's property).

Plot B: cutting off a body part as proof of murder.

Plot C: a letter of death that orders the murder of its bearer.

Plot D: rewriting a part of the letter, an act which the bearer is unaware, for a beneficial consequence.

Plot E: the plotter's son falls prey to the former's conspiracy and is murdered.

These plots correspond to the AT-type numbers of international folktales as described by Hans-Jörg Uther as follows:

Plot A-C-D = AT930: 'The prophecy' or 'The rich man and his son-in-law'[15]

Plot B = AT462: 'The outcast queen and the ogress queen'[16]

Tales Sharing Similar Plots

Drawing on earlier studies, it is possible to list tales sharing plots with the story of Chandrahāsa.

India before the Jaimini-bhārata

(I-1) 'Dharma-dāna prince Jātaka' in the *Rokudojikkyo* (Chinese translation of *Jātaka*, third century). The original version, which may be in Sanskrit, is lost. (Plot B only.)

(I-2) 'Kumāra Jātaka' in the *Rokudojikkyo*. In this story, the target of the murder has been accidentally changed to the beloved son of the commander, who has plotted the crime. The role of the delivery of a letter of death is changed. A potter recognizes the unknown person as the target and throws him into a furnace exactly as per the command in the letter. Here we should set another plot F.

Plot F: The replacement of the beloved son of the commander as the target of the murder.

Plots A-F-C-D. This telling corresponds to AT910K: 'Walk to the Ironworks', previously 'the Precepts and the Uriah Letter'.[17]

(I-3) 'The story of merchant Ghosaka' in the Pāli *Manoratha-purāṇī*[18] and in the *Dhammapaṭṭhakathā*[19] by Buddhaghoṣa (fifth century).[20] (Plots A-F-C-D.)

India in the Period of the Jaimini-bhārata

(I-4) 'The Sanskrit and Prakrit story of Damannaka, who was first born as a fisherman and then as the son of a merchant', in the *Kathākośa* by an unknown author (eleventh century; before the Apabhraṁśa version by the Jaina Śrīcandra).[21] (Plots A-B-C-D-E.) This story bears a striking resemblance to the story of Candrahāsa, so much so that the name of the daughter who rewrites the letter is 'Viṣā' and the word to be rewritten is 'viṣa'.[22]

(I-5) 'The Story of Parabhūti' in the Sanskrit *Kathā-sarit-sāgara* by Somadeva (eleventh century, Kashmīr).[23] (Plot F only.)

(I-6) 'The Jaina Sanskrit story of Śrīpuñja' in the *Prabandha-cintāmaṇi* (twelfth century)[24] (Plot A only.)

India After the Time of the Jaimini-bhārata

(I-7) The Sanskrit *Campakaśreṣṭhi-kathānaka* by Jinakīrti (fifteenth century, Jaina).[25] (Plot A-C-D-E.)

(I-8) Only the name of Candrahāsa in the *Bhaktamāl* by Nābhādās (early seventeenth century).

(I-9) Priyādās' *Bhaktirasabodhinī*[26] (1712). The story is told in eleven [*kavitt*]-metre verses (III, 58-68).

(I-10) The *Amar Chitra Katha* comics (Plots A-B-C-D-E.)

(I-11) The Hindi drama, *Bhakta Candrahāsa*, by Bābū Jamunādās Meharā. As there is neither a preface nor a postscript in this edition, it is not possible to determine its origin. It differs in many details from the Schick version. One main difference is that Candrahāsa's fate is decided not by the *śālagrāma* but by the saint Gālava. In this respect, the drama more closely resembles the Wheeler version even though its plots conform to the former. (Plots A-B-C-D-E.)

Europe[27]

(E-1) 'The letter of Bellerophon' in the *Iliad* (Plot C).

(E-2) 'The letter of Uriah' in the *Old Testament* (Plot C).

(E-3) 'The Pope Pelagius' in the Latin *Legenda aurea* by Jacobus de Voragine (1230?-1298). (Plots A-B-C-D.)

(E-4) 'Of Tribulation and Anguish' (No. 20) in the Latin *Gesta Romanorum* (thirteenth century, Britain). (Plots A-B-C-D.)

(E-5) 'Flidolin, schlechter ahtem' (No. 283) in the *Gesta Romanorum* (Plot F). In this story, the commander of the murder becomes the target of murder because the loyal murderer does not recognize his face.

(E-6) *Le dit de l'Empereur Coustant* (thirteenth century). (Plots A-B-C-D.)

(E-7) *Hamlet, Prince of Denmark* by Shakespeare, Act 4, Scene 3 (1601). (Plots C-D.)

(E-8) The Italian *Pentamerone* (Third day, Story 2) by Gian Alesio Abbatutis (Giambattista Basile 1573?-1632). (Plots B-D.)

(E-9) *Der Gang nach dem Eisenhammer* by Johann Christoph Friedrich von Schiller (1759-1805). (Plot F only.)

(E-10) 'Der Teufel mit den drei goldenen Haaren' (KHM29) in the *Kinder- und Hausmärchen* by the Grimm Brothers (1819). (Plots A-C-D.)

The Middle East

(M-1) 'Ahmed' in *Sindbad* (eighth-ninth century, in Pahlavi. However, this story is contained in an Arabic version, fifteenth century). (Plot F.)

(M-2) Vardan 119 & 120 (thirteenth-fourteenth century, the Armenian version of M-1). (Plot F.)

Transmission of the *Candrahāsa* between India and the West

According to a Indologist, H. Winternitz,[28] A. Weber was the first scholar who noticed the similarity between episodes of the *Jaimini-bhārata* and various tales in Europe.[29] At the beginning of the last century, Schick investigated the origin of the motif of Shakespeare's *Hamlet,* tracing its transmission from India to the West.[30] Another famous Finn folklorist, A. Aarne,[31] and the Indologist Winternitz[32] also advocated the introduction of 'the letter of death' motif from India to Europe. On the other hand, by comparing the *Jaimini-bhārata* as a whole with the Alexander romance, the Gospels and some Arabic tales, D. Derret stated that there was a prominent gospel-type theme in the Candrahāsa story, which is a development from that of the Bellerophon, the oldest example sharing plots in Europe.[33] Furthermore, he argues that the story of Candrahāsa could have multiple pedigrees: it could have part-classical, part-Indian, part-Christian and, perhaps, part-Arab roots.[34] In the face of serious opposition, he held that the Hindu Puranic material was heavily indebted to the Biblical story.[35]

Plot F, in which the target of murder changes to the beloved one or to the commander himself, may have originated in India and then was transmitted westwards, since the plot pattern A-F-C-D is peculiar to the Buddhist and older versions. Plot B, however, may have arrived in India from Europe, as Derret argues, with regard to the *Jaimini-bhārata*. However, it is impossible to precisely determine the transmission of the other plots.

Transmission of *Candrahāsa* Story in India

From early times, well before the composition of the extant Sanskrit Candrahāsa story, people—perhaps in Buddhist circles since the earliest occurrence of the 'Candrahāsa plots' is in the *Jātakas*—enjoyed tales with plots similar to the Candrahāsa story.

While innumerable similar stories have been shared by people in various languages, these stories were transmitted orally and not in writing because narrative stories have had no scripts from the outset and have sometimes been recorded by the one who wants to preserve them in the form of collected works. During the eleventh or twelfth centuries, a bhakta or bhaktas recomposed the story of Candrahāsa as a part of the *Jaimini-bhārata* and, almost simultaneously, one or several Jainas reformulated the story of Damannaka as a section of the *Kathākośa*, based on various tales that include some of the aforementioned plots. Lakṣmīśa, who may also have been a Vishnu bhakta, adapted the *Jaimini-bhārata* into Kannada. While Nābhādās only made a passing mention of Candrahāsa, Priyādās narrated his story in brief.[36] On the other hand, there may have been numerous streams of oral transmission of this story, some of which are found in the form of dramas or folktales as newly recorded in Mumbai.[37] On the basis of these two phases—denominational and no such-denominational—it is possible to imagine that Nābhādās adopted the name of Candrahāsa because of the latter's popularity as a pious bhakta, who, after overcoming considerable affliction, achieved happiness under the protection of Vishnu. The story of Candrahāsa must have been popular in oral lore, hence Nābhādās did not feel the need to retell the story. Priyādās merely had to remind the audience of its outline.

The story in the *Amar Chitra Katha* series has also been simplified. While the scene of little Candrahāsa finding the *śālagrāma* is narrated, no emphasis is placed on the greatness of the latter. As we have not yet explored the preceding version in Kannada by Lakṣmīśa, the stage at which these minor alterations were made is not precisely known. However, we may suppose that this change reflects the intentions of the comics' editor, Anant Pai.[38]

In the following section, I would like to enumerate some elements in order to elucidate the narrative nature of Schick's *Jaimini* version. These elements are not recognizable in the *Bhaktirasabodhinī*'s version due to its brevity.

Puranic Elements

Ekādaśī

It is interesting to observe the various aspects of a pious bhakta's manners and customs in Schick's *Jaimini* version. Candrahāsa reveres Vishnu just as he does his own parents[39] and constantly chants the name Hari.[40] In chapter LII, when Candrahāsa becomes a feudal lord, he enacts the strict practice of fasting on the day of *ekādaśī*.[41] During the visit of Candrahāsa's attendants to the suzerain in Kauntalaka, the former refuse food offered by the minister, Dhṛṣṭabuddhi, because they adhere to the praxis of the Vishnu bhaktas on the day of *ekādaśī*.[42] Such observance of the fast of *ekādaśī* is found in many of the Purāṇas.[43]

Worship of the Śālagrāma

The power of the *śālagrāma* is described in twenty-two verses at the end of the story (LVIII, 80-102). In the narrative, the sage, Nārada, states that because of its abundance, he cannot explain the virtues of the *śālagrāma* and, in apparent embarrassment, makes a sudden departure.[44] Thus, the greatness of the *śālagrāma* is the main theme of this story.

I found the following parallel verses regarding the meaning of the greatness of the *śālagrāma* in Schick's *Jaimini* version and in the Purāṇas, as introduced by W. Kirfel,[45]

yadi yuktā mahāpāpair janma-koṭi-samudbhavaiḥ.
mucyante nātra saṁdehaḥ śālagrāma-śilārcanāt (LVIII, 89cd, 90ab)

If the people who are debased by major sins because of ten million instances of births can attain moksha, there is no doubt about the fact that their worship of the *śālagrāma* will be beneficial.

In the Purāṇas,

prasaṅgāt kathayiśyāmi śālagrāmasya lakṣaṇam,
śālagrāma-śilā-sparśāt koṭi-janmāghanāśanam.
(*Garuḍa Purāṇa* 45,1, *Padma Purāṇa*, IV,78,16, *Agni Purāṇa*,48,1)[46]

> I will zealously tell you the distinguishing feature of *śālagrāma*. By merely touching the *śālagrāma*, the sins of ten million instances of births will be purged out.

The same is also mentioned in the *Bhāgavata Purāṇa* (vv. 95cd-96ab). This fact indicates that the composer of Schick's *Jaimini* version depended on Puranic authority to explain the value of the *śālagrāma*. In contrast, Priyādās omits praise of the *śālagrāma*, although he still mentions it twice (at the first attempt on Candrahāsa's life and at his falling asleep on his way to deliver the letter of death).

Folk Elements

A transmitter sometimes inserts popular ideas rooted in his time and society into a work in order to make it more accessible or enjoyable to his audience. The descriptions of oneiromancy, i.e. the interpretation of dreams (LVII, 30cd-36) and of omens of disaster (LVI, 22cd-23, LVII, 65, 67, etc.) are such elements present in Schick's *Jaimini* version. Needless to say, Priyādās did not portray such scenes.

Conclusion

Every plot of the story of Candrahāsa must have originated in folklore. Each anonymous plot has been arranged or inserted into new folktales or other literary works from early times not only in India but also across the world. Besides the above-mentioned works, innumerable folktales with the same plots exist in various parts of the world.[47]

The composer of the *Jaimini-bhārata* (Schick's version), with the intention of retelling the *Mahābhārata* and of advocating Vishnu bhakti, must have adapted this rather completed story with every plot A-B-C-D-E from folktales or (lost) earlier works, as the Jaina composer of the *Kathākośa* did, and tried to make it similar to a Purāṇa by adding aspects such as the description of the *ekādaśī* fast and the efficiency of the *śālagrāma*. Thus, the tale popularizes Vishnu bhakti to a wider audience interested in stories soon after the appearance of the *Bhāgavata Purāṇa*[48] and before its flourishing in medieval India. The more popular the *Jaimini-bhārata* became,[49] the wider the story of Candrahāsa in it must have spread, especially among the Vishnu bhaktas. There must have been another current of orally-transmitted tales with almost the same pattern of plots. These tales may have been integrated under the title of Candrahāsa induced by the popularization of his story. Then this story may have become part of the repertoire of innumerable story-tellers crossing the borders of languages. That is the reason why the story of Candrahāsa has various versions independent of the *Jaimini-bhārata.*

In this study, I examined the story from a broader perspective, including that of Europe. It is clear that phases similar to the hagiographies of Hindu bhakti are observed in European Christianity. For example, the *Legenda aurea* also adopted many folktales. It is worth noting that a story in the *Legenda aurea* shares motifs with the story of Candrahāsa.

As R.P. Bahuguna states, Nābhādās does refer to occasional episodes in the lives of certain individual devotees but those references are brief and assume a certain degree of knowledge of events on the part of the listeners or readers.[50] His *Bhaktamāl* does not contain any biographical story that listeners can enjoy. For this reason, P. Lutgendorf states that the *Bhaktamāl* appears to have been intended as a kind of mnemonic for Vaishnava storytellers;[51] he follows G.A. Grierson in pointing out that it is written in an extremely compressed style and that every epithet is intended as a clue to some unrecorded legend.[52]

Neither in its commentary, the *Bhaktirasabodhinī* by Priyādās, a work that readers or listeners can accept directly. Thus, P.G. Friedlander states that the *Bhaktamāl* by Nābhādās is an important textual landmark in the tradition of telling tales about the lives of Vaishnava devotees, and it is almost certain that both the *mūl* text and its commentaries were composed by drawing on a stock of oral traditions current at that time.[53] H.R.M. Pauwels argues that all hagiographers seem to have had access to oral sources that were circulating stories and songs of holy men, and that hagiographic stories reveal which songs were popular at the time of their writing.[54]

As we focused on the story of Candrahāsa in this paper, we cannot argue the whole work of the *Bhaktamāl* and the *Bhaktirasabodhinī*. However, an investigation into that of structure of the story of Candrahāsa and how it and of similar versions have been transmitted from the viewpoint of folktales seems to indicate why Nābhādās adopted Candrahāsa. It is fortunate for us that we can see the same peculiarity of depending on popular tales in our hagiographies, especially in the *Bhaktamāl* by Nābhādās and in its commentary, the *Bhaktirasabodhinī*, through the story of Candrahāsa.

NOTES

1. The text has been edited three times: J. Schick, ed., *Das indische Hamlet-Epos, Aus dem Jaiminibhārata, Separatabdruck aus dem Corpus Hamleticum (1912)*, Leipzig, no date, R.S. Shastri, ed., *Śrī Jaiminīyāśvamedha-parva, hindī ṭīkā-sahit*, Gorakhpur: Gita Press, 1961; and K. Aggarwal, 'Jaiminīya Mahābhārata: Āśvamedhika Parva: Part 2', *Kalyāṇ Kalpataru*, vol. 54, no. 1, 2008. This Jaimini is probably not identical with the author of the *Mīmāṁsā-sūtra*. However, there are traces of a legend, particularly in south India, that both works belong to the same author. See Schick, ed., *Das indische Hamlet-Epos*, pp. 1-2 and A. Pai, S. Rao, and P. Mulick, *Chandrahasa*, Bombay: Indian Book House, no date.
2. W.L. Smith, 'The Jaiminibhārata and its Eastern Vernacular Versions', *Studia Orientalia*, vol. 82, 1997, pp. 195-6.
3. J.D.M. Derrett, 'Greece and India Again: the Jaimini-Aśvamedha, the Alexander-romance and the Gospels', *Zeitschrift für Religions-und Geistesgeschichte*, vol. 22, no. 1, 1970, p. 46.
4. Each chapter has 44, 55, 91, 75, 64, 50, 57, 75 and 105 verses. In Schick's edition some verses (L-30, 39, 57; LI-15, 22, 23, 36; LII-16, 52, 74; LIII-27; LIV-38; LV-25, 50; LVI-52; LVII-24, 73; LVIII-51, 56) have three lines and other verses (LII-90; LVI-33, 40; LVII-69) have only one; numbers 52 and 53 in Ch. LIV are duplicated, and number 61 in Chapter LVIII is omitted. There is a verse inserted between verse 20 and 21. According to R.S. Shastri's and K. Aggarwal's editions, a sequel to the story of Candrahāsa is narrated in the subsequent chapter.
5. It also uses a variety of metres such as *upajāti* (54 verses), *vaṁśamālā* (2), *vasantatilakā* (2) and *puṣpitāgrā* metres (1). The *upajāti* metre is shown at the end part of almost all chapters except Ch. LV and LVIII (*upajāti*: L-40-

42, 44; LI-55; LII-48-49, 91; LIII-74-75; LIV-25-26, 64; LV-14-19; LVI-24-25, 30-45, 47-52, 53cd-57; LVII-70-72; 73cd-75, *vaṁśamālā*: L-43; LVII-73ab, *vasantatilakā*: LIII-73; LVI-53ab, *puṣpitāgrā*: LVI-46).

6. J. Brockington, *The Sanskrit Epics*, Leiden: Brill, 1998, p. 493.
7. Wheeler depends upon the English translation of the *Mahābhārata* from a manuscript preserved in the Library of the Asiatic Society of Bengal (J. T. Wheeler, *The History of India from the Earliest Ages* vol. 1, London: Trubner & Co., 1867, p. vii). This *Mahābhārata* may be a vernacular one but we have no full information.
8. The 'k' in *Bikya* is developed from the typical north-Indian 'kh' pronunciation of the character 'ṣ'. The loss of aspiration would link the story to the Deccan where it is a typical change (cf. Dakkhin—> Dekkan).
9. A. Datta et al., eds., *Encyclopaedia of Indian Literature*, vol. 3, Delhi: Sahitya Akademi, 1989, p. 2229. It has only an incomplete edition without the story of Candrahāsa: D. Sanderson, ed., *The Jaimini Bharata: A Celebrated Canarese Poem, with Translation and Notes*, Bangalore: The Wesleyan Mission Press, 1852.
10. Smith, 'The Jaiminibhārata', p.194.
11. Pai, Rao, and Mulick, *Chandrahasa.*
12. Smith, 'The Jaiminibhārata', p. 203.
13. J.H. Knowles, *Folk-tales of Kashmir*, 2nd edn, Delhi: Low Price Publications, 2004; rpt., 2004, pp. 42-50, A. Stein and G. Grierson, eds., *Hatim's Tales: Kashmiri Stories and Songs*, Delhi: Gian Publishing House, 1989, pp. 93-5; W. Crooke, 'Note on the Folklore of the Tales', in *Hatim's Tales: Kashmiri Stories and Songs*, ed. A. Stein and G. Grierson, Delhi: Gian Publishing House, 1989, pp. xliv-xlvii and S.H. Blackburn, *Moral Fictions: Tamil Folktales from Oral Tradition*, Helsinki: Suomalainen Tiedeakatemia, Academia Scientiarum Fennica, 2001, pp. 62-4, 244-5.
14. S. Thompson, ed., *Motif Index of Folk-Literature*, 6 vols., Bloomington: Indiana University Press, 1955, S. Thompson and J. Balys, *The Oral Tales of India*, Bloomington: Indiana University Press, 1958 and H.-J. Uther, *The Types of International Folktales: A Classification and Bibliography, Based on the System of Antti Aarne and Atith Thompson*, 3 vols., Helsinki: Suomalainen Tiedeakatemia, Academia Scientiarum Fennica, 2004.
15. S. Thompson, *The Folklore*, Berkeley and Los Angeles: California University Press, 1946; rpt., 1977, p. 139; H.-J. Uther, *The Types of International Folktales: A Classification and Bibliography: Based on the System of Antti Aarne and Atith Thompson*, vol. I, pp. 568-9.
16. Uther, *The Types of International Folktales*, p. 273.
17. Ibid., pp. 535-6.
18. E. Hardy, 'The Story of the Merchant Ghosaka (Ghosaka-seṭṭhi) in its Twofold Pāli Form, with Reference to Other Indian Parallels', *Journal of the Royal Asiatic Society*, 1898, pp. 741-94; E.W. Burlingame, *Buddhist Parables*, New Haven: Yale University Press, 1922, pp. 128-38.

19. H.C. Norman, ed., *The Commentary on the Dhammapada*, vol. 1, Part 1, *Pali Text Society*, London: Luzac, 1970, pp. 174-88 and E.W. Burlingame, *Buddhist Legends Translated from the Original Pali Text of the Dhammapada Commentary*, Part 1, Cambridge, Mass.: Harvard University Press, 1990 (1st edn 1921), pp. 256-66.
20. Norman admits that Buddhaghoṣa is the author of the *Manoratha-Purāṇī* but not of the *Dammapadaṭṭhakathā* because of the difference in the style of the story of Ghosaka (Norman, ed., *The Commentary on the Dhammapada*, p. xvii).
21. C.H. Tawney, tr., *The Kathākośa: or Treasury of Stories*, Delhi: Oriental Books Reprint Corporation, 1975.
22. This work and the Jaimini version and another story of Candrahāsa in the *Bhaktirasabodhinī* have been comprehensively compared by Gupta (R.D. Gupta, 'The Story of Candrahāsa as Narrated by Priyā Dās and Jaimini and its Comparison with the Kathākośa Version', *Orientalia Lovaniensia Periodica*, vol. 2, 1971, see n. 9). Penzer mentions this story in the column 'the letter of death' and its appearance in the *Bhaktamāl* of Nābhādās N.M. Penzer, ed., *The Ocean of Story: Being C.H. Tawney's Translation of Somadeva's Kathā sarit sāgara*, 10 vols., Delhi: B.R. Publishers, 2001, vol. III, pp. 277-81, but he misunderstands its date.
23. Penzer, ed., *The Ocean of Story*, vol. II, p. 113.
24. Merutuṅga, *Prabandhacintāmaṇi*, ed. Jinvijay Muni, Santiniketan: Siṁghī Jain Jñānpīṭh, 1933 and C.H. Tawney, ed., *The Prabandhacintāmaṇi or Wishing-Stone of Narrative*, Calcutta: The Asiatic Society, 1901.
25. J. Hertel, 'The Story of Merchant Campaka', *Zeitschrift der Deutschen Morgenländischen Gesellschaft*, vol. 65, 1911, pp. 1-51, 425-71.
26. H. Bhagirath, ed., *Śrī nābhādās jī viracit bhaktamāl, śrī priyādās jī kṛt bhaktirasabodhinī ṭīkā sahit*, Bombay, 1903, pp. 15-17. See also P. Dikshit, *Nābhādās kṛt bhaktmāl, ek adhyayan*, Allahabad: Sāhitya Bhavan, 1961, pp. 57, 176-7.
27. M. Winternitz, *A History of Indian Literature*, vol. 1, Delhi: Motilal Banarsidass, 1987, pp. 557-9. A. Weber, 'Über eine Episode im Jaimini-Bharata (entsprechend einer Sage von Kaiser Heinrich III und dem 'Gang nach dem Eisenhammer')', *Monatsberichte der Preussischen Alademie der Wissenschaften, Philosophisch-Historische Klasse*, 1869 and A. Aarne, *Der reiche Mann und sein Schweiegersohn, vergleichende Marchenforschungen*, Hamina: Suomalaisen tiedeakatemian kustantama, 1916.
28. Winternitz, *A History of Indian Literature*, p. 557.
29. Weber, 'Über eine Episode im Jaimini-Bharata (entsprechend einer Sage von Kaiser Heinrich III und dem "Gang nach dem Eisenhammer")'.
30. A newspaper article of unknown authorship, 'A Literary Detective on the Trail of Hamlet', *New York Times*, 19 November 1911.
31. Aarne, *Der reiche Mann und sein Schweiegersohn*.
32. Winternitz, *A History of Indian Literature*, p. 558.

33. Derrett, 'Greece and India Again', p. 34.
34. Ibid., note.
35. Ibid., p. 39.
36. Gupta compares the texts of three versions namely the story of Damannaka in *Kathākośa*, that of Candrahāsa in the *Jaimini-bhārata* and that of the *Bhaktirasabodhinī*. His philological study is centred on the analysis of variations in these three versions. However, Gupta does not include a comprehensive discussion on the background of these texts; he merely states that the setting of the *JV* (*Jaimini-bhārata* version) is more realistic and worldly, and that the author was obviously out to amuse and entertain his audience. Gupta, 'The Story of Candrahāsa as Narrated by Priyā Dās and Jaimini and its Comparison with the Kathākośa Version', p. 187.
37. N.B. Godabole, 'Folklore—The Story of Chandrahāsya', *The Indian Antiquary*, vol. 11, 1882, pp. 84-6.
38. Cf. J.S. Hawley, 'The Saints Subdued: Domestic Virtue and National Integration in Amar Chitra Katha', in *Media and the Transformation of Religion in South Asia*, ed. Lawrence A. Babb and Susan S. Wadley, Philadelphia: University of Pennsylvania Press, 1995, pp. 129-31.
39. *mama mātā-pitā kṛṣṇas tenāhaṁ paripālitaḥ* (LI, 16ab) (My mother and father is Krishna, by whom I am guarded).
40. *saptābdikaś candrahāso nānākṣara-vinirṇayam. vicārya samyaṅ manasā harir ity akṣaradvayam; sa jajāpa sadā kruddhas tadā so 'kṣara-pāṭhakaḥ.* (LI, 26cd, 27). (When Candrahāsa was seven, he selected the two-letter word Hari which is a set of various letters after careful consideration and he was always chanting it. This angered his teacher.)
41. LII, 31-40ab.
42. *na garvitā vayaṁ svāmin na bhuñjāmo harer dine* (LII, 70ab) (Not for the sake of pride, lord, we do not eat on the day of Hari).
43. P.V. Kane, *History of Dharmaśāstra*, 2nd edn, vol. 5, part 1, Poona: Bhandarkar Oriental Research Institute, 1974, pp. 95-121. See also P.V. Das, ed., *Ekādaśī Māhātmya, the Glories of Ekādaśī*, Vrindavan: Rasbihari Lal & Sons, 2000.
44. *śālagrāma-śilāyās tu mahimā varṇatuṁ mayā. na śakyate bahutvāc ca gamiṣyāmi surālayam* (LVIII, 102cd-103ab).
45. W. Kirfel, 'Vom Steinkult in Indien', in *Studien zur Geschichte und Kultur des Nahen und Fernen Ostens*, ed. Willi Heffening and Willibald Kirfel, Leiden: Brill, 1935, pp. 167-70.
46. Kirfel, 'Vom Steinkult in Indien', p. 167.
47. Uther, *The Types of International Folktales*, pp. 273, 535-6, 568-9.
48. As I already noted, the story of Candrahāsa in the Jaimini version has a quotation from the *Bhāgavata Purāṇa*. Winternitz, *A History of Indian Literature*, p. 559.
49. The high number of its manuscripts is mentioned; Winternitz, *A History of Indian Literature*, p. 557, n. 3.

50. R.P. Bahuguna, 'Conflict and Assimilation in Medieval North Indian Bhakti: An Alternative Approach', in *SAP-History Monograph*, Delhi: Department of History and Culture, Jamia Millia Islamia, no date, p. 20.
51. P. Lutgendorf, 'Dining Out at Lake Pampa: The Shabari Episode in Multiple Ramayanas', Paula Richman, ed., *Questioning Ramayana: A South Asian Tradition*, Berkeley: University of California Press, 2001, p. 127.
52. G.A. Grierson, 'Gleanings from the Bhakta-mala', *Journal of the Royal Asiatic Society*, 1909, p. 608.
53. P.G. Friedlander, 'The Struggle for Salvation in the Hagiographies of Ravidās', in *Myth and Mythmaking: Continuous Evolution in Indian Traditon*, ed. Julia Leslie, Richmond: Curzon, 1996, p. 117.
54. H.R.M. Pauwels, *In Praise of Holy Men: Hagiographic Poems by and about Harirām Vyās*, Groningen: Egbert Forsten, 2002, p. 294.

BIBLIOGRAPHY

Aarne, A., *Der reiche Mann und sein Schweiegersohn, vergleichende Marchenforschungen, Folklore Fellows Communications*, 23, Hamina: Suomalaisen tiedeakatemian kustantama, 1916.

Aggarwal, K., 'Jaiminīya Mahābhārata: Āśvamedhika Parva: Part 2', *Kalyāṇ Kalpataru*, vol. 54, no. 1, 2008.

Bahuguna, R.P., 'Conflict and Assimilation in Medieval North Indian Bhakti: An Alternative Approach', in *SAP-History Monograph*, Delhi: Department of History and Culture, Jamia Millia Islamia, no date, pp. 1-47.

Bhagirath, H., ed., *Śrī nābhādās jī viracit bhaktamāl, śrī priyādās jī kṛt bhakti-rasabodhinī ṭīkā sahit*, Bombay, 1903.

Blackburn, S.H., *Moral Fictions: Tamil Folktales from Oral Tradition, FF Comunications*, 278, Helsinki: Suomalainen Tiedeakatemia, Academia Scientiarum Fennica, 2001.

Brockington, J., *The Sanskrit Epics, Handbuch der Prientalistik*, Leiden: Brill, 1998.

Burlingame, E.W., *Buddhist Legends Translated from the Original Pali Text of the Dhammapada Commentary, Part 1, Harvard Oriental Series*, 28, Cambridge, Mass.: Harvard University Press, 1990, 1st edn 1921.

———, *Buddhist Parables*, New Haven: Yale University Press, 1922.

Crooke, W., 'Note on the Folklore of the Tales', in *Hatim's Tales: Kashmiri Stories and Songs*, ed., A. Stein and G. Grierson, Delhi: Gian Publishing House, 1989, pp. xxx-xlvii.

Dasa, P.V., ed., *Ekādaśī Māhātmya, the Glories of Ekādaśī*, Vrindavan: Rasbihari Lal & Sons, 2000.

Datta, A., et al., eds., *Encyclopaedia of Indian Literature*, vol. 3, Delhi: Sahitya Akademi, 1989.

Derrett, J.D.M., 'Greece and India Again: The Jaimini-Aśvamedha, the Alexander-romance and the Gospels', *Zeitschrift für Religions- und Geistesgeschichte,* vol. 22, no. 1, 1970, pp. 19-44.

Dikshit, P., *Nābhādās kṛt bhaktmāl, ek adhyayan*, Allahabad: Sāhitya Bhavan, 1961.

Friedlander, P.G., 'The Struggle for Salvation in the Hagiographies of Ravidās', in *Myth and Mythmaking: Continous Evolution in Indian Traditon*, ed. J. Leslie, Richmond: Curzon, 1996, pp. 106-23.

Godabole, N.B., 'Folklore—The Story of Chandrahāsya', *The Indian Antiquary,* vol. 11, 1882, pp. 84-6.

Grierson, G.A., 'Gleanings from the Bhakta-mala', *Journal of the Royal Asiatic Society,* vol. for 1909, pp. 607-44 , vol. for 1910, pp. 87-109, 269-306.

Gupta, R.D., 'The Story of Candrahāsa as Narrated by Priyā Dās and Jaimini and its Comparison with the Kathākośa Version', *Orientalia Lovaniensia Periodica,* vol. 2, 1971, pp. 163-89.

Hardy, E., 'The Story of the Merchant Ghosaka (Ghosaka-seṭṭhi) in its Twofold Pāli Form, with Reference to Other Indian Parallels', *Journal of the Royal Asiatic Society,* vol., 1898, pp. 741-94.

Hawley, J.S., 'The Saints Subdued: Domestic Virtue and National Integration in Amar Chitra Katha', in *Media and the Transformation of Religion in South Asia*, ed. L.A. Babb and S.S. Wadley, Philadelphia: University of Pennsylvania Press, 1995, pp. 107-34.

Hertel, J., 'The Story of Merchant Campaka', *Zeitschrift der Deutschen Morgenländischen Gesellschaft*, vol. 65, 1911, pp. 1-51, 425-71.

Kane, P.V., *History of Dharmaśāstra*, 2nd edn., vol. 5, part 1, *Government Oriental Series, Class B*, 6, Poona: Bhandarkar Oriental Research Institute, 1974.

Kirfel, W., 'Vom Steinkult in Indien', in *Studien zur Geschichte und Kultur des Nahen und Fernen Ostens*, ed. W. Heffening and W. Kirfel, Leiden: Brill, 1935, pp. 163-72.

Knowles, J.H., *Folk-tales of Kashmir*, 2nd edn, Delhi: Low Price Publications, 2004.

Lutgendorf, P., 'Dining Out at Lake Pampa: The Shabari Episode in Multiple Ramayanas', Paula Richman, ed., *Questioning Ramayanas: A South Asian Tradition*, Berkeley: University of California Press, 2001, pp. 119-36.

Merutuṅga, *Prabandhacintāmaṇi*, ed. J. Muni, Santiniketan: Siṁghī Jain Jñānpīṭh, 1933.

Norman, H.C., ed., *The Commentary on the Dhammapada*, vol. 1, part 1, *Pali Text Society*, London: Luzac, 1970.

Pai, A., S. Rao, and P. Mulick, *Chandrahasa*, Amar Chitra Katha 97, Bombay: Indian Book House, no date.

Pauwels, H.R.M., *In Praise of Holy Men: Hagiographic Poems by and about Harirām Vyās, Groningen Oriental Studies*, v 18, Groningen: Egbert Forsten, 2002.

Penzer, N.M., ed., *The Ocean of Story: Being C.H. Tawney's Translation of Sōmadeva's Kathā sarit sāgara*, 10 vols, Delhi: B.R. Publishers, 2001.

Sanderson, D., ed., *The Jaimini Bharata: A Celebrated Canarese Poem, with Translation and Notes*, Bangalore: The Wesleyan Mission Press, 1852.

Schick, J., ed., *Das indische Hamlet-Epos, Aus dem Jaiminibhārata, Separatabdruck aus dem Corpus Hamleticum (1912)*, Leipzig, no date.

Shastri, R.S., ed., *Śrī Jaiminīyāśvamedha-parva, hindī ṭīkā-sahit*, Gorakhpur: Gita Press, 1961.

Smith, W.L., 'The Jaiminibhārata and its Eastern Vernacular Versions', *Studia Orientalia,* vol. 82, 1997, pp. 193-208.

Stein, A., and G. Grierson, eds., *Hatim's Tales: Kashmiri Stories and Songs*, Delhi: Gian Publishing House, 1989.

Tawney, C.H., tr., *The Kathākośa: or Treasury of Stories*, Delhi: Oriental Books Reprint Corporation, 1975.

Tawney, C.H., ed., *The Prabandhacintāmaṇi or Wishing-Stone of Narrative*, Calcutta: The Asiatic Society, 1901.

Thompson, S., *The Folklore*, Berkeley and Los Angeles: California University Press, 1946, rpt., 1977.

Thompson, S., ed., *Motif Index of Folk-Literature*, 6 vols, Bloomington: Indiana University Press, 1955.

Thompson, S. and J. Balys, *The Oral Tales of India*, Bloomington: Indiana University Press, 1958.

Uther, H.-J., *The Types of International Folktales: A Classification and Bibliography, Based on the System of Antti Aarne and Atith Thompson,* 3 vols, *FF Comunications* 286, Helsinki: Suomalainen Tiedeakatemia, Academia Scientiarum Fennica, 2004.

Weber, A., 'Über eine Episode im Jaimini-Bharata (entsprechend einer Sage von Kaiser Heinrich III und dem 'Gang nach dem Eisenhammer')', *Monatsberichte der Preussischen Alademie der Wissenschaften, Philosophisch-Historische Klasse,* vom 14, Januar 1869, pp. 10-48, 377-87.

Wheeler, J.T., *The History of India from the Earliest Ages*, vol. 1, London: Trubner & Co., 1867.

Winternitz, M., *A History of Indian Literature*, vol. 1, Delhi: Motilal Banarsidass, 1987.

BHAKTI AND SOCIETY

CHAPTER 6

Shiva and Parvati Assist Young Couples in their Marriage as Referred to in Hindi Devotional Literature and Folk Songs

TEIJI SAKATA

Shiva and his consort, Parvati, play important roles in everyday life of the people in south Asia. In north India, Shiva and Parvati are worshipped on the occasion of Shivaratri festival in early spring; their son, Ganesha, is worshipped on the day of Ganesh Chauth or Ganesha Chaturthi in early autumn. Moreover, Ganesha is expected to remove obstacles and therefore invoked before undertaking important activities, including marriage ceremony. Although there is no substantial Shaiva literature in Hindi, there are many references to Shiva and Parvati in early Hindi devotional literature and in folk songs. Ganesha is invoked regularly in the same sources. From among the various roles of Shiva and Parvati, this paper gives focus to the role of their assistance to young couples in their marriage.

In early Hindi devotional literature, assistance of Shiva and Parvati to young couples for their marriage is referred to in Malik Muhammad Jāysī's *Padmāvat*[1] (*c.*1540), and Tulsīdās's *Rāmcaritmānas*[2] (*c.*1574). The former is a Sufi romance, the latter an adaptation of the ancient story of Rama. The author of *Padmāvat,* Jāysī (hereafter to be written as Jaysi), was a Sufi who adapted popular romances to Islamic mysticism in which the hero leaves his fort in search of the supreme being, who appears in the human form of a princess, Padminī. The author of *Rāmcaritmānas*, a brahman Tulsīdās (hereafter to be written as Tulsidas), had access to Vālmīki's Sanskrit *Rāmāyaṇa*[3] and later related works such as *Adhyātma Rāmāyaṇa*.[4]

Padmāvat and *Rāmcaritmānas* are narratives that are labelled as a romance and an epic, respectively. The former was composed to popularize Islamic mysticism, the latter to offer a guideline on daily life to the Hindus of the time. Although both literary works have their own religious sources at the centre, they seem to have incorporated various elements of folk culture.

Both the authors hailed from the eastern Hindi area of Avadh and composed their works in literary Avadhi. We also find many references to the assistance of Shiva and Parvati to young couples in Hindi folk songs of Avadhi and the neighbouring Bhojpuri, but less in western Hindi dialects such as Braj and Khari Boli.

The References in *Padmāvat*

Padmāvat, the story of Padminī or 'Princess Lotus' was composed by Malik Muhammad Jāysī, an ascetic living in the town of Jāyas. The author draws on popular folk romances and historical memory of the day to create an allegorical story in which King Ratnasen of Chittor assumed the form of an ascetic to attain Padminī of Simhala and, after severe trials, succeeds in marrying her. His love, *pem*, symbolizes divine love.

The first half of the romance is centered on attaining the union of an ideal couple, symbolizing the union of the human being with the supreme being. Here, Shiva and Parvati were invoked by both the hero and heroine of the story. On arriving in the town of Padminī, Ratnasen visits *Mahādev kar maṇḍap* (the temple of Shiva) [164.8, 9] and, wishing to see Padminī, prays to Shiva [165.2, 166.1-9]. Affected by the sincere prayer of Ratnasen and having the report on him conveyed by her messenger parrot, Hīrāman, Padminī wishes to get united with the king [168.1, 175-82], and goes to Shiva's temple to request the god to offer

Ratnasen as her bridegroom [189.1-9]. Gaurā ('the fair goddess', Parvati) observing that both Ratnasen and Padminī are eager to get united, advises Shiva to assist them for a happy marriage [211.1-9]. The king of Chittor, in this way, succeeds in attaining princess Padminī of Simhala and the human soul reaches the supreme being.

This is only the first half of this allegorical romance by Jaysi with many references to Shiva and Parvati. In contrast with this part, the latter half of the narrative hardly ever refers to Shiva and Parvati.

The References in *Rāmcaritmānas*

Rāmcaritmānas or *The Holy Lake of the Acts of Rama* relies primarily on the long tradition of the Rama story. It was composed a few decades after *Adhyātma Rāmāyaṇa*, one of its principal sources. It is noteworthy that although most of his sources were in Sanskrit, Tulsidas wrote his epic in the literary vernacular. This fact, accompanied by a non-sectarian understanding of the acts of Rama, soon made his Hindi Rama story popular and a point of reference for solving the problems of everyday life.

Tulsidas suggests that the people who are sincerely devoted to the supreme deity Vishnu, who appears on earth sometimes as Rama, attain harmony in this life. Thus, for example, the tribulations of Rama and Sita eventually leads to a peaceful life in his version, whereas in Valmiki's *Rāmāyaṇa*, Sita is expelled by Rama at the concluding section of the story.

Parvati is already present at the first meeting of Rama and Sita. When Rama and Lakshmana arrive in Janaka's capital, Sita happens to be on her way to 'Gaurī niketā' (Parvati's abode, i.e. temple) [1.227.3]. It is there that Rama catches sight of Sita and it is there that Sita is advised by her attendants to mediate on Parvati and look at the prince. Sita glimpses Rama and is enchanted by his beauty [1.234.1-1.235.2] and, afraid that the young and slender Rama may fail in lifting the huge heavy bow, returns to 'Bhavānī bhavan' (temple of Parvati) and entreats the goddess to assist her to be united with Rama. Parvati then assures her heart's desire would be fulfilled [1.235.2-1.236.4]. During the contest, Sita prays to Ganesha, the remover of obstacles, to reduce the weight of the bow to a mere trifle [1.257.4].

References to the assistance by Shiva, Parvati and Ganesha are limited to these portions of the epic. This assistance singles out Tulsidas's work since neither of the preceding important Sanskrit epics, Valmiki's *Rāmāyaṇa* [1.67.1-27] and *Adhyātma Rāmāyaṇa* [1.6.1-82], has any reference to it. Neither is the mutual acquaintance of Rama and Sita before marriage referred to in them.[5]

The case in which Sita prayed to Ganesha during the bow contest should be understood that he is not expected to assist the marriage directly, but to remove the obstacle, namely the heaviness of the bow.

The References in Avadhi and Bhojpuri Folk Songs

Hindi has a rich tradition of folk songs sung and published in many dialects. A particularly high number of songs relate to weddings and have been the subject of studies on folk literature. As for the assistance offered by Shiva and Parvati for marriages, we find many folk songs in Avadhi and Bhojpuri. In these folk songs, other gods also join the wedding ceremony to celebrate it.

A girl anxious to get married may pray to Siu (Shiva) in a folk song in Avadhi.[6] In a Bhojpuri folk song, when a marriage is arranged, three gods (Brahma, Vishnu, Mahesha/Shiva) are invited in the morning of wedding ceremony to celebrate the couple.[7] Bhavānī (Parvati) sometimes personally joins the wedding ceremony.[8] Shiva and Parvati are kind enough to offer auspicious gifts to the couple.[9]

From this brief survey of references in Hindi folk songs, we find that all the three Hindu gods Brahma, Vishnu and Shiva are invited to the marriage ceremony. Here too, Siu and Bhavānī perform the important role of arranging marriage. They also sometimes offer auspicious gifts.

It should also be noted that in Hindi folk songs, it is not the

TABLE 1: AN OVERVIEW OF DIVINE INVOLVEMENT IN DEVOTIONAL LITERATURE AND FOLK SONGS

Padmāvat	*Rāmcaritmānas*	Avadhi Folk Songs	Bhojpuri Folk Songs
Ratnasen visits Shiva's temple to pray for a sight of Padminī (166).	Sita visits Parvati's temple and begs for a handsome spouse (1.227.3).	Siu (Shiva) is prayed to by a young girl for a suitable bridegroom.	
Affected by Ratnasen's prayer, Padminī prays to Shiva that Ratnasen be her bridegroom (189).	Rama glimpes Sita in a garden near the temple (1.230,231). Sita sees Rama in the same garden and is enchanted by him (1.234, 235). Sita returns to the temple of Parvati and entreats the goddess to assist her to be united with him (1.235.1-236.2).		
Seeing this situation, Parvati advises Shiva to assist their marriage (211).	Parvati reassures Sita (1.236.3-4).		
	Sita prays to Ganesha to reduce the weight of the bow (1.257.4).		
			Brahma, Vishnu and Shiva are invited to the marriage ceremony.
With the assistance of the gods, the young couple marries, circumambulating the fire (286).	Rama and Sita marry, circumambulating the fire (1.325.1).	Shiva and Parvati offer auspicious gifts to the couple.	Bhavānī (Parvati) joins marriage ceremony on her own.

people who visit the temples of the gods, but the gods who come to celebrate the couple and their families are either invited or are visiting on their own. In this manner, gods and goddess appear like revered and familiar neighbours.

Contributions of Lord Shiva and Goddess Parvati in Arranging and Celebrating Marriage

When young couples aspiring to get married are suffering from difficulties or obstacles, Shiva and his consort, Parvati, offer them assistance or the power to overcome them. Their son, Ganesha, may sometimes assist young couples but his role is more removal of obstacles than assisting marriage directly.

The description of difficulties or obstacles in the way of a happy union in devotional literature leads to religious interpretation. In *Padmāvat*, the hero wishes to be united with the Lotus Princess who is allegorically interpreted as the human form of the divine being. His *pem* stands for divine love in Islamic mysticism. His story is that of a transcendental endeavour. In *Rāmcaritmānas*, the hero, Rama, is expected to govern a country. He must be suitable and fully qualified for it. The heavy bow to be stringed stands for the obstacles in his way.

In contrast to the aristocratic setting of these literary works, the world of folk songs is that of the common people. For them, there is no obstacle if they pray sincerely in their everyday life. Gods and goddess are not usually expected to remove obstacles but to celebrate the young couples and offer auspicious gifts.

On the whole, gods and goddess in devotional literature prepare the way for the happy marriage of couples who are confronting severe obstacles, while in folk songs, deities visit the scene of the marriage ceremonies of the people in keeping with social codes and lavish them with gifts.

Conclusion: Traditions, Synthesis/ Reconciliation and Creation

Works of devotional literature convey religious ideas to the recipients. Alongside their religious message, both *Padmāvat* and

Rāmcaritmānas incorporate religious outsiders, including Shiva and Parvati. Folk songs usually take topics from everyday life and folk beliefs. They may share the imagery or narrative plots of devotional literature by offering or by receiving material from it or drawing on collective heritage. We may assume that all these works, *Padmāvat, Rāmcaritmānas* and the Avadhi and Bhojpuri folk songs, drew on the shared lore of their geographical area.

Ravindra Bhramar's meticulous study of folk elements in Hindi devotional literature notes that *Padmāvat* picked up many folk beliefs or fictional motifs known to the people of the day, including the role of Shiva and Parvati in assisting people or in offering opportunities to the young couples to meet in Shiva's temple.[10] This synthesis of Islamic and folk elements, including popular Hinduism, contributed to the success of this romance and Sufi mysticism in general.

The importance of Tulsidas's worship of Shiva has already been underlined by Mataprasad Gupta.[11] In *Rāmcaritmānas*, for example, Rama declares that 'without adoring Sankara, no man can attain devotion to me' (*saṅkarabhajana binā nara bhagati na pāvai mori*, 7.45).

In this way, Tulsidas created a synthesis of popular Shaivism and his Rama devotion. Philip Lutgendorf explains it as follows: 'Reconciliation and synthesis are indeed underlining theme of Tulsidas's epic: the reconciliation of Vaishnavism with Shaivism through a henotheistic vision that advocates worshiping Shiva as Father of the Universe while making him the archetypal devotee of Rama.'[12] Camil Bulcke, in his comprehensive study on many Rama stories writes, that in describing Rama's marriage ceremony, many poets incorporated folk traditions: in certain Oriya Rama stories, King Dasharatha attended Rama's marriage ceremony with his queens; in *Rāmcaritmānas*, along with King Dasharatha (1.325), deities attend the ceremony assuming priestly roles (1.319 chand).[13]

Bulcke also studied the scene in which Rama and Sita get to know each other before marriage. According to him, the idea of mutual pre-marital acquaintance of Rama and Sita has long been present in Rama stories. It is found in *Mahāvīra Carita*, a Sanskrit drama of the eighth century, in *Ānanda-rāmāyaṇa* of the fifteenth century and elsewhere.[14] It is clear that this plot was not created by Tulsidas; he preferred this plot over the versions of Vālmīki and of *Adhyātma Rāmāyaṇa*.

Above-cited Hindi devotional literary works and Hindi folk songs were composed at a time when Vaishnavism was on the way forward to an unprecedented establishment. They very often incorporated traditions or folk beliefs of the preceding or current period to earn wider audiences. As for the folk songs studied in this paper, they must have substantialy changed during transmission but their transmission history still remains to be studied.

It should also be emphasized that the sixteenth century in north India was the crossroads of the classical language and various modern literary languages. All the sources of this paper are told, sung and written in the vernaculars accessible to most common people. Thus, the roles performed by Shiva, Parvati and other deities reflect the views of the people communicating in their own tongues.

NOTES

1. M. Gupta, ed., *Padmāvat*, Allahabad: Bhārtī Bhaṇḍār, 1963.
2. H.P. Poddar, ed., *Rāmcaritmānas*, Gorakhpur: Gita Press, 1961.
3. J. Sharma, ed., *Maharṣi vālmīkipraṇīta śrīmadvālmīkīya rāmāyaṇa: hindī bhāṣāntarasahita*, 12th edn., Gorakhpur: Gītā Press, 1982.
4. *Adhyātma rāmāyaṇa: hindī anuvādasahita*, tr., Munilal, Gorakhpur: Gītā Press, 1967.
5. Tulsī seems to have adopted this scene from Jayadeva's drama *Prasannarāghava*. See C. Vaudeville, *Étude sur les sources et la composition du Rāmāyaṇa de Tulsīdās*, trs. J.K. Balbir, Pondichéry: Institut Français d'Indologie, 1959, p. 116.
6. 'Sita prays to Shiva to grant her a suitable bridegroom, Rama'. See K. Upadhyay, *Avadhī lokgīt*, Allahabad: Sāhitya Bhavan, 1978, p. 42.
7. 'Brahma, Vishnu, Mahesh, all three of you bless the couple, they should live for hundred thousand years'; see C. Singh, *Marriage Songs from the Bhojpuri Region*, Jaipur: Champalal Ranka and Company, 1979, p. 23; 'Brahma, Vishnu, Mahesh, you three please bless the couple to live happily for centuries'; see H. Tivari and R. Sharma, *Bhojpurī saṁskār-gīt*, Patna: Bihār Rāṣṭrabhāṣā Pariṣad, 1977, p. 193.
8. 'Oh, dear cute bride, I will join your wedding ceremony and give you golden flowers'; see Tivari and Sharma, *Bhojpurī saṁskār-gīt*, p. 217.

9. 'Mahādev offered ten coconuts, Gaurā Deī (Parvati) gave the box full of garlands to the bride'; I. Pande, *Avadhī lokgīt aur paramparā*, 2nd edn, Allahabad: Rāmnārāyaṇ Lāl, 1958, p. 210.
10. R. Bhramar, *Hindī bhakti sāhitya mẽ lok-tattva*, Delhi: Bhārtī Sāhitya Mandir, 1965, pp. 65-6.
11. M. Gupta, *Tulsīdās*, Allahabad: Hindī Bhavan, 1953, pp. 440-1.
12. P. Lutgendorf, *The Life of a Text: Performing the Rāmcaritmānas of Tulsīdās*, Berkeley: University of California Press, 1991, p. 10.
13. C. Bulcke, *Rāmkathā*, Allahabad: Hindī Pariṣad Prakāśan, 1971, pp. 351-2.
14. Ibid., pp. 353-5.

BIBLIOGRAPHY

Bhramar, Ravindra, *Hindī bhakti sāhitya mēm lok-tattva*, Delhi: Bhārtī Sāhitya Mandir, 1965.

Bulcke, Camil, *Rāmkathā*, 3rd edn., Allahabad: Hindī Pariṣad Prakāśan, 1971.

Gupta, Mataprasad, ed., *Padmāvat,* Allahabad: Bhārtī Bhaṇḍār, 1963.

Lutgendorf, Philip, *The Life of a Text Performing the Rāmcaritmānas of Tulsidas,* Berkeley: University of California Press, 1991.

Munilal, tr., *Adhyātma rāmāyaṇa—hindī-anuvādasahita,* Gorakhpur: Gītā Press, n.d.

Pande, Indprakash, *Avadhī lokgīt aur paramprā*, 2nd edn., Allahabad: Rāmnārāyaṇ Lāl, 1958.

Poddar, Hanumanprasad, ed., comm., *Rām-carit-mānas* 12th edn., Gorakhpur: Gītā Press, 1961.

Sharma, Jankinath, ed. and tr., *Maharṣ vālmīkipranītaśrīmadvālmīkīya rāmā-yaṇa—hindī bhāṣantarasahita*, 12th edn., Gorakhpur: Gītā Press, 1982.

Singh, Chandramani, *Marriage Songs from Bhojpuri Region,* Jaipur: Champalal Ranka and Company, 1979.

Tivari, Hanskumar and Radhavallav Sharma, *Bhojpurī saṁskār-gīt*, Patna: Bihār Rāṣṭrabhāṣā Pariṣad, 1977.

Upadhyay, Krishndev, *Avadhī lokgīt*, Allahabad: Sāhitya Bhavan, 1978.

Vaudeville, C., *Étude sur les sources et la composition du Rāmāyaṇa de Tulsīdās,* tr. J.K. Balbir, Pondicherry: Institut Français d'Indologie, 1959.

CHAPTER 7

Devotion Rewarded: The Attitude towards Wealth in the Religious Literature of Medieval Gujarat

FRANÇOISE MALLISON

Kaccā siddha, māyā priya, 'The false saint is eager to gain', states Kabīr in a 'saying' which has become proverbial. Yet the hagiographic tales we shall look into state the opposite: if the holy man is chosen by his god, he will not lack wealth. This is a widespread belief among the Krishnaite Vaishnavas of Gujarat who often belong to well-to-do merchant and peasant castes, and are a dominant model for the local society.

God Provider

Vaishnavism became increasingly important in Gujarat from the fifteenth century onwards[1] as the Puṣṭimārga, 'Path of Grace', preaching of Vallabha reached the region and as the cult of Ranchod-Krishna (Raṇachoḍa-Kr̥ṣṇa) spread from its Dwarka sanctuary.[2] However, although emblematic for the Gujaratis, the Vaishnava saint, Narasiṁha (Narsī) Mahetā (1414-80?) is not a Vallabhan (and not even held in esteem by the Puṣṭimārgīs), nor does he belong to any sect; and he never alludes to the Lord of Dwarka (except in hagiographic tales). Even more than to his *pads*, 'devotional hymns', his popularity is due to hagiographic tales apparently attributing him preoccupations unconnected with the spiritual quest as met with in his most authentic poems. He is credited with miracle tales said to be 'autobiographic stories in verse', *ātma-caritra-kathānāṁ kāvyo,*[3] in which God Krishna offers material aid especially when called for on the occasion of splendid family rituals such as are compulsory in the upper caste Nāgara brahman community to which he belongs. K.M. Munshi, in his history of Gujarati literature,[4] rightly affirms that Narasiṁha Mahetā 'became the centre of a new mythology of *bhakti*'. Numerous miracle tales, initially orally transmitted, finally took the written form of either *pad*, 'short verse pieces', or *caritra-ākhyāna*, 'biographic tales in verse' whose heroes always belong to mythology, except for the case of the historical Narasiṁha Mahetā. One might think that Narasiṁha could have reached the level of his Puranic archetype, Sudāmā, the poor brahman friend of Krishna's youth, whose fidelity was rewarded by the god with wealth, treasury and palace. Among the miracles belonging to Narasiṁha's golden legend, I shall consider three of them, i.e. his son's wedding, the ceremony for his daughter's first pregnancy and the bill of exchange.[5]

Putrano vivāha 'The Son's Wedding'

According to the autobiographical version,[6] the *purohita*, 'priest', of Madana Mahetā, a wealthy Nāgara brahman of Vadnagar (Vaḍanagara) in north Gujarat, surprisingly chooses poor Narsī's son as a bridegroom for Madana's daughter. Madana objects and, believing that Narasiṁha would not be able to rapidly face the expense entailed by the ceremony, has the marriage fixed on an early date. So Narasiṁha's wife starts worrying and the saint decides to see Krishna at Dwarka. The following episode copies the Puranic tale of how the pious brahman, Sudāmā, paid a visit to his friend Krishna as told in the Gujarati *ākhyāna*: similar images are used to describe the same motives, as, for instance, Krishna's emotional welcome in hurrying to wash his friend's feet. Loaded with gifts, Narsī returns home with the promise that Krishna will participate in the wedding procession. Narsī is now able to assume the preparations and to feed all his caste fellows in Junagadh abundantly with sweets. The moment of the procession's departure arrives but Krishna is missing. As a matter of fact, he is asleep and only the fervent prayers of his devotee succeed in wakening him, a motive met with in every tale and which enables the narrator to put into Narsī's mouth the litany of the *mahābhaktas*, i.e. to enumerate all the mythological saints saved by Krishna not only Sudāmā but also Gajendra, Prahlāda, Ambarīṣa, Dhruva, Draupadī and the Pāṇḍavas, and even Hariścandra, to whom are added the names of the great bhaktas belonging to our present Kaliyuga era: Nāmdev whose roof was repaired through Krishna's intervention, Jayadeva whose wife he resuscitated, Mīrā who was able to drink poison without harm, and Kabīr, Senā and Raidās. To this list is sometimes added a summoning-up of Vishnu (Viṣṇu)'s avatāras. Krishna, awakened thanks to Narsī's prayer, takes part in the procession of the bridegroom (which, deploying unheard-of splendour, takes twelve days) in the company of elephants, armed men, girls and married women—to reach Vadnagar. Krishna either plays the part of an influential friend who is beneficial for social decorum or appears in the first rank of the divinities who admire the festivity from a balcony in the sky. It so happens that even Narsī, as his name suggests, takes the traits of an avatāra of Krishna: Narasiṁha, the man-lion. Madana Mahetā is obliged to acknowledge his error, admits defeat and, unable to rival the splendour of his son-in-law's family, trembles to think he might not accede to the other party's demands, as any girl's father would do. He finally gives in and Krishna leaves Narsī. Whosoever might be the *ākhyāna*'s author, one feels his evident pleasure in describing and illustrating the extreme munificence and lavishness of this fantastic wedding despite of the fact that the real aim of this hagiographical story was to depict the miraculous conversion of Madana Mahetā, the wedding splendours being merely the way to achieve it.

Māmeruṁ, 'The Daughter's First Pregnancy'

According to the *ākhyāna* by Premānanda, a celebrated author of the second half of the seventeenth century whose masterpiece it is,[7] Narsī's daughter, Kuṁvara Bāī, sends a message to her father as she reaches the seventh month of her first pregnancy. Her family is now expected to pay a visit, loaded with gifts, to the household of her husband. Her mother has already died. Narsī, lacking everything needed for the occasion, sets out on a miserable cart drawn by skinny bullocks in the company of a few other bhaktas who are carrying their instruments to accompany their hymns such as the *karatāla*s.[8] Narsī is met with as befits his appearance, and housed off the road in a flea and mosquito-infested place. The mother-in-law dictates to Kuṁvara the list of expected goods and gifts, i.e. 700 coconuts, 300 loin pieces, 240 saris—a breathtaking enumeration! Narsī is given boiling water for his bath. The bhakta poet plays *malhāra*, a monsoon raga, and rain starts falling despite the season. The in-laws of Kuṁvara Bāī remain unimpressed by the miracle and present the basket in which the gifts, clothes and jewels must pile up. Once more, Krishna is asleep, this time not in Dwarka but at Vrindaban, as, in Premānanda's times, Krishnaism was under the sway of Vallabhism, which from Braj had come to Gujarat. The bhakta then prays, reciting the list of the *mahābhakta*s whose devotion had been rewarded, who had been saved by avatāras and who had been gratified by Krishna. Narsī adds in his prayer that Krishna will be blamed for the fault of his bhakta, and that he must also recall Kabīr, Nāmdev, Mīrā Bāī and Senā. Narsī's prayers and reproaches having been listened to, Krishna, unrecognizable in the guise of a wealthy merchant by the name of Dāmodara, and accompanied by his wife, Kamaḷā, arrives on the scene followed by his servants who are carrying the gifts. Kamaḷā must explain to Kuṁvara Bāī's mother-in-law that she and Dāmodara are not Narsī's parents but Baniyās called by Narsī to repay what was due to him as they had borrowed from him in order to start their business. Thus, Krishna becomes a vaishya among brahmans and the debtor of a Nāgara in order to save the face of his devotee. Premānanda is especially good at depicting the protests and complaints resulting from the self-love of the different family members during the gift distribution. Finally, everybody receives more than his due and everyone bows to Narasiṁha Mahetā with satisfaction. According to Premānanda, the lesson stops there but the description of a Nāgara family and the society in which it lives in the years around 1680 is remarkable.

Hūṁḍī, 'The Bill of Exchange'

This is by far the most popular of Narsī's miracles. There are many versions, one of them in the form of a song known by every Gujarati, regardless of religion.[9] Here, the context changes from the Nāgara family rituals. Pilgrims on their way to Dwarka reach Junagadh looking for a banker to issue them a bill of exchange[10] for Rs. 700 to be encashed at Dwarka. To make fun of him, the Nāgaras send them to Narasiṁha Mahetā. In spite of the strange aspect of his poor lodging and the essentially religious activities going on there, the pilgrims remain confident as they recognize a brother bhakta in Narsī. Narsī, not wanting to disappoint them, issues a bill on the name of Krishna, or rather of Śāmaḷa Śeṭha at Dwarka. The pilgrims leave and Narsī, who spends Rs. 700 to feed bhaktas, implores god to honour his bill and not to shame his devotee, the prayer accompanied by the habitual list of saints. After reaching Dwarka the pilgrims look for Śāmaḷa Śeṭha's bank in vain. They start distrusting Narsī. Then, at nightfall, they encounter a wealthy Śeṭha, well-clothed and covered with jewels, followed by his servants. He introduces himself as Śāmaḷa. The transaction unfolds in minute detail, the validity of the money is checked and the percentage of the commission fee is agreed upon. After this, Krishna has a receipt written for Narsī and the pilgrims slowly become aware that they have seen Krishna in person. Their gratitude is boundless not because of the advantageous money transfer but for the vision that the bhakta had made possible for them. Thus, down-to-earth pecuniary worries led to a miraculous vision. Narsī joyfully breaks into tears on reading his receipt.

This miracle evokes Vallabhism even more than the two preceding ones. A pretext, sometimes futile, may be the occasion of Krishna's divine grace. The *Vārtā*, 'biographies of Vallabhan saints in Braja language', do not lack similar situations where Kr̥ṣṇa-Śrīnāthajī is said to miraculously provide money or wealth, particularly the *Vārtā* telling the lives of Gujarati saints such as Kṛṣṇadāsa Adhikārī[11] or the Sāṭhodara Nāgara called Nāgajī Bhaṭṭa.[12] The leads taken by the hagiographical tales, and their concessions to a world-view where economic and social success are visible signs of divine favour, are more extraordinary as Narasiṁha Mahetā remains, in the eyes of the Vallabhans, a very imperfect bhakta, a *maryādā bhakta* (a follower of rituals) and not a *puṣṭi-bhakta* (blessed with the grace of god).

Some tension can be observed between what, on the one hand, could be a spiritual biography of Narasiṁha Mahetā and the tales of his hagiography, on the other. Narsī, belonging to the most prestigious group in Gujarat, the Vadnagar Nāgara brahmans, leads an apparently secular life with his wife and children, not unlike the bhaktas and Sants of his time, yet wanting to be at the service of god alone whom he sings of day and night. His only profession, he says, is 'the service of the Sants'. Unable to provide for his daily life, he refuses to face his duties as a Nāgara *gṛhastha* 'householder' or to align his conduct on that of his caste brethren. He is unconcerned with earthly goods and despises all ritual formalism. 'Only the Vaishnavas are dear to my heart', he says, and dares to go to the quarter of the untouchables in order to lead an assembly for the singing of religious songs (*bhajan*).[13] Utterances about himself are rare found here and there in his *pad*s, more precisely among those grouped under the title *bhakti-jñāna*, such as *Evā re amo evā* 'I am like that, as you say I am . . . the only bad one, worse than the worst! Treat me as you like, but my love is still stronger.'[14] Why then does his public cherish his image of a beggar chasing after goods and riches? First of all, maybe because every society 'produces the saints it needs'.[15] A saint is recognized as such from the outside, by a group of people projecting its dreams and fantasms into hagiographical tales shaped by an author-narrator. The community substitutes itself to the author, suggests to him its desires and finally appears as the actual collective author of the hagiographical tale, its redactor assuring its conformity with the demands of the community.[16] The hagiographies, thus, inform us not on the actual personality of the saint but rather on the society around him, i.e. the dominant

Gujarati merchant society whose dharmic success is measured by its accumulation of wealth. The Vallabhan doctrine of dedicating all riches to God Krishna without, however, ceasing to enjoy it for one's own advantage certainly meets with success in this region.[17] Yet, at the same time, a non-sectarian saint like Narsī is equally identified with the regional mercantile society.

Perhaps an explanation is offered by the concept of Krishna's divinity within this framework of self-interested devotion. André Couture, in his article 'Le Kṛṣṇa du *Harivaṁśa*: Un Dieu qui distribue ses richesses'[18] stresses the immoderate love for descriptions of welfare, wealth, treasures and affluence in texts from ancient India, showing that Krishna 'est représenté comme une grande divinité qui ne cesse de vaincre ses ennemis et de leur arracher les biens qu'ils ont égoïstement accumulés pour les redistribuer', '*is put forward as an important divinity ceaselessly defeating his enemies, depriving them of their egoistically acquired wealth and giving it back to his devotees*'. Krishna is a generous and wealthy god, enriching his faithful according to the author's perception. One understands why Krishna was successful in Gujarat. The very title of Ranchod that the Vaishnava god takes on in the sanctuary of all-India importance at Dwarka, and whose cult spread all over Gujarat and Rajasthan, is explained by this fact. If indeed, as I propose, the etymology of *raṇa* leads to *ṛṇa* 'debt', Ranchod (Raṇachoḍa) would mean 'the one who takes away the debt' and, thus, would rather favourably incline to his worship the merchant castes of Gujarat.[19]

The *Sudāmā-caritra*

Under these circumstances, it is not surprising that the episode of the poor brahman Sudāmā, loaded with benefits by his childhood friend, Krishna, should be popular in Gujarat. The version contained in the tenth book of the *Bhāgavata Purāṇa* (chapters 80-1) is by no means the only source for the medieval tale handing down elements of oral and folkloric versions.[20] Besides, a local cult to Sudāmā had got implanted at Porbandar (called Sudāmāpurī) in Saurashtra in replacement of the town of Avantī where Sāṁdīpani's *āśrama* was located, according to Puranic tradition.[21]

Among its numerous versions, I would like to offer a few remarks on the atypical version by Soma. The *Sudāmāsāra*, known from a single manuscript, was published in 1922 by M.R. Majmudar[22] as an appendix to his edition of the *Sudāmā-caritra* by Premānanda. According to the editor, the language points to the fifteenth century. There is no other work by Soma except for a few *pad*s in an undated manuscript belonging to the collection of the Forbes Gujarātī Sabhā in Mumbai.[23] The arrangement of the text into seventy-one verses is surprising. If the end of the tale from the departure of Sudāmā for Dwarka onwards is quite conventional, the first half projects the strong personality of Sudāmā's wife (a trait taken up in later versions) and the dialogue unfolds in a lyrical mode, unusual in this literary genre.

The poem starts with the list of grievances put forward by Sudāmā's wife on their doorstep: 'Your friend Mukunda is grand and generous (v. 2), why remain thirsty on the banks of river Ganges? (v. 5) Ask him for money'. Verses 8 to 13 all start with the words *vita vamṇa* 'without money' and expose the inconvenience of poverty according to her: 'without money, no inter-family relations are possible, nor any social life, no possibility of performing sacrifices to divinities, no means for fulfilling religious duties, no poet-singer in the courtyard of a poor man, even your relatives tend to ignore you'. Verses 14 to 18 harp on Sudāmā's lack of imagination as he knows nothing but the name of 'Nārāyaṇa' despite the fact that there are so many ways of making money: 'Some people (*ko*, repeated at the beginning of each line) do business, some know how to put medicinal herbs to use, some are good at spells and enchantments, some make skilful use of their astrological know-how, some are able to exploit their knowledge of magic or religious rites, some are soldiers, some dig wells, some write poems or are good at music, some are small farmers, some grow wheat, some are weavers or seafarers, some preach in public, some save other people's lives, some are cunning and resort to illegal means to earn their lives'.

Sudāmā's wife does not seem to be worried about harmonizing her husband's caste with his profession! To all this, Sudāmā answers that he will not importune Krishna. His wife insists: 'You must request the Beloved (*Yācavā velā*), eleven times and, after another rebuke by Sudāmā (vv. 26-7) she lists, very knowingly and competently, instances of Nārāyaṇa's goodness in the past (vv. 21-40). Her thorough knowledge of Bhakti mythology finally convinces Sudāmā.

This texts surprises with a wealth of striking details in an unusual social environment. The portrait of the wife of Sudāmā, for instance, her arguments, are more those of a merchant's wife than of a brahman. Could the text be of Jaina origin? The colophon '*iti Śrī Sadāmāsāra sa pūrṇa* [*sic*] *samāpta/celā rāja-pāla paṭhanārtha*', 'thus the story of Sudāmā is completed for the instruction of the disciple Rājpāla' indeed reminds one of the manner of Jaina didactic works in Gujarati.

God Provided

Vaishnava hagiography, prevailing in Gujarat among sectarians as well as non-sectarians, shows how god, especially Krishna, is attentive to the well-being of his devotees. But what about a completely different religious domain, although essentially Gujarati and Indianized, namely the Nizārī-Ismā'īlī Shi'a community of the Khojās?

One of their essential religious obligations consists in offering to their Imām one 'tenth' part of their income, the tithe called *Dasonda*. If they are unable to offer it, their despair is great as they then cannot receive the spiritual benefits attached to the tithe and remain orphans of the Imām who is a divine incarnation to them. The offer of the tithe is the very first gesture of the newly-converted who must understand that this is his sacred duty. In case he is a renouncing mendicant, he must again go back to work. A serious reminder to pay one's tithe appears here and there in the devotional hymns, the *ginān*s. Thus, Pīr Shams, in his *gārabī* no. 19,[24] says, 'It was at that time laid down that the payment of the tithe was to be the means of salvation. Tithes should be paid from income honestly calculated . . .'; in *gārabī* no. 27 'All devotees were purified by paying the tithes.'[25]

Pīr Shams is one of those who started Ismā'īlī preaching in the north-west of the Indian subcontinent, the second after the almost mythological Pīr Nur Satgur. Pīr Shams is said to have lived during the twelfth-thirteenth centuries;[26] his hagiography abounds in details. One of his miracle stories tells of how he converted animals. In a *ginān*,[27] he, at first, preaches to pigeons: 'The Guide showed the way. Humbly they tied bags on their shoulders, and the Guide told them the secret: 'If you give the offering of the tithe, your sins will be destroyed. Nine parts are for you to consume, and the tenth is our portion. Keep this carefully for it is our due!' (vv. 3-5) Then he converted a tiger. How could it offer the tenth part of its revenues? 'The tiger contracted to pay the tithe, and it gave up the business of one forest grove. It would not enter the forest, and did no mischief there' (v. 13). The attitude of the tiger who does not give but renounces probably puts light on the nature of the gift of the tithe. It is a means of ascetic renunciation in order to obtain spiritual benefits.

Mainly from the time of the third Aga Khan, Sultan Mohammad Shah (r. 1883-1957), onwards, the Khojā community became busy in merchant and trading occupations and accumulating wealth as proof of meritorious divine reward,[28] an attitude which was in accordance with the regional merchant ideal. But the special relation with the divine that was obtained thanks to the payment of the tithe, which the faithful must *give* in order to obtain spiritual benefit, is radically opposed to that of the bhakta who must *receive* from god to prove that he belongs to the chosen. However, in both cases, the texts, mainly hagiographical speak obsessively of money—a feature which stresses, once more, the homogeneity of Gujarati culture, whatever the religious affiliation.

NOTES

1. F. Mallison, 'Early Kṛṣṇa Bhakti in Gujarat: The Evidence of Old Gujarati Texts Recently Brought to Light', in *Studies in South Asian Devotional*

Literature, Research Papers 1988-1991, ed. A.W. Entwistle and F. Mallison, New Delhi and Paris: Manohar and École Française d'Extrême-Orient, 1994, pp. 51-64.

2. F. Mallison, 'Development of Early Krishnaism in Gujarāt: Viṣṇu-Raṇchoḍ-Kṛṣṇa', in *Bhakti in Current Research, 1979-1982*, ed. M. Thiel-Horstmann, Berlin: Dietrich Reimer, 1983, pp. 245-55.
3. K.K. Shastri, ed., *Narasiṁha Mahetā-kṛta ātmacaritanāṁ kāvyo: Jhārī, Vivāha, Māmeruṁ, Hūṁḍi, Hāra*, Junagadh: Śrī Narasiṁha Mahetā Corā Samiti, 1969.
4. K.M. Munshi, *Gujarāt and its Literature from Early Times to 1852*, Bombay: Bharatiya Vidya Bhavan, 1954, p. 185.
5. For a survey of the hagiographic literature of Narasiṁha Mahetā, see F. Mallison, 'Notes on the Biography of Narasiṁha Mahetā', *Annals of the Bhandarkar Oriental Institute*, vol. 55, 1974, pp. 189-201; F. Mallison, *Au point du jour: Les Prahhātiyāṁ de Narasiṁha Mahetā, poète et Saint vishnouite du Gujarat, Paris: École française d' Extrême-Orient, 1986*, pp. 17-32; F. Mallison, 'Le discours hagiographique dans les hagiographies du saint-poète gujarati Narasiṁha Mahetā (XVème siècle, Inde occidentale)', *Bulletin de l'École Française d'Extrême-Orient*, vol. 85, 1998, pp. 265-83.
6. Shastri, ed., *Narasiṁha Mahetā-kṛta ātmacaritanāṁ kāvyo*, pp. 6-50.
7. K.K. Shastri and S. Jesalpura, eds., *Premānandanī kāvyakṛtio*, vol. 1, Ahmedabad: Sāhitya-saṁśodhana Prakāśana, 1978, pp. 277-325. The date given to the text is 1682.
8. *Karatāla*s are either small cymbals or the small wooden instruments tied to the thumbs of the singer to allow him to beat a rhythm. The popular iconography of Narsī always shows him singing with his *karatāla*s.
9. The song is published in H.V. Divetia, ed., *Narasiṁha Mahetānāṁ bhajano*, Ahmedabad: Sastuṁ Sāhitya Vardhaka Kāryālaya, 1950, pp. 89-90. The so-called autobiographical version is in Shastri, ed., *Narasiṁha Mahetā-kṛta ātmacaritanāṁ kāvyo*, pp. 73-82. The *Huṁḍī* of Premānanda, dated 1674, is published in Shastri and Jesalpura, eds., *Premānandanī kāvyakṛtio*, pp. 254-69.
10. The practice of the bill of exchange came into general use in Europe during the fourteenth century. It is not known when it started in India but it was in extensive use in the seventeenth century. See A.M. Bagchi, *Money Credit in Indian History*, Delhi: Tulika Books, 2002, p. 47.
11. In the last *vārtā* in D. Parikh, ed., *Caurāsī vaiṣṇavana kī vārtā: tīna janma kī līlā bhāvanā vālī*, Mathura: Śrī Govardhana Granthamālā Kāryālaya, 1970, pp. 526-71.
12. In the fifth *vārtā* in N. Sharma, ed., *Dosau bāvana vaiṣṇavana kī vārtā*, Mathura: Śrī Govarddhana Granthamālā Kāryālaya, 1965, pp. 31-6.
13. *Pada 'Giri taḷāṭīne'*, in I.S. Desai, ed., *Ādi-bhakta-kavi Narasiṁha Mahetākṛta kāvyasaṁgraha*, Bombay: Gujarati Printing Press, 1915, *Bhakti-jñānanāṁ pado* no. 4, p. 470.

14. *Pada 'Evāre amo'*, in Desai, ed., *Narasiṁha Mahetākṛta kāvyasaṁgraha, Bhakti-jñānanāṁ pado* no. 5, p. 471.
15. J.-Y. Tillette, 'Introduction', in *Les fonctions des saints dans le monde occidental (IIIe-VIIIe siècles): Actes du colloques*, Rome: École Française de Rome, 1991, p. 5.
16. F. Mallison, 'Introduction', in *Constructions hagiographiques dans le monde indien: Entre mythe et histoire*, ed. Françoise Mallison, Paris: Honoré Champion, 2001, p. xv.
17. On 'Businessman and Devotee' in the Puṣṭimārga, see P. Bennett, *The Path of Grace: Social Organization and Temple Worship in a Vaishnava Sect*, Delhi: Hindustan Publishing Corporation, 1993, pp. 180-2.
18. A. Couture, 'Le Kṛṣṇa du Harivaṁśa: Un dieu qui distribue des richesses', in *Divines richesses: Religion et économie en monde marchand indien*, ed. P. Lachaier and C. Clémentin-Ojha, Paris: École Française d'Extrême-Orient, 2008, pp. 31-48. We may add Vaudeville's observation to the remarks of Couture, 'The worship of the Cowherd-god and that of the Great Goddess [a provider deity] have coalesced', in C. Vaudeville, 'Krishna Gopāla, Rādhā and the Great Goddess', in *Myths, Saints and Legends in Medieval India*, ed. Vasudha Dalmia, Delhi: Oxford University Press, 1996, p. 157.
19. Mallison, 'Development of Early Krishnaism in Gujarāt', pp. 247-8; on the ancient brahmanic conception of the debt and the different meanings of *ṛṇa*, see Ch. Malamoud, 'La théologie de la dette dans le brahmanisme', in C. Malamoud, 'La théologie de la dette dans le brahmanisme', in *Puruṣārtha, sciences sociales en asie du sud*, vol. 4, Paris: École des Hautes Études en Sciences Sociales, 1980, pp. 39-62. I thank Prof. Monika Boehm-Tettelbach for pointing out to me how often 'Bhakti is likened to the merchant activities' in the Sant literature of northern India and how the 'public sphere of Bhakti in the period of early modernity was dominated by merchants' (electronic mail, 7 July 2010). On the particularism of Gujarat, I am thankful to Dr. Imre Bangha who sent me the text and translation of the *pad Mudaḷa thoḍo re bhāīḍā* . . . by the seventeenth-century Jain poet, Ānandghan. These verses are surprisingly written in Gujarati instead of the usual Braj-Rajasthani idiom used by the author for rendering a metaphoric description of the 'business' of God (electronic mail, 11 January 2011).
20. On the comparison between the *Bhāgavata Purāṇa* version and the Gujarati versions, see F. Mallison, 'Saint Sudāmā of Gujarat: Should the Holy be Wealthy', *Journal of the Oriental Institute*, vol. 29, nos. 1-2, 1979, p. 93 fol.
21. F. Mallison, 'The Cult of Sudāmā in Porbandar-Sudāmāpurī', *Journal of the Oriental Institute*, vol. 29, nos. 3-4, 1980, pp. 216-83.
22. M.R. Majmudar, ed., *Mahā kavi premānanda tathā bījā āṭha kavionāṁ sudāmācaritra*, Baroda, 1922, pp. 105-9.
23. It is also possible that the short *Rambhā-śuka saṁvāda* of a Soma (ed. J. Sandesara in *Sambodhi,* vol. 8, nos. 1-2, 1980, pp. 43-4) belongs to the

same author as it is taken from the Gujarati manuscript no. 127 of the M.S. University of Baroda, which contains the 'unpublished *Jainetara*' compositions.

24. V.D. Hooda, 'Some Specimens of Satpanth Literature', in *Collectanea*, vol. 1, Leiden: E.J. Brill and Ismaili Society, 1948, p. 77.
25. Ibid., p. 84.
26. Z. Moir, 'The Life and Legends of Pir Shams as Reflected in the Ismaili Ginans: A Critical Review', in *Constructions hagiographiques dans le monde indien: Entre mythe et histoire*, ed. Françoise Mallison, Paris: Honoré Champion, 2001, pp. 380-2.
27. *Ginan* 37 in C. Shackle and Z. Moir, *Ismaili Hymns from South Asia: An Introduction to the Ginans*, London: School of Oriental and African Studies, 1992, pp. 132-3.
28. M. Boivin, 'Enrichissement et quête du salut chez les Khojas ismaéliens d'Asie du Sud', in *Divines richesses: Religion et économie en monde marchand indien*, ed. P. Lachaier and C. Clémentin-Ojha, Paris: École Française d'Extrême-Orient, 2008, pp. 169-88.

BIBLIOGRAPHY

Bagchi, A.M., *Money Credit in Indian History*, Delhi: Tulika Books, 2002.

Bennett, P., *The Path of Grace: Social Organization and Temple Worship in a Vaishnava Sect*, Delhi: Hindustan Publishing Corporation, 1993.

Boivin, M., 'Enrichissement et quête du salut chez les Khojas ismaéliens d'Asie du Sud', in *Divines richesses: Religion et économie en monde marchand indien*, ed. P. Lachaier and C. Clémentin-Ojha, *Études thématiques*, 21, Paris: École française d'Extrême-Orient, 2008, pp. 175-84.

Couture, A., 'Le Kṛṣṇa du Harivaṁśa: Un dieu qui distribue des richesses', in *Divines richesses: Religion et économie en monde marchand indien*, ed. P. Lachaier and C. Clémentin-Ojha, *Études thématiques*, 21, Paris: École française d'Extrême-Orient, 2008, pp. 31-48.

Desai, I.S., ed., *Ādi-bhakta-kavi Narasiṁha Mahetākṛta kāvyasaṁgraha*, Bombay: Gujarati Printing Press, 1915.

Divetia, H.V., ed., *Narasiṁha Mahetānāṁ bhajano*, Ahmedabad: Sastuṁ Sāhitya Vardhaka Kāryālaya, 1950.

Hooda, V.D., 'Some Specimens of Satpanth Literature', in *Collectanea*, Leiden: E.J. Brill and Ismaili Society, 1948, pp. 55-137.

Majmudar, M.R., ed., *Mahā kavi premānanda tathā bījā āṭha kavionāṁ sudāmācaritra*, Baroda, 1922.

Malamoud, C., 'La théologie de la dette dans le brahmanisme', in *Puruṣārtha, sciences sociales en asie du sud*, Paris: École des Hautes Études en Sciences Sociales, 1980, pp. 39-62.

Mallison, F., *Au point du jour: Les Prahhātiyāṁ de Narasiṁha Mahetā, poète et Saint vishnouite du Gujarat*, Paris: École Française d' Extrême-Orient, 1986.

——, 'The Cult of Sudāmā in Porbandar-Sudāmāpurī', *Journal of the Oriental Institute,* vol. 29, nos. 3-4, 1980, pp. 216-23.

——, 'Development of Early Krishnaism in Gujarāt: Viṣṇu-Raṇchoḍ-Kṛṣṇa', in *Bhakti in Current Research, 1979-1982*, ed. M. Thiel-Horstmann, Berlin: Dietrich Reimer, 1983, pp. 245-55.

——, 'Early Kṛṣṇa Bhakti in Gujarat: The Evidence of Old Gujarati Texts Recently Brought to Light', in *Studies in South Asian Devotional Literature, Research Papers 1988-1991*, ed. A.W. Entwistle and F. Mallison, Delhi and Paris: Manohar and École française d'Extrême-Orient, 1994, pp. 51-64.

——, 'Introduction', in *Constructions hagiographiques dans le monde indien: Entre mythe et histoire*, ed. F. Mallison, *Bibliothèque de l'École des Hautes Études, Sciences historiques et philologiques* 338, Paris: Honoré Champion, 2001, pp. VII-XXVIII.

——, 'Le discours hagiographique dans les hagiographies du saint-poète gujarati Narasiṁha Mahetā (XVème siècle, Inde occidentale)', *Bulletin de l'École Française d'Extrême-Orient,* vol. 85, 1998, pp. 265-83.

——, 'Notes on the Biography of Narasiṁha Mahetā', *Annals of the Bhandarkar Oriental Institute,* vol. 55, 1974, pp. 189-201.

——, 'Saint Sudāmā of Gujarat: Should the Holy be Wealthy?', *Journal of the Oriental Institute,* vol. 29, nos. 1-2, 1979, pp. 90-9.

Moir, Z., 'The Life and Legends of Pir Shams as Reflected in the Ismaili Ginans: A Critical Review', in *Constructions hagiographiques dans le monde indien: Entre mythe et histoire*, ed. F. Mallison, *Bibliothèque de l'École des Hautes Études, Sciences historiques et philologiques* 338, Paris: Honoré Champion, 2001, pp. 380-2.

Munshi, K.M., *Gujarāt and its Literature from Early Times to 1852*, Bombay: Bharatiya Vidya Bhavan, 1954.

Parikh, D., ed., *Caurāsī vaiṣṇavana kī vārtā: tīna janma kī līlā bhāvanā vālī*, Mathura: Śrī Govardhana Granthamālā Kāryālaya, 1970.

Sandesara, J., 'Rambhā-śuka saṁvāda of Soma', *Sambodhi,* vol. 8, nos. 1-2, 1980, pp. 43-4.

Shackle, C. and Z. Moir, *Ismaili Hymns from South Asia: An Introduction to the Ginans, SOAS Asian Texts*, 3, London: School of Oriental and African Studies, 1992.

Sharma, N., ed., *Dosau bāvana vaiṣṇavana kī Vārtā*, Mathura: Śrī Govardhana Granthamālā Kāryālaya, 1965.

Shastri, K.K., ed., *Narasiṁha Mahetā-kṛta ātmacaritanāṁ kāvyo: Jhārī, Vivāha, Māmeruṁ, Hūṁḍi, Hāra*, Junagadh: Śrī Narasiṁha Mahetā Corā Samiti, 1969.

Shastri, K.K. and S. Jesalpura, ed., *Premānandanī kāvyakṛtio*, vol. 1, Ahmedabad: Sāhitya-saṁśodhana Prakāśana, 1978.

Tillette, J.-Y., 'Introduction', in *Les fonctions des saints dans le monde occidental (IIIe-VIIIe siècles): Actes du colloque*, Rome: École Française de Rome, 1991, pp. 1-11.

Vaudeville, C., 'Krishna Gopāla, Rādhā and the Great Goddess', in *Myths, Saints and Legends in Medieval India*, ed. V. Dalmia, Delhi: Oxford University Press, 1996, pp. 140-57.

IDEOLOGY

CHAPTER 8

Vaishnava *Sampradayas* on the Importance of Ritual: A Comparison of the Two Contemporaneous Approaches by Viṭṭhalanātha and Jīva Gosvāmī

MONIKA HORSTMANN AND ANAND MISHRA

Topic and Method

Reading the theological treatises of the north Indian Vaishnava *sampradaya*s feels like standing in a hall of mirrors. The sects resonate with doctrines of each other, though they rarely acknowledge their mutual indebtedness. One can take for granted, and can also point to, cross-fertilization. But how is one to grasp that process without becoming caught in the hen-and-egg conundrum or entering into a comparison that states the obvious without disclosing the historical dynamics at work? This paper will not be able to redress the elusiveness of this issue. It will rather restrict itself to documenting a test case which exhibits close similarities and subtle differences, though these, unfortunately, disclose relatively little of the processes of doctrinal exchange regarding the problem examined. This contribution then fails to trace these historical processes. We found, however, that in the early eighteenth century, the quotations shared in our test case by different sects, though initially used to underpin divergent doctrinal opinions, seemed to have provided a basis that was robust enough to build a consensus between two sects, the Gauḍīyas of the northern type (not fully representative of the entire Gauḍīya fold and exposed to various doctrinal counter-currents from Bengal) and the Puṣṭimārgīyas. The consensus was insinuated by the Mahārājā of Jaipur, Savāī Jaisingh.[1] Our present exercise sparked off from the doctrinal debates conducted during his regnal period and orchestrated by him. The most substantial intellectual impact in this came from these two sects and it is, accordingly, only their views that we wish to compare here.

We wish to emphasize that in what follows we are only concerned with the doctrinal positions of the teachers of these two sects and not with the practical interaction of the priests and devotees of the period of our study. Both are, of course, interdependent, but doctrine and practice must not be lumped together straightaway or the former dismissed as a transparent strategy to sustain sectarian power. The fact that strategic thinking was inevitably involved is a truism, but one needs to grasp the points of agreement and disagreement in their own right to understand how they could serve as strategic tools.

The issue at stake is ritual as enjoined upon the devotees of both these orthodox Vaishnava sects. Both sects were brahman dominated. Both enjoined good conduct conforming to the *varṇāśrama-dharma* in which ritual was mandatory. Both sects had to address the perpetual tension between the concept of bhakti as the free flow of love or grace and the idea of ritual discipline as a pre-condition and concomitant of bhakti. That tension is, of course, already present in the *Bhāgavata Purāṇa*, the 'modern' Veda of both sects.

The Gauḍīya author, Rūpa Gosvāmī, while naming, in his *Bhaktirasāmṛtasindhu*,[2] the categories or stages of bhakti based, on the one hand, on ritual and other instruments (*sādhana*) of bhakti (*sādhana-bhakti*) and, on the other, pure bhakti (*rāgānugā-bhakti*) as the culmination of that first category or stage, mentions the identical position of Vallabha, the founder of the Puṣṭimārga.[3] In so doing, he uses the technical terms used by Vallabha which, as would be expected, shows his familiarity with the system of this famous Vaishnava scholar, who was for some time active in the same region as Rūpa, who survived him by twenty-six years. Rūpa completed his *Bhaktirasāmṛtasindhu* in 1541, ten years after the death of Vallabha. However, for all the similarities with Vallabha exhibited by Rūpa's treatise (and his other works), Rūpa's reflections also proliferate in a different direction, namely the aesthetics of devotion. There prevails, thus, an indebtedness of Rūpa to concepts prior to him but also coming from a spectre broader than just Vallabha's theory, and a certain chronological imbalance between the two sects, the first and second generations of Gauḍīya teachers lagging behind the Puṣṭīmārga by some decades.

Puṣṭimārga	Gauḍīya
Vallabha, 1479-1531	Rūpa, between 1470 and 1490-1557, Sanātana, died in *c.* 1555
Viṭṭhalanātha, 1516-86	Jīva, 1546-1608

When trying to define what was common Vaishnava doctrine, the eighteenth-century debate built upon a number of authoritative passages from the *Bhāgavata Purāṇa*, on which the founding fathers of both sects had written exegetical commentaries. Was their ostensibly shared opinion also perceived as similar in the period of these foundational exegetical treatises? What were their commonalities and differences in those earlier days?

The second generation of teachers of the two sects continued to be marked by their different periods, the tradition of Vallabha still being thirty years ahead. Jīva's familiarity with Viṭṭhalanātha's writings can be taken for granted, all the more so because both teachers resided in Braj. This had not been so during the first generation when Vallabha was busy spreading his doctrine and sect outside Braj.[4] In the period of the second generation, the sectarian authorities of both sects were running religious bodies that relied on the patronage of the wealthy and mighty, which enabled them to run temples and conduct opulent worship of their deities. This worship needed doctrinal underpinnings as did the organizational manifestations of the bhakti religion. Moreover, soliciting patronage required doctrinal justification to distinguish oneself from competitors. There was also tension at work *within* the various sects. The *varṇāśrama-dharma*, as it was enjoined upon the upper castes, with its ritual obligations to be fulfilled regularly meant little to the devotees from the lower castes. It, therefore, needed continuous vindication. There were also radical upper caste voices criticising the orthodox, ritual stance of the bhakti doctrine.

Viṭṭhalanātha, in pleading for mandatory ritual, based his arguments on proofs from the *Bhāgavata Purāṇa*, passages also emphasized by Jīva. We wish to examine these passages to find out if the theologians of the second generation of the two sects involved responded overtly to each other.

Both Vallabhācārya and Viṭṭhalanātha were confronted by the challenge to create and establish an independent identity for their doctrinal systems as well as their religious community. Carving out a separate niche requires the presence of distinctive elements and establishing it in the traditional system calls for reconciling the new with the accustomed. The new *Śuddhādvaita-brahmavāda* had to be established as the essence of Vedānta and the upcoming Puṣṭimārga had to take roots as a Vaishnava *sampradaya*. The task of intertwining these two divergent threads was attempted by them (as well as by later scholars of the *sampradaya*), as can be gleaned from their words and deeds. *Bhaktihaṃsa*[5] and *Bhaktihetunirṇaya*[6] are two important examples of Viṭṭhalanātha's response to the above challenge.

These texts become especially interesting as one reads them against the *Bhaktisaṃdarbha*[7] of Viṭṭhalanātha's slightly younger contemporary, Jīva Gosvāmī. Jīva treats the various aspects salient to his system in six discrete treatises which together form his *Ṣaṭsaṃdarbha*. This enables him to present his case for *varṇāśrama-dharma*-conformed ritual obligations quite specifically in the fifth of these six works in an approach which confirms Rūpa's *Bhaktirasāmṛtasindhu* and also follows the sequence of the citations as they occur in the *Bhāgavata Purāṇa*. Thereby he submits a specified treatise in the form of a selective running commentary on the *Bhāgavata Purāṇa*. Viṭṭhalanātha and Jīva both prove their case by numerous quotations from this text.

There are virtual clusters of identical quoted passages from the *Bhāgavata Purāṇa* which both of them use to vindicate their individual arguments. The question which attracts our attention is: how do the two Vaishnava *ācāryas* respond to a similar challenge? (Here, another radical but valid question would be whether they are responding to a similar challenge or whether these works represent a response at all.) Their tantalizing closeness in terms of time and space, not to speak of their religious affinities, compels one to look for substantial mutual exchange of doctrinal ideas and practices. Is it possible to identify such an exchange? Does a comparison open a window on such an exchange? Or do the two scholars ignore each other deliberately?

Viṭṭhalanātha

Both in the *Bhaktihaṃsa* and the *Bhaktihetunirṇaya*, the primary focus of Viṭṭhalanātha is on delineating a theological space for his *sampradaya*. Right in the beginning, he postulates that Bhagavān[8] is untouched by any conventional means to attain him. Kṛṣṇa sports among his 'chosen' devotees (upon whom he bestows his grace or *anugraha*). In the rest of the *Bhaktihaṃsa*, he shows that methods or means like the recitation of mantras, worshipping God through constant prayers and meditation (*upāsanā*), and through Vedic or tantric initiation (*dīkṣā*), and worshipping some form or representation of God (*arcana*) and other means like *japa* or *dāna,* etc. do not come close to Bhagavān. Puruṣottama is totally untouched by and unconnected with all these, or, in fact, any means created by *jīvas*. It is bhakti alone which connects one with him. Bhakti, however, is achieved only through the grace or *anugraha* of Bhagavān. This is the proposition Viṭṭhalanātha proves in the *Bhaktihetunirṇaya* by hypothesizing contrary positions and refuting them one after another. Following the Vedānta tradition, he establishes his thesis by proving—with the help of logical reasoning—that his premises are in conformity with *śruti* and *smṛti*, which, according to Vallabha, consist of the Upaniṣads, the *Brahmasūtras*, the *Bhagavadgītā* and the *Bhāgavata Purāṇa*, the so-called *prasthāna-catuṣṭayī*.

Any other path is partial, relative and incomplete, and cannot connect one to Puruṣottama. It is only the 'path of divine grace' or Puṣṭimārga which is capable of associating one with god.

There is, thus, an attempt to prove that any means other than bhakti is unsuitable for attaining god. Moreover, there is a general laxity in the Puṣṭimārga in the deliberations on bhakti as a means to something. Thus, Viṭṭhalanātha wrote a book on the 'cause of bhakti' and not on 'the one whose cause is bhakti'. In the system of Vallabha, there is, in fact, greater emphasis on bhakti as the result of the grace of Bhagavān. So, whereas normally it is held that one attains god through bhakti, i.e. bhakti is the means and Bhagavān is the goal, in the Puṣṭimārga, a reversal takes place with god considered as the means and bhakti as the goal.

The argumentation in *Bhaktihaṃsa* sets in by stating that there cannot be any connection (*sambandha*) of Bhagavān with any of the conventional means of worship or traditional injunctions (*vidhi*s). Specifically: (1) Bhagavān cannot be the effect or result (*phala*) of these injunctions (*vidhi*s), (2) Bhagavān is also not that which is taught by the injunctions (*vidheya*), and, finally, (3) Bhagavān is also not their object or *uddeśya*. Bhagavān cannot be the result or *phala* of these injunctions because he is not attainable through any means which are made by the *jīva*s (*jīvakṛta*) but only through the grace or *anugraha* of god. This is established through Upaniṣadic testimony.[9] Bhagavān is also not what is taught by the injunctions because he is permanently existent (*sarvadā-siddha*) and not finite like the ritual sacrifice, which again is made by a *jīva*. Nor is Bhagavān directly implicated as the object of these injunctions. It is only some attribute of Bhagavān (*vibhūti-rūpa*) which is the object of worship. This is because Bhagavān is impartial (*aviśiṣṭa*) to all and is to be worshipped by everyone (*sarvopāsya*). Consequently, his name and the ways to worship him should also be impartial to all. This, however, is not the case. A particular mantra (specifically named is the *rāma-mantra*) is friend to some and foe to others.

Thus, according to Viṭṭhalanātha, no injunction can form a means to associate oneself with god because

(1) worship based on injunctions is not impartial (*aviśiṣṭa*),

(2) worship based on injunctions brings about desired results (*iṣṭasādhaka*) as long as it is performed without mistakes but, if one belongs to god, undesired results never occur,

(3) even the *gopāla-mantra*, which always brings about desired results, cannot be considered connected with Bhagavān because it can also bring forth undesirable results, which is not the case with bhakti, which dispels all undesired results (*anarthopaśama*) as testified by the *Bhāgavata Purāṇa* 1.7.6[10] and 11.20.35cd.[11]

There is a fundamental difference between conventional means of worship like *pūjā* and bhakti. The *Bhāgavata Purāṇa* (11.27.52-53) makes this explicit when it emphasizes a clear difference between the results or *phala* of worship and bhakti.[12] As the *phala* of *pūjā* and bhakti is different, they must be different in their intrinsic nature (*svarūpa*) as well. If there are two dissimilar effects, their causes cannot be similar. Thus, there is not a trace of bhakti in *karma* or *jñāna*, which bring forth *phala*s that are different from *bhagavat-svarūpa*. Moreover, bhakti produces no other result than the attainment of *bhagavat-svarūpa*. As we will see, Jīva also uses the second of these stanzas (*Bhāgavata Purāṇa* 11.27.53) in *Bhaktisaṃdarbha* 235 to explain that *pūjā*, *bhajana*, etc., are the means to attain *ahaitukī-bhakti*, which, in turn, takes one to Bhagavān. He also mentions *vaidhī-* and *rāgānugā-bhakti* in this context.

Here, one can object, Viṭṭhalanātha argues, that since the *Bhāgavata Purāṇa* (11.20.32-33) enumerates many results of bhakti, and hence if one and the same bhakti (or cause) can have many results, the argument that difference in results implies difference of causes is not tenable. Viṭṭhalanātha clarifies that instances like the *Bhāgavata Purāṇa* 11.20.32-33 explain the special nature of bhakti which is its endless potential, i.e. its *kalpa-taru-svabhāva*. It also shows that the results which one attains through other means are also attained through bhakti but are ancillary (*ānuṣaṅgika*) to it. Viṭṭhalanātha concludes that all this indicates that one should depend only on bhakti and practice only bhakti. All other benefits, even liberation (*mukti*), come as fringe benefits. As for Jīva, he reads these verses in a similar manner.

Again, Viṭṭhalanātha carries on that one could object, that the use of the word *mām* in the *Bhāgavata Purāṇa* verse 11.27.53 indicates that the object of *pūjā* is Puruṣottama. He declares this to be unacceptable, arguing that the object of *pūjā* is only some attribute (*vibhūti*) of god, and it is only since *vibhūti-rūpa* is a *rūpa* of himself that Vyāsa uses *mām* in that stanza; or through the use of *mām*, it is indicated that if one meditates only on Puruṣottama, discarding all other results, Puruṣottama enters the object of *pūjā* as well as the devotee's heart (*antaḥkaraṇa*). This resembles Jīva's exegesis *ad locum* where he says that a real *bhakta* should neither desire heaven nor release.

After postulating that it is only grace or *anugraha* which is instrumental in attaining bhakti, Viṭṭhalanātha goes on to state another principle to account for the existence of other ways and to prove the supremacy of his path. He posits that there are two different ways in which Bhagavān chooses or accepts his devotees, namely, (i) the *maryādā-mārga* or the path guided by conventional injunctions as well as that of *jñāna* and *karma* and (ii) the *puṣṭi-mārga* or the path of the direct grace of god.

Viṭṭhalanātha groups all other ways within the *maryādā-mārga*. Here a devotee is either drawn towards *jñāna* or *karma*, towards the performance of different means including *pūjā*, *bhajana*, *arcana*, etc., or towards fulfilling the injunctions (*vidhi*s). All this causes the emergence of *sneha* or deep attachment to god. In Jīva's words, this is *vaidhī-bhakti*. After the emergence of *sneha*, one is drawn towards the service of god not because of any injunction but out of attachment (*rāga*) originating from *sneha*.

In the Puṣṭimārga, however, both engrossment (*pravṛtti*) and the lack of it (*apravṛtti*) are futile and pointless (*aprayojaka*) because Bhagavān himself is the means as testified by the *Bhāgavata Purāṇa* 2.7.31.[13] This division is justified and recorded in this text. The path of *karma* only leads to the *vibhūti*s of god;[14] Puruṣottama is not the object of *karma*. This is evident from the difference in the results of actions (*phalabheda*) as testified by the *Bhagavadgītā*.[15] Further, the *gopī*s attained Bhagavān only through bhakti (*Bhāgavata Purāṇa* 11.12.8) and, in fact, Bhagavān is not attainable through any other means except bhakti (*Bhāgavata Purāṇa* 11.12.9). As for Jīva, he uses these verses of the *Bhāgavata Purāṇa* to prove and emphasize the efficacy of *satsaṅga* for the attainment of bhakti and Bhagavān, while Viṭṭhalanātha employs them to prove that bhakti is different from and unique as compared to other means. The *jñāna-mārga* also does not take one to Puruṣottama and is, thus, inferior to the *bhakti-mārga*. Viṭṭhalanātha illustrates all this by referring to the beginning of the *Bhāgavata Purāṇa* 11.12. This passage also forms a compact block of quotations in Jīva's *Bhaktisaṃdarbha*:

no rodhayati māṃ yogo na sāṅkhyā dharma eva ca;
na svādhyāyas tapas tyāgo neṣṭā-pūrtaṃ na dakṣiṇā. (1)
vratāni yajñaś chandāṃsi tīrthāni niyamā yamāḥ;
yathāvarundhe sat-saṅgaḥ sarva-saṅgāpaho hi mām. (2)
sat-saṅgena hi daiteyā yātudhānā mṛgāḥ khagāḥ;
gandharvāpsaraso nāgāḥ siddhāś cāraṇa-guhyakāḥ. (3)
vidyādharā manuṣyeṣu vaiśyāḥ śūdrāḥ striyo'ntyajāḥ;
rajas-tamaḥ-prakṛtayas tasmiṃs tasmin yuge yuge. (4)
bahavo mat-padaṃ prāptās tvāṣṭra-kāyādhavādayaḥ;
vṛṣaparvā balir bāṇo mayaś cātha vibhīṣaṇaḥ. (5)
sugrīvo hanumān ṛkṣo gajo gṛdhro vaṇik-pathaḥ;
vyādhaḥ kubjā vraje gopyo yajña-patnyas tathāpare. (6)
te nādhīta-śruti-gaṇā nopāsita-mahat-tamāḥ;
avratātapta-tapaso sat[16]*-saṅgān mām upāgatāḥ.* (7)
kevalena hi bhāvena gopyo gāvo nagā mṛgāḥ;
ye'nye mūḍha-dhiyo nāgāḥ siddhā mām īyur añjasā. (8)
yaṃ na yogena sāṅkhyena dāna-vrata-tapo-'dhvaraiḥ;
vyākhyā-svādhyāya-sannyāsaiḥ prāpnuyād yatnavān api. (9)

Yoga, reasoning, *dharma* do not capture me, nor do study, austerities, relinquishment, sacrifices and patronage of buildings, or honoraria to priests. (1)
Vows, sacrifice, Vedic recitation, pilgrimages, prescriptions and proscriptions do not capture me in the same way as the community of devotees[17] which is free of any other attachment. (2)
Only by contact with the community of devotees the Daiteyas, Yātudhānas, the deer and birds, Gandharvas and Apsarases, snakes, Siddhas, Cāraṇas and Guhyakas, (3)

Vidyādharas, and, amongst men, the Vaiśyas, Śūdras, women and the lowest castes who have a *rajas*- and *tamas*-nature, found me in age by age. (4)
Many were those who found my place, Vṛtra, Prahlāda, Vṛṣaparvā, Bali, Bāṇa, Maya and Vibhīṣana, (5)
Sugrīva, Hanumān, the bear, the elephant, the vulture, the trader, the hunter, Kubjā, the herdsmen of Vraja, the herdswomen, the wives of the sacrifice patrons, and others, (6)
that host of creatures uneducated in the *śruti*, of darkest nature, practising no worship, no vows, no austerities, they reached me by way of contact with the community of devotees. (7)
By love alone, the herdswomen, cows, trees, deer, dull-witted beings, and snakes became accomplished and promptly reached me, (8)
whom one cannot attain, even if he strives hard, by yoga, reasoning, gifts, vows, austerities, sacrifices, exegesis, study, or renunciation. (9)

Speaking of the ninefold bhakti (*navadhā-bhakti*) consisting of *śravaṇa*, 'listening', etc., Viṭṭhalanātha says that this is also directed towards the *vibhūti* of god. There are intermediate categories based on the difference of competence or *adhikāri-bheda*. Thus, there is *karma-mārgīya-śravaṇa, jñāna-mārgīya-, upāsanā-mārgīya-, prāvāhikī-bhakti-, maryādā-bhakti-* and *puṣṭi-bhakti-śravaṇa*.

After emphasizing the distinctive character of his path, Viṭṭhalanātha takes up the task of establishing the practices of his *sampradāya*. It is interesting to note that even his *sampradāya* enjoins *śravaṇa, kīrtana*, and other nine forms of bhakti (*navadhā-bhakti*). The issue consists in the status of the *puṣṭimārgīya-upadeśa*. Should a person who does not have *sneha* for Bhagavān follow the instructions of a *puṣṭimārgīya-ācārya* or not? For if someone acts without *sneha*, this cannot be called *puṣṭi-bhakti*; he also does not act with the intention to attain bhakti and, therefore, not out of *maryādā-bhakti*; neither does he act with a desire for liberation and, therefore, not out of *prāvāhikī-bhakti*; and, finally, since his acting is a part of bhakti (as it is enjoined by a *puṣṭimārgīya-ācārya*), it cannot even be called *upāsanā*. So the *upadeśa* to practise the nine forms of bhakti is useless and pointless. Viṭṭhalanātha solves this by giving the example of a child following the instructions of his father to perform *sandhyā*. That child does not yet know about Vedic injunctions, yet his actions are called Vedic *karmas* and, as in the case of that child, these *karmas* produce their results, so that following the instructions of *puṣṭimārgīya-ācāryas*, one attains Puruṣottama in due course. In this way *śravaṇa* and other nine forms of bhakti become a means to attain god. And since the original *ācāryas* had the grace of god, it is justified to follow their instructions because god sides with those who are his own.

After emphasizing the importance of his path, Viṭṭhalanātha goes on to reconcile or harmonize it with established traditions. First of all, the *sampradaya* injunctions only relate to the worship of Bhagavān and the practice of bhakti and not to *vaidika-dharma* or to *varṇāśrama-dharma*. After perceiving these as the wish of god,[18] one should follow the respective *vidhis* or injunctions concerned with *agnihotra* and other rituals.

Finally, Viṭṭhalanātha rebuts any possibility of castigating the teachings of his *sampradaya* as *aprāmāṇika*, 'lacking authenticity', for not being enjoined by Śruti and Smṛti. He does that by stating that *śiṣṭācāra*, 'demeanour of the learned', is an equally forceful source of authenticity and that it is, furthermore, not possible to teach love (*vidhāna*) for it can only be recounted (*anuvādamātra*).

Jīva Gosvāmī

In the introduction to his *Bhaktisaṃdarbha*, Jīva rests his foundational argument largely on the evidence of the *Bhāgavata Purāṇa* (1.2) as briefly summarized below. Only a *jīva* oriented towards Bhagavān will be liberated from distress. This orientation is essentially expressed by worship (*upāsanā*), which is the issue (*abhidheya*) of the *Bhaktisaṃdarbha*. Worshipful single-mindedness focusing on Bhagavān is regarded as leading to the experience of god (the *prayojana* of the treatise). The central issue of the *Bhāgavata Purāṇa* is, of course, to show which *dharma* has to be followed so that the soul may find peace: this is the *bhakti-dharma*, with all human means and all insight subservient to the end of bhakti but invalid if applied to other ends (*Bhāgavata*

Purāṇa 1.2.6). *Bhakti-dharma* is invariably one's own *dharma* (*Bhāgavata Purāṇa* 1.2.13). It has no material cause and no ulterior end; it is practised only to please Bhagavān. It passes stages that lead from dutifulness to eagerness to apply oneself to matters relating to Bhagavān and *bhakti-yoga* (consisting of the *bhakti-sādhanas*). *Dharma* conducive to liberation is *bhakti-yoga* executed according to one's caste-specific duties (*Bhāgavata Purāṇa* 1.2.9-10, strengthened by *Bhāgavata Purāṇa* 5.19.19-20). Bhakti liberates whereas egotistical desire for a result (*kāma*) fetters man. And what is the essence of being? It is knowledge 'without another' (*Bhāgavata Purāṇa* 1.2.11-12). In bhakti, this is the knowledge of Bhagavān inclusive of all his *śakti*s. This is at the heart of Gauḍīya theology. The fulfilment of one's *varṇāśrama-dharma* gives Hari pleasure (*Bhāgavata Purāṇa* 1.2.13) and to give him this pleasure is the devotee's only motive. This splits the fetters of *karma* (*Bhāgavata Purāṇa* 1.2.14-15). People who have a mental block which hinders them from finding delight in this practice eventually acquire the same delight in the *satsaṅga*. The fulfilment of good conduct (*sad-ācāra*), as is inherent in the *varṇāśrama-dharma*, unties the knot of egotism; it is easy and grants nothing but happiness. Therefore, the means is the end (identity of *sādhana* and *sādhya*: *Bhāgavata Purāṇa* 1.2.17). Gods other than Bhagavān may be worshipped if they are understood to be essentially his forms. True knowlege is not dry bookish knowledge, but bhakti and *bhāva*, 'emotion, interior realisation'. True *karma* is that which is dedicated to Bhagavān. If someone renounces his *svadharma* because he has attained god, this is not objectionable but it may turn out to be fatal for one not yet advanced (*Bhāgavata Purāṇa* 1.5.12, 15,17). These principles are elaborated in the course of *Bhaktisaṃdarbha*, the exposition proliferating into the principles of aesthetics as established by Rūpa.

The *Bhāgavata Purāṇa* passages on which Jīva and Viṭṭhala-nātha base the mandatory status of ritual occur at an advanced stage of the *Bhaktisaṃdarbha*, logically so because they belong to the last and final book of the *Bhāgavata Purāṇa*, namely 11.11 and 11.12. Before going into these passages, Jīva Gosvāmī argues as follows: there are two ways of bhakti, *vaidhī* (in two modes, *pravṛtti* and *jñāna*) and *rāgānugā* (235). Only *vaidhī-bhakti* will lead the devotee to take *śaraṇāpatti*, 'refuge in God' (236). This result is attained by the true *sevā* of the guru, etc. The guru will instruct the disciple in the *śāstra*s referring to Bhagavān and also in the appropriate *bhagavan-mantra*. The grace of the guru is the root of the grace of Bhagavān. There is no other means but the true *sevā*. The guru is instrumental for enlightenment (*jñāna*, 237). This enlightenment has two forms; the first of which takes one to brahman (and is, therefore, rejected in the bhakti systems), the other takes the devotee to Bhagavān. He proceeds by the rituals enjoined by the 'Veda'. The now valid Vedic rituals have their substitutes in bhakti rituals (*ijyā* = *saṃskāra*s and *pūjā*; *prajāti* = *vaiṣṇava-dīkṣā; tapas* = *samādhi; upaśama* = *bhagavan-niṣṭhā*).

From the next paragraph (*Bhaktisaṃdarbha* 238), the use of *Bhāgavata Purāṇa* passages parallel to that in the two Puṣṭimārgīya texts sets in. The nucleus of the quotations (explicitly or implicitly shared) are long passages of the *Bhāgavata Purāṇa* 11.12, supplemented by passages from 11.11. and also 11.14. The nucleus consists of the *Bhāgavata Purāṇa* verses 11.12.1-9, which has been quoted and translated above.[19]

If no guru can be found with the qualities described in the foregoing paragraphs of the *Bhaktisaṃdarbha*, then the devotee should worship a perfect *mahābhāgavata* instead. In fact, everyone who bears the distinguishing marks of a Bhāgavata needs to be served. Service (*sevā*) is performed according to two alternate modes, *prasaṅga-rūpā* and *paricaryā-rūpā*. The first kind of service is characterized by quoting the *Bhāgavata Purāṇa* (11.12.1-2), already quoted above as occurring in Viṭṭhalanātha's exegesis:

> Yoga, reasoning, *dharma* do not capture me, nor do study, austerities, relinquishment, sacrifices and patronage of buildings, or honoraria to priests. (1)
> Vows, sacrifice, Vedic recitation, pilgrimages, prescriptions and proscriptions do not capture me in the same way as the community of devotees which is free of any other attachment. (2)[20]

The same passage is quoted in the *Bhaktihetunirṇaya* and the *Bhaktihaṃsa*.[21] In explaining the passage, Jīva, in his *Kramasaṃdarbha*,[22] his commentary on the *Bhāgavata Purāṇa*, follows the commentaries of Śrīdhara Svāmī and Sanātana, whose exegesis is, in turn, an elaboration of Śrīdhara's commentary, supported by specifications based on further quotations from the *Bhāgavata Purāṇa*. The *Kramasaṃdarbha* on the *Bhāgavata Purāṇa* 11.12.1-6 is identical with the *Bhaktisaṃdarbha* 237 ff., not accounting for minor variants. The *Kramasaṃdarbha* sums up quotations which appear in full in the *Bhaktisaṃdarbha*. Service is further explained by the *Bhāgavata Purāṇa* (11.11.47):

iṣṭāpūrteṇa mām eva yo yajeta samāhitaḥ;
labhate mayi sadbhaktiṃ matsmr̥tiḥ sādhusevayā.

He who worships only me by sacrifices and patronage of buildings gains the true bhakti of me by serving the devout while remembering me.

The *iṣṭa* are the Vedic sacrifices (*Bhāgavata Purāṇa* 7.15.48-49 is given as testimony), whereas *pūrtā* comprises the patronage of buildings, gardens, wells, etc., for the sake of Bhagavān, that is for the sake of the *sampradāya* and the service of the devout. In mentioning pious acts for the sake of the *satsaṅga* and the remembrance of god through the service of his *bhaktas* as enjoined by the *Bhāgavata Purāṇa* (11.11.47), Jīva points to instruments of worship which have a different and superior quality to those described by the *Bhāgavata Purāṇa* (11.12.1-2). They are applied solely in remembrance of Krishna. This attitude transforms exterior bhakti (*bahiraṅga-bhakti*) into intrinsic bhakti (*antaraṅga-bhakti*). The *satsaṅga* has a transforming quality and wields its power independently. No other means equivalent to the power of the *satsaṅga* exists. In this, Jīva elaborates and goes beyond Sanātana.[23] His emphasis is on the service of the *sādhu*s, that is, of the *satsaṅga*. For Jīva, the *satsaṅga* is an independent instrument effecting bhakti. He says that the means mentioned in the *Bhāgavata Purāṇa* (11.12.1-2) are invalid if applied as a means to an ulterior end. If they are, however, applied as ends in themselves (while solely focusing on Bhagavān), they are valid. Moreover, says Jīva, from the futility of mechanically or ingenuinely applied ritual instruments, it cannot be concluded that the rituals enjoined upon a Vaishnava should not be performed. This would violate one's Vaishnavahood, of the characteristics of which Sanātana had reminded his readers. In consequence, all regular Vaishnava rituals have to be performed.

The next paragraph (*Bhaktisaṃdarbha* 239) talks about the way in which Bhagavān can be subdued to the will of the devotee. Here too, two methods are taught: (1) principal and (2) secondary. This is linked with and also extrapolated from the *Bhāgavata Purāṇa* (11.12.3-6), already referred to above as quoted by Viṭṭhalanātha in his exegesis:

> Only by contact with the community of devotees the Daiteyas, Yātudhānas, beasts and birds, Gandharvas and Apsarases, snakes, Siddhas, Cāraṇas and Guhyakas, (3)
> Vidyādharas, and, amongst men, the Vaiśyās, Śūdras, women and the lowest castes who have a *rajas*- and *tamas*-nature, found me in age by age. (4)
> Many were those who found my place, Vṛtra, Prahlāda, Vṛṣaparvā, Bali, Bāṇa, Maya and Vibhīṣana, (5)
> Sugrīva, Hanumān, the bear, the elephant, the vulture, the trader, the hunter, Kubjā, the herdsmen of Vraja, the herdswomen, the wives of the sacrifice patrons, and others, . . . (6)[24]

The *Bhaktisaṃdarbha* follows Śrīdhara, whose commentary on these four aggregate stanzas is limited to the identification of eight of the characters occurring in the passage. The principal method, says Jīva, is that of the *gopī*s, the secondary that of the other characters enumerated in the *Bhāgavata Purāṇa* passage. For the *gopī*s, *satsaṅga* is the unmediated, direct contact with Krishna; for all others, including the latter-day devotees, the *satsaṅga* is the community of the *bhakta*s of Krishna.

Paragraph 240 underscores that the characters mentioned in the *Bhāgavata Purāṇa* (11.12.3-6) had no access to the instruments of bhakti except the *satsaṅga*. It starts with 11.12.7:

> . . . that host of creatures uneducated in the Śruti, of darkest nature, practising no worship,

> no vows, no austerities, they reached me by way of contact with the community of devotees. (7)[25]

These devotees of reduced means achieved everything through the *satsaṅga*. The paragraph culminates in two identifications, namely *bhāgavata-saṅga* = *sat-saṅga; sat* = *avatāra*. These equations take their development from the exegesis of Śrīdhara Svāmī (*sat-saṅgāt iti sadbhiḥ saṅgo nāma mayaiva saṅga ity abhipretyoktam; yad vā, sva-saṅgasyāpi sat-saṅgatvaṃ vivakṣyate, svasyāpi sattvāt; yad vā, madīya-saṅgād ity arthaḥ*) which Jīva quotes verbatim. He emphasizes that there is no other means of generating alignment to Bhagavān than the *satsaṅga*. It alone is an independently effective instrument upon which all other instruments depend. Bhagavān, who is subservient to the *satsaṅga*, will hardly accord his grace independently of it. Nonetheless, it cannot be disputed that he accords his grace unconditionally. Therefore, it cannot be ruled out that creatures perceive him by virtue of this unconditional grace. In such a case, however, it needs to be remembered that Bhagavān became an *avatāra* to taste the *rasa* of love. The flow of *rasa*, however, can only be realized thanks to the community of the devout (*sādhusaṅga*). This, according to Jīva, proves that the *satsaṅga* is the instrumental cause (*nimitta*) of Bhagavān's only seemingly independent grace.

Paragraph 241 proceeds to show how the *gopī*s, the practitioners of the principal method of subduing Bhagavān to their will, have no other means but love. To authenticate this, Jīva quotes the *Bhāgavata Purāṇa* (11.12.8):

> By love alone, the herdswomen, cows, trees, deer, dull-witted beings, and snakes became accomplished and promptly reached me, . . . (8)[26]

While Śrīdhara *ad locum* distinguishes between the characters mentioned in 11.12.7 who all depended on the *satsaṅga*, and the *gopīs*, etc., enumerated in verse 8 who attained Bhagavān by *bhāva* alone, Jīva asserts: the *gopīs* are distinguished by *bhāva*, and *bhāva* is the instrument of subduing Bhagavān. *Bhāva* is the same as bhakti, and according to the *Bhāgavata Purāṇa* passage 11.14.20:

na sādhayati māṃ yogo na sāṃkhyaṃ dharma uddhava;
na svādhyāyas tapas tyāgo yathā bhaktir mamorjitā.

Yoga, reasoning, *dharma*, oh Uddhava, study, austerities, or relinquishment do not lead to me in the same way as does powerful bhakti towards me.

Only bhakti can attain Bhagavān. Bhakti, however, as Jīva stresses, is produced by the *satsaṅga.*

Paragraph 242 proceeds to explain *bhāva*, quoting the *Bhāgavata Purāṇa* (11.12.9):

> . . . [me,] whom one cannot attain, even if he strives hard, by yoga, reasoning, gifts, vows, austerities, sacrifices, exegesis, study, or renunciation. [27]

Here, the commentary of Śrīdhara is confirmed by Jīva. Śrīdhara says:

> He (i.e. Vyāsa) said that it was difficult to find [Bhagavān] independently. . . . And here first of all the *gopīs*, the animals, etc. joined Kṛṣṇa. These are the *sat*. For all others, the contact with these primeval companions of Kṛṣṇa is the *satsaṅga*. By this, they acquire bhakti. This is what is meant.

The community of the *gopī*s, the animals, etc., and Kṛṣṇa was the primeval *satsaṅga. Satsaṅga* has before been defined as meaning both *mama saṅga*, 'contact with me (i.e. Kṛṣṇa)'and *madīyānāṃ saṅga[ḥ]*, 'contact with those who are mine'.

Paragraphs 243 to 245 finally declare worshipping the *bhakta*s as more powerful than worshipping Bhagavān.

The *Bhaktisaṃdarbha* then moves on to the delicate issue of who deserves worship and notes that it is only the Vaishnava; a topic no longer covered by the quotations from the *Bhāgavata Purāṇa* shared by the two sectarian exegetes and, therefore, beyond the limits of the present paper.

Conclusion

For the *Bhaktisaṃdarbha* and, implicitly the *Kramasaṃdarbha*, it is evident that within his treatment of the *Bhāgavata Purāṇa*

(11.12.1-9), Śrīdhara's commentary forms the backbone of Jīva's reasoning, with Jīva putting the accent differently by strengthening the power of the *satsaṅga* as the only agent, almost in the sense of an institutionalized body, dispensing bhakti.

In Jīva's *Bhaktisaṃdarbha*, bhakti as grace accorded unconditionally recedes. Foregrounded is the power of the *satsaṅga* to accord the bond with Krishna. While the instruments of bhakti are not sufficient, they are, nonetheless, indispensable for a Vaishnava for he has to act according to his *svadharma* as it corresponds to Vaishnava characteristics. *Svadharma* is the *dharma* by which the soul finds peace; in other words, by which the quest of bhakti is fulfilled. The observance of *svadharma* is the quintessential *bhakti-dharma*.

Viṭṭhalanātha and Jīva are informed by different traditions, sharing, however, reliance on the ubiquitous *Bhāgavata Purāṇa* as the 'modern' Veda. Viṭṭhalanātha restricts himself to Vallabha and the scriptural proofs accepted by his school. Jīva relies on the tradition established by Rūpa and Sanātana, and takes the guidance of Śrīdhara Svāmī's commentary on the *Bhāgavata Purāṇa*. Moreover, Jīva sees his own exegesis as in compliance with the teachings of the Purāṇas and of the *Pāñcarātra*, both of which, along with a host of other texts, he quotes profusely.[28] Jīva just passes over in silence the position of the Puṣṭimārga and argues in vindication of the *satsaṅga*; in other words, the body of the devotees of his own sect, as the mediator of grace. Exclusiveness, let alone denying the authenticity and legitimation of other orthodox Vaishnavas, does not figure overtly in the part of his agenda reviewed here. But, as for the passages of the treatises reviewed here, the positions of Viṭṭhalanātha and Jīva emphasize different *modus operandi* of grace. The Puṣṭimārgīya position has god accord unconditional grace which anticipates all human acts of bhakti, whereas the Gauḍīya position ascribes to the *satsaṅga* the power to coerce Bhagavān to give his grace. What unites the two positions is their firm commitment to the *varṇāśrama-dharma* on which the two sects, like the other orthodox Vaishnavas, could also rest their pragmatic cooperation.

NOTES

1. M. Horstmann, *Der Zusammenhalt der Welt: Religiöse Herrschaftslegitimation und Religionspolitik Mahārājā Savāī Jaisinghs (1700-1743)*, Wiesbaden: Harrassowitz Verlag, 2009 and M. Horstmann, 'Theology and Statecraft', in R. O'Hanlon and David Washbrook, ed., *Religious Cultures in Early Modern India: New Perspectives*, London: Routledge, 2012. In these two publications, attention has been drawn, respectively, to the contributions of the Gauḍīya scholar, Kṛṣṇadeva Bhaṭṭācārya, and the Puṣṭimārgīya scholar, Bālakṛṣṇa Bhaṭṭa. Portions of Kṛṣṇadeva's otherwise unpublished works have been edited and translated in the first-mentioned book. For Bālakṛṣṇa's particularly relevant *Prameyaratnārṇava*, see Bālakṛṣṇa, *Prameyaratnārṇava*, ed. with Hindi translation and commentary by Kedarnath Mishra, Varanasi: Ānand Prakāśan Saṃsthān, 1971, and Bālakṛṣṇa, *Śrībālakṛṣṇa-granthāvalī*, ed. Shyam Manohar Gosvami, Kolhapur: Śrīvallabhavidyāpīṭh-Śrīviṭṭhaleśprabhucaraṇ Ashram Hospital Trust, vs 2054.
2. D.L. Haberman, ed., *The Bhaktirasāmṛtsindhu of Rūpa Gosvāmin*, Delhi: Indira Gandhi National Centre for the Arts and Motilal Banarsidass, 2003.
3. *Bhaktirasāmṛtasindhu* 1.2.269 and 309, respectively.
4. For the spread of the Puṣṭimārga and socio-economic conditions shaping its history, see S. Saha, 'The Movement of Bhakti along a North-West Axis: Tracing the History of the Puṣṭimārg between the Sixteenth and Nineteenth Centuries', *International Journal of Hindu Studies*, vol. 11, no. 3, 2007, pp. 299-318.
5. Viṭṭhalanātha, *Bhaktihaṃsa*, ed., tr. into Hindi, comm. by Kedarnath Mishra, Varanasi: Ānand Prakāśan, 1971.
6. Viṭṭhalanātha, *Bhaktihetunirṇaya*, with the comm. of Raghunātha, ed., tr. into Hindi, comm. by Kedarnath Mishra, Varanasi: Ānand Prakāśan, 1978.
7. Jīva Gosvāmī, *Bhaktisaṃdarbha*, ed. Haridas Shastri, Vrindaban: Śrīgadādharagaurahari Press, 1986.
8. In Vallabhācārya's philosophy, *brahman* which is *saccidānanda* (being, consciousness and bliss) has *Jagat* (world), *Akṣara* (eternal being) and *Puruṣottama* (the highest divinity) as his own form (*svarūpa*) according to the prominence of *sat* (being), *cit* (consciousness) and *ānanda* (bliss) respectively. Puruṣottama, Bhagavān and Kṛṣṇa are the terms interchangeably employed for the supreme *brahman* (cf. *Bhāgavata Purāṇa* 1.2.11, 1.3.28; *Bhagavadgītā* 8.21, 15.18 and *Siddhānta-muktāvalī* of Vallabhācārya).
9. *nāyam ātmā pravacanena labhyo na medhayā na bahunā śrutena; yam evaiṣa vṛṇute tena labhyaḥ* . . . , 'This self cannot be grasped by teachings or by intelligence, or even by great learning. Only the man he chooses can grasp him . . .' (*Kaṭha Upaniṣad* 2.23, tr. Olivelle in P. Olivelle, tr., *Upaniṣads*, New York: Oxford University Press, 1996, p. 238).

10. *anarthopaśamaṁ sākṣād bhaktiyogam adhokṣaje; lokasyājānato vidvāṁś cakre sātvatasaṁhitām*, 'People do not know that the *bhakti-yoga* directed to Adhokṣaja puts these evils immediately to rest. Therefore, the wise man composed the *Sātvatasaṁhitā* (the *Bhāgavata Purāṇa*).'
11. . . . *tasmān nirāśiṣo bhaktir nirapekṣasya me bhavet*, '. . . therefore he who does not desire anything and is indifferent has *bhakti* in me.'
12. *pratiṣṭhayā sārvabhaumaṁ sadmanā bhuvanatrayam; pūjādinā brahmalokaṁ tribhiḥ matsārṣṭitām iyāt. mām eva nairapekṣyeṇa bhaktiyogena vindati; bhaktiyogaṁ sa labhata evaṃ yaḥ pūjayeta mām*, 'By installing images, he attains universal rule; by building temples, the three worlds; by worship and so forth, the heaven of Brahmā; by doing all these three things, he becomes my equal. Me he finds only through disinterested *bhaktiyoga*. In this way, he who worships me attains *bhaktiyoga*.'
13. *nandaṃ ca mokṣyati bhayād varuṇasya pāśād, gopān bileṣu pihitān mayasūnunā; ahnyāpṛtaṁ niśi śayānam atiśrameṇa, lokaṃ vikuṇṭham upaneṣyati gokulaṁ sma*,'He will liberate Nanda from the fear of Varuṇa's sling and the cowherds held captive in the caves by the son of Maya. The cowherd people, busy in their daily course and sleeping at night from great fatigue, he will lead to the Vikuṇṭha-abode.'
14. *Bhāgavata Purāṇa* 10.72.3.
15. *Bhagavadgītā* 7.23, 8.6. See *Bhagavadgītā with English translation*, Gorakhpur: Gita Press, 1969.
16. A variant reading for this word is *mat*.
17. *Satsaṅga* is, literally, the community of those who really are; that is the good ones who enjoy unperishable life.
18. *śrutismṛtī mamaivājñe yas te ullaṅghya vartate; ājñocchedī mama dveṣī madbhakto'pi na me priyaḥ*, 'Śruti and Smṛti have been ordained by me. He who ignores them in violation of my command hates me; he is neither my devotee nor do I love him' (*Bhaktihetunirṇaya*, pp. 17-18).
19. See pp. 155-6.
20. For the original passage, see p. 155.
21. Pp. 26 and 57, respectively.
22. *Śrīmadbhāgavatam*, 1983.
23. Sanātana had explained how the power of phenomena extrinsic to bhakti could be annihilated, and he went on explaining the distinguishing marks of a Vaishnava by quoting the *Bhāgavata Purāṇa* 11.19.34: *ahiṃsā satyam asteyam asaṅgo hrīr asañcayaḥ; āstikyaṁ brahmacaryaṁ ca maunaṁ sthairyaṁ kṣamābhayam. śaucaṁ japas tapo homaḥ śraddhātithyaṁ madarcanaṁ; tīrthāṭanaṁ parārthehā tuṣṭir ācāryasevanam*).
24. For the original passage, see p. 155.
25. For the original passage, see p. 155.
26. *kevalena hi bhāvena gopyo gāvo nagā mṛgāḥ; ye'nye mūḍha-dhiyo nāgāḥ siddhā mām īyur añjasā.*

27. *yaṁ na yogena sāṅkhyena dāna-vrata-tapo-'dhvaraiḥ; vyākhyā-svādhyāya-saṃnyāsaiḥ prāpnuyād yatnavān api.*
28. For the texts that Jīva relied upon, see S.K. De, *Early History of the Vaisnava Faith and Movement in Bengal: From Sanskrit and Bengali Sources*, 2nd edn., Calcutta: K.L. Mukhopadhyay, 1961, pp. 413-21.

BIBLIOGRAPHY

Bālakṛṣṇa, *Prameyaratnārṇava*, with Hindi tr. and notes ed. Kedarnath Mishra, Varanasi: Ānand Prakāśan Saṃsthān, 1971.

——, *Śrībālakṛṣṇa-granthāvalī*, ed. Shyam Manohar Gosvami, Kolhapur: Śrīvallabhavidyāpīṭh-Śrīviṭṭhaleśprabhucaraṇ Ashram Hospital Trust, vs 2054, 1997.

Bhagavadgītā with English translation, Gorakhpur: Gita Press, 1969.

[*Bhāgavatapurāṇa*.] *Śrīmadbhāgavatam. Maharṣi śrī kṛṣṇadvaipāyanapraṇītam: prathamaḥ skandhaḥ. Śrī śrīdharasvāmīkṛta bhāvārthadīpikā, śrī jīva-gosvāmikṛta kramasaṁdarbhaḥ, śrī viśvnātha cakravarti kṛta sārārtha-darśinī, śrī nātha cakravarti kṛta śrī caitanyamatamañjuṣā, śrī baladeva vidyābhūṣaṇa kṛta vaiṣṇavānandinī, śrīman madhvācāryyakṛta bhāga-vatatātparyyanirṇayaḥ, śrī haridāsa śāstri kṛta vinodinīti ṭīkābhir anvayānuvādena cālaṃkṛtam*, ed. Haridas Shastri, Vrindaban: Śrī Gadā-dharagaurahari Press, 1983.

[*Bhāgavatapurāṇa*.] *Śrīmadbhāgavatamahāpurāṇa hindī anuvād sahit*, Gorakh-pur: Gita Press, 2000.

De, S.K., *Early History of the Vaisnava Faith and Movement in Bengal: From Sanskrit and Bengali Sources*, 2nd edn., Calcutta: K.L. Mukhopadhyay, 1961.

Gosvāmī, J., *Bhaktisaṁdarbha*, ed. H. Shastri. Vrindaban: Śrīgadādharagaurahari Press, 1986.

——, *Kramasaṁdarbha*, see *Bhāgavatapurāṇa*, 1983.

Haberman, D.L., ed., *The Bhaktirasāmṛtsindhu of Rūpa Gosvāmin*, Delhi: Indira Gandhi National Centre for the Arts and Motilal Banarsidass, 2003.

Horstmann, M., *Der Zusammenhalt der Welt: Religiöse Herrschaftslegitimation und Religionspolitik Mahārājā Savāī Jaisinghs (1700-1743)*, Wiesbaden: Harrassowitz Verlag, 2009.

——, 'Theology and Statecraft', in R. O'Hanlon and David Washbrook, ed., *Religious Cultures in Early Modern India: New Perspectives*, London: Routledge.

Olivelle, P., tr., *Upaniṣads*, New York: Oxford University Press, 1996.

Saha, S., 'The Movement of *Bhakti* along a North-West Axis: Tracing the History of the Puṣṭimārg between the Sixteenth and Nineteenth Centuries', *International Journal of Hindu Studies*, vol. 11, no. 3, 2007, pp. 299-318.

Viṭṭhalanātha, *Bhaktihaṁsa*, ed., tr. into Hindi, comm. by Kedarnath Mishra, Varanasi: Ānand Prakāśan, 1975.
——, *Bhaktihetunirṇaya*, with the comm. of Raghunātha, ed., tr. into Hindi, comm. by Kedarnath Mishra, Varanasi: Ānand Prakāśan, 1978.

CHAPTER 9

Jayatrām's *Jogpradīpakā*: Between Hatha-yoga and Bhakti in the Eighteenth Century

MAYA BURGER

Introduction

Most pre-twentieth-century yoga texts that have received scholarly attention are in Sanskrit.[1] The *Jogpradīpakā* of Jayatrām stands out as an important testimony in the history of yoga[2] as one of the very few available texts on it written in the vernacular or, more precisely, the new Indo-Aryan languages.[3] Although the discussion of the relation between bhakti and yoga goes back to the Upanishads, the relation of hatha-yoga with bhakti deserves more specific attention. This paper focuses on what one may call the 'bhaktification' of the hatha-yoga tradition. The *Jogpradīpakā* of Jayatrām belongs to the hatha-yoga tradition, maintaining an explicit interest in specific hatha-yoga concepts such as the asanas, *prāṇāyāma,* the *cakra*s, the mudras, *kuṇḍalinī* or the *bandha*s. The author is a Rama-bhakta and his hatha-yoga is imbued with a vision of yoga as leading to the eternal contemplation of Sītārāma (Siyārām). After a brief summary of aspects linked to physical yoga, this essay will focus on the passages that relate to samadhi and to Jayatrām's spiritual perspective.

Jayatrām's particular view of bhakti and the intricate relationship he establishes between hatha-yoga and bhakti can be clarified by examining his view of the aim of yoga. Indeed, it is the deviation from the classical understanding of samadhi that qualifies him as a bhakta. His teaching about yoga does not exclude the devoted attitude that a yogi may have for his master or for Shiva[4] but the goal of his yoga, the core of samadhi for him, is the love of and surrender to a personified divine couple.

The boundaries between various currents that characterize pre-modern Indian 'religiosity' are not clearly marked, and 'religious' trends and different world-views overlap. Besides manifesting the cumulative and non-exclusive character of Indian writings, many texts testify to a crisscrossing of attitudes[5] and Jayatrām's *Jogpradīpakā* is no exception. Certain passages clearly show a Nāth background, whereas others place the work in a Vedantic tradition. Several strands converge in what can be seen as the major strand (bhakti) and the 'bhaktification' of the hatha tradition. The hatha-yoga exemplified in this text belongs to a tradition emphasizing work on the physical and the yogic body[6] and the practice of asana, but it contains a number of peculiarities that invite us to consider the relation between bhakti and hatha-yoga in this context.[7]

Author, Text, Structure and Content

The Author

The author, Jayatrām, provides some information on himself such as that he is a resident of Vrindavan and that he wrote the text in 1737 on Vijayadaśamī.[8] He states, moreover, that he is the disciple of a certain Payaharibābā. Payaharibābā is considered another name of Kṛṣṇadāsa who occupied the seat of Galta (near Jaipur). This information has to be related to the fact that Galta by that time had become a seat of a Vaishnava sect, the Rāmānandīs,[9] which, in turn, may have had an influence on the type of yoga developed by Jayatrām.[10]

The Text and Its Structure

In the middle of the eighteenth century, the hatha-yoga tradition was already well-established and could rely on important texts in Sanskrit and the living oral tradition of yoga surrounding the texts.[11] The first thing to note is that Jayatrām names his own text after the *Haṭhayogapradīpikā* of Svātmārāma. In many ways, his text resembles this work but also clearly feeds more on the Nāth tradition, which offers techniques for making the body strong and capable of defeating death or reversing the course of time, and allowing the yogi to unite with Shiva/Shakti.[12]

The edition I am working with was edited by M.L. Gharote and published by the Rajasthan Oriental Research Institute of Jodhpur in 1999. It brings together two incomplete but complementary manuscripts from Pune and Varanasi, the main text being that of the Varanasi manuscript.[13] No translation of the text has yet appeared, although Gharote has produced a summary of the contents along with a commentary.

The language of the text is a mixture of old Hindi (*kharī bolī, braj*) and many Sanskrit terms.[14] It is clear that Jayatrām had some knowledge of Sanskrit because he refers to yoga texts in Sanskrit and uses a Sanskritized idiom. His choice of a vernacular in a highly Sanskritic tradition needs more investigation. Could it be that he did not know enough Sanskrit? Did he want to popularize yoga knowledge among people with a limited command of Sanskrit or confirm an oral tradition and secure it in writing? We should consider that his choice of idiom may have been motivated by the intention to combine traditions and thereby preserve them.

Jayatrām's *Jogpradīpakā* has eight chapters, which follows the division of the *aṣṭāṅga* part of the *Yoga-sūtra* of Patañjali: *yama, niyama, āsana, prāṇāyama, pratyāhāra, dhāraṇā, dhyāna, samādhi.*[15] The *Haṭhayogapradīpikā*, apparently the primary source of inspiration for Jayatrām, does not follow this division.[16]

It is important to note that the *Haṭhayogapradīpikā* correlates hatha-yoga with raja-yoga (and not with bhakti), showing their interdependence: one yoga needs that of the other type. Hatha-yoga is the more physically oriented tradition, whereas raja-yoga refers to the higher limbs of the *aṣṭāṅga* tradition of the Patañjali yoga, which deals with mental processes.[17] In spite of the fact that the Sanskrit *Haṭhayogapradīpikā* does not follow this division into eight chapters, it is clear that the emphasis on the upper *aṣṭāṅga* represents the more meditation-oriented raja-yoga.[18] Jayatrām follows the *aṣṭāṅga* division, but the content differs from the classical *Yoga-sūtra* and is closer to the *Haṭhayogapradīpikā*.

Content

The differences between hatha, *nātha* and *aṣṭāṅga* yogas and bhakti are manifest in their contrasting aims, termed as samadhi. The following presentation of the eight chapters, thus, concentrates on the question of samadhi.

The invocation at the beginning of the text is addressed to Rama and Sita, which is a programmatic deviation from the more conventional role of Shiva as 'god' of the yogis in the hatha-yoga tradition. Obviously Jayatrām wants to be identified as a follower of Rama. Chapters 1 (1-35) and 2 (36-48) are dedicated to *yama* and *niyama*. Jayatrām explains that the aim of yoga is samadhi and that it follows a path of eight limbs. It is a yoga by which all afflictions and diseases are cured. Samadhi is obtained where the moon and sun reside (13) and through the grace of the master.[19]

Chapter 3 (49-363) describes the eighty-four asanas.[20] Many of the asanas examined in this text are not part of the modern yoga repertoire. Only twenty-six of these postures are also named in *Haṭhayogapradīpikā*.[21] Judging from the number of lines devoted to each topic, this is the most important chapter in the book with 314 lines. Postures are described and their benefits are indicated. With the help of the asanas and exercises of purification, the body becomes pure (*nirmala*) and obtains its natural (*sahaja*) state. Most of the benefits are physical and therapeutic: diseases and disorders are cured. This chapter clearly deals with the question of purifying the body and mind, whereas it hardly mentions the investigation into samadhi as the goal of these practices.[22]

Chapter 4 (364 to 442)[23] is devoted to *prāṇāyāma* as well as to various kinds of *mantras* (Vedic, tantric) and practices of purification. *Prāṇāyāma* is said to be particularly efficient in bringing about samadhi, which reflects the fact that for hatha-yoga, *prāṇāyāma* is the central practice to control the mind. As for the higher limbs (*aṅga*) of yoga, it is said that the retreat of the senses (*pratyāhāra*) is successful when the mind is freed from happiness and sadness; concentration (*dhāraṇā*) when *buddhi* is purified; meditation (*dhyāna*) when the ego consciousness (*ahaṁkāra*) is stable. *Samādhi* finally occurs when the soul (*jīva*) has no more distinguishing properties (*upādhi*) and the yogi, thus, becomes like a dead body.[24] Full yoga is obtained by the person who is devoted to *prāṇāyāma* (437-40).

Chapter 5 (450 to 727) deals with *pratyāhāra* (retreat of the senses), the *mudras*, and the syllable *oṁ*. It is a long chapter and most of the emphasis is laid on the *mudras*.[25] It begins with an explanation of the eight *kuṁbhakas* (aspects of *prāṇāyāma*), followed by a discussion of the twenty-four *mudras* and reflections on the syllable *oṁ* before devoting the last few lines to *pratyāhāra*. The chapter confirms that *pratyāhāra* is the way to stop the agitation of the mind (*citivṛti,* [*cittavṛtti*] 720); Jayatrām stipulates that he obtained this state by the grace of the guru. This would imply that he had had a vision of Siyārām and experienced samadhi and was, therefore, himself a practising yogi. *Samādhi* is also mentioned in the context of *kevala kuṁbhaka,* a way to control breathing that results in samadhi (503-4).

Chapter 6 (728-60) concerns *dhāraṇā* and develops an essentially therapeutic perspective. Disturbances of the five elements distributed in the body can be healed by concentration. The text emphasizes the combination of *tattvas* and *dhāraṇās*. For example, the ability to fly in the sky is mentioned as being a result of *vāyutattva dhāraṇā,* whereas *ākāśa dhāraṇā* opens the door to liberation.

Chapter 7 (761-96) has only 35 lines. It concerns *dhyāna* and concentrates on the question of death and how to control it. Attention is paid to the role deities can play. When it comes to meditation on the lotus of the heart, one should concentrate (or meditate) on Rama and Sita. Rama is imagined as dark in colour like rain-filled clouds with his beautiful body decorated with ornaments (7.788-90). The yogi meditates on such a form from foot to face, as well as on Jānakī. Meditating on the all-pervading nature of Rama is said to pacify the mind: the result is *sahaja samādhi.* In the last *dohā* of the chapter, Jayatrām recognizes himself as Rama's servant, who has abandoned all differentiations and obtained *sahaja samādhi* (7.796).

The Samadhi Chapter

In the *aṣṭāṅga* sequence, the eighth chapter with 167 lines (797-964) is entitled samadhi (*atha samādhi varanan*) but, like the other chapters, it covers other topics as well. It sets up the entire edifice of yoga as a progressive path: through cleansing, purifying, breathing, and numerous difficult exercises and *siddhi*s, the yogi will finally reach his goal—samadhi.[26] The culmination is indeed samadhi, treated specifically in lines 932-52.

It is in the lotus of the thousand petals that the yogi can obtain samadhi (932). This is the abode of Rama and Sita.[27] Rama is the sun, Jānakī the rays (935). The place is described with words for light and splendour such as *sūr*, *tej*, *ābhās* (933); it is *sat cit ānanda* (934). With the help of the metaphor of water and the reflection of the sun (Rama) in the water, Rama, the sun, is said to absorb all the water, hence leaving an ultimate state of samadhi which has no reflection (*pratibiṁba*; 936-7). This state represents the destruction of the duality of *nirguṇa* and *saguṇa*. Rama is both: all-pervasive (938).

The yogi wishes only to be the servant of Rama.[28] The yogi's mind is centred exclusively on the divine couple, as the mind of the thirsty person is centred on water (945).[29] What is happening in the body is called *saṁprajñāta* 'conscious (of its object)'; whereas what is happening in *dhāraṇā*, *dhyāna* and samadhi is *asaṁprajñāta* ('unconscious of its object', as James Haughton Woods translates the terms (942),[30] which means that it is pure knowledge, an undifferentiated state. Jayatrām chose this state of samadhi where there is nothing but Siyārām, whether in a state of waking, sleeping or absorption (946-8).

Yoga is compared to a tree that takes away all suffering and bestows the fruit of natural (*sahaja*) liberation (950): '*yama* and *niyama* are the seed, *āsana* and *kumbhaka* are the leaves, *pratyāhāra* the flowers, *dhāraṇā*, *dhyāna* and samadhi the fruits' (949).[31] Samadhi removes all darkness: just as the light brought to the temple removes the dark, so is this book a light and the exercises like the lamp oil. The goal of yoga, the chapter concludes, is hence to render service to the all-pervading divine couple who bestows grace and brightness (951-2).

Concluding Remarks: The Changing Relations between Bhakti and Hatha-yoga

There can be no doubt that by the middle of the eighteenth century, this hatha-yoga text had absorbed and integrated many elements of the yoga tradition into a vernacular medium and provided a text of its own independent compilation. Although it is a body-oriented hatha-yoga text, containing predominantly, chapters on asanas, the final aim of yoga here departs from the concept found, for instance, in the *Haṭhayogapradīpikā*; at the same time, despite the fact that the structure of the book follows the *aṣṭāṅga* division of classical yoga, Jayatrām's concept of samadhi has also very little to do with the exposition of yoga in the *Yoga-sūtras*. The chapter on samadhi in the *Haṭhayogapradīpikā*, Jayatrām's supposed source of information, reveals some similarities but also substantial differences. In the *Haṭhayogapradīpikā*, the samadhi chapter begins by stating synonyms for the state of samadhi such as *unmanī*, *rāja-yoga*, *manonmanī*, etc. (4, 3-4). The yogic path is summed up as leading to immortality for those whose *śakti* is awakened, who have renounced action, and who know how to control *prāṇa*. The *Haṭhayogapradīpikā* emphasizes the hearing of the *anāhata* sound in the last stage of realization. The union of *anāhata* and mind (4.76) is called raja-yoga, and the real yogi becomes the creator and destroyer of the universe, like god. The yogi is entirely absorbed and happy. Hatha-yoga is said to be vain if not related to raja-yoga as the ultimate goal, as revealed in sound. Once this ultimate sound ceases, the state of *paramātman* is reached (*Haṭhayogapradīpikā*, 4.100). The yogi is liberated alive, though he looks like a dead person. He is beyond the reach of worldly affairs as a result of his complete control of the yogic body.

In the *Haṭhayogapradīpikā*, hatha-yoga is included in raja-yoga[32] and the yogi in samadhi 'cannot be killed by any instrument, and is beyond the controlling power of beings. He is beyond the reach of incarnations and charms' (4, 112).[33] As for Jayatrām's *Jogpradīpakā*, although it is also primarily a hatha-yoga text, the strategy of subordinating hatha-yoga is similar but effected through bhakti rather than raja-yoga. Jayatrām, however, places more emphasis on the corporality of yoga than the *Haṭhayogapradīpikā*, relating bodily control to medical treatment, for instance. The primacy given to physical yoga may also be underlined by the fact that samadhi is not related to hearing the *anāhata* sound,[34] which is so important to the the *Haṭhayogapradīpikā*. From the perspective of bhakti, it is bhakti that has been transformed by being brought closer to the yoga tradition. From the point of view of the yoga tradition, it can be said that yoga has been 'bhaktified'.

The last chapter on samadhi explains Jayatrām's spiritual position. Although he has written a hatha-yoga text that reveals all the physiological and medical benefits of these techniques, and demonstrated his allegiance to the Patañjali tradition by a programmatic outline spelt out in his eight chapters, in the end, his religious attitude is one of allegiance to divine love. His concept of samadhi does not translate into an identification with Shiva/ Shakti, nor is it the total cessation of any relation to the manifested world and a final retreat into a state of undifferentiation. Rather, his samadhi requires the recognition of Siyārām, the all-pervading divine couple, whom the yogi contemplates upon and wants to serve with devotion.[35]

The parts of the text that have a clear Nāth connotation (and they are the greater part of the work) invoke Shiva as the generic name of the divinity. Jayatrām knows and recognizes Shiva as the god of the yogis and mentions this belief as if quoting somebody else's conviction. By implication, the relation of a Nāth yogi to Shiva would not be 'bhakti' and perhaps should, therefore, not be called bhakti. However, the higher steps of yoga and, in particular, its goal are permeated with bhakti to Siyārām. One could argue that the author has simply framed a hatha text with bhakti experiences (offering the text to the god at the beginning and invoking him again at the end as the ultimate bliss). The historical network of religious strands, the constellation of spiritual typologies and the terminologies for identifying any one of them in a scholarly context are definitely more complicated, however. Throughout the text Jayatrām favours a yogi who depends on the grace of his god.

Hatha-yoga was an important step in the codification of yogic practices when it was sytematized in treatises during the pre-modern period. The *Haṭhayogapradīpikā* related it to the more philosophical tradition of classical yoga. Jayatrām's Hindi text operates yet another change by 'bhaktifying' hatha-yoga, which had been a more ascetic tradition. His text is not simply another version of a traditional hatha text but is coloured by unmistakable bhakti shades. The attitude and the spirituality that the work transmits are grounded in a vision that places Siyārām above all, without whom nothing is possible.[36] Samadhi is a visionary experience of the divine couple and not samadhi in its classical sense of a content-free state of mind (*citta-vṛtti-nirodha*).

The *Jogpradīpakā* stresses more palpable forms of yoga—oriented towards the body and asceticism—and approaches samadhi through more tangible means than does raja-yoga. Hence, this text may well be an important step in orienting yoga in a more and more worldly direction. Conquering death would not imply liberation from the body (including the transfer of the life principle to another body). Understanding samadhi as a vision of Siyārām may lead to a state of mind and mode of consciousness that have room for content, an object, a relationship (perhaps even emotions).

Hatha-yoga and bhakti are two different strands but Jayatrām has merged them. Hence, his text documents the existence of a certain combination of hatha-yoga and bhakti in Vrindavan during the eighteenth century. Knowing this, we may wonder whether this type of yoga was an exception or whether it is typical and important in the history of yoga. One aspect of the reception history of Jayatrām's text has been documented by G. Bühnemann.[37] At the end of the nineteenth century, an unknown painter illustrated the 84 asanas of his *Jogpradīpakā*. He painted the yogi in accurate postures corresponding to the text and placed him in a surrounding that reminds us of certain miniatures, especially those related to the mythology of Krishna.[38] The beautiful natural landscape is completed with representations of temples and often a disciple is depicted as serving his master. The atmosphere does not invite us to think of yoga as a path detached from the world. Perhaps we have with this text, as well as with the pictures (painted more than a century later), the first indications of the new type of yoga that would characterize twentieth-century yoga with a more worldly orientation.

NOTES

1. G. Larson and R.S. Bhattacharya, *Yoga Philosophy*, Delhi: Motilal Banarsidass, 2008 admittedly only deals with Sanskrit texts; G. Feuerstein, *The Yoga Tradition: Its History, Literature, Philosophy and Practice*, Delhi: Motilal Banarsidass, 2002 has a larger ambition but does not mention vernacular texts either. The hatha-yoga tradition is the topic of D.G. White, *The Alchemical Body: Siddha Traditions in Medieval India*, Chicago: University of Chicago Press, 1996 but his sources are in Sanskrit. This is however different in the recent edited volume by D.G. White, *Yoga in Practice*, Princeton and Oxford: University of Princeton Press, 2012.
2. To use the word yoga in the singular is certainly inadequate and the plural should be preferred.
3. There might, of course, be more texts in vernacular idioms but, for the time being, they are not available for research. It should be noted that yoga texts also exist in south Indian languages.
4. It is a common trend to address a personal deity or a supreme master at the beginning of a treatise but this does not mean that the content is bhakti. In the same line, the injunction of *īśvarapranidhāna* (surrender to a deity) in the *Yoga-sūtra* of Patañjali has been the object of various interpretations and extrapolations but does not refer at all to the type of bhakti that characterizes the *Jogpradīpakā* of Jayatrām.

5. For examples, see W. Pinch, *Warrior Ascetics and Indian Empires*, Cambridge: Cambridge University Press, 2006, and White, *The Alchemical Body: Siddha Traditions in Medieval India*, Chicago: University of Chicago Press, 1996.
6. This type of yoga is known from sources that incorporate influences from different texts and traditions such as the Shaiva tantric traditions, the Nāth tradition, the *Yoga Upanishads* or the *Śivasaṁhitā*.
7. This paper represents work in progress. There are many parameters that I am not able to bring into the argument for the time being such as the historical background of the author, his confirmed affiliation, textual references or intertextuality.
8. M.L. Gharote, ed., *Jayatrām: Jogpradīpakā, Rājasthān Purātan Granthmālā*, 192, Jodhpur: Rajasthan Oriental Research Institute, 1999, p. 1. There are other works attributed to Jayatrām, such as a *Yogāsanmālā* preserved in a manuscript at the Rajasthan Oriental Research Institute, which might indeed be by the same author. See Gharote, ed., *Jogapradīpakā*, p. 2.
9. Galta is a shrine connected to a natural spring that has attracted important religious activities. See Pinch, *Warrior Ascetics*, pp. 18-22. On the Rāmānandīs of Galta, see M. Horstmann, 'The Rāmānandīs of Galta (Jaipur, Rajasthan)', in *Multiples Histories: Culture and Society in the Study of Rajasthan*, ed. L.A. Babb, V. Joshi and M.W. Meister, Jaipur and Delhi: Rawat Publications, 2002, pp. 141-97.
10. Pinch notes that since the legendary dispute between Tārānāth (representing the yogic tradition) and Paihari (Payahari; the bhakti tradition) in the sixteenth century, the Vaishnavas took over Galta and reformed religiosity in a new direction: 'Taranath's reputation was based on his ability to generate supernormal power within himself: not only did this render him an unpredictable and unruly ally, it meant that his power (and popular appeal) could always be challenged by other yogis. Paihar Krishandas, by contrast, disclaimed any hint of ascetic wizardry [. . .] His reputation was based on his love for Krishna, pure and simple. This not only made him a predictable ally, it offered a concept of a loving God who was ready and willing to tend to the needs of even the most destitute supplicant.' Pinch, *Warrior Ascetics*, p. 20. For the reform movements occurring around this time and the transformation of the Nāth yogis, see also D.G. White, *Sinister Yogis*, Chicago and London: University of Chicago Press, 2009, pp. 240-3.
11. Jayatrām lists his sources of inspiration at the end of his text (lines 955-7). They comprise eleven works: *Pātañjal jog prakās, Cūḍāmaṇī, Jognidh, Jog prakās, Jogsaṁghitā, Jog saṁdhi, Mūrat saṁghitā, Haṭhapradīpikā, Gorakhasat, Tatpradīpikā*, and *Jog nāgvali* (transliterated according to the text). Jayatrām does not mention the *Gheraṇḍasaṁhitā*, a text dating probably from the seventeenth or eighteenth century (P. Thomi, ed., *Gheraṇḍasaṁhitā*: Institut für Indologie Wichtrach, 2006, available online at http://www.indologiewichtrach.ch/site/werkstatt/werkstatt.html). This

text may not have been known to him, yet the similarities between these two texts, especially regarding the question of bhakti, are intriguing. Could it have been a rival text?

12. Vasudeva observes that the differences between individual yoga systems may be greater than what it seems at first sight, despite the similarities among the terms used. The Shaiva systems of yoga seem to be strictly theistic, which is, of course, not the case with the *Yoga-sūtra*. S. Vasudeva, *The Yoga of the Mālinīvijayottaratantra: Chapters 1-4, 7-11, 11-17*, Pondicherry: Institut Français de Pondichéry, École Française d'Extrême-Orient, 2004, pp. 367-436; Vasudeva, *Mālinīvijayottaratantra*, quoted by G. Bühnemann, *Eighty-four Āsanas in Yoga: A Survey of Traditions (with Illustration)*, Delhi: D.K. Printworld, 2007, p. 18, n. 43.
13. Ms. 117/A (1883-1884) deposited at the Bhandarkar Oriental Research Institute, Pune, and Ms. 3035/1894, Nāgarīpracāriṇī Sabhā, Varanasi. See Gharote, ed., *Jogapradīpakā*, p. 1.
14. The little we know about the author leaves important questions unanswered: was he, for instance, a yogi or not? It is certain that he was a learned person.
15. Although the chapters are clearly named and demarcated, from the point of view of the content, there are many overlaps between them. It is interesting to note that by the eighteenth century, this reference to the eightfold path is normative and it has remained a standard reference in yoga in modern times.
16. Various manuscripts divide the *Haṭhayogapradīpikā* into four, six or ten chapters. For a summary of the different manuscripts of the *Haṭhayoga-pradīpikā*, see Gharote, ed., *Jogapradīpakā*, p. xvi, table 1.
17. On the history of the raja-yoga, see P. Schreiner, 'Le rāja-yoga dans une perspective historique', in *L'héritage spiritual de l'Inde: Des Védas à la Bhagavad-Gita*, vol. 1, ed. S. Berti-Rossi and D. Chaille, Gollion: Infolio, 2007, pp. 15-76; Bühnemann, *Eighty-four Āsanas*, pp. 11-16 and White, *Sinister Yogis*, pp. 45-8.
18. The *Haṭhayogapradīpikā* '[...] explains Haṭha Yoga for the attainment of Râja Yoga. Owing to the darkness arising from the multiplicity of opinions, people are unable to know the Râja Yoga. Compassionate Swâtmârâma composes the Haṭha Yoga Pradîpikâ like a torch to dispel it' (chapter 1, lines 2-3), P. Sinh, tr., *The Hatha Yoga Pradipika*, tr. Pancham Sinh, Allahabad, 1915; rpt., New York: AMS, 1974.
19. *candra-sūra ekaiṁ dhari rahai; jogī joga samādhi hī lahai.* (*Jogpradīpakā* 13). When he explains the *niyama* related to *īśvarapūjā*, he refers to the nine kinds of bhakti of the *Bhāgavata Purāṇa* (42).
20. The number of 84 asanas has been discussed by G. Bühnemann, op. cit., 2007, pp. 25-36.
21. It is important to note this difference from the perspective that the *Haṭhayogapradīpikā* is the source of inspiration for Jayatrām. The latter

seems to be far more interested in postures; hence, he might come from a posture-oriented tradition.

22. The term is mentioned only with *mṛtyabhañjīkāsana* ('death-breaking-posture'; 157) and *gohī āsana* ('secret-posture'; 174).
23. The division between chapters three and four is not clear. I follow Gharote's division.
24. *aisī eka samādhi jaba pāvai apanī jīva upādhi miṭāvai; jaisai mṛtaka tana visarāvai aisai jogī sadā rahāvai* (439).
25. For example, the *ākarṣaṇī mudrā* is a combination of posture, breathing and meditation upon the lotus of the thousand petals, where one remembers (*sumare*) Siyārām; when the Lord looks with his side-glance of grace (*kṛpā-kaṭācha*), two fruits, *bhukti* (enjoyment) and *mukti* (liberation), are experienced; *sahasradala kamala hai puni tahā siyārāma ko sumare jahāṁ, prabhu kripā-kaṭācha jaba dekhai bhukti mukti dou phala pekhai.* (527)
26. The beginning of the chapter deals with the possibility offered to advanced practitioners to enter the body of a dead person (*parakāyā praveśana*), which means leaving the old body and taking on a new one, including the memories of its previous life. This is followed by considerations on *cakra*s, *nāḍī*s and divinities—a full-fledged tantra panorama! Such preoccupations are shared with Nāth yogis. Gharote notes the similarity with *Gorakh–śatak*, lines 26-9 (Gharote, ed., *Jogapradīpakā*, p. 29). On the importance of entering a new body with Nāth yogis and yogis of 'old', see White, *Sinister Yogis*, pp. 45-8.
27. There is, of course, no reference to the episodes of the *Rāmāyaṇa*, as the bhakti developed here concerns an attitude towards the divine, rather than the relation to the story connected with these figures.
28. *prabhu sevya mai sevaga soī; yahai vṛtya sadā mama hoī.* (940)
bhakti sahita prabhu caraṇa ju sevai; cyāro mukti kade nahī levai.
deha māhi varatai hai jau lau; dāsabhāva so rakhai to lau. (941)
29. [. . .] *pyāsa ko mana nīra hī jāno; jogī mana siyārāma hī mānau.* (945)
30. These terms are not mentioned in the *Haṭhayogapradīpikā* but are from the Patañjali text.
31. *jama aru nema bīja kari jānau āsana kuṁbhaka patra ju mānau;*
pratyāhāra yahu phūla soī dhāraṇā dhyāna samādhi phala hoī. (949)
32. 'Those who are ignorant of the Râja-Yoga and practice only Haṭha-Yoga, will, in my opinion, waste their energy fruitlessly' (4, 78). *The Hatha Yoga Pradipika*, p. 58.
33. Ibid., p. 62.
34. This is mentioned superficially, however, in other parts of the book.
35. The text mentions words such as *prabhu*, *sevā*, *kṛpā*, *bhakti* (once) that stand for the relation Jayatrām has with his godhead, which is one of surrender, acceptance and service. These terms are absent from the *Haṭhayogapradīpikā*.

36. Bhakti and yoga have an intricate history; a good example for the need to reflect on their relationship is the figure (or tradition) of Kabīr. The work attributed to him is a testimony to the cohabitation of bhakti and yoga. The present example, however, stands for a different case. Here, we are dealing with a manual of hatha-yoga blended with bhakti spirituality.
37. Bühnemann, *Eighty-four Āsanas.*
38. See also M. Burger, 'Illustrating Yoga: From the Master to the Book', in *Religiöse Blicke—Blicke auf das Religiöse: Visualität und Religion*, ed. B. Beinhauer-Köhler, D. Pezzoli-Olgiati and J. Valentin, Zurich: TVZ, 2010.

BIBLIOGRAPHY

Bühnemann, G., *Eighty-four Āsanas in Yoga: A Survey of Traditions (with Illustration)*, Delhi: D.K. Printworld, 2007.

Burger, M., 'Illustrating Yoga: From the Master to the Book', in *Religiöse Blicke—Blicke auf das Religiöse: Visualität und Religion*, ed. B. Beinhauer-Köhler, D. Pezzoli-Olgiati and J. Valentin, Zurich: TVZ, 2010, pp. 165-84.

Feuerstein, G., *The Yoga Tradition: Its History, Literature, Philosophy and Practice*, Delhi: Motilal Banarsidass, 2002.

Gharote, M.L., ed., *Jayatrām: Jogpradīpakā, Rājasthān Purātan Granthmālā*, 192, Jodhpur: Rajasthan Oriental Research Institute, 1999.

The Hatha Yoga Pradipika, tr. P. Sinh, Allahabad, 1915; rpt., New York: AMS, 1974.

Horstmann, M., 'The Rāmānandīs of Galta (Jaipur, Rajasthan)', in *Multiple Histories: Culture and Society in the Study of Rajasthan*, ed. L.A. Babb, V. Joshi and M.W. Meister, Jaipur and Delhi: Rawat Publications, 2002, pp. 141-97.

Larson, G., and R.S. Bhattacharya, *Yoga Philosophy: The Encyclopaedia of Indian Philosophy*, 12, Delhi: Motilal Banarsidass, 2008.

Pinch, W., *Warrior Ascetics and Indian Empires*, Cambridge: Cambridge University Press, 2006.

Schreiner, P., 'Le rāja-yoga dans une perspective historique', in *L'héritage spiritual de l'Inde: Des Védas à la Bhagavad-Gita*, ed. S. Berti-Rossi and D. Chaille, Gollion: Infolio, 2007, pp. 15-76.

Thomi, P., ed., *Gheraṇḍasaṁhitā*, Institut für Indologie Wichtrach, 2006.

Vasudeva, S., *The Yoga of the Mālinīvijayottaratantra: Chapters 1-4, 7-11, 11-17*, Pondicherry: Institut Français de Pondichéry, École Française d'Extrême-Orient, 2004.

White, D.G., *The Alchemical Body: Siddha Traditions in Medieval India*, Chicago: University of Chicago Press, 1996.

——, *Sinister Yogis*, Chicago and London: University of Chicago Press, 2009.

——, *Yoga in Practice*, Princeton and Oxford: University of Princeton Press, 2012.

CHAPTER 10

From *Śabda-brahman* to *Sabad*: The Way from a Transpersonal Concept to Personal Experience

FLORINA DOBRE-BRAT

Vedic Literature

In Vedic literature there are a number of hymns more or less[1] dedicated to the Word-Speech (*Vāc*), the very source of the many *nāmas* (names). Primarily hypostatized as the female aspect of Puruṣa, the androgynous, *Vāc* is the first sacrificial substance (X, 125, 3b). She has three secret quarters which do not 'stir' (i.e. move) and a quarter that is spoken speech (I, 164, 45), which the gods divided in many ways so that she has many abodes and revelations (I, 125, 3cd). Hymn X.125 of the *Rigveda* speaks about the goddess of Speech, Vāgāmbhṛṇī, the queen, companion of gods, 'sustainer and nourisher of Soma, Tvaṣṭṛ, Pūṣan and Bhaga' the gatherer of treasures, the one with penetrating perception, the first of those who should be worshipped, and who says of herself:

> I myself declare this which is liked by the gods as well as by men. I make whomsoever I like: a fierce (warrior), a priest, a sage or a wise poet.[2]

The sovereignty of *Vāc* over the other gods is taken to a new philosophical dimension in the literature of the Āraṇyakas and the Upanishads, where it becomes the same as Ātman-Brahman.

Equating Speech with the Brahman means to admit that speech and the supreme reality coexist: 'Verily the Word-Speech is the Brahman' (*vāg vai brahmeti*, *Bṛhadāraṇyaka Upaniṣad* 4.1.2). It is also the first born of the Vedic lore (*ṛta*)[3] that is above all gods. The consequent identity joins together the mystical syllable *oṁ* that encompasses within the whole linguistic and supra-linguistic reality, in both sound (*nāda-dhvani*) and meaning (*artha*) forms, and the Brahman.

When analysing the nature of the word, philosophers and grammarians refer to it as *śabda*, and no longer as *Vāc*, the latter remains somehow confined to a more mystic and poetical reality.[4] Retaining the *in illo tempore* quality of primary *Vāc*, *śabda* is also acknowledged by all orthodox philosophical schools as the means of right, correct and true knowledge (*śabda pramāṇa*), without being necessarily equated with the body of the Vedas, which tradition holds as not human creation (*apauruṣeya*), but revealed and eternal.

Bhartṛhari

In the fifth century, as if out of nowhere, given the scarcity of grammatical commentaries at the time, the grammarian-philosopher, Bhartṛhari, not only aimed to reinstate the genuine grammatical Pāṇinian tradition,[5] but also caught the hanging threads of the *Vāc* mysticism warp[6] and created a pattern of World Unity that folds and unfolds as the Brahman Word Principle (*śabda-tattva brahman*). According to Bhartṛhari, the world is but the outcome of the manifestation (*vivarta*) of the Brahman Word Principle (*brahman-śabda-tattva*). The Veda as well as the syllable *oṁ* are the way and the symbol (*anukāra*) to attain it,

> That without any beginning or end is Brahman, the Principle of Word-Speech, which is imperishable and which manifests itself in states of things, from which the world proceeds to evolve. Although he is taught as one, he appears divisible because of his powers, and [although] his powers are not distinctive, he manifests as if they are distinctive; that whose six types of modifications such as birth, etc. depend upon the power of Time, they being the sources of different types of existence;

that whose unity, One, the seed of all [is perceived] as multiple: the agent, the object and the action, that for which the Veda is a means of attainment and a symbol. Although it is one, the great sages transmitted it distinctively in different traditions.[7]

Moreover, the transformation of the Word in the form of Vedic verse as the creator of the phenomenal world is repeatedly emphasized: 'Knowers of tradition have declared that all this is the transformation (*pariṇāma*) of the word. It is from the *chandas* that this universe has evolved.'[8]

The Brahman that Bhartṛhari refers to is the *parā-brahman* and not the Upanishadic *śabda-brahman* which, however, is more understood as related to ritual worship in the form of the Vedic hymns.[9]

Alongside the theoretical argument of his Word-World vision, Bhartṛhari does point out the means of reaching the Word-principle:

It has been said that the Self, which is within the speaker, is the Word, the great Bull with whom one desires union. Therefore, the purification of the word (*śabdasaṁskāra*) is the means of realization of the Supreme Ātman.[10]

Can this purification of the word be done within the framework of grammar as a shastra? The grammar can act in Bhartṛhari's vision as a door to salvation:

It is the door of salvation, the remedy for all the impurities of speech, the purifier of all the sciences and shines in every branch of knowledge. (. . .) This is the first step in the ladder leading to liberation, this is the straight royal road for all those who desire salvation.[11]

Do these assertions involve a great deal of the meta-linguistic approach that not many grammarians are ready to digest? Bhartṛhari says that *śabdasaṁskāra* is the very means of realization of the Supreme Ātman. In this state of things, *śabdasaṁskāra* cannot merely be a linguistic process of the correct verbal derivation and elimination of corrupted verbal forms (*apabhraṁśa*), but it might hint at special techniques of the yogic type on which the commentary, unfortunately, does not shed much light, presenting the readers are familiar with it.[12] The commentary also speaks of *śabdayoga* or *śabda-pūrva yoga* (union with the previous [correct, purified] word), presumably through *śabdasaṁskāra*. This *śabda yoga* of Bhartṛhari was interpreted either as a 'kind of meditation aimed at rising the level of consciousness to the highest stage of word',[13] or, in more recent studies, as exploring the grammar's resources.[14] However, what we can get from the commentary is that this possible technique seems to be the way in reaching the intuitive flash of insight or the super-sensuous knowledge (*pratibhā*). What puts one back on the track of following the linkage between the Word Principle and the Sants who took up the divine name, such as Kabīr, is a rather obscure observation that the *vṛttikāra*, according to tradition—and most likely—Bhartṛhari himself, makes in the commentary of the most proclaimed verse which analyses the three, or rather four, stages of the Word (*vaikharī, madhyamā, paśyantī* and *parā*),[15] a verse that has been always compared to the often-disputed verse I.165,45 of the *Rigveda*.

> The scripture of some say that it is the form of this [state of the word, i.e. *paśyantī*] which can be attained *either* by the knowledge of grammar through achieving the knowledge of the proper [words] *or* through the union with the word previously [purified] (*śabda-pūrva yoga*).[16]

The expression *iti ekeṣāṁ*, 'according to some', might also refer to those other than the grammarians who, from their position, were bound to defend the instrumentality of their shastra in reaching the Supreme Reality. This Reality can also be approached with the help of another more debatable means (*śabda-pūrva yoga*) now taken out of the framework of grammar. It can be argued that *śabda-pūrva yoga* is a reference to a genuine form of yogic practice and philosophy other than *vyākaraṇa* that must have always been known to some Tantric sects who transmitted it during initiatory practices and guarded it to preserve its esoteric power. There are only a few, scattered references to it, as shown above, and unfortunately not enough to recompose its full picture. It is also the point identified in Bhartṛhari's work, where we can find a possible hint at the fact that the grammarians of the fifth century (and possibly a few centuries later if the author of the *vṛtti* is not Bhartṛhari himself) were also aware of some techniques which were more common to esoteric and Tantric traditions.

Kabīr

The link between the poetry attributed to Kabīr and the concepts of the Nāths has already been the subject of several studies.[17] Considering the inflated corpus of the poems ascribed to him and the fact that no research has convincingly established what the historical Kabīr wrote, Kabīr-poetry can be perceived as a poetic tradition which was shaped in different social, religious, and historical environments. This tradition has been regionalized by late twentieth-century scholarship, dividing it into eastern (*Bījak*), northern or Punjabi (*Ādī Granth*) and western or Rajasthani (Shyam Sundar Das' *Kabīr granthāvalī* and most poems from the *Millennium Kabīr Vāṇī*) traditions. The publication of the *Millennium Kabīr Vāṇī* and of new studies and translations, such as Vinay Dharwadker's,[18] do not essentially modify our perception of Kabīr as a tradition.

A lot has been said about Kabīr's *sabad* focused on the Name, more precisely the name of Rama.[19] Therefore, I shall dwell no more on this aspect. Similarly, Linda Hess, Charlotte Vaudeville[20] and others have discussed Kabīr's usage of the language and paradoxes in detail, which follows, more or less, the pattern of the Nāth *sandhyābhāṣā*.

When looked from a different light Kabīr's usage of the Word—as the soteriological vehicle of the individual fully engaged in his quest for salvation—two key concepts[21] might enlarge one's perspective when looking at Kabīr's *sabad*. One is what Kabīr calls *parcā*: the seeing, the direct experiencing (*pratyakṣa*—what is in front of one's eyes, without an intermediary), and the other is the verbal understanding (*śābdabodha*) that we have while trying to get the gist of the paradoxes which give the specific flavour and rich imagery of Kabīr's world.

Parcā and Pratibhā

For a scholar, understanding is based on or rather influenced by data acquired through consulting glossaries, commentaries, lists of esoteric terms and reference books. For the practitioner, initiation is the minimum premise required. But in both cases understanding is not always recomposing piece-by-piece the intricate puzzle which the changing paradigms in historical and social layers and textual interpolations lay between us and Kabīr. Real understanding may come eventually at the end of strenuous effort or in an instantaneous flash of understanding. What Kabīr calls *parcā* seems to be very close to what Bhartr̥hari names *pratibhā*[22]—the means which challenges and eventually supersedes the other means of correct understanding (*pramāṇa*).

The meaning of *pratibhā* in Indian schools of thought covers a wide range but its core generally is 'the sense of wisdom characterized by immediacy and freshness (. . .) supersensuous and supra-rational apperception, grasping truth directly'.[23] In the grammarians' school, *pratibhā* and *prajñā* are identical with the *paśyantī* stage of *Vāc*. The *pratibhā* theory is based on the *śabda brahman* as the source of all phenomena and knowledge, and the objective world. Although Bhartr̥hari and his commentators relate the *śabda* to the Vedas, which is the self-revelation of the supreme *śabda*, while Kabīr utterly rejects it, the features of the *pratibhā* are highly akin to Kabīr's kind of mystical encounter with what is beyond all. If Kabīr would have commented scholarly on his *parcā*, it would probably have sounded like Bhartr̥hari's words:

> Having reached to that purified state of the word, one goes to intuition (*pratibhā*), the origin of all word's modifications. From this state named intuition (*pratibhā*) due to its similarity to pure existence, by the repetition of the meditation on the union with the previous [purified] word, one reaches the supreme origin where all attempts of modification disappears.[24]

The commentator, Puṇyarāja, describes *pratibhā* as the purest form of *prajñā* (*bhagavatī vidyā viśudhiprajñā pratibhākhyā, VP,* II, 493) and equals it with the *paśyantī* stage of *Vāc* for exactly retaining its luminous character as the name indicates. Explanations and detailed descriptions of *pratibhā* continue in several places in Bhartṛhari's work, but what would be of interest in those descriptions is to retain the *characteristic* of *pratibhā* as the capacity of seeing the real thing in that spontaneous flash of understanding, a feature that is also shared by *parcā*.

Thus for Bhartṛhari, *pratibhā* refers to seeing and experiencing directly the last resort of the sensible world and for Kabīr, experiencing *parcā* means transcending the mundane experience and witnessing the real, subtle thing. In Kabīr's words: 'Seeing is the only proof'[25] since 'without the Experience (*parcā*) man goes puffed with pride having grasped but the shadow of the śabda'.[26] The Word hypostasized in the words of the *sākhīs*[27]—which are but expressions of witnessing encounters with the Satguru, the highest experience (*paricaya*)—is, thus, a constant witness of the Satguru. The divine *sabad* is communicated by the Satguru, who is identical with the supreme divinity or Reality through direct experience.

gura sisikaligara kījie gyāna masakalā dei;
sabada cholanā̃ choli ke cita darpaṇa kari lei. (*Sākhī*, 1.8)

Let the Guru be the Burnisher/let wisdom be his tool,
Graping with the scraper of śabda/let Him polish your soul as a mirror.

The description of Kabīr's seeing or witnessing[28] experience abound in direct references to light, such as 'the effulgence of the supreme being/is beyond imagination' or 'all darkness vanishes/ when I found the lamp within'; 'Pearls were scattered on the path but those who came by were blind/without the Light of the Lord the world steps over them.'[29] The experience is compared to a diamond in several places such as 'Hari is the Diamond, the devotee is the Jeweller/who displays his wares on his stall/ If a connoisseur be found/they will fetch a good price!', 'I found stability and salvation when the Satguru made me firm/Kabīr, the Diamond is for sale on the bank of Mansarovar.'[30]

Although both *pratibhā* and *parcā* seem to have a great deal in common, there is a difference between the two. For Bhartṛhari, *pratibhā* is a means and a state in itself, impersonal, at which one arrives after consuming and internalizing certain stages. The highest mystical experience which Kabīr emphatically speaks of as the only real encounter of the seeker with the truth, although deeply rooted in the sincere effort of craving salvation, dawns upon the bhakta spontaneously and graciously.

Śābdabodha

In terms of verbal understanding, the *ulaṭbāṁsī* (upside down language) of Kabīr give us a peculiar type of *śābdabodha*, 'true cognition or knowledge'. Three conditions are to be fulfilled to have a proper verbal understanding of a syntactic construction: *saṁnidhī* or *āssatī*, 'physical proximity'; *ākāṅkṣā*, 'intention of the speaker', and *yogyatā*, 'the logic, possibility or compatibility of two connected terms on the semantic plan of the construction'. As is clear, the first two conditions are more or less fulfilled with every *ulaṭbāṁsī* poem but the *yogyatā* condition is systematically broken. Yet there are levels of understanding from puzzling (which, however, sets the mind in motion) to that revelatory comprehension taking place in the mind of the hearer. It depends upon the capacity of the hearer to get to the meanings of it. The quality that ensures the production of the meaning is given by Kabīr's 'qualification' to trigger many possibilities of realities beyond our grasp or comprehension: 'A tree stands without root/ without flowers bears fruits. . . . Dance done without feet/tune played without hands/Praises sung without tongue. . . .'[31] (*Bījak, Śabda*, 24)

That paradoxical case of *śābdabodha* can also be supported by reconsidering the meaning of *ulṭā* as Linda Hess does.[32] Thus 'upside down' or 'reversed' does not necessarily mean mere reversing of the view depicted, in the unusual description of a town, for example:

> Littered with meat/where the watchman is a vulture/Mouse in the boat/ cat at the oars;/frog sleeping,/snake on guard;/bull giving birth/cow sterile/calf milked/morning, noon and night/lion forever leaping to fight

the jackal/.Kabīr says, rare listeners/hear the song right. (*Bījak, Śabda,* 95)[33]

Kabīr probably wants to say that one should get the awareness of, or at least reflect upon, the world which we exist in, and which is governed by certain, immovable rules. It may not be the absolute one, and there could be other worlds governed by other rules. This is why all the sacred lore either of the Hindus or the Turks (as he calls the followers of Islam), commented upon and preached with bigotry by pedant pandits, could very well apply up to a certain limit but that is not the end. He invites us through this rich imagery to think upon what might be—and that is the yoga of liberated minds. The *ulṭā* insight which effulgently reveals assertions such us *nirvāṇa is saṁsāra* eventually eliminates dualistic thinking in the omnipresent pair of contradictions.

Conclusion

After this brief attempt to place the pattern of the Word-Principle (*śabda-tattva brahman*) and the Word (*sabad*) in a comparative light as put forward by Vedic literature, Bhartṛhari and Kabīr, it can be said that the later views are not necessarily a development of the former, although they have a certain soteriological inclination in common. On the one hand, Bhartṛhari's *śabda-tattva* is an impersonal, cosmological principle by the manifestation (illusory or substantial) of which the world evolves and is intertwined with the knowledge of this world. On this basis, grammar and its techniques such as *śabdasaṁskāra* or possibly *śabda* (*pūrva*) *yoga* are the doors and means to liberation. On the other hand, Kabīr's *sabad* is something real, yet almost impossible to be grasped by any of our organs and perception faculties (including the mind); (*Sākhīs* 5, 35, 89) but is, nevertheless, the only path to salvation.

The link I have tried to establish between *śabda-tattva* and *sabad* shows that these concepts are not fully independent of each other although developed in different epochs. The philosophical concept of the *śabda-tattva*, although unique to Bhartṛhari, had the force to cut its way through centuries. Kabīr's *sabad*, although sharing philosophical (mostly Upanishadic) impersonal features, tends to concentrate on *nāma*, 'the name of God', which is a devotional path to union with god—establishing, thus, a very personal relation between the subject and god.

Both concepts eventually serve shared practical purposes but they refer to different ways of approach. One is highly philosophical and elaborately constructed as a system, and the other one is more empirical but equally strong due to the force of the personal and devotional credo behind it.

NOTES

1. There is controversy whether hymn I.164 of the *Rigveda*, also known as the *Asyavāmīya sūkta*, or hymn X.81, precisely refers to *Vāc*, the Word-Logos.
2. *aham eva svayamidaṁ vadāmi jṛṣṭaṁ devebhiruta mānuṣebhiḥ; yaṁ kāmaye taṁtamugraṁ kṛṇomi taṁ brahmāṇaṁ tamṛṣiṁ taṁ sumedhāmm/* (*Rigveda* X. 125.5) Hymns from the *Rigveda* are quoted from *Ṛksūktaśatī, Selected Hymns from the Ṛg Veda with Important Padapaṭha*, ed. and tr. H.D. Velankar, Bombay: Bharatiya Vidya Bhavan, 1972, pp. 297-8.
3. *vāg akṣaram prathamā ṛtasya* (*Taittirīya Brāhmaṇa* 2.8.8.5) quoted in G. Rath, *Linguistic Philosophy in Vākyapadīya*, Delhi: Bharatiya Vidya Prakashan, 2000, p. 34.
4. It is interesting to note that though there are several Sanskrit words signifying speech or language, such as *bhāṣa, vāṇī, gir* and *śabda*, none of them except *śabda* covers the meaning of *vāc*.
5. 'The Pāṇinian tradition seems to be lost due to the grammarians who were fond of abridgements and had little knowledge, or dry reasoning. When tradition slipped away from the hands of Patañjali's disciples, the mere text survived only in the South. Ācarya Candra received the true tradition from the "mountain" and from him was transmitted to Bhartṛhari.' (*VP* II, 476-8) The text of the *Vākyapadīya* is quoted on the basis of Bhartṛhari; *Vākyapadīya of Bhartṛhari with the Vṛtti and the Paddhati of Vṛṣabhadeva*, ed. K.A Subramanya Iyer, Poona: Deccan College Postgraduate and Research Institute, 1966. Other published editions and commentaries consulted for this paper are W. Rau, ed., *Bhartṛharis Vākyapadīya: Die mūlakārikās nach den Handschriften herausgegeben und mit einenm Pada-Index versehen, Abhandlungen für die Kunden des Morgenlandes*, Wiesbaden: Franz Steiner, 1977 and Bhartṛhari *Vākyapadīya Containing the Ṭīka of Puṇyarāja and the Ancient Vṛtti*, ed. K.A. Subramanya Iyer, Delhi: Motilal Banarsidass, 1995.
6. 'Bhartṛhari is the oldest available and clearest link so far to the tradition of *Vāc* mysticism that has obviously survived in India right down from the

Vedic period, albeit without receiving recognition in literature as a *darśana* in itself.' A. Aklujkar, 'An Introduction to the Study of Bhartṛhari', in *Bhartṛhari Philosopher and Grammarian*, ed. S. Bhate and J. Bronkhorst, Delhi: Motilal Banarsidass, 1994, p. 18.

7. *anādinadhanaṁ brahma śabdatattvaṁ yad akṣaram;*
vivartate 'rthabhāvena prakriyā jagato yataḥ.
ekam eva yad āmnātaṁ bhinnaśaktivyapāśrayāt;
apṛthaktve 'pi śaktibhyaḥ pṛthaktveneva vartate.
adhyāhitakalāṁ yasya kālaśaktim upāśritāḥ;
janmādayo vikārāḥ ṣaḍ bhāvabhedasya yonayaḥ.
ekasya sarvabījasya yasya ceyam anekadhā;
bhokṛbhoktavyarūpeṇa bhogarūpeṇena ca sthitiḥ;
prāptyupāyo 'nukāraś ca tasya vedo maharṣibhiḥ;
eko 'py anekavartmeva samāmnātaḥ pṛthak pṛthak. (*VP* I.1- 5). The English translations from Bhartṛhari are by K.A. Subramanya Iyer, except the first and last quotations which were made by Florina Dobre-Brat, Ph.D. thesis.
8. *śabdasya pariṇāmo 'yam ity āmnāyavido viduḥ;*
chandobhya eva prathamam etad viśvaṁ vyavartate (*VP* I, 124), tr. K.A. Subramanya Iyer.
9. See *Maitrī Upaniṣad* 6.22. Bhartṛhari does not refer to the *śabda-brahman* as some commentators presume. See also N. Isayeva, *From Early Vedanta to Kashmir Shaivism: Gauḍapada, Bhartṛhari and Abhinavagupta*, Albany: State University of New York Press, 1997, p. 101.
10. *api prayoktur ātmānaṁ śabdam antaravasthitam;*
prāhur mahāntam ṛṣabhaṁ yena sāyujam iṣyate.
tasmād yaḥ śabdasaṁskāraḥ sā siddhiḥ paramātmanaḥ;
tasya pravṛttitattvajñās tad brahmāmṛtam aśnute (*VP* I.143-4).
11. *tad dvāram apavargasya vāṅmalānāṁ cikitsitam;*
pavitraṁ sarvavidyānām adhividyam prakāśate (*VP* I.14).
idam ādyam padasthānaṁ siddhisopānaparvaṇām;
iyaṁ sā mokṣamāṇānām ajihmā rājapaddhatiḥ (*VP* I.16).
12. See F. Dobre-Brat, 'Śabdasaṁskāra, a Mere Grammatical Technique?', in *Lucrarile Simpozionului International Cartea. Romania. Europa* (*Proceedings of the International Symposium 'The Book. Romania. Europe'*), Bucureşti: Biblioteca Bucureştilor, 2010, pp. 491-502.
13. K.A. Subramanya Iyer, *Bhartṛhari: A Study of the Vākyapadīya in the Light of the Ancient Commentaries*, Poona: Deccan College Postgraduate and Research Institute, 1969, p. 145.
14. J.E.M. Houben, *The Saṁbandha-Samuddeśa and Bhartṛhari's Philosophy of Language*, Groningen: Egbert Forsten, 1995, p. 281.
15. For a detailed description of these word stages, see the commentary to verse 159 of the *Brahmakāṇḍa*. The *paśyantī* stage is the stage where the sound and mental sequence of speech does not manifest itself although it is present. Unlike its commentary, the text itself does not mention the *parā* stage.

16. *paraṁ tu paśyantīrūpam anapabhraṁśaṁ asaṇkīrṇaṁ lokavyavahārātītam; tasyā eva vaco vyākaraṇena sādhutvajñānalabhyena vā śabdapūrvena yogenādhigamyata ityekeṣām āgamaḥ* (*VP*, I vṛtti 159).
17. See, for example, P. Barthwal, *Traditions of Indian Mysticism Based Upon the Nirguna School of Hindi Poetry*, New Delhi: Heritage, 1978, Preface, pp. xiii-xiv; H.P. Dvivedi, *Kabīr*, 2nd edn, Delhi: Rājkamal Prakāśan, 1980, pp. 28-9; M. Offredi, 'Kabīr and the Nāthpanth', in *Images of Kabir*, ed. M. Horstmann, Delhi: Manohar, 2002, p. 128; C. Vaudeville, *A Weaver Named Kabir: Selected Verses with a Detailed Biographical and Historical Introduction*, Delhi and Oxford: Oxford University Press, 1993, pp. 67-86; L.B. Hess and S. Singh, *The Bijak of Kabir*, 1st Indian edn, Delhi: Motilal Banarsidass, 1986, p. 143.
18. V. Dharwadkar, *Kabir: The Weaver's Songs*, Delhi and New York: Penguin Books, 2003.
19. W.J. Dwyer, *Bhakti in Kabir*, Patna: Associated Book Agency, 1981, pp. 57-119; Vaudeville, *A Weaver Named Kabir*, pp. 89-90.
20. Hess and Singh, *The Bijak of Kabir*, pp. 136-61; Vaudeville, *A Weaver Named Kabir*, pp. 102-3.
21. When discussing the philosophical tenets of Kabīr's world, there is a constant *ativyaptī* temptation which may do more harm than justice to the original idea behind the verses. In order to sustain the parallel proposed in this paper, the above two concepts seemed more appealing to Kabīr's poems than others also present in Bhartṛhari's thought. Although it might look a Procrustes bed, these concepts may act as indicatory signs of a reality that might be named in different ways.
22. The meaning of *pratibhā* in Bhartṛhari's work is threefold: (1) instinct or the structural pattern of each type of being and action, (2) intuitive knowledge, the spontaneous flash of understanding spoken of above, (3) meaning of a sentence.
23. 'Other two main allied senses are: (i) any kind of knowledge which is not sense-born nor of the nature of inference. But as such knowledge may range over a wide variety of subjects, it is possible to distinguish it again as lower and higher. The phenomena of ordinary clairvoyance and telepathy are instances of the former, while the latter is represented in the Supreme Wisdom of the Saint; (ii) In the latter sense, however, the use of the term is restricted to the *Āgamic* literature, where it stands for the Highest Divinity, understood as Principle of Intelligence and conceived as Female. In other words, *pratibhā*, otherwise known as *parā saṁvit* (or *citiśakti*) in the *Āgama*, especially in the *Tripurā* and *Trika* section, is the power of self-revelation or self-illumination of the Supreme Spirit which is essentially and eternally identical. The employment of the word in the meaning of "guru" (as in Abhinavagupta's *Tantrasāra*), comes under this second head.' G. Kaviraj, 'The Doctrine of Pratibhā in Indian Philosophy', *The Annals of the Bhandarkar Institute*, vol. 5, no. 1, 1923, pp. 1-2.

24. *so'vyatikīrṇāṁ vāgavasthām adhigamya vāgvikārāṇām prakṛtim pratibhām anuparaiti.tasmācca sattānuguṇyamātrāt pratibhākhyācchabdapūrvayogabhāvanābhyāsākṣepāt pratyastamitasarvavikārollekhamātraṁ parāṁ prakṛtiṁ pratipadyate.* (*VP*. I.14).
25. As the text indicates, Kabīr refers to *pramāṇa*, as proof the valid means of right knowledge 'certified' by Indian philosophies. See Vaudeville, *A Weaver Named Kabir*, p. 178. All translations of Kabīr's verses except the last two are by Vaudeville.
26. *parcā bina phūlā phire pakaḍi sabada kī chā̃hī* (*Sākhī* 19, 10b). If not indicated otherwise, Kabīr-texts are quoted from the *Kabīr granthāvalī* as published in W.M. Callewaert and B.O. d. Beeck, *Nirguṇ Bhakti Sāgar: Devotional Hindī Literature: A Critical Edition of the Pañc-Vāṇī or Five Works of Dādū, Kabīr, Nāmdev, Raidās, Hardās with the Hindī Songs of Gorakhnāth and Sundardās, and a Complete Word-index* vols. 1-2, Delhi: Manohar, 1991, vol. 1, pp. 281-343. The capitalization in the translation is by Vaudeville.
27. Vaudeville makes a thorough observation about *sākhī* when saying: 'Sākhī is not merely a literary genre, but a privileged form of expression, or rather the evocation of the highest truth', Vaudeville, *A Weaver Named Kabir*, p. 112.
28. Nevertheless, the sound quality of mystic *vāc* – *śabda* (*śruti*), which is communicated and heard by sages, and which all mystics, including Kabīr, identify eventually with silence, cannot be overlooked. This paper does not touch upon this aspect but it would represent a development of the present comparison.
29. *pārabrahma ke teja ka kaisā hai unamā̃na* (*Sākhī*, 9.2); *sab aṅdhiyārā miṭi gayā jaba dīpaka dekhā mā̃hī* (*Sākhī*, 9,1); or, *paidai moti bīṣare andhā nikasā āi; joti bināṁ jagdīsa kī jagada alandhai jāi* (*Sākhī* 18,3).
30. *hari hīrā jana jauharī lai lai mā̃ḍī hāṭī; jaba re milaigā pāriṣū taba hīrā kī sā̃ṭi* (*Sākhī*, 18,1); *thāpni pāi thiti bhai satguru dīnhi dhīra; kabīra hīrā banijiyā maṁnasarobara tīra* (*Sākhī*, 1.11).
31. Hess and Singh, *The Bijak of Kabir*, p. 49.
32. Ibid., p. 158.
33. Ibid., p. 73.

BIBLIOGRAPHY

Aklujkar, A., 'An Introduction to the Study of Bhartṛhari', in *Bhartṛhari Philosopher and Grammarian*, ed. S. Bhate and J. Bronkhorst, Delhi: Motilal Banarsidass, 1994, pp. 7-36.

Barthwal, P., *Traditions of Indian Mysticism Based upon the Nirguna School of Hindi Poetry*, Delhi: Heritage, 1978.

Bhartṛhari, *Vākyapadīya Containing the Ṭīka of Puṇyarāja and the Ancient Vṛtti*, ed. K.A. Subramanya Iyer, Delhi: Motilal Banarsidass, 1995.

——, *Vākyapadīya Bhartṛhari with the Vṛtti and the Paddhati of Vṛṣabhadeva*, ed. K.A. Subramanya Iyer, Poona: Deccan College Postgraduate and Research Institute, 1966.

Callewaert, W.M., and B.O. d. Beeck, *Nirguṇ Bhakti Sāgar: Devotional Hindī Literature: A Critical Edition of the Pañc-Vāṇī or Five Works of Dādū, Kabīr, Nāmdev, Raidās, Hardās with the Hindī Songs of Gorakhnāth and Sundardās, and a Complete Word-index*, vols. 1-2, *South Asian Studies*, no. 25, Delhi: Manohar, 1991.

Dharwadkar, V., *Kabir: The Weaver's Songs*, Delhi, New York: Penguin Books, 2003.

Dobre-Brat, F., 'Śabdasaṁskāra, a Mere Grammatical Technique?', in *Lucrarile Simpozionului International Cartea. Romania. Europa (Proceedings of the International Symposium 'The Book. Romania. Europe')*, Bucureşti: Biblioteca Bucureştilor, 2010, pp. 491-502.

Dvivedi, H.P., *Kabīr*, 2nd edn., Delhi: Rājkamal Prakāśan, 1980.

Dwyer, W.J., *Bhakti in Kabir*, Patna: Associated Book Agency, 1981.

Hess, L.B., and S. Singh, *The Bijak of Kabir*, 1st Indian edn., Delhi: Motilal Banarsidass, 1986.

Houben, J.E.M., *The Saṁbandha-Samuddeśa and Bhartṛhari's Philosophy of Language*, Groningen: Egbert Forsten, 1995.

Isayeva, N., *From Early Vedanta to Kashmir Shaivism: Gauḍapada, Bhartṛhari and Abhinavagupta, SUNY Series in Religious Studies*, Albany: State University of New York Press, 1997.

Kaviraj, G., 'The Doctrine of Pratibhā in Indian Philosophy', *The Annals of the Bhandarkar Institute,* vol. 5, no. 1, 1923, pp. 1-18.

Ṛksūktaśatī, Selected Hymns from the Ṛg Veda with Important Padapaṭha, ed. H.D. Velankar, Bombay: Bharatiya Vidya Bhavan, 1972.

Offredi, M., 'Kabīr and the Nāthpanth', in *Images of Kabir*, ed. M. Horstmann, Delhi: Manohar, 2002, pp. 127-41.

Rath, G., *Lingustic Philosophy in Vākyapadīya*, Delhi: Bharatiya Vidya Prakashan, 2000.

Rau, W., ed., *Bhartṛharis Vākyapadīya: Die mūlakārikās nach den Handschriften herausgegeben und mit einenm Pada-Index versehen, Abhandlungen für die Kunden des Morgenlandes*, Wiesbaden: Franz Steiner, 1977.

Subramanya Iyer, K.A., *Bhartṛhari, A Study of the Vākyapadīya in the Light of the Ancient Commentaries*, Poona: Deccan College Postgraduate and Research Institute, 1969.

Vaudeville, C., *A Weaver Named Kabir: Selected Verses with a Detailed Biographical and Historical Introduction*, French Studies in South Asian Culture and Society 6, Delhi and Oxford: Oxford University Press, 1993.

CHAPTER 11

From Ontology to Aesthetics: A Bengal Vaishnava Interpretation of the Upanishadic Passage *So'ham*[1]

KIYOKAZU OKITA

Introduction

The Upanishads contain two types of passages, the *abhedaśruti*s, which declare the oneness between Brahman and the *jīva* (the individual self), and the *bhedaśruti*s, which declare the difference between them. One of the greatest challenges to all the schools of Vedānta is to reconcile these seemingly contradictory statements and to establish a cohesive system of thought. The proponents of absolute monism (*kevalādvaita*) develop their system focusing on the *abhedaśruti*s such as *ahaṁ brahmāsmi* (I am Brahman) at the expense of the *bhedaśruti*s, whereas the proponents of Vaishnava Vedānta attempt to reconcile those *abhedaśruti*s with the *bhedaśruti*s in such a way that they will fit into their theistic scheme.

The Upanishadic passage *so'ham* (I am He) is one of the *abhedaśruti*s, which occurs in the *Chāndogyopaniṣad* (*ChāU*), the *Īśopaniṣad* (*ĪśaU*) and the *Gopālatāpanyupaniṣad* (*GoTāU*), and is widely used in post-Vedic traditions, such as Haṭha-yoga, Jainism and Nirguṇa bhakti. While other schools of Vedānta interpret this passage from an ontological perspective, Baladeva Vidyābhūṣaṇa, a Bengal Vaishnava Vedantist of the eighteenth century offers an aesthetic interpretation based on his examination of the *GoTāU* within his commentary on the *Brahmasūtra*s (*BraSū*) called the *Govindabhāṣya* (*GoBhā*).[2]

One of the contributions of Bengal Vaishnavism, which was inaugurated by Krishna Caitanya in the fifteenth century, to the history of Indian thought is that it developed a refined theory of devotional sentiment (*rasa*). According to the school, the highest bhakti is expressed in the cowherdesses' (*gopī*s') love for Krishna, which is portrayed in the *Bhāgavata Purāṇa* (*BhāPu*). In his commentary on *BraSū* 3.3.46, Baladeva applies this theory to the interpretation of the Upanishadic passage and says that it expresses the state of consciousness attained by the cowherdesses in their extreme emotional pain caused by separation from Krishna.

In this paper, I first discuss the interpretations of the Upanishadic passage offered by the schools of Advaita, Viśiṣṭādvaita and Dvaita Vedānta. Then I will examine Baladeva's interpretation of the passage based on his *GoBhā* 3.3.46 and argue that he offers a distinct solution to deal with the tension between the *bhedaśruti*s and the *abhedaśruti*s by shifting the focus of his discussion from ontology to devotional aesthetics.

Advaita, Viśiṣṭādvaita and Dvaita Interpretations

In this section, we examine different interpretations of the passage *so'ham* offered by Śaṅkara, Vedāntadeśika and Madhva. I limit myself to their commentaries on the *ĪśaU*, and point out that their interpretations mainly concern the ontological relationship between what is denoted by the term *saḥ* and what is denoted by the term *aham* in the passage.

In the *ĪśaU*, the passage occurs in verse 16:

> *pūṣann ekarṣe yama sūrya prājāpatya vyūha raśmīn samūha tejaḥ; yat te rūpaṁ kalyāṇatamaṁ tat te paśyāmi yo 'sāv asau puruṣaḥ so 'ham asmi.*
>
> (Śaṅkara 2000: 11)

The verse belongs to the final four verses (15-18) of the Upanishad, which comprise a prayer to the one who nourishes (*pūṣan*). Although the passage is not as famous as other 'great statements (*mahāvākya*)' such as *aham brahmāsmi*, Śaṅkara and other Advaitins cite the passage to prove the ontological oneness of Brahman and the *jīva*. According to Śaṅkara, the last four verses of the *ĪśaU* comprise the prayer of a person to the deity in the sun at the time of his death and he thereby becomes the deity himself. Śaṅkara adds that the deity to whom the prayer is offered is lower Brahman (*aparabrahman*).[3] The first *pāda* of verse 16 is a series of vocatives addressing the deity in the sun. Śaṅkara identifies the deity as the nourisher, the lone traveller, the controller, the sun, and the son of Prajāpati.[4] Then he gives the following explanation on the fourth *pāda, yo 'sāv asau puruṣaḥ so 'ham asmi*, which includes the phrase *so 'ham*:

> *yaḥ asau*, the Person who is there, in the solar orb [. .], and who is called a Person (*Puruṣa*) because he has the figure of a person: [. . .] *saḥ aham asmi*, that Person am I.[5]

Śaṅkara gives 'I become (*bhavāmi*)' as a gloss of *asmi*. It is clear that, according to him, the passage suggests the oneness of the person offering the prayer with lower Brahman, who is the object of the prayer.

Vedāntadeśika was the first one to write a full commentary on the *ĪśaU* from the perspective of Viśiṣṭādvaita Vedānta. In contrast to Śaṅkara who says that the person who is the object of the prayer is lower Brahman, Vedāntadeśika says that the person is the supreme self (*paramātman*).[6] Commenting on the fourth *pāda* of verse 16, Vedāntadeśika first says that the repetition of *asau* expresses great respect.[7] Śaṅkara did not offer any interpretation on this point. Then Vedāntadeśika explains that *puruṣa* in the fourth *pāda* indicates the supreme person (i.e. Vishnu), '*Puruṣa* (indicates) the great person, who has qualities such as completeness and being the old existence, who has a special body with the colour of the sun, who is famous in the *Puruṣasūkta* and so on, which are dedicated to none other than He who is mentioned in all the Vedas (i.e. Vishnu)'.[8]

Then Vedāntadeśika explains that the word *aham* in the *pāda* indicates the supreme self within (*paramātman*) and does not refer to the individual self (*jīva*),

[The verse says] *so 'ham asmi*. Through the individual self [*jīva*], the word 'I [*aham*]' here indicates the inner self [i.e. *paramātman*]. Precisely because of this, the first person copula 'am [*asmi*]' also refers to the supreme self [*paramātman*], who is characterized by the individual self, [the individual self] who has a separate nature. For, exactly this is taught [by Pāṇini as] *asmady uttamaḥ*. When the word 'I' indicates the Supreme Self through the individual self, still [the use of] the first person copula does not cease.[9]

According to Vedāntadeśika, 'I' (*aham*) indicates the Supreme Self who is distinct from the individual self. If that is the case, it may be asked why the first person copula 'am' (*asmi*) is used. In other words, the third person copula 'is' (*asti*) may be more appropriate if 'I' actually denotes the third person, the Supreme Self. To answer the question, Vedāntadeśika refers to the *Aṣṭādhyāyī* 1.4.107: *asmady uttamaḥ*. This rule teaches that when the first person pronoun *asmad*, which is the root form of *aham*, is used, the verb must have the first person ending (*uttama*). In conclusion, according to Vedāntadeśika, the fourth *pāda* '*yo 'sāv asau puruṣaḥ so 'ham asmi*' means that venerable *puruṣa* (Vishnu), who is mentioned in the *Puruṣasūkta* and so on, is identical with the supreme self (*paramātman*) within.

Madhva offers yet another interpretation. He comments on the first and fourth *pāda*s of verse 16 (*pūṣann ekarṣe yama sūrya prājāpatya [...] yo 'sāv asau puruṣaḥ so 'ham asmi*) as follows:

Since he has the most excellent knowledge, Vishnu is known as *Ekarṣi*. Hari is (known as) *Yama* because he is the controller. (He is known as) *Sūrya* because he is accessible to the learned people. (He is known as) *Prājāpatya* because he is especially accessible to *Prajāpati*. And He (is known as) *Aham* because he cannot be rejected.[10] (He is known as) *Asmi*, abiding in all the *jīva*s, because he is proud of his eternal existence. But supreme Hari Himself is separate from all the *jīva*s.[11]

Here, Madhva is explaining the verse in the way of *nirukta*, that is, a word packed with semantic meanings based on phonetic similarity.[12] Vishnu is called *Yama* because he controls (*niyamanāt*). He is called *Sūrya* because he is accessible to the learned people (*sūrigamyatvāt*). He applies the same method in interpreting the phrase *so 'ham asmi*. Instead of explaining *aham* as the first person pronoun and *asmi* as a copula, Madhva says that they are both secret names of Vishnu. According to him, Vishnu is called *Aham* because he cannot be rejected (*aheyatas*) and *Asmi* because he is proud of his eternal existence (*nityāstitamānāt*).

According to Madhva, therefore, the words *aham* and *asmi* in the phrase *so 'ham asmi* have nothing to do with the individual self. Furthermore, explaining the repetition of *asau* which occurs in *yo 'sāv asau puruṣaḥ* of the fourth *pāda*, he says that one of them is a locative of *asu*, which means the life air (*prāṇa*).[13] The entire fourth *pāda* would then mean that the person in the life air is Vishnu, who cannot be rejected and who is conscious of his own eternal existence.

So 'ham in the *Gopālatāpanyupaniṣad*

So far we have examined different interpretations of the phrase *so 'ham* offered by three prominent Vedantists. Although their interpretations differ from each other, they have one thing in common. All of them understand the phrase *so 'ham* to be a sentence which suggests some kind of ontological oneness between two entities that are denoted by the words *saḥ* and *aham*, respectively.

In contrast to the three Vedantists discussed above, Baladeva Vidyābhūṣaṇa, a Gauḍīya Vaishnava Vedantist in the eighteenth century, suggests that the phrase *so 'ham* is an emotional expression of a lover to her beloved, which occurs as a result of the extreme pain of separation from each other. According to Gauḍīya theologians such as Rūpa Gosvāmī, this feeling of separation is the highest devotional sentiment (*rasa*) which a devotee can experience toward God. Thus, bringing the theory of *rasa* into the realm of Vedānta, Baladeva explains the phrase from the perspective of devotional aesthetics.

Baladeva's unique interpretation of the phrase *so 'ham* is found in his *GoBhā*. Instead of commenting on the *ĪśaU*, however, he discusses the same phrase in the *GoTāU*. The Upanishad is divided into two sections, *pūrva* and the *uttara*. The *uttara* section starts with a conversation between a lady of Braj called Gandharvī and Durvāsas. Gandharvī, who is Rādhā according to the Gauḍīya commentators, asks about Krishna's birth, his *mantra*, his abode, and the method of worship. In reply, Durvāsas refers to a conversation between Brahmā and Nārāyaṇa. In the conversation quoted by Durvāsas, Brahmā asks Nārāyaṇa the following questions: Which incarnation is the best? By whom are people satisfied? Remembering whom do they become liberated from the circle of birth and death? How can such an incarnation be Brahman?[14] In reply, Nārāyaṇa answers that Krishna, accompanied by Balarāma, Pradyumna, Aniruddha and Rukmiṇī, is the supreme ruler.[15] Then he explains a meditation by which one obtains Brahman. This is where we come across the phrase *so 'ham* in the *GoTāU*:

> [. .] after having a determinate cognition 'I am He' (*so 'ham*), he should contemplate oneself with the thought 'I am Gopāla'. He obtains liberation. He realizes the state of being Brahman. He becomes the knower of Brahman.[16]

After explaining how to achieve liberation, Nārāyaṇa says that the supreme Brahman is Krishna, who is identical with him.[17] Then he explains Gopāla's oneness with *auṁ* and gives a detailed description of his appearance.

Baladeva's Interpretation

Baladeva discusses the *GoTāU* in his *GoBhā* 3.3.46, and explains that the phrase *so 'ham* expresses a type of bhakti. At the beginning of his commentary on *BraSū* 3.3.46, Baladeva raises a question about the phrase *so 'ham*, which occurs in the *GoTāU*. As we saw above, the Upanishad teaches that to obtain liberation, one should meditate on phrases such as 'I am He' (*so 'ham*), 'I am Gopāla' (*gopālo 'ham*). The question here is whether or not these phrases teach the oneness of Brahman and the *jīva*. The *prima facie* view says that these phrases indeed teach such oneness, because of the naturalness of the words.[18]

Baladeva then brings in the conclusive view (*siddhānta*), rejecting the *prima facie* view. According to him, *sūtra* 3.3.46 (*pūrvavikalpaḥ prakaraṇāt syāt kriyāmānasavat*) teaches that the phrase *so 'ham* is a particular type of devotional meditation, and it does not teach the ontological oneness of Brahman and the *jīva*. The formulation of this *sūtra* is according to inference (*anumāna*) taught in the Nyāya school. In *BraSū* 3.3.46, *pūrvavikalpa* is the first step, the proposition to be established (*pratijñā*). According to Baladeva, the proposition is that the meditation *so 'ham* is an optional type of devotion previously taught in the *GoTāU*. Then the phrase *prakaraṇāt* expresses the second step, the reason for the proposition (*hetu*). Baladeva explains that the meditation *so 'ham* is a type of devotion because of the context of the *GoTāU* in which the phrase appears. In his *GoBhā,* Baladeva examines this context of the Upanishad by applying the method of the sixfold criteria (*tātparyaliṅga*), which is an exegetical tool employed by Vedantists to determine the meaning of texts. We shall come back to this point later. Finally, *kriyāmānasavat* expresses the third step, giving two examples (*udāharaṇa/dṛṣṭānta*). According to Baladeva, action and mental activities are given as examples of devotion. Just as they are types of devotion, so is the meditation *so 'ham*.

It is, however, not immediately clear in what sense the meditation *so 'ham* can be a kind of devotion. Therefore, Baladeva explains that extreme emotional absorption in an object causes a cognitive identification between the subject and the object. He writes, 'When there is excessive absorption from passion and fear, the feeling "I am He" arises. [From passion to Krishna arises the feeling] "I am Krishna" and [from fear of a lion arises the feeling] "I am a lion".'[19] The emotional identification 'I am Krishna', which Baladeva gives as an example, alludes to the *gopīs*' identification with Krishna out of their extreme attachment to him. Such an instance is seen in *BhāPu* 10.30. After the *rāsa* dance described in the *BhāPu* 10.29, Krishna suddenly disappears since the *gopīs* have become proud of their close contact with him during the dance. The *gopī*s' search for Krishna is described in the 30th chapter. Being unable to find him and unable to bear their separation from him, they start imitating the pastimes of Krishna:

> With their minds overcome by [His] gait, lustful smile, coquettish glance, mind-captivating speech, sport and restlessness, [those] maddened [*gopī*s], being devoted to Him, performed various pastimes of the Lord of Lakṣmī [i.e. Krishna].[20]

The expression 'I am Krishna (*kṛṣṇo 'ham*)' occurs in *BhāPu* 10.30.19: 'Another [*gopī*], with [her] mind intent on Him [i.e. on Krishna], placing her arms on another [*gopī*] and walking, said, "I am Krishna. Behold [my] lovely gait!"'[21] According to the Gauḍīya tradition, this emotional absorption in Krishna as a result of one's separation from him is called *vipralambha rasa*. This sentiment is considered the highest expression of devotion to god. According to *BhaRaASi* 3.1-5 of Rūpa Gosvāmī, there are five primary devotional sentiments (*rasa*) which devotees can engage with in relation to Krishna. These are peacefulness (*śānta*), servitude (*dāsya*), friendship (*sākhya*), parental love (*vātsalya*) and erotic love (*mādhurya*). The last one among these five is considered the highest and most intimate relation between a devotee and Krishna. In *Ujjvalanīlamaṇi* 15.1, Rūpa further explains that the relation of erotic love consists of separation (*vipralambha*) and contact (*saṃbhoga*).[22] Jīva Gosvāmī, a nephew of Rūpa, then explains in his *Prītisandarbha Anuccheda* 370 that separation is higher than contact because a devotee becomes more conscious of Krishna when there is separation.[23] According to Baladeva, therefore, the *so 'ham* meditation is a particular type of devotion because it is a mental state in which a devotee cognitively identifies herself with Krishna as a result of her extreme emotional absorption in him.

As shown above, Baladeva says that the *so 'ham* meditation is an optional type of devotion. The reason given for such an inference is *prakaraṇāt*, which, according to him, means 'because of the context of the GoTāU'. Baladeva's point is that the phrase *so 'ham* is a type of devotion, and it does not indicate the ontological oneness between the *jīva* and Brahman because the whole point of the *GoTāU* is devotion to Krishna. To explain that the *GoTāU* teaches devotion, Baladeva employs the six criteria of determining the content of a text. His predecessors such as Śaṅkara, Rāmānuja, Madhva and Jīva also employ this particular exegetical method.[24] For example, Jīva in his *Paramātmasandarbha Anuccheda* 105 mentions these six signs: 'The (1) opening and concluding sentences [*upakrama* and *upasaṁhāra*], (2) repetition [*abhyāsa*], (3) unprecedentedness [*apūrva*], (4) fruit [*phala*], (5) praise [*arthavāda*], (6) reasoning [*upapatti*] are the signs in determining a purport [of a text].'[25]

Baladeva selects different passages from the *GoTāU* which fulfil the sixfold criteria:

(1) The opening and concluding sentences	*GoTāU* 1.14, 2.63
(2) Repetition	*GoTāU* 2.17
(3) Unprecedentedness (4) reasoning	*GoTāU* 1.2, 1.3, 1.6, 1.7, 1.11, 1.14
(5) Fruit	*GoTāU* 1.5, 1.23
(6) Praise	*GoTāU* 1.33

For the opening and closing sentences, Baladeva chooses *GoTāU* 1.14 and 2.63 which say:

> Devotion means to worship him [i.e. Krishna]. It [the worship of Krishna] means to fix [one's] mind on that [i.e. Krishna] by not expecting [any] condition in this life and next. And exactly this is the state of being without [any] action.[26]
>
> [Glorious Krishna] exists in loving devotion whose sole essence is existence, consciousness, and bliss.[27]

Both sentences point towards devotion to Krishna.

Then Baladeva cites a part of the conversation between the sages and Brahmā. In *GoTāU* 1.2, the sages ask, 'Who is the highest God?'[28] and in *GoTāU* 1.3, Brahmā answers, 'Glorious Krishna is indeed the highest God.'[29] Baladeva further quotes another set of questions and answers between the sages and Brahmā. In *GoTāU* 1.6 the sages ask three questions, 'What is his form (*rūpa*)? What is taste (*rasa*)? How do we worship (*bhajana*) him? Tell [us] who want to know all these.'[30] To the first question, Brahmā answers in *GoTāU* 1.7, '[Krishna] is dressed as a cowherd, having the colour of rain clouds. He is a fresh youth and sitting under a wish-fulfilling tree.'[31] The answer to the second question is given in *GoTāU* 1.11: 'Furthermore, the flavour is palatable.'[32] The answer to the last question is given in *GoTāU* 1.14: 'Worship is devotion to Him [i.e. Krishna].'[33] I suggest that these two sets of conversations between the sages and Brahmā fulfil two criteria, unprecedentedness and reasoning. These conversations fulfil the criteria of unprecedentedness because knowledge concerning Krishna is a revelation through Brahmā and was not known before. They fulfil the criteria of reasoning because Brahmā's answer explains why worship means devotion to Krishna. It is so because Krishna is the highest God.

Between his citations of these two sets of conversations, Baladeva cites *GoTāU* 1.5, 'He who meditates, praises and serves this [supreme reality called Krishna] becomes immortal.'[34] This sentence fulfils the criteria for fruit since it shows the result of devotion to Krishna. Baladeva also cites *GoTāU* 1.23:

> He [i.e. Krishna] would show the nature of the Self to those who mutter the incantation, which is covered by the letter *oṁ*, the incantation consisting of five words. Therefore those who desire liberation should repeat this incantation for the sake of eternal peace.[35]

The incantation covered by the syllable *oṁ* refers to the Gopāla-Krishna *mantra*, *auṁ klī̃ kr̥ṣṇāya govindāya gopījanavallabhāya svāhā auṁ*. The passage shows that chanting this prayer to Krishna results in liberation.

Baladeva does not specify which phrase he is citing for fulfilling the criteria of praise. *GoTāU* 1.33 is one of the sentences which he quotes without any specification with regard to the six criteria. This is the one, which seems to be closest to the criteria of praise:

> By the best praise, I, together with the group of the *Marut*s, always appease that Govinda only, whose form is existence, consciousness, and bliss, who is consisting of five words, who sits at the base of wish-fulfilling trees in Vrindavan.[36]

This is the first in the series of prayers that Brahmā offers to Krishna towards the end of the *pūrva* section of the *GoTāU*. The fact that he praises Krishna shows the importance of devotion to the latter.

At this stage, the only criterion left to be fulfilled is repetition. For this, Baladeva cites *GoTāU* 2.17:

He [i.e. the sage Durvāsas] said to her [i.e. Gāndharvikā Rādhā]: Formerly [there existed] only divine Nārāyaṇa, in whom the worlds are both interwoven and fixed. The lotus-born one [i.e. Brahmā] was born from his [i.e. Nārāyaṇa's] lotus-like heart. After performing austerity, [Nārāyaṇa] indeed granted a boon for him [i.e. Brahmā]. He [i.e. Brahmā] did choose [a boon] to ask questions as he desires. [Nārāyaṇa] granted that [boon] for him [i.e. Brahmā].[37]

This is the beginning of Duruvāsas' reply to Gāndharvikā's questions regarding Krishna's nature, on how to worship him, etc., expressed in *GoTāU* 2.16.[38] To answer the questions asked by Gāndharvikā, Durvāsas refers to the conversation between Brahmā and Nārāyaṇa, which was on the same topic. Baladeva points out that this is a sign of repetition. In other words, the fact that Brahmā asked the same questions earlier indicates the significance of the knowledge of Krishna and devotion to him. After citing the passages from the *GoTāU* and explaining how they fulfil the sixfold criteria, Baladeva concludes that the phrase *so 'ham*, which occurs in the *GoTāU*, teaches a type of devotion.[39]

Conclusion

In this paper, we have examined four different interpretations of an Upanishadic passage, *so 'ham*, offered by Śaṅkara, Vedāntadeśika, Madhva, and Baladeva. While Śaṅkara suggests that the passage indicates the ontological oneness of Brahman and the *jīva*, Vaishnava Vedantists such as Vedāntadeśika and Madhva reject such a monistic interpretation and offer alternative interpretations. As a Vaishnava Vedantist, Baladeva also rejects the Advaitic interpretation. However, while his Vaishnava predecessors offered ontological interpretations of the passage, Baladeva takes an entirely new approach based on the Gauḍīya aesthetic theory of *rasa*.

In his commentary on *BraSū* 3.3.46, he first interprets the *sūtra* according to the model of an inference articulated by the

Nyāyasūtras of Gautama. According to Baladeva, the passage *so 'ham* is a type of devotion because of the context of the *GoTāU*. Alluding to the state of the *gopīs* described in the tenth book of the *BhāPu*, Baladeva explains that extreme attachment to Krishna can create a mental state where a devotee identifies herself with him, thinking 'I am Krishna'. Then, in his explanation of the second step of the inference, Baladeva skilfully applies the six criteria of textual interpretation to the *GoTāU*. By this method, he shows that the context of the Upanishad in which the phrase *so 'ham* occurs does not teach the ontological oneness of Brahman and the *jīva* but devotion to Krishna instead.

NOTES

1. A previous version of this paper was presented at the Fourteenth World Sanskrit Conference (Kyoto University, Japan, September 2010). I would like to thank Dr. Imre Bangha, Prof. John Cort, Prof. Jack Hawley, Prof. Monika Horstmann and Prof. Harunaga Isaacson for their comments.
2. Baladeva Vidyābhūṣaṇa, *Vedāntasūtram śrīgovindabhāṣyeṇa sūkṣmāṭīkayā ca sametam*, Calcutta: Śrī Sārasvata Gauḍīyāsana Mission, 1968.
3. *tatra niṣekādiśmaśānāntaṁ karma kurvan jijīviṣedyo vidyayā sahāparabrahmaviṣayayā taduktaṁ 'vidyāṁ cāvidyāṁ ca yas tad vedobhayaṁ saha; avidyayā mṛtyuṁ tīrtvā vidyayāmṛtam aśnute' [...] brahmopāsīno yathoktakarmakṛc ca yaḥ so 'ntakāle prāpte satyātmānam ātmanaḥ prāptidvāraṁ yācate 'hiraṇmayena pātrena'.* (Śaṅkara, *Ten Principal Upanishads with Śāṅkarabhāṣya*, vol. I, Delhi: Motilal Banarsidass, 2000, p. 11).
4. *he pūṣan! jagataḥ poṣaṇāt pūṣā; ravis tathaika eva ṛṣati gacchati ity ekarṣiḥ he ekarṣe! tathā sarvasya saṁyamanād yamaḥ he yama! tathā raśmīnāṁ prāṇānāṁ rasānāñ ca svīkaraṇāt sūryaḥ he sūrya! prajāpater apatyaṁ prājāpatyaḥ he prājāpatya!* (ibid.).
5. The translation is from *Eight Upanishads*, tr. Gambhirananda, Calcutta: Advaita Ashrama, 1972, pp. 27-8. The original reads: *[...] yo 'sāv ādityamaṇḍalastho vyāhṛtyavayavaḥ puruṣaḥ puruṣākāratvāt pūrṇaṁ vānena prāṇabuddhayātmanā jagatsamastam iti puruṣaḥ puri śayanād vā puruṣaḥ so 'ham asmi bhavāmi*; *Ten Principal Upanishads with Śāṅkarabhāṣya*, p. 12.
6. *atha evaṁ phalaparyantasāṅgabrahmavidyāniṣṭhasyānusandheyā mantrā upadiśyante; teṣu ca pūṣādiśabdāḥ sarvaśabdavācyaṁ paramātmānam anusandadhatām [...]. Vedāntadeśika, Śrīmad Vedāntadeśikaviracitam Īśāvāsyopaniṣadbhāṣyam*, ed. Uttamur Viraraghavacharya, Chennai: Shri Uttamur Viraraghavachariar Centenary Trust, 2004, p. 153.

7. *vīpsā atyādaravyañjanārthā* (*Īśāvāsyopaniṣadbhāṣyam*, p. 157).
8. *puruṣaḥ pūrṇatvapūrvasattvādiguṇakaḥ ādityavarṇavigrahaviśiṣṭaḥ sarvavedapaṭhitānanyaparapuruṣasūktādiprasiddho mahāpuruṣaḥ* (*Īśāvāsyopaniṣadbhāṣyam*, pp. 157, 185). All the translations in this paper are mine unless otherwise stated.
9. *so 'ham asmi; ahaṁśabdo 'tra jīvadvārā tadantarātmaparyantaḥ; ata evāsmīty api pratyagrūpasvaviśiṣṭe paramātmani viśrāmyati; 'asmady uttamaḥ' ity etāvad eva hy anuśiṣṭam; na punar asmacchabdasya pratyagātmadvārā paramātmaparyantatāyām uttamanivṛttiḥ* (*Īśāvāsyopaniṣadbhāṣyam*, pp. 185-6).
10. Mesquita construes *prājāpatyaḥ* with *prajāpateḥ*, *ahaṁ* with *viśeṣenaiva gamyatvād*, and *asau* with *aheyataḥ* in his translation: 'Er ist Prajāpatya, weil er Herr über die Völker ist. Und er ist "ich", weil er in besonderer Weise zu erkennen ist. Er ist "dieser", weil er [in seinem Wesen absolut uneingeschränk bzw.] unaufhebbar ist'; R. Mesquita, *Madhvas Zitate aus den Purāṇas und dem Mahhābhārata: Eine analytische Zusammenstellung nicht identifizierbarer Quellenzitate in Madhvas Werken nebst Ubersetzung und Anmerkungen*, Wien: Institut für Südasien-, Tibet- und Buddhismuskunde der Universität Wien, 2007, p. 328. However, *ahaṁ cāsāv aheyataḥ* must be construed together. *Aheyataḥ* is the reason why Brahman is called *ahaṁ*. This is evident since commenting on the phrase *ahaṁ brahmāsmi*, which occurs in *BṛĀU* 1.4.10, Madhva says *ahaṁ aheyaṁ brahma paripūrnam; asmi sarvadāstīti meyam [. . .]*; Madhva, *Śrīmad-Ānandatīrthabhagavatpāda-praṇīta sarvamūlagranthāḥ tṛtīyaṃ sampuṭam daśopaniṣadbhāṣyāṇi*, Bangalore: Śrī Vyāsa Madhwa Sevā Pratiṣṭhāna, 1999, p. 552. Therefore *asau* here is not another name of Brahman as Mesquita understands it but must be understood as a pronoun referring to Vishnu.
11. *pradhānajñānarūpataḥ viṣṇur ekarṣir jñeyo yamo niyamanād dhariḥ; sūryaḥ sa sūrigaymatvāt prājāpatyaḥ prajāpateḥ; viśeṣenaiva gamyatvād ahaṁ cāsāv aheyataḥ; asmi nityāsitāmānāt sarvajīveṣū saṁsthitaḥ; svayaṁ tu sarvajīvebhyoḥ vyatiriktaḥ paro hariḥ* (Madhva, *Daśopaniṣadbhāṣyāṇi*, p. 10.)
12. This explanation is Prof. H. Isaacson's given in his class (30 June 2009).
13. *eko 'sauśandaḥ prāṇe sthita iti* (Madhva, *Daśopaniṣadbhāṣyāṇi*, p. 10).
14. *yo 'vatārāṇāṁ madhye śreṣṭho 'vatāraḥ ko bhavati; yena lokās tuṣṭā devās tuṣṭā bhavanti; yaṁ smṛtvā muktā asmāt saṁsārād bhavanti; kathaṁ vāsyāvatārasya brahmatā bhavati*; *GoTāU* 2.18; *The Vaiṣṇava Upaniṣads with the Commentary of Śrī Upaniṣad Brahmayogin*, ed. A.M. Shastri, Chennai: Adyar Library and Research Centre, 2005, p. 67.
15. *yatrāsau saṁsthitaḥ kṛṣṇas tribhiḥ śaktyā samāhitaḥ; rāmāniruddhapradyumnai rukmiṇyā sahito vibhuḥ.* (*GoTāU* 2.28; *The Vaiṣṇava Upaniṣads*, p. 71.)

16. *tasmād eva paro rajaseti so 'ham ity avadhāryātmānaṁ gopālo 'ham iti bhāvayet. sa mokṣam aśnute; sa brahmatvam adhigacchati; sa brahmavid bhavati.* (*GoTāU* 2.30; *The Vaiṣṇava Upaniṣads*, p. 72.)
17. *paraṁ brahma kṛṣṇātmako nityānandaikarūpaḥ so 'ham.* (*GoTāU* 2.30; *The Vaiṣṇava Upaniṣads*, p. 72.)
18. *śabdasvārasyāt*; Baladeva Vidyābhūṣaṇa, *Vedāntasūtram*, p. 491.
19. *rāgād bhayāc ca gāḍhāveśe sati so 'ham iti bhāvo 'bhyudeti; kṛṣṇo 'ham iti siṁho 'ham iti ca*; Ibid., p. 492. It is difficult to see why the identification 'I am a lion' occurs from fear of a lion. A possible interpretation is that fear arises from the perception of duality between the subject and the object (See *BṛĀU* 1.4.2: *dvitīyād vai bhayaṁ bhavati.*). Therefore, fear can be overcome by identifying oneself with the object of fear. Prof. H. Isaacson suggests that *siṁha* in this context may refer to Narasiṁha, the man-lion incarnation of Vishnu.
20. *gatyānurāgasmitavibhramekṣitair manoramālāpavihāravibhramaiḥ; ākṣiptacittāḥ pramadā ramāpates tās tā viceṣṭā jagṛhus tadātmikāḥ* (*BhāPu* 10.30.2.; *Bhāgavata Purāṇa of Kṛṣṇa Dvaipāyana Vyāsa with Sanskrit Commentary Bhāvārthabodhinī of Śrīdhara Svāmin*, ed. J.L. Shastri, Delhi: Motilal Banarsidass, 1983, p. 494).
21. *kasyāñcit svabhujaṁ nyasya calanty āhāparā nanu; kṛṣṇo 'haṁ paśyata gatiṁ lalitām iti tanmanāḥ*; *Bhāgavata Purāṇa*, p. 494. I thank Prof. J.S. Hawley for pointing out this verse to me.
22. *atha śṛṅgārabhedaprakaraṇam; sa vipralambhaḥ sambhoga iti dvedhojjvalo mataḥ*; Rūpa Gosvāmī, *Ujjvalanīlamaṇiḥ Śrīmaj-Jīva-Gosvāmī-viracitayā Locanarocany-ākhyayā, Śrīmad-Viśvanāthacakravarti-viracitayā Ānanda-candrikā-vyākhyayā ca bhāsitaḥ*, Delhi: Chaukhamba Sanskrit Pratishthan, 1985, p. 506.
23. Jīva cites *BhāPu* 10.33.20, 10.47.34-35 as evidence.
24. The verse is quoted in Jīva's *Paramātmasandarbha Anuccheda* 105, *GoBhā* 1.1.3, Vijñānabhikṣu's *BraSū* commentary, the *Vijñānamṛtabhāṣya*, Rāghava Bhaṭṭa's *Śāradātilakatantra* and also in van Buitenen, *Rāmānuja's Vedārthasaṁgraha*, Poona: Deccan College, 1956, p. 200, n. 134. Madhva in his *Pramāṇalakṣaṇa* has the following passage: *upakramopasaṁhāra tadaikarūpābhyāsāpūrvatā phalārthavāda upapattiviśeṣāḥ*; Madhva, *Śrīmad-Ānandatīrthabhagavatpāda-praṇīta Sarvamūlagranthāḥ Saptamaṃ Sampuṭam Prakaraṇagranthā, Saṅkīrṇagranthā*, Bangalore: Śrī Vyāsa Madhwa Sevā Pratiṣṭhāna, 1999, p. 5.
25. *upakramopasaṁhārāv abhyāso 'pūrvatā phalam; arthavādopapattī ca liṅgaṁ tātparyanirṇaye*; Jīva Gosvāmī, *Śrī-paramātmasandarbha*, tr. H. Shastri, Vrindavana: Gadadharagaurahari Press, 1986, p. 291.
26. *bhaktir asya bhajanam; tad ihāmutropādhinairāśyenāmuṣmin manaḥkalpanam; etad eva ca naiṣkarmyam*; Pandit Mahadeva Shastri, *The Vaiṣṇava Upaniṣads with the Commentary of Śrī Upaniṣad Brahmayogin*, p. 47.

27. *saccidānandaikarase bhaktiyoge tiṣṭhati*; ibid., p. 78.
28. *kaḥ paramo devaḥ?*; ibid., p. 43.
29. *śrīkṛṣṇo vai paramaṁ daivatam*; ibid., p. 43.
30. *kiṁ tadrūpam; kiṁ rasanam; kathaṁ vāho tadbhajanam; tatsarvaṁ vividiṣatām ākhyāhīti*; ibid., p. 45.
31. *gopaveṣam abhrābhaṁ taruṇaṁ kalpadrumāśritam*; ibid., p. 45.
32. *rasyaṁ punā rasanam*; ibid., p. 46.
33. *bhaktir asya bhajanam*; ibid., p. 47.
34. *etad yo dhyāyati rasati bhajati so 'mṛto bhavatīti*; ibid., p. 44.
35. *oṁkāreṇāntaritaṁ ye japanti govindasya pañcapadaṁ manum; teṣām asau darśayed ātmarūpaṁ tasmān mumukṣur abhyasen nityaśāntyai*; ibid., p. 50.
36. *tam ekaṁ govindaṁ saccidānandavigrahaṁ pañcapadaṁ vṛndāvana-surabhūruhatalāsīnaṁ satataṁ samarudgaṇo 'haṁ paramayā stutyā toṣayāmi*; ibid., p. 58.
37. *sa hovāca tāṁ ha vai; eko ha vai pūrvaṁ nārāyaṇo devaḥ yasmin lokā otāś ca protāś ca; tasya hṛtpadmāj jāto 'bjayonis; tapitvā tasmai hi varaṁ dadau; sa kāmapraśnam eva vavre; taṁ hāsmai dadau*; ibid., p. 67.
38. *sā hovāca gāndharvī kathaṁ vāsmāsu jāto 'sau gopālaḥ; kathaṁ vā jñāto 'sau tvayā mune kṛṣṇaḥ; ko vāsya mantraḥ; kiṁ vāsya sthānaṁ; kathaṁ vā devakyāṁ jātaḥ; ko vāsya jyāyān rāmo bhavati; kīdṛśī pūjāsya gopālasya bhavati; sākṣāt prakṛtiparo yo 'yam ātmā gopālaḥ kathaṁ tv avatīrṇo bhūmyāṁ hi vai*; ibid., p. 67.
39. *sa coktahetor bhakter eva pūrvopadiṣṭāyāḥ prakārabhedo bhavituṁ yuktaḥ*; Baladeva Vidyābhūṣaṇa, *Vedāntasūtram*, p. 493.

BIBLIOGRAPHY

Baladeva Vidyābhūṣaṇa, *Vedāntasūtram śrīgovindabhāṣyeṇa sūkṣmāṭīkayā ca sametam*, Calcutta: Śrī Sārasvata Gauḍīyāsana Mission, 1968.

Bhāgavata Purāṇa of Kṛṣṇa Dvaipāyana Vyāsa with Sanskrit Commentary Bhāvārthabodhinī of Śrīdhara Svāmin, ed. J.L. Shastri, Delhi: Motilal Banarsidass, 1983.

Eight Upanishads, tr. Gambhirananda, Calcutta: Advaita Ashrama, 1972.

Jīva Gosvāmī, *Śrī-paramātmasandarbha*, tr. H.H. Shastri, Vrindavana: Gadadharagaurahari Press, 1986.

Madhva, *Śrīmad-Ānandatīrthabhagavatpāda-praṇīta Sarvamūlagranthāḥ Saptamaṁ Sampuṭam Prakaraṇagranthā, Saṅkīrṇagranthā*, Bangalore: Śrī Vyāsa Madhwa Sevā Pratiṣṭhāna, 1999.

——, *Śrīmad-Ānandatīrthabhagavatpāda-praṇīta sarvamūlagranthāḥ tṛtīyaṁ sampuṭam daśopaniṣadbhāṣyāṇi*, Bangalore: Śrī Vyāsa Madhwa Sevā Pratiṣṭhāna, 1999.

Mesquita, R., *Madhvas Zitate aus den Purāṇas und dem Mahhābhārata: Eine analytische Zusammenstellung nicht identifizierbarer Quellenzitate in*

Madhvas Werken nebst Ubersetzung und Anmerkungen, Wien: Institut für Südasien-, Tibet- und Buddhismuskunde der Universität Wien, 2007.

Rūpa Gosvāmī, *Ujjvalanīlamaṇiḥ Śrīmaj-Jīva-Gosvāmī-viracitayā Locana-rocany-ākhyayā, Śrīmad-Viśvanāthacakravarti-viracitayā Ānandacand-rikā-vyākhyayā ca bhāsitaḥ*, Delhi: Chaukhamba Sanskrit Pratishthan, 1985.

Śaṅkara, *Ten Principal Upanishads with Śāṅkarabhāṣya, Works of Śaṅkarācārya in Original Sanskrit*, vol. 1, Delhi: Motilal Banarsidass, 2000.

The Vaiṣṇava Upanishads with the Commentary of Śrī Upaniṣad Brahmayogin, ed. A.M. Shastri, Chennai: Adyar Library and Research Centre, 2005.

van Buitenen, J.A.B., *Rāmānuja's Vedārthasaṁgraha*, Poona: Deccan College, 1956.

Vedāntadeśika, *Śrīmad Vedāntadeśikaviracitam Īśāvāsyopaniṣadbhāṣyam*, ed. U. Viraraghavacharya, Chennai: Shri Uttamur Viraraghavachariar Centenary Trust, 2004.

FORMS

CHAPTER 12

Loving God through Sanskrit Grammar: Jīva Gosvāmī's Use of Krishna's Names in *Harināmāmṛta-vyākaraṇa*

RITA JENEY

The *Harināmāmṛta-vyākaraṇa*

In his *Harināmāmṛta-vyākaraṇa* Jīva Gosvāmī rendered the rules of Sanskrit grammar in sutra form. Although writing in this genre is an old tradition, he wrote them in a way so as to add a devotional meaning to the grammar. The pun in the title, *The Ambrosial Grammar of Hari's Names* or *Immortality with Sanskrit Grammar*, reflects the double purpose of the work. On the one hand, it is a handbook of classical Sanskrit grammatical rules and, on the other, its recitation leads to devotional advancement. Its religious layer has been achieved by using Krishna's names as grammatical terms. In this paper I will point out Jīva Gosvāmī's unique method of inventing a new self-consistent terminology by typologically analysing his terms.

Jīva Gosvāmī lived during the sixteenth century and spent most of his life in Vrindavan. As a follower of Caitanya (1486-1534), the founder of the Gauḍīya Vaishnava school, and a perpetuator of his teachings, he left behind a broad range of philosophical and literary works. In his youth Caitanya was mainly famous for his expertise in the field of Sanskrit grammar and logic. In the beginning he taught grammar to his students through the *Kalāpa-vyākaraṇa.*[1] Later, after returning from Gayā, where he received spiritual initiation from Īśvara Purī, Caitanya explained all grammatical topics in connection with Krishna.[2] This initiative was eventually accomplished by Jīva Gosvāmī in the *Harināmāmṛta-vyākaraṇa.*

The *Harināmāmṛta-vyākaraṇa* has two versions. The general opinion is that the *Laghu-harināmāmṛta-vyākaraṇa* was written first. Either Rūpa[3] or Sanātana Gosvāmī[4] is thought to have been the author of this work of 750 sutras. The *Laghu-harināmāmṛta-vyākaraṇa* is more like an outline, which was developed by Jīva Gosvāmī to its fullness in his *Bṛhad-dharināmāmṛta-vyākaraṇa* containing over 3,000 sutras. He himself wrote grammatical commentaries and *vṛtti*s containing examples to the sutras.

Jīva Gosvāmī's *Harināmāmṛta*, inclusive of the *vṛtti*s, has several editions and my paper is based on the following three: (1) A *Harināmāmṛta-vyākaraṇa* without commentaries published by the Sadgrantha Prakāśak in Vrindavan.[5] (2) The version containing the *Bālatoṣaṇī-ṭīkā* published in Mayapur by the Caitanya Math.[6] (3) The version containing both the *Bālatoṣaṇī-ṭīkā* and the *Amṛtāsvādinī-ṭīkā* edited by Bābā Śrīkṛṣṇadāsa Jī Mahārāja and published after his death by the Ḍalamiyā Jain Trust in New Delhi.[7]

The *Harināmāmṛta-vyākaraṇa* contains seven chapters:[8]

Chapter 1 (147 sutras): Nomenclature and phonetic changes
Chapter 2 (218 sutras): Declension
Chapter 3 (586 sutras): Conjugation of verbs
Chapter 4 (275 sutras): Use of cases
Chapter 5 (466 sutras): Formation of verbal derivatives
Chapter 6 (373 sutras): Compounds
Chapter 7 (1,127 sutras): Rules of secondary word formation

This is supplemented by the *Dhātu-saṁgraha*, Jīva Gosvāmī's collection and list of 1,135 verbal roots.[9] Every chapter starts with an invocation which establishes the theme of the chapter. These verses have both a grammatical meaning and a secondary meaning of prayer or glorification in which the author connects Sanskrit grammar with Vaishnava philosophy. Thus, in the beginning of the chapters, he does not just introduce the grammatical phenomena that he wishes to discuss but also connects them to Krishna. In this way he casts light upon the double purpose of his book.

Following the Tradition

The *Harināmāmṛta-vyākaraṇa* is a late work in the history of Sanskrit grammar and Jīva Gosvāmī relied upon the tradition of his predecessors in several aspects. In its genre and usage, namely the sutra form, the *Harināmāmṛta-vyākaraṇa* fully follows the tradition of Sanskrit grammatical works.

Jīva Gosvāmī also relied on previous grammarians in the formulation of his sutras, restating earlier grammatical rules and definitions without essential changes if he did not find it logically necessary to make adjustments. He had studied numerous grammatical works before writing the *Harināmāmṛta-vyākaraṇa*. In his commentaries he makes references to the following grammarians and their treatises: Pāṇini: *Aṣṭādhyāyī*, Kātyāyana: *Vārttika*, Patañjali: *Mahābhāṣya*, Jayāditya and Vāmana: *Kāśikā*, Puruṣottamadeva: *Bhāṣāvṛtti*, *Bhāgavṛtti*, Rāmacandra: *Prakriyā-Kaumudī*, Sarvavarman: *Kalāpa/Kātantra*, Candragomin: *Cāndra*, Anubhūtisvarūpācārya: *Sārasvata*, Kramadīśvara: *Saṁkṣiptasāra*, *Rasavatī*, and Padmanābha: *Supadma*.

Innovation

Content Structure and Form

With regard to the content, Jīva Gosvāmī strived for practicality. He summarized classical Sanskrit grammar and avoided forms that were not in use.[10] Thus the rules of Vedic Sanskrit grammar are not included. The conscious endeavour for easy usage can be best seen in the structure of the treatise. As opposed to Pāṇini, Jīva Gosvāmī arranged the sutras not according to the *anuvṛttis*, but the description of the derivation of a certain grammatical form is immediately followed by the presentation of all the pertaining rules. This arrangement is especially helpful for beginners.[11]

The prime cause of Pāṇini's method of structuring was a strong endeavour for brevity, to keep the text to be memorized brief, but this leads to a highly codified outcome. However, at the time of Jīva Gosvāmī, many of the flourishing Sanskrit schools broke away from brevity and gave a religious content to grammatical works.[12] Jīva Gosvāmī took the lead in this innovation. He gives greater importance to the religious content than to conciseness.

Objections

Some indologists criticize this kind of mixture of grammar and religious philosophy. S.K. Belvalkar calls the religious philosophical elements sectarian and says they do not add to the grammatical text. In his book *Systems of Sanskrit Grammar* he gives a brief description of the *Harināmāmṛta-vyākaraṇa* where he notes that 'the whole subject is presented to us in a dull, uninteresting manner'[13] but adds that this text is one of the most significant endeavours of grammarians to make grammar the vehicle of religion.[14]

Belvalkar wrote his book at the beginning of the twentieth century. In his brief review of the *Harināmāmṛta-vyākaraṇa* we can discover several inaccurate statements and he is also unaware of the commentaries.[15] R.S. Saini (whose book was published in 1999 but who had done most of his research in the 1960s)[16] stated that the original work was not available.[17] In his grammar-dictionary published in 1961, K.V. Abhayankar only mentions the title of the book.[18] H.G. Coward and K.K. Raja in their *The Philosophy of the Grammarians* do not mention it at all.[19] On the other hand, A.C. Barthakuria analyses the *Kāraka-prakaraṇam* in detail in his doctoral thesis written on the *kāraka*s in 1972,[20] which was published as late as 1997.

All this shows that in the circle of Indologists, including Indian scholars, this work of Jīva Gosvāmī was barely known before the 1990s. For most of them the text itself was not available, not to mention the commentaries. Thus their statements on the practicality and interest of the book cannot be considered well-established. This tendency changed only recently as a new interest arose for grammars belonging to religious groups.[21]

An analytical study of the terminology introduced by Jīva Gosvāmī leads to a completely different point of view: the nomenclature was chosen in an original way based on several correlations and as they are connected to the grammatical meaning, in some way, they help in the easy recall of the grammatical rules. I have reached this conclusion by typologically analysing the terminology. In each *saṁjñā-sūtra* I examined the correlations of terms and arranged them in groups. For philosophical explanations I relied mainly on the *Amṛtāsvādinī-ṭīkā*.

Terminology

With regards to its genre and usage, Jīva Gosvāmī's grammar book fits into the grammar tradition. The innovations primarily concern structure and form. Regarding form, Jīva Gosvāmī sacrifices brevity for the sake of religious content. The main innovation in his grammar book is the introduction of a new terminology that contains Krishna's names. Jīva Gosvāmī introduces more than a hundred new terms. There are two fundamental reasons for his choices: (1) how the term sounds, and (2) what the term means.

TERMS CHOSEN ON THE BASIS OF SOUND

(1) *The sound of the new term resembles the traditional term:* Jīva Gosvāmī changes the names of phenomena already existing in the tradition of grammar. In certain cases he does this by choosing a name which sounds similar to the original term but that carries an additional philosophical content (Table 12.1).

(1b) *The sound of the new term resembles the grammatical phenomenon:* The sound of the new term that also carries a philosophical content in some way accords with or evokes the grammatical phenomenon that it designates. In many cases this means that the new term includes one of the sounds that it designates. The naming of re-duplication is somewhat different. During re-duplication the first sounds of a root or stem are

TABLE 12.1

traditional term	new term	literal meaning	grammatical phenomenon	saṁjñā-sūtra
val	vala	strength, Balarāma	consonants except y	1.18
saṁyoga	satsaṅga	association of devotees, true people	consonant cluster	1.82
guṇa	govinda	Krishna, the king of cows	guṇa grade of vowels	2.32
vṛddhi	vṛṣṇīndra	the best of the Vṛṣṇis, Vāsudeva, Krishna	vṛddhi grade of vowels	2.43
upadhā	uddhava	the minister of the Vṛṣṇis, friend of Krishna, disciple of Bṛhaspati	the penultimate letter	2.80
pada	viṣṇupada	Vishnu's feet	a word including its ending as used in a sentence	2.7
vibhakti	viṣṇubhakti	loving devotion to Vishnu	case affixes and personal endings	2.1
saṁbuddhi	buddha[22]	Buddha, the ninth member of the daśāvatāra	singular vocative ending	2.24
ghuṭ, sarvanām-asthāna	kṛṣṇasthāna	Krishna's place, dhāman, meaning Vrindavan	sg.N.m, du.N/Ac.m, pl.N.m, pl.N/Ac.n endings	2.81
bha	bhagavat	possessing six opulences (bhaga), Nārāyaṇa	case endings starting with a vowel (except kṛṣṇasthāna) and taddhita endings starting with a vowel or y	2.88
sarvanāman	kṛṣṇanāman	Krishna's name	pronouns	2.166
laṅ, (past tense is bhūta)	bhūteśvara	the controller of beings, spirits, Shiva	past imperfect endings	3.6
luṅ, (past tense is bhūta)	bhūteśa	the Lord of beings, spirits, Shiva	aorist endings	3.7

vidhi-liṅ	vidhi	rule, ordinance, act, Brahmā, the creator	optative endings	3.4
carkarīta, yaṅluk	cakrapāṇi	who has a wheel/ discus in his hand	secondary roots expressing the intensive	3.497-498
parasmai-pada	parapada	the supreme place	active voice	3.19
ātmane-pada	ātmapada	the place of the ātmā/paramātmā	middle voice	3.20
upasarga	upendra	Upendra, another name for Vāmana, son of Kaśyapa and Aditi, born after Indra	verbal prefix	3.42
karma-pravacanīya	kṛṣṇa-pravacanīya	the speaker of Krishna's characteristics and pastimes	post-position	4.107
niṣṭhā	viṣṇuniṣṭhā	Vishnu's position, Vishnu's unflinchingness	past passive participle and active participle derived from it	4.44; 5.27
sārvadhātuka	kṛṣṇa-dhātuka		affixes applied to verbs and kṛt affixes marked with the mute letter ś (ś-it)	3.22
ārdhadhātuka	rāma-dhātuka		affixes applied to verbs and kṛt affixes marked without the mute letter ś	3.23

Note: The sūtra numbers in the Tables are from the *HNV* (Vrindavan) edition.

duplicated, prefixed to the root or the stem. Re-duplication thus involves a re-duplicated syllable and a re-duplicative syllable. Jīva Gosvāmī calls these *nara* and *nārāyaṇa*, respectively. Grammatically *nara-nārāyaṇa* is not a re-duplication but sounds like one (Table 12.2).

TABLE 12.2

grammatical phenomenon	new term	literal meaning	traditional term	saṁjñā-sūtra
voiceless unaspirated plosives (k c ṭ t p)	harikamala	Hari's lotus flower	prathama, cay	1.21
voiceless aspirated plosives (kh ch ṭh th ph)	harikhaḍga	Hari's sword	dvitīya	1.22
voiced unaspirated plosives (g j ḍ d b)	harigadā	Hari's mace	tṛtīya, jaś	1.23
voiced aspirated plosives (gh jh ḍh dh bh)	harighoṣa	Hari's conch shell	caturtha, jhaṣ	1.24
nasals (ṅ ñ ṇ n m)	hariveṇu	Hari's flute	pañcama, anunāsika, ñam	1.25
liquids and semi-vowels (y r l v)	harimitra	Hari's friend	antastha, yaṇ	1.27
affixes marked with the mute letter k and/or ṅ	kaṁsāri	Krishna, Kaṁsa's enemy	kit és ṅit	3.17
affixes marked with the mute letter k	kapila	Kapila	kit	3.15
affixes marked with the mute letter ṅ	nirguṇa	having no material qualities	ṅit	3.16
affixes marked with the mute letter ṇ	nṛsiṁha	half man-half lion incarnation	ṇit	3.14
affixes marked with the mute letter p	pṛthu	Pṛthu	pit	3.13
affixes marked with the mute letter ś	śiva	Śiva	śit	3.18

roots such as dā and dhā	dāmodara	Krishna, having a rope around his waist	ghu	3.54
re-duplicative syllable	nara	Nara	abhyāsa	3.73
re-duplicated syllable	nārāyaṇa	Nārāyaṇa	abhyasta	3.74

TERMS CHOSEN ON THE BASIS OF MEANING

(2a) *The meaning of the new term is in quantitative relation with the grammatical phenomenon:* The philosophical meaning of the new term can be connected with a number which corresponds to the number connected to the grammatical phenomenon that the term designates (Table 12.3).

TABLE 12.3

grammatical phenomenon	new term	literal meaning	traditional term	saṁjñā-sūtra
i ī u ū (4 in number)	catuḥsana	four boys; four Kumāras	iṇ	1.11
u ū r̥ r̥̄ (4 in number)	caturbhuja	four-armed	uk (u ū r̥ r̥̄ l̥ l̥̄)	1.12
diphtongs (e ai o au) (4 in number)	caturvyūha	having four kinds of appearance	saṁdhyakṣara, ec	1.13
monophtongs (a ā i ī u ū r̥ r̥̄ l̥ l̥̄) (10 in number)	daśāvatāra	ten incarnations/ having ten incarnations	samāna, ak	1.3
two adjacent vowels of the alphabet (1 pair)	dvaya	pair, Lakṣmī-Nārāyaṇa		1.38
sg. N/Ac, du. N/Ac, pl. N. case endings (5 in number)	pāṇḍava	Pāṇḍu's five sons	ghuṭ, suṭ	2.44
sparśas, except ñ (viṣṇuvarga - ñ)	viṣṇugaṇa	Vishnu's associates (gaṇa is a smaller group than varga)	may	1.20

(2b) *The meaning of the new term is in visual connection with the grammatical phenomenon:* The new term with philosophical meaning brings to mind a picture which can be connected to the grammatical phenomenon the term designates (Table 12.4).

TABLE 12.4

grammatical phenomenon	new term	literal meaning	traditional term	saṁjñā-sūtra
short vowels (a i u ṛ ḷ)	vāmana	dwarf incarnation	hrasva (one mātrā long)	1.5
long vowels (ā ī ū ṝ ḹ)	trivikrama	giant incarnation who made three steps	dīrgha (two mātrās long)	1.6
lengthened vowels	mahā-puruṣa	Mahā-Viṣṇu whose body includes everything	pluta (three mātrās long)	1.7
anusvāra[23]	viṣṇucakra	Vishnu's wheel	aṁ, anusvāra, bindu, lava	1.14
anunāsika,[24] candrabindu	viṣṇucāpa	Vishnu's bow	anunāsika	1.15

(2c) *The meaning of the new term is in grammatical connection with the grammatical phenomenon:* The new term with philosophical meaning is itself an example of the grammatical phenomenon that the term designates (Table 12.5).

TABLE 12.5

grammatical phenomenon	new term	literal meaning	traditional term	saṁjñā-sūtra
nominal stems in -a	kṛṣṇa	Krishna		2.11
feminine nominal stems in -ā	rādhā	who fulfils Krishna's desires (rādhayati)	śraddhā	2.63
masculine nominal stems in -i and -u	hari	Vishnu who takes away all inauspicious things; Krishna who	agni, ghi	2.30

		takes away the mind with his love		
feminine nominal stems in -ī and -ū	gopī	Vraja's cowherd girls	nadī	2.73
karmadhāraya compound	śyāmarāma	green[25] Rāma, son of Daśaratha	karmadhāraya	6.9
dvigu compound	trirāmī	three Rāmas: Rāma, Paraśurāma and Balarāma	dvigu	6.48
bahuvrīhi compound	pītāmbara	having yellow clothes; Krishna whose clothes are yellow	bahuvrīhi	6.102
dvandva compound	rāmakṛṣṇa	Balarāma and Krishna	dvandva	6.117

(2d) *The meaning of the new term is in a philosophical connection with the grammatical phenomenon:* The philosophical content of the new term is parallel with the function of the grammatical phenomenon that the term designates.

Among the categories of phonetics, the term for short and long monophtong vowel pairs belongs to this category. The short and long vowel pairs are one in essence and only the time of articulation is different. A short vowel is exactly the same as an identical short vowel, whereas it is only slightly different from its long pair but the same in essence. This oneness in essence is expressed by calling the short and long vowel pairs *ekātmaka*. The literal meaning of the word *ekātmaka* is 'having one nature, one essence'. As two vowels which are also the same in length are completely the same, Krishna also has expansions which look exactly like him (*prakāśa-rūpa*).[26] For example, during the *rāsa* dance, Krishna danced with every single *gopī* as a separate expansion which was not different from him in any way. On the other hand, although vowels which only differ in length are essentially the same, we still find a difference. Similarly, certain expansions of Krishna are essentially the same with him but their external appearances are different (*vilāsa-rūpa*),[27] such as Balarāma who is essentially one with Krishna, the only difference being that while Krishna's complexion is blackish, Balarāma's is white. The term *ekātmaka* refers to this quality of Krishna.[28]

A plosive[29] is called *viṣṇudāsa*. *Viṣṇudāsa*s are similar to *viṣṇuvarga*s[30] and *viṣṇugaṇa*s[31] in that they are all *vrajavāsī*s but due to their role of servitude, they are a separate group. Similarly, the plosives (*viṣṇudāsa*s) are also *sparśa*s (*viṣṇuvarga*s) but, excluding the nasals, they have specific roles in certain rules.[32] Thus the term *viṣṇudāsa* is also based on a philosophical connection.

Jīva Gosvāmī introduces the term *rāma* to name a sound. Thus, for example, *a-rāma* means the sound *a*. The word *rāma* thus always connects to a single sound. Similarly, Rāma was famous for having only accepted one woman as his wife during his entire life.[33]

While applying certain grammatical rules, some sounds are to be exchanged for something else, to be added or to be dropped. Jīva Gosvāmī calls the phenomenon of changing a sound to another sound *viriñci*. Viriñci is a name for Brahma who performs the secondary creation, making something into something else. The appearance of a sound is called *viṣṇu*. Vishnu maintains the world by appearing at the proper time. There are two ways in which a sound can disappear; one is named *hara* and the other *mahāhara*. Both Hara and Mahāhara are names of Shiva who is the deity responsible for destroying the world.[34]

Apart from the above-mentioned terms of phonetics, this category includes certain terms connected to verb conjugation. Jīva Gosvāmī introduces the term *acyuta* to designate the verb endings expressing present tense. The word *acyuta* literally means 'not fallen, solid, imperishable, permanent'.[35] At the same time, Acyuta is also a name for Krishna.[36] The philosophical parallel between the term *acyuta* and the present tense is that as the present is imperishable, Krishna is also eternal and, therefore, his name is Acyuta.

To express the future tense, there are two groups of suffixes which are both named by Jīva Gosvāmī after Kalki, the incarnation in the *daśāvatāra* who is to appear in the future. Thus a philosophical connection is created between the term and the grammatical phenomenon. Future is called *kalki*, whereas periphrastic future is called *bālakalki*, the child Kalki.

The precative, or aorist optative, is used to express benedictions or wishes. Jīva Gosvāmī calls it *kāmapāla*, which literally means the fulfiller of desires. Kāmapāla is a name for Balarāma who protects (*pālayati*) Krishna (*kāmadevam*) as his elder brother.[37]

In Sanskrit, the conditional tense expresses unreal conditions of the past. Jīva Gosvāmī calls this verb mode *ajita* as Ajita is a name for Vishnu who has never been conquered by anyone.[38] The philosophical connection with the grammatical phenomenon in regard to this term is that as the conditional tense expresses something that did not happen, similarly the conquering of Vishnu cannot happen and, therefore, Vishnu is Ajita (Table 12.6).

TABLE 12.6

grammatical phenomenon	new term	literal meaning	traditional term	saṁjñā-sūtra
short and long vowel pairs (a ā) (i ī) (u ū) (ṛ ṝ) (ḷ ḹ)	ekātmaka	having one nature, one essence	savarṇa	1.4
plosives	viṣṇudāsa	Vishnu's servant	jhay	1.26
the sound itself	rāma	Rāma	kāra, -t	1.37
changing, replacement	viriñci	Brahma	ādeśa	1.39
adding, insertion	viṣṇu	Vishnu	āgama	1.40
dropping, removal	hara	Shiva	lopa	1.41
complete disappearance	mahāhara	Shiva	luk	1.41
present tense verb endings	acyuta	not fallen, firm, solid, imperishable, permanent, Krishna	vārtāmāna, laṭ	3.3
future tense verb endings	kalki	the future incarnation of Vishnu	bhaviṣyat, lṛṭ	3.11

periphrastic future tense verb endings	bālakalki	child Kalki, the tenth member of daśāvatāra in child-form	śvastanī, luṭ	3.10
precative (aorist optative) verb endings	kāmapāla	fulfiller of desires	āśīr-liṅ	3.9
conditional (unreal conditions of the past)	ajita	who has never been conquered	kriyātipatti, lṝṅ	3.12

(3) *The new term is in a philosophical connection with other terms:* In some cases there is no definable connection between the new term and the grammatical meaning in itself. The choice of the term in these cases is governed by the philosophical content the term gains by coming in contact with other terms in certain rules.

Of the terms in connection with phonetics, *harigotra* refers to the *ś ṣ s h* sound group. It may have two interpretations: the mountain of Hari', namely Govardhana, Nandīśvara or other mountains in Vraja,[39] or the 'family, lineage of Hari'. In this case the word *harigotra* refers to Aniruddha (son of Pradyumna, grandson of Krishna), Vajra (son of Aniruddha, great-grandson of Krishna) and other descendants of Hari.[40] The word *harigotra* has no definable connection with the *ś ṣ s h* sounds. In this case the naming can be explained by the term *harigotra* coming in philosophical relation with other terms in rules applying to the *ś ṣ s h* sounds.

An example of this is the *saṁjñā-sūtra* defining the term Vaishnava: *viṣṇudāsa-harigotrāṇi vaiṣṇavāḥ.* The term Vaishnava refers to a larger group of sounds containing all the consonants except the semi-vowels and nasals. Jīva Gosvāmī takes advantage of the terms he has created for sound groups and thus easily defines the term Vaishnava: the *viṣṇudāsa*s (explosives without the nasals) and the *harigotra*s (spirants and *h*) together are the Vaishnavas. The word Vaiṣhnava means 'the devotee of Vishnu' and thus the sutra may also be interpreted from a philosophical perspective. Vishnu's servants (*viṣṇudāsa*), as well as Govardhana and the other hills (*harigotra*), are Vishnu's followers. Besides Hari's servants in human forms such as Raktaka, the Govardhana hill is also known as *hari-dāsa-varya*[41] as he serves the pastimes of Hari with every particle of his body and thus he is also called a Vaishnava. The statement that the *harigotras* are Vaishnavas is also true in the second interpretation of the word *harigotra* (Hari's descendants, namely Pradyumna, Aniruddha and others) as the other meaning of the word Vaishnava is 'the descendant of Vishnu'.[42]

Jīva Gosvāmī calls the voiced consonants *gopāla* and defines it as *harigadā-harighoṣa-hariveṇu-harimitrāṇi haś ca gopālāḥ*. The voiced unaspirated explosives (*harigadā*), the voiced aspirate explosives (*harighoṣa*), the nasals (*hariveṇu*), the semi-vowels (*harimitra*) and the *h* sound are voiced consonants. Apart from the grammatical meaning, the sutra also has a philosophical one: Krishna's sticks (*harigadā*),[43] horns (*harighoṣa*), flutes (*hariveṇu*), friends (*harimitra*) and Shiva (*ha*) are themselves *gopālas*. *Gopāla* literally means 'cowherd' and because Krishna takes care of cows, his name is also Gopāla. The instance when we see Krishna's sticks, horns, flutes and friends being non-different from him is during the *brahma-vimohana-līlā*.[44] Once Brahma wanted to test Krishna's power and stole all the calves and cowherd boys, and hid them in a secret place. When Krishna could not find them anywhere, he understood that it was due to Brahma's trick. Then to please Brahma, as well as his friends and their mothers, he expanded himself into calves and boys that looked exactly like the ones that disappeared, and kept in their hands the same things (stick, horn, flute) as the original boys had.[45] In the grammatical sense the word *ha* in the sutra refers to the *h* sound whereas philosophically it means Shiva.[46] Shiva being a *gopāla* is supported by the following verse of *Śrī Gaura-gaṇoddeśa-dīpikā: śrī-kṛṣṇasya prasādena dvividho 'bhūt sadāśivaḥ / ekas tatra śivaḥ sākṣād anyo gopāla-vigrahaḥ,*[47] according to which one of Sadāśiva's forms is Shiva and the other is Gopāla.

The voiceless consonants are called *yādava*. While defining the voiced consonants, Jīva Gosvāmī lists all the sounds belonging to the group but all he says about voiceless consonants is *yādavā anye,* meaning that besides the listed ones (*gopāla*), all other consonants are voiceless (*yādava*). The word *yādava* means a descendant of Yadu. Although all members of the Yadu dynasty are called *yādava*s in a general sense, when the word *gopāla* (cowherd) is mentioned, it specifically refers to the residents of Vrindavan, whcreas *yādava* refers to all the other descendants of the family who live in Mathura and Dvaraka.[48] In this way the definition '*yādavā anye*' has a double meaning.

Voiceless sounds have two major groups: voiceless explosives and spirants. Voiceless explosives are called *sātvata* while spirants are *śauri*.[49] Sātvata is a devotee of Vishnu who took birth in the Yadu dynasty and his descendants are called *sātvata*s.[50] This term is in connection with the terms *yādava* and *śauri*. As both Sātvata and Śūra and all their descendants are the descendants of Yadu, so both the voiceless explosives (*sātvata*s) and the spirants (*śauri*s) are voiceless (*yādava*s).

For the sake of exactness in defining grammatical rules, there are also terms for the position of letters within words. The term *saṁsāra* refers to the final syllable beginning with a vowel in the word. One of the meanings of *saṁsāra* is the circle of material existence but the other meaning is Krishna, the essence of everything (*samyak sāra*).[51] There is no direct connection between the term and the grammatical phenomenon but, in certain rules, when the term comes in contact with other terms, the philosophical meaning is relevant. For example: *saṁsārasya haraś citi*.[52] The grammatical meaning is: [While declining stems in *i*] the last vowel of the stem (*saṁsāra*) before an *it* containing a *c* (*cit*) disappears (*hara*). The philosophical meaning is that when pure knowledge (*cit*) awakens, the circle of repeated birth and death (*saṁsāra*) disappears (*hara*).[53]

The case endings introduced while describing noun declensions other than the singular nominative and accusative, the dual nominative and accusative, and the plural nominative (whose the endings are called *pāṇḍava*) are called *yadu*. Yadu is the eldest son of King Yayāti of the Candravaṁśa. Krishna also appeared in this dynasty.[54] Within the endings named *yadu* is a smaller group including the singular dative, genitive, ablative and locative endings that are called *vṛṣṇi*. Vṛṣṇi is the eldest son of King Madhu of the Yadu dynasty.[55] The *yadu* and *vṛṣṇi* terms have no direct connection with the grammatical phenomena they are designating but are in connection with each other: as Vṛṣṇi is a descendant of Yadu, so the *vṛṣṇi* case endings are included among the *yadu* case endings.

Of the verbal modes, the optative and the imperative are close to each other in meaning. This may be the reason why Jīva Gosvāmī named both of them after the same individual. The term for the optative is *vidhi*, which sounds similar to the traditional term *vidhi-liṅ* and means the creator Brahma, while the term for the imperative is *vidhātṛ*, another name for Brahma.[56]

The present and past participle get their names from the imperfect present tense (*acyuta*) and the perfect past tense (*adhokṣaja*). The reason behind this is that they are formed from these stems. The present participle is called *acyutābha* and the past participle is called *adhokṣajābha*, which mean 'similar to *acyuta/adhokṣaja*'.

The *taddhita* endings containing *ṭ-it* are called *keśava* while the *taddhita* endings containing *ṭ-* or *ṇ-it* are called *mādhava*. *Keśava* and *Mādhava* are names of Krishna that often occur together. Keśava means Krishna who has long hair, and Mādhava means Krishna who is a descendant of Madhu (Table 12.7).

TABLE 12.7

new term	literal meaning	grammatical phenomenon	traditional term	saṁjñā-sūtra
harigotra	Hari's mountain; Hari's lineage	spirants and h (ś ṣ s h)	ūṣman, śiṭ, śal	1.28
vaiṣṇava	Vishnu's devotee, Vishnu's descendant	plosives plus spirants and h	dhuṭ , jhal	1.30
gopāla	cowherd	voiced consonants	ghoṣavat, haś	1.31
yādava	Yadu's descendant	voiceless consonants	aghoṣa, khar	1.32
sātvata	Sātvata's descendant	voiceless explosives	khay	1.33

saṁsāra	essence of everything; circle of material existence	final syllable of the word beginning with a vowel	ṭi	1.75; 2.38
yadu	the eldest son of King Yayāti of the Candravaṁśa	sg. I-L., du. I-L. and pl. Ac-L. case endings		2.27
vṛṣṇi	the eldest son of King Madhu of the Yadu dynasty	sg. D/G/Ab/L. case endings	ṅit	2.33
vidhātṛ	arranger, creator, Brahma	imperative verb endings	loṭ	3.5
acyutābha	similar to Acyuta	present participle	sat	4.41; 5.2
adhokṣajā-bha	similar to Adhokṣaja	past participle		4.45; 5.19
keśava	Krishna who has long hair	endings marked with the mute letter ṭ	ṭit	7.246
mādhava	Krishna who is the descendant of Madhu	endings marked with the mute letter ṭ or ṇ	ṭaṇit	7.246

(4) *The traditional term is preserved:* In some cases Jīva Gosvāmī does not change the traditional term but takes advantage of its philosophical meaning.

Besides keeping the traditional terms *prakṛti*, *pratyaya*, *laghu* and *guru*,[57] Jīva Gosvāmī also refrains from introducing new terms for the three persons of verb conjugation. The term for the third person is *prathama-puruṣa*, for the second *madhyama-puruṣa*, and for the first *uttama-puruṣa*. The literal meaning of these words refers to a custom in Indian grammar in which the form of the third person (*prathama* = first) is said first, then the form of the second person (*madhyama* = middle) and finally that of the first person (*uttama* = last). Jīva Gosvāmī does not change these terms but takes advantage of their second meaning, namely that the three *puruṣa*s mean the three *puruṣa-avatāra*s of Vishnu. The first (*prathama-puruṣa*) is Kāraṇodakaśāyī-Viṣṇu who creates the *mahat-tattva*. The middle (*madhyama-puruṣa*) is Garbhodakaśāyī-Viṣṇu who enters the universes. The last (*uttama-puruṣa*) is Kṣīrodakaśāyī-Viṣṇu, who enters every living entity (Table 12.8).[58]

TABLE 12.8

traditional term	new term	literal meaning	grammatical phenomenon	saṁjñā-sūtra
prakṛti	prakṛti	original or natural form or condition of anything; origin; nature; the passive energy of creation; material nature	base, root, uninflected word	2.2
pratyaya	pratyaya	belief, firm conviction, faith; notion, idea	affix or suffix	2.3
laghu	laghu	light, short	light syllable	1.79
guru	guru	difficult, heavy, long; master	heavy syllable	1.80-1
prathama-puruṣa	prathama-puruṣa	first person; Kāraṇodakaśāyī-Vīṣṇu	third person (he/she/it)	3.21
madhyama-puruṣa	madhyama-puruṣa	middle person; Garbhodakaśāyī-Viṣṇu	second person (you)	3.21
uttama-puruṣa	uttama-puruṣa	last person; Kṣīrodakaśāyī-Viṣṇu	first person (I)	3.21

SUMMARY OF THE CHOICE OF TERMS:

(1) The new term sounds similar to
   (a) the traditional term
   (b) the grammatical phenomenon
(2) The meaning of the new term
   (a) is in a quantitative connection with the grammatical phenomenon
   (b) is in a visual connection with the grammatical phenomenon
   (c) is in a grammatical connection with the grammatical phenomenon

(d) is in a philosophical connection with the grammatical phenomenon
(3) The new term is in a philosophical connection with other terms
(4) The traditional term is preserved

All the terms created by Jīva Gosvāmī fit into the above typology. Besides these, he also creates terms with not just one but two or even three observable correlations. The following paragraphs will describe these terms.

TERMS WITH TWO CORRELATIONS

The different groups of consonants are named after Krishna's associates. The consonants from *ka* to *ma* are called *viṣṇuvarga*, whereas the traditional term is *varga* (meaning 'group') or *sparśa*. Not only is the new term similar to the traditional term but there is also a quantitative connection between the term and the grammatical phenomenon. *Sparśa*s are assigned to five groups based on the locus of their formation (*ka-varga*, *ca-varga*, *ṭa-varga*, *ta-varga*, *pa-varga*). Krishna's *vrajavāsī* associates (the *viṣṇuvarga*s) are also five in kind: *vaiśya*s, *ābhīra*s, *gurjara*s, *vipras*, *bahiṣṭha*s. The first three are keepers of animals (*vaiśya*s are cowherds, *ābhīra*s keep buffaloes and *gurjara*s keep goats), the *vipra*s conversant with the Vedas perform sacrifices, and the *bahiṣṭha*s are craftsmen.[59]

The traditional term for the *ś ṣ s* spirants is *śar,* which Jīva Gosvāmī changes to *śauri*. This term sounds similar to the traditional term and refers to the first sound of the group. The Śauris are the descendants of King Śūrasena.[60] Śūrasena was the father of Vasudeva and Kuntī. Vasudeva was the father of Krishna and Kuntī was the mother of the three elder Pāṇḍavas.

Jīva Gosvāmī changes the term *saṁprasāraṇa* to *saṅkarṣaṇa.* Literally, both words mean contraction and refer to the grammatical phenomenon where the sounds *y*, *r*, and *v* followed by the vowels *a* or *ā* become *i*, *ṛ* and *u*. The two terms sound similar and the meaning visually brings to mind the grammatical phenomenon. However, the word *saṅkarṣaṇa* also has a philosophical meaning as it refers to Balarāma, Krishna's brother. Balarāma appeared in Devakī's womb before Krishna but was later transferred to Rohiṇī's womb. This transference is called *saṅkarṣaṇa* in the *Bhāgavata Purāṇa*.[61] The other reason for Balarāma being called Saṅkarṣaṇa is that he united the *kṣatriya* family of Vasudeva and the *vaiśya* family of Nanda with this transfer.[62]

For the three nominal genders Jīva Gosvāmī chooses the terms *puruṣottama*, *lakṣmī* and *brahman*. These terms have a visual connection with the grammatical phenomena they designate. The word *puruṣottama* means 'best of men' and designates masculine words. Lakṣmī, the Goddess of Fortune, designates feminine words. *Brahman*, the all-pervading impersonal Absolute refers to words of the neuter gender. Besides this, the terms also have a grammatical connection with the grammatical phenomena they designate, as the word *puruṣottama* is masculine, *lakṣmī* is feminine and *brahman* is neuter.

Jīva Gosvāmī does not change the term for words without gender but keeps the term *avyaya* and takes advantage of its philosophical meaning. The word *avyaya* means 'not liable to change, imperishable'. From the grammatical point of view it refers to the unchanging form of the word as it is indeclinable. As Krishna is also characterized as being changeless and imperishable, he is called Avyaya.[63]

The term for the *avyayībhāva* compound was kept in Jīva Gosvāmī's terminology for very similar reasons. The word *avyayībhāva* means 'unchangeable state'. From the grammatical point of view it means that the *avyayībhāva* compound is always indeclinable. Similarly, Krishna's nature is also unchangeable.

Jīva Gosvāmī changes the name of *tatpuruṣa* compounds to *kṛṣṇapuruṣa*. This sounds similar to the original term, and, just like the traditional one, is also an example of the specific compound. The word *kṛṣṇapuruṣa* means 'Krishna's man, Krishna's devotee'.

One way of expressing the past tense is to use the perfect aspect, which in Sanskrit is also used to narrate an activity of the past that was not witnessed by the speaker. This is expressed by the traditional Sanskrit name for the perfect, *parokṣabhūta*, which means the past that is invisible to the eye. The term chosen by Jīva Gosvāmī, *adhokṣaja*, sounds similar. Adhokṣaja is a name for Krishna which has a meaning parallel to the grammatical phenomenon: Krishna is not visible to the eye (*akṣa*), he is beyond the senses.[64]

The traditional term *kṛtya* for the gerundive has been changed to *viṣṇukṛtya*,[65] meaning 'to be done for Vishnu'. Besides sounding like the traditional term, it is also an example of the grammatical phenomenon. The term *viṣṇujana* also has two correlations but due to its connections with other terms, I will explain it in the next section (Table 12.9).

TABLE 12.9

new term	literal meaning	grammatical phenomenon	traditional term	saṁjñā-sūtra
viṣṇuvarga	Vishnu's groups	consonants from ka to ma	sparśa, varga: ku cu ṭu tu pu	1.19
śauri	Śūra's descendant	spirants (ś ṣ s)	śar	1.29
saṅkarṣaṇa	drawing together, Balarāma	contraction	samprasāraṇa	3.244
puruṣottama	best of men	masculine gender	puṁliṅga	2.6
lakṣmī	good fortune, prosperity, success, wealth, beauty, goddess of fortune, wife of Nārāyaṇa	feminine gender	strīliṅga	2.6
brahman	the all-pervading impersonal Absolute	neuter gender	napuṁsaka-liṅga	2.6
avyaya	not liable to change, imperishable; Vishnu's name	indeclinable words	aliṅga	2.6
avyayī-bhāva	unchangeable state	avyayībhāva compound	avyayībhāva	6.151
kṛṣṇapuruṣa	Krishna's man, Krishna's devotee	tatpuruṣa compound	tatpuruṣa	6.8

adhokṣaja	who exists beyond the senses	perfect verb endings	parokṣabhūta, liṭ	3.8
viṣṇukṛtya	to be done for Vishnu	gerundive	kṛtya	4.60; 5.149
viṣṇujana	Vishnu's follower, devotee	consonants	vyañjana, hal	1.17

TERMS WITH THREE CORRELATIONS

In Jīva Gosvāmī's terminology the introduction of certain terms may be accredited to three reasons. One such term is *sarveśvara* used to designate vowels. *Sarveśvara* means 'the controller of everything', namely Shri Krishna. As it is possible to pronounce vowels independently, Krishna is also independent of everyone.[66] Consonants are called *viṣṇujana* which means the 'devotee of Vishnu', the *bhakta*. The *bhakta* is always in connection with Krishna and is dependent on him. In the same way, the articulation of a consonant always depends on a vowel.[67] Thus the grammatical phenomenon is parallel with the philosophical content. Furthermore, both *sarveśvara* and *viṣṇujana* sound similar to the traditional terms for vowels and consonants, *svara* and *vyañjana*. There is also a quantitative connection between the meaning of the word *sarveśvara* and the vowels. In Sanskrit there are fourteen vowels. Krishna or Sarveśvara has fourteen *manvantara-avatāra*s.

To facilitate the description of grammatical rules, vowels are further divided into groups. Vowels other than *a* or *ā* (i.e. *i ī u ū ṛ ṝ ḷ ḹ e ai o au*) are called *īśvara*. Pāṇini calls this group *ic*. The two terms also sound similar. Another reason for the term *īśvara* is that this group of vowels starts with the sound *i* and, thus, the first sound of the term resembles the grammatical phenomenon. The word *īśvara* means 'lord, master'. Sarveśvara (Krishna) has twelve forms responsible for the months (*māsa-adhidevata-rūpa*), which are called Īśvaras.[68] The vowels designated by the term *īśvara* are also twelve in number.

The monophtongs other than *a* and *ā* (*i ī u ū ṛ ṝ ḷ ḹ*) are called *īśa*. Pāṇini calls this group *ik*, so the first sound of the terms is the same. This group also starts with the sound *i* and, thus, the first sound of the term refers to the first sound of the group. The word *īśa* means 'supreme proprietor' or 'supreme controller'. *Īśa*s are the presiding deities of the eight layers covering the universe: Varāha (earth), Matsya (water), Sūrya (fire), Pradyumna (air), Aniruddha (ether), Saṅkarṣaṇa (false ego), Vāsudeva (*mahat-tattva*) and Parameśvara (*prakṛti*).[69] Thus the eight *īśa*s and the eight monophtongs in the group have a quantitative connection.

The six sounds *a ā i ī u ū* are called *ananta*. There are again three reasons for the choice of this name. It sounds similar to Pāṇini's term *aṇ*, the term's first letter refers to the first sound of the group and there is also a quantitative connection. The word *ananta* literally means infinite and is the name of the thousand-hooded snake who keeps the universes on his heads. He has six expansions. In Kṛṣṇaloka the original Ananta is Baladeva. In the *paravyoman* (the spiritual sky) it is Saṅkarṣaṇa. His expansions are Kāraṇa-, Garbha- and Kṣīra-udakaśāyī-Viṣṇu, and the thousand-hooded Śeṣa on Pātāla.[70]

Jīva Gosvāmī changes the traditional term *visarga* to *viṣṇusarga*. The word *viṣṇusarga* means 'the creation of Vishnu'. The originator of the material creation is Mahā-Viṣṇu who is lying on the Causal Ocean. Millions of universes come into being when he exhales in his slumber on the ocean and they are all destroyed when he inhales.[71] Vishnu's creation (*viṣṇusarga*) appears with Vishnu's exhaling. Similarly, the articulation of *visarga* (*viṣṇusarga*) is the pronunciation of a voiceless *h* and, thus, there is a philosophical parallel between the term and the grammatical phenomenon that it designates. The sign of *visarga* in the Devanāgarī script is shaped like a colon. This is in visual connection with the interpretation of the word *viṣṇusarga*, according to which it refers to Vishnu's *sargodhāman*. Vishnu's three eternal residences are Gokula, Mathurā and Dvārakā. According to the *Laghu-bhāgavatāmṛta*, the word Māthura includes Gokula and Mathura. Thus, from the two dots of *visarga*, one refers to Māthura (i.e. Gokula and Mathura), and the other refers to Dvaraka (Table 12.10).[72]

TABLE 12.10

new term	literal meaning	grammatical phenomenon	traditional term	saṁjñā-sūtra
sarveśvara	the controller of everything, having 12 manvantara-avatāras	vowel (a ā i ī u ū ṛ ṝ ḷ ḹ e ai o au) (12 in number)	svara, ac	1.2
īśvara	lord, master, having 12 forms responsible for the months	vowels except a and ā (i ī u ū ṛ ṝ ḷ ḹ e ai o au) (12 in number)	nāmin, ic	1.8
īśa	supreme proprietor, supreme controller, presiding deities of the 8 layers	monophtongs except a and ā (i ī u ū ṛ ṝ ḷ ḹ) 8 in number)	ik	1.9
ananta	infinite; name of the thousand-hooded snake, having 6 expansions	a ā i ī u ū (6 in number)	aṇ	1.10
viṣṇusarga	Vishnu's creation	visarga ḥ	visarga, visarjanīya, visṛṣṭa, abhiniṣṭhāna	1.16

The Levels of Term Choices

Apart from one, two or three reasons for the choice of a particular term, the new terms are often not just consistent in themselves but also in connection with each other. Thus there are three levels governing the choice of terms:

I. The term should include a name of Hari or a name connected to him
II. There should be a connection between the term and the grammatical phenomenon.
III. The terms for grammatical phenomena that interact with each other should also have a philosophical connection.

Level I is discernible for all the terms. In terms where level II is not discernible, level III is always discernible. Thus the choice of every single term has at least two levels but, in most cases, all three levels are visible. I will now proceed to demonstrate examples of terms that reflect all three levels of choice.

As the philosophical parallel of vowels (*sarveśvara*) is Krishna, all the vowel groups bear the names of Krishna and his different appearances. At the same time, as the philosophical parallel of consonants (*viṣṇujana*) is the devotee, all the terms connected to consonants refer to devotees of Krishna. The terms for Krishna's attributes (*harikamala*, etc.) are no exceptions because although physically they appear to be objects, they eternally accompany Hari and are servants of his pastimes, and therefore they fit into the *viṣṇujana* category.

Jīva Gosvāmī calls consonant clusters *satsaṅga*. The word *sat* means 'true man, devotee', and *saṅga* means 'association'. In this way the grammatical definition *mithaḥ saṁlagno viṣṇujanaḥ satsaṅga-saṁjñaḥ*[73] means that consonants (*viṣṇujana*) that directly follow each other are called a consonant cluster (*satsaṅga*). The philosophical meaning is that when the devotees (*viṣṇujana*) are together, there is an association (*satsaṅga*) of devotees.

The terms *vāmana* and *trivikrama* introduced to designate short and long vowels appear in the same story.[74] In the form of a dwarf brahman, Vāmanadeva went to the court of King Bali and asked for three steps of land from him. However, when he started taking the steps, he assumed a gigantic form. In this way, he crossed the three worlds with two steps. For his third step, there was no other place than the head of Bali. With this trick, Vāmanadeva in a gigantic form, which is called Trivikrama, took away all the wealth of Bali and made him his devotee. Jīva Gosvāmī explains that from the short and long vowel pairs, it is always the short one that comes first in the alphabet and the long one second; *pūrvo vāmanaḥ, paras trivikramaḥ*.[75] This also means that in the story of Bali, Vishnu first assumes the form of Vāmana and later turns into the gigantic Trivikrama who takes the three steps.[76]

From the perspective of prosody syllables may be either light or heavy. Jīva Gosvāmī keeps the traditional terms *laghu* and *guru* but, in their definitions, they gain a philosophical content while coming in contact with other terms. The definition of the light syllable is *vāmano laghuḥ*.[77] The grammatical meaning is that the short vowel is a light syllable. The philosophical meaning is that the dwarf incarnation is small. The definition of the heavy syllable is *trivikramo guruḥ*.[78] The grammatical meaning is that the long vowel is a heavy syllable. The philosophical meaning is that the giant incarnation is big. Apart from long vowels, a short vowel followed by a consonant cluster also makes for a heavy syllable: *satsaṅgāt pūrvo vāmano 'pi guruḥ*.[79] The grammatical meaning is that a short vowel (*vāmana*) preceding several consonants (*satsaṅgāt pūrvaḥ*) is also heavy (*guru*). The philosophical meaning is that even one who has been a small, insignificant person (*pūrvo vāmanaḥ*) can become a master (*guru*) due to the association of devotees (*satsaṅgāt*).

Jīva Gosvāmī introduces terms for basic concepts connected to nominal declension in the following way: the declined word is called *viṣṇupada* made up of a stem (*prakṛti*) and an ending (*viṣṇubhakti*). *Viṣṇupada* is the form of the word containing the ending and eligible to be placed into a sentence, and literally means 'the abode of Vishnu' or 'Vishnu's foot'. The word *viṣṇubhakti* means 'devotion to Vishnu'. The three terms and the grammatical phenomena they designate have a philosophical connection. The definition of *viṣṇupada*, *viṣṇubhaktisiddhaṁ viṣṇupadam*[80] may be interpreted in two ways: (1) The grammatical meaning is that a word root with its ending is called *viṣṇupada*, namely the declined word, (2) The philosophical meaning is that Vishnu's feet or Vishnu's abode (*viṣṇupada*) can be reached (*siddham*) by devotion to Vishnu (*viṣṇubhakti*).[81] The term *prakṛti* for the stem also has a philosophical connection with the other two terms. The word root (*prakṛti*) and the ending (*viṣṇubhakti*) together constitute the declined word (*viṣṇupada*). From the philosophical perspective, the word *prakṛti* refers to material energy. One who is able to use material energy (*prakṛti*) in devotional service (*viṣṇubhakti*) can return to the spiritual abode of Vishnu (*viṣṇupada*).[82]

Conclusion

By typologically analysing the terminology used in the *Harināmāmṛta-vyākaraṇa*, I have demonstrated that in his creation of a new terminology, Jīva Gosvāmī did not substitute traditional grammatical terms with names referring to Krishna simply because of religious sentimentalism. The terms he introduced are in correlation with grammatical phenomena and several terms can be shown to have two or three correlations. Furthermore, the terms for grammatical phenomena interacting with each other can, in most cases, also be explained philosophically. Thus three levels are discernible in Jīva Gosvāmī's choice of terms. The sutras of the *Harināmāṛta-vyākaraṇa* do not only describe the complete system of rules of classical Sanskrit grammar in an easy-to-use manner but can also be interpreted from a philosophical perspective. This, on the one hand, makes it easier to remember the rules and, on the other, results in spiritual advancement. Due to the resourcefulness and consistency of the choice of terms, the *Harināmāmṛta-vyākaraṇa* might claim intellectual interest not only from a grammatical perspective, but also from the perspective of bhakti.

NOTES

1. The author of the *Kalāpa-vyākaraṇa* or *Kātantra* is Śarvavarman and it was compiled in the first centuryh CE. This is the oldest grammatical system after Pāṇini. The *Śrī Caitanya-caritāmṛta, Ādi-līlā* 16.32 refers to Caitanya using it.
2. *Śrī Caitanya-bhāgavata, Madhya-līlā* 1.147, 1.252, 1.256, 1.324-34. Vṛndāvana Dāsa Ṭhākura, *Śrī Caitanya-bhāgavata*: Vrajraj Press, 1998.
3. *Amṛtāsvādinī-ṭīkā, Granthārambha*, 1, commentary, *HNV* (Delhi), vol. 1, p. 1.
4. *Bālatoṣaṇī-ṭīkā*, Haridās Śāstrī's introduction, *HNV* (Delhi), vol. 1, p. 4.
5. Jīva Gosvāmī, *Savṛttikaṁ Śrī-harināmāmṛta-vyākaraṇam*, Vrindavan: Sadgrantha Prakāśak, 1985, hereafter: *HNV* (Vrindavan).
6. Jīva Gosvāmī, *Savṛttikaṁ Śrī-harināmāmṛta-vyākaraṇam*, Mayapur: Shri Caitanya Math, n.d., hereafter: *HNV* (Mayapur).
7. Jīva Gosvāmī, *Savṛttikaṁ Śrī-śrī-harināmāmṛta-vyākaraṇam*, ed. Baba Shrikrishnadas, Delhi: Ḍālamiyā Jain Trust, n.d., hereafter: *HNV* (Delhi).

8. The *Harināmāmṛta-vyākaraṇa* contains 3,192 sutras although the number varies in different publications. In this paper I follow the numbering of *HNV* (Vrindavan) while quoting the commentaries my references are to *HNV* (Delhi) with page numbers.
9. The *Dhātu-saṁgraha* is not an integral part of the *Harināmāmṛta-vyākaraṇa* but is included at the end of certain publications such as *HNV* (Vrindavan).
10. This may be observed in sutra 12 of Chapter 1: *u-ū-ṛ-ṝ caturbhujāḥ. ukaś ca.* Jīva Gosvāmī names the *u-ū-ṛ-ṝ* sound group *caturbhuja* and mentions that its traditional name is *uk*. But the term *uk* also encompasses the short and long *ḷ* sound beyond the *u-ū-ṛ-ṝ* group. In his *vṛtti* Jīva Gosvāmī explains the cause of the difference: *prayojanābhāvād ḷ ḹ na gṛhyete.* The short and long *ḷ* sounds are not included because they do not appear in the rules dealing with this sound group.
11. *HNV* (Delhi), vol. 1, p. 29.
12. According to R.S. Saini, the tendency to use grammar as a vehicle of religion started with Vopadeva's *Mugdhabodha* and reached its pinnacle with *Harināmāmṛta*. He also mentions Balarāma-pañcānanda's *Prabodha-prakāśa* where Shaiva religious terms are used, and discusses Jaina grammars such as the *Jainendra-vyākaraṇa*, the *Śākatāyana-vyākaraṇa* and the *Haima-vyākaraṇa*, as well as the Buddhist *Cāndra-vyākaraṇa*. R.S. Saini, *Post-Pāṇinian Systems of Sanskrit Grammar*, Delhi: Parimal Publications, 1999, p. 239. The most important non-sectarian rearrangement of Pāṇini's sutras for the sake of easier usage was done by the seventeenth-century, Bhaṭṭojī Dīkṣita, whose work has been well-researched in recent years. See J. Bronkhorst, 'Innovation in Seventeenth Century Grammatical Philosophy: Appearance or Reality?', *Journal of Indian Philosophy*, vol. 36, nos. 5-6, 2008, pp. 543-50.
13. S.K. Belvalkar, *Systems of Sanskrit Grammar*, Delhi: The Bharatiya Book Corporation, 1997, p. 95.
14. Ibid., p. 94.
15. Ibid., p. 95.
16. Saini, *Post-Pāṇinian Systems of Sanskrit Grammar*, Introduction.
17. Ibid., p. 242.
18. K.V. Abhayankar, *A Dictionary of Sanskrit Grammar*, Baroda: Oriental Institute, 1986, p. 444.
19. H.G. Coward and R. Kunjunni, *Encyclopedia of Indian Philosophies: The Philosophy of the Grammarians*, Princeton: Princeton University Press, 1990.
20. A.C. Barthakuria, *The Philosophy of Sanskrit Grammar: A Critical Study of Kāraka*, Calcutta: Punthi-Pustak, 1997, Preface.
21. R. Manring notes that the *Harināmāmṛta-vyākaraṇa* is 'intriguing in and of itself, all the more so because few scholars to date have taken the sectarian grammars seriously' (p. 257). Then she says 'the sectarian grammars are indeed worth our intellectual attention. Their authors had significant reasons

for producing them, which merit our attention' (p. 268). R.J. Manring, 'Does Kṛṣṇa Really Need His Own Grammar? Jīva Gosvāmin's Answer', *International Journal of Hindu Studies*, vol. 12, no. 3, 2008, pp. 257-82.

22. The additional philosophical meaning of Jīva Gosvāmī's new terms also takes effect in many grammatical definitions. An example of this is the rule that follows the sutra defining the term *buddha: e o vāmanebhyo buddhasyādarśanam* (*H*NV [Vrindavan] 2.25). The grammatical meaning of the sutra is that after e, o and short vowels (*vāmana*) the singular vocative ending (*buddha*) disappears (*adarśanam*). At the same time *buddhasyādarśanam* can also be interpreted from a philosophical point of view meaning that Buddha's views do not belong to any of the six traditional philosophical schools (*ṣaḍ-darśana*) thus they are *adarśana*. The fact that the sutra may also be interpreted philosophically is supported by the usage of the word *adarśana* which Jīva Gosvāmī may have chosen with intention to create the philosophical meaning, as he already defined two terms earlier for the disappearance of a sound (*hara* and *mahāhara*) (*HNV* [Vrindavan], 1.41) but did not use them here.
23. In Devanāgarī writing *anusvāra* is written as a dot above a syllable.
24. In Devanāgarī writing *anunāsika* is written as a half-moon sign above a syllable.
25. According to the *Amṛtāsvādinī-ṭīkā*, it is *green* Rāma. *HNV* (Delhi), vol. 1, p. 459.
26. 'When the Lord married 16,108 wives at Dvārakā, He expanded Himself into many forms. These expansions and the expansions at the *rāsa* dance are called *prābhava-prakāśa*, according to the directions of revealed scriptures'; *Śrī Caitanya-caritāmṛta, Madhya-līlā* 20.168.
27. *Vilāsa-rūpa:* expansions that are slightly different in appearance, e.g. Balarāma is white; Nārāyaṇa has four arms; *Śrī Caitanya-caritāmṛta, Ādi-līlā* 1.76-8.
28. *Amṛtāsvādinī-ṭīkā, HNV* (Delhi), vol. 1, p. 13.
29. Plosives do not include nasal consonants.
30. See under 'Terms with Two Correlations'.
31. For the meaning of *viṣṇugaṇa*, see above.
32. *Amṛtāsvādinī-ṭīkā, HNV* (Delhi), vol. 1, p. 22.
33. Ibid., p. 26.
34. Ibid., pp. 27-8.
35. M. Monier-Williams, *A Sanskrit-English Dictionary*, Delhi: Motilal Banarsidass, 1997, p. 9.
36. The *Amṛtāsvādinī-ṭīkā* quotes the *Amarakośa: pitāmbaro 'cyutaḥ śrāṅgī*; *Amṛtāsvādinī-ṭīkā, HNV* (Delhi), vol. 1, p. 206.
37. The *Amarakośa* also mentions this name of Balarāma: *kāmapālo halāyudhaḥ*; ibid., p. 208.
38. Ibid.

39. *Bhāgavata Purāṇa* 3.2.33. also refers to the Govardhana hill with the word *gotra*.
40. *Amṛtāsvādinī-ṭīkā, HNV* (Delhi), vol. 1, p. 23.
41. *Bhāgavata Purāṇa* 10.21.18.
42. *Amṛtāsvādinī-ṭīkā, HNV* (Delhi), vol. 1, p. 23.
43. The club appears in Vraja as a stick (*yaṣṭi*); ibid., pp. 21-2.
44. *Bhāgavata Purāṇa* 10.13.
45. Ibid., 10.13.19.
46. Monier-Williams, *Sanskrit-English Dictionary*, p. 1286.
47. *Amṛtāsvādinī-ṭīkā, HNV* (Delhi), vol. 1, pp. 23-4.
48. Ibid., p. 24.
49. See under 'Terms with Two Correlations'.
50. *Amṛtāsvādinī-ṭīkā, HNV* (Delhi), vol. 1, p. 24.
51. *Bālatoṣaṇī-ṭīkā, HNV* (Delhi), vol. 1, p. 47.
52. *HNV* (Vrindavan) 2.39.
53. Matsyāvatāra Dāsa's *Harināmāmṛta-vyākaraṇa* translation. Personal communication (February 2007).
54. *Amṛtāsvādinī-ṭīkā, HNV* (Delhi), vol. 1, p. 97.
55. Ibid., p. 100.
56. To prove that both epithets signify Brahma, the *Amṛtāsvādinī-ṭīkā* quotes the list of his names from the *Amarakośa*: *vidhātā viśvasṛd vidhiḥ*; ibid., p. 207.
57. See under 'The Levels of Term Choices' for an explanation of the Vaishnava philosophical corralations of these terms.
58. *Amṛtāsvādinī-ṭīkā, HNV* (Delhi), vol. 1, p. 210.
59. The *Amṛtāsvādinī-ṭīkā* refers to Rūpa Gosvāmī's *Śrī-Rādhā-Kṛṣṇa-Gaṇoddeśa-dīpikā* in this content; ibid., p. 20.
60. Ibid., p. 23.
61. *Bhāgavata Purāṇa* 10.2.13.
62. Ibid. 10.8.12.
63. *Bhagavad-gītā* 7.25.
64. *Amṛtāsvādinī-ṭīkā, HNV* (Delhi), vol. 1, p. 207.
65. *HNV* (Vrindavan) 5.149.
66. *Amṛtāsvādinī-ṭīkā, HNV* (Delhi), vol. 1, p. 12.
67. *HNV* (Vrindavan) 1. *vṛtti* 17.
68. *Amṛtāsvādinī-ṭīkā, HNV* (Delhi), vol. 1, p. 16.
69. Ibid.
70. Ibid.
71. See *Brahma-saṁhitā* 48; *Śrī Brahma-saṁhitā*, ed. B.S. Goswami, Bombay: The Bhaktivedanta Book Trust, 1989.
72. *Amṛtāsvādinī-ṭīkā, HNV* (Delhi), vol. 1, pp. 18-19.
73. *HNV* (Vrindavan) 1.82.
74. *Bhāgavata Purāṇa* 8.18-22.
75. *HNV* (Vrindavan) 1.5-6.

76. *Bālatoṣaṇī-ṭīkā, HNV* (Delhi), vol. 1, pp. 14-15.
77. *HNV* (Vrindavan) 1.79.
78. Ibid. 1.80.
79. Ibid. 1.81.
80. Ibid. 2.7.
81. *Amṛtāsvādinī-ṭīkā, HNV* (Delhi), vol. 1, p. 89.
82. Matsyāvatāra Dāsa, personal communication (February 2007).

BIBLIOGRAPHY

Abhayankar, K.V., *A Dictionary of Sanskrit Grammar*, Baroda: Oriental Institute, 1986.

Barthakuria, A.C., *The Philosophy of Sanskrit Grammar: A Critical Study of Kāraka*, Calcutta: Punthi-Pustak, 1997.

Belvalkar, S.K., *Systems of Sanskrit Grammar*, Delhi: The Bharatiya Book Corporation, 1997.

Bhagavad-gītā: The Bhaktivedanta Book Trust, 1992.

Bronkhorst, J., 'Innovation in Seventeenth Century Grammatical Philosophy: Appearance or Reality?', *Journal of Indian Philosophy,* vol. 36, nos. 5-6, 2008, pp. 543-50.

Coward, H.G. and R. Kunjunni, *Encyclopedia of Indian Philosophies: The Philosophy of the Grammarians*, Princeton: Princeton University Press, 1990.

Jīva Gosvāmī, *Savṛttikaṁ Śrī-harināmāmṛta-vyākaraṇam*, Vrindavan: Sadgrantha Prakāśak, 1985.

——, *Savṛttikaṁ Śrī-harināmāmṛta-vyākaraṇam*, Mayapur: Shri Caitanya Math, n.d.

——, *Savṛttikaṁ Śrī-śrī-harināmāmṛta-vyākaraṇam*, ed. Baba Shrikrishnadas, Delhi: Ḍālamiyā Jain Trust, n.d.

Kṛṣṇadāsa Kavirāja, *Śrī Caitanya-caritāmṛta*, Los Angeles: The Bhaktivedanta Book Trust, 1992.

Manring, R.J., 'Does Kṛṣṇa Really Need His Own Grammar? Jīva Gosvāmin's Answer', *International Journal of Hindu Studies,* vol. 12, no. 3, 2008, pp. 257-82.

Monier-Williams, M., *A Sanskrit-English Dictionary*, Delhi: Motilal Banarsidass, 1997.

Saini, R.S., *Post-Pāṇinian Systems of Sanskrit Grammar*, Delhi: Parimal Publications, 1999.

Śrī Brahma-saṁhitā, ed. B.S. Goswami, Bombay: The Bhaktivedanta Book Trust, 1989.

Śrīmad-Bhāgavatam, Los Angeles: The Bhaktivedanta Book Trust, 1972-7.

Vṛndāvana Dāsa Ṭhākura, *Śrī Caitanya-bhāgavata*: Vrajraj Press, 1998.

CHAPTER 13

God Outside and God Inside: The North Indian Digambar Jain Performance of Bhakti

JOHN E. CORT

Digambar Bhakti

This essay is part of a larger project on Jain bhakti, which I have been researching for the past decade and more. This project has a twofold goal: first, to see what the Jain tradition looks like if we intentionally frame it as a bhakti tradition; and second, to see what the broader history of bhakti and devotional religion in South Asia looks like when we include the Jains in our portrait.[1] As the most recent part of this project, I spent four months in Jaipur in 2007-8 researching the contemporary Digambar performance of bhakti. My analysis, in other words, is not solely textual, but is based, importantly, on fieldwork.[2]

When we apply this twofold interpretation framework, we find that bhakti has been central to Jain practice and doctrine for two millennia. Bhakti, in its Jain iteration, involves enthusiasm for, and veneration and glorification of, the Jinas who have shown the path to liberation. It also involves the same attitudes and practices directed toward a wide array of unliberated deities, religiously superior humans, and even laudable abstract concepts such as liberation, asceticism and ethical conduct. We see the many ways in which Jain bhakti is similar to other bhakti traditions, yet at the same time remains distinctly Jain. Finally, this framework brings into focus major elements of the Jain tradition to which scholars (in India and elsewhere, and both Jain and non-Jain) have paid insufficient attention. One of these is the north Indian Digambar lineage of hundreds of poets, who composed hymns in all the vernacular languages and dialects of north India.

At the heart of this north Indian Digambar bhakti tradition are the hymns in regionalized Hindi of five poets who lived between the seventeenth and nineteenth centuries: Dyānatrāy (Agra and Delhi, 1676-1726); Bhūdhardās (Agra, fl. 1724-49); Budhjan (Jaipur, fl. 1778-1838); Daulatrām (Mathura, Gwalior and Delhi, d. 1866); and Bhāgcand (Gwalior, fl. 1850s). In contrast to the Śvetāmbar tradition, as well as the earlier Digambar tradition, in which almost all poets and authors were mendicants, all of these poets were laymen. They were not the first Digambar lay poets to compose hymns in Hindi, but they are the most popular of the earlier poets today. There are several possible reasons for this. One, I suspect, is that the language of even earlier poets such as Banārsīdās (1586-*c.*1643) and his contemporaries is sufficiently distant from contemporary Hindi usage (whether Modern Standard Hindi, or vernaculars such as the Dhundhari Rajasthani spoken in Jaipur) that it poses difficulties of comprehension for many people today. This was certainly an answer I was given when I asked why people did not sing hymns by Banārsīdās. Another reason, at least in the case of Banārsīdās, is that his compositions tend to be rather long and philosophical, and so lend themselves more to reflection and study than to singing and performance. Many of the compositions of Banārsīdās are close in style to the Śvetāmbar genre known as the *sajjhāy*. These are short metrical texts in the vernacular that are easy to memorize, and are the principal way many Śvetāmbar mendicants and in which laity learn the basics of Jain doctrine and practice.[3]

The tradition of composition of hymns did not die out in the nineteenth century. Every year, hundreds and thousands of new hymns are composed, sung and recorded. Many of these are in contemporary genres such as *cālīsā*s, *ghazal*s and *filmī gīt*, in addition to hymns that imitate older forms. They do not, however, have the staying power of the older hymns (although scholars, a century hence, may conclude otherwise).

The Digambar Hindi hymn tradition has very deep historical roots in Digambar literature and practice. One root is a set of ritual texts known as the Ten Bhaktis (*Daśa Bhakti*), the recitation of which structures the daily practice of mendicants. These exist in both Prakrit and Sanskrit forms, and were composed in the first millennium CE. While the Prakrit Bhaktis are older and share significant textual material with the Śvetāmbar mendicant liturgical material known as the *āvaśyaka*s, it is in the Sanskrit form that they are performed today. The Bhaktis are liturgies in which the performer proclaims his or her intention to venerate various concepts, ideals and exemplary beings within the Jain world, such as the Siddhas, the twenty-four Jinas, Mahāvīra, the scriptures, right conduct, the mendicant *ācārya*, and *nirvāṇa*.[4]

Second, there is a rich Digambar tradition of *stotra*s composed in classical languages—mostly Sanskrit but also Prakrit and Apabhramsha. The Sanskrit *stotra* tradition remains vitally alive in contemporary Digambar practice as tens of thousands of Jains recite the most popular of them daily. In the past few centuries, a tradition developed of five Sanskrit *stotra*s being quasi-canonical; but these by no means are the only Sanskrit (and occasionally Prakrit) *stotra*s in contemporary Digambar devotional culture. The five are: *Bhaktāmara Stotra* of Mānatuṅga (*c*. sixth century); *Viṣāpahāra Stotra* of Dhanañjaya (*c*. eighth century); *Ekībhāva Stotra* of Vādirāja (*c*. eleventh century); *Kalyāṇamandira Stotra* of Kumudacandra (*c*. eleventh-twelfth century); and *Jinacaturviṁśati Stotra* of Bhūpāla (*c*. thirteenth century).[5]

Hindi Bhakti

The Hindi hymns that I discuss in this essay emerged in a vibrant Digambar intellectual, ritual and devotional culture in the urban centres of north India in the seventeenth century. In cities throughout the region, laymen gathered in circles known as *maṇḍalī*s (circles), *goṣṭhī*s (seminars), *śailī*s (poetic lineages), *sabhā*s (assemblies) and, in a term that seems to have been specific to Jaipur, *sahailī*s (friends). On a regular basis, Digambar laymen met in temples. Most Digambar temples in north India have courtyards (open or covered) and verandas precisely for meetings and other rituals. There the men (in terms of the composition of texts, this was largely, if not exclusively, a male tradition; any female aspects of it did not get written down) listened to sermons by local and visiting scholars. They studied doctrinal, philosophical and devotional texts, usually with the aid of Sanskrit and vernacular commentaries. They translated many of the classic Digambar texts from Sanskrit, Prakrit and Apabhramsha into the vernacular.[6] They performed extended congregational rituals to icons of the Jinas (and, less often, to other deities). Finally, they composed and sang vernacular hymns (*bhajan*s, *pad*s). Many of these hymns have remained among the most popular Digambar hymns today, and are sung on a daily basis in temples and homes from Bundelkhand in the east to Rajasthan and Gujarat (and, of course, Mumbai) in the west, and from the Punjab and Uttar Pradesh in the north to Maharashtra in the south.[7]

In an article in 2003, I made a preliminary foray into the world of these hymns.[8] I had been in Jaipur in 2000-1 conducting fieldwork on other questions—in particular, on Digambar sectarian practices and ideologies concerning icons. In this research, I had unavoidably come across the works of Digambar poets. In my article, I translated the liturgy of the most popular Digambar *pūjā* (the *Dev-śāstra-guru pūjā*) and five *pad*s, all by Dyānatrāy. The enthusiastic response I received from several Digambar Jains (including Padmanabh S. Jaini, who fondly recalled singing one of the *pad*s regularly as a child in a Jain boarding school at Karanja in Vidarbha, Maharashtra) indicated that I had chosen my texts well. In my brief introduction to the poems, I indicated several conceptual frameworks for interpreting them. Among these was that of the well-known and, by now, thoroughly problematized distinction in Hindi devotional poetry between *saguṇ* and *nirguṇ*: hymns addressed to God as having identifiable attributes, and to God as being beyond all attributes and description.[9] While this was not a framework used by Digambars themselves in discussing the hymns, I found it helpful to distinguish between a *pūjā* and what I called a *nirguṇ pad*. In the former, the poet enumerates the visible virtuous qualities (*guṇ*) inherent in the Jina and other Jain divinities, the Jain scriptures and the Digambar *muni*. In the latter, the poet insists that true religiosity should focus solely upon the pure soul within the worshipper.

I returned to Jaipur for four months of fieldwork in 2007-8, this time with the express purpose of investigating Digambar bhakti. I arrived with a rather expansive usage of this term to include a range of rituals and texts. In a 2002 article, I have argued for this expansive definition of bhakti as an analytical category for the study of South Asian religion.[10] I quickly found through conversations that people were puzzled by my use of it. My use of bhakti as a second-order concept did not correspond with the first-order usage among contemporary Digambars. On the one hand, I used it to cover congregational rituals known as *maṇḍal-vidhāns*, which, while certainly involving elements of bhakti, are understood to be located in a kind of ritual technology that we might more aptly call Tantric.[11] Informants—including *paṇḍits* who compose and regularly perform *maṇḍal-vidhāns*—disagreed that the texts and performances of these rituals were bhakti.

Of more immediate relevance to this essay, I used the word bhakti to cover a wide range of *pads* sung regularly, both on an individual and a congregational basis. My informants, however, again disagreed with my usage, and applied 'bhakti' only to hymns in which the poet and singer worships the Jina in person in the icon in the temple and in principle as an enlightened soul. In a bhakti *pad*, the poet praises the Jina, enumerates the latter's infinite and perfect virtues or qualities, recognizes his own failings, and seeks to inculcate and arouse the Jina's virtues in his or her own soul.

Informants did not see as 'bhakti' the other hymns that I also labelled as such, and which constitute anywhere from one-third to two-thirds of the hymns found in the many hymnals I collected. These hymns, my informants told me, were *adhyātma*. We can translate this term as 'spiritual' as long as we understand 'spirit' in its literal sense—synonymous with soul (*ātmā*, *jīv*)—and not the common use of 'spiritual' in contemporary English to refer to a wide range of non-institutional and/or non-traditional religious practices, beliefs and orientations.[12] These are the *pads* that in my 2003 article I had said resembled *nirguṇ pads*. I still think this is a useful way to categorize them. My informants did not agree with the second-order, methodological point I had made in my 2002 article. Instead, they would probably agree wholeheartedly with Charlotte Vaudeville's argument, 'if we admit that there can be no real bhakti (from *bhaj*, "to participate" or "to adore") without some distinction between the Lord (Bhagvan) and the devotee (bhakta), the very notion of "*nirguṇa* bhakti" seems to be a contradiction in terms'.[13]

My informants' resistance of my framework helped clarify for me a basic distinction that one finds, for example, in the hymnals, of which there are dozens of well-worn copies in every north Indian Digambar temple.[14] My interest in the older hymns found in many hymnals also led me to several elderly gentlemen—almost inevitably, the most valuable of informants for historical questions—who helped me to see ritual articulations of the difference in genres. These ritual forms used to be widespread but have died out in recent decades.

Digambar Bhakti in Jaipur

Jaipur, in common with most Indian cities, has undergone profound demographic changes in recent years. Increasingly, the old walled city, where everyone lived in the nineteenth century, is becoming a commercial district. Those who still live in the old city now tend to be poorer people who cannot afford to join the flight to the ever more far-flung suburbs, which are now where the vast majority of Jaipur's residents live. The Jains, many of whom are sufficiently middle-class to be mobile, have mostly left the old city. Neighbourhoods that used to be almost all Jain are now increasingly empty of them. These neighbourhoods are full of Jain temples dating to the eighteenth and nineteenth centuries. Formerly, so many people lived near them that the temples were full of worshippers every morning, and saw many congregational and personal rituals and activities in the evenings. Nowadays, most inner-city temples see, at best, a handful of worshippers on any given day.

With this shift to the suburbs, religious performance styles have changed.[15] In particular, my discussions with several elderly men revealed to me ritual patterns that held sway for much of the twentieth century but have disappeared in the past twenty-five years. Of interest here is the former method of the congregational performance of hymns in temples in all-night devotional music sessions (*rātrī jāgaraṇ*) by groups of men known as *sahailī*s (also spelled *sahelī*).

The Performance of Bhakti

The most famous of the Jaipur *sahailī*s was the *Śukravār kī bāl sahailī* (The Friday Young Friends), which was founded in 1902.[16] Its founder, Gaindilal Bhanvsa, was interested in Jain *bhajan*s from childhood, when he regularly accompanied his grandmother to the temple. He decided to regularize this singing, and so began to gather with a group of men every evening in the Kālāderā temple, dedicated to a main icon of Mahāvīra.[17] At first, the group was small and the men could sit in the main altar room directly in front of the main icon. When more and more people began to attend, they shifted to an outer courtyard. As the popularity of the programmes continued to grow, the men started meeting at different temples in the city every evening.

Several people suggested that the singers add instruments; this led to a number of men undertaking the formal study of music. It was not possible for such structured programmes to be held every night, so from 1905 they met every Friday evening, as Friday was the weekly governmental holiday in pre-Independence Jaipur. This also gave the name to the group. A photograph of the group taken some time in the first half of the twentieth century in the courtyard of the Digambar temple Choṭe Divān[18] shows eight distinguished-looking gentlemen seated in a row, flanked by three musicians, who played sarangi, tabla and harmonium [Fig. 13.1]. The caption to the photograph says that the twelfth man was in charge of the dance (*nṛtya*) performance, indicating the use of this performance

Figure 13.1: Śukravār kī bāl sahailī. From Gaindīlāl Bhāṅvsā, *Prācīn Jain Bhajan Saṅgrah*, Jaipur: Author, 1956.

medium as well. The commemorative hymnal published in 1956 organized the several hundred *pad*s, all of which the group sang, according to the *rāga*s and *rāginī*s, further indicating the level of technical artistic proficiency exhibited by the members of the *sahailī*.

While the Śukravār kī bāl sahailī and other older singing groups are no longer active, there are still occasions when people gather for congregational singing in Jaipur, both in the old city and, increasingly, in the suburbs. People also meet for music programmes on the annual festivals of temples in villages outside the city as well. It is customary to invite a trained singer to lead the singing; he[19] is responsible for bringing musicians (nowadays the instruments are usually the synthesizer, tabla and dholak; the musicians are often not Jain) and the accompanying singers.[20] If the temple is a newer one designed with a large space for congregational rituals in the main altar room, then everyone gathers there. Otherwise, the singers and the crowd sit in a courtyard facing the main altar room, which allows for a direct *darśan* of the main icon on the part of the performers. Performances last from anywhere between an hour or two (if it is a weekday evening) to all night, an event known as *rātrī jāgaraṇ*, held nowadays only on special occasions. Here, we see one of the effects of modernity upon this performance tradition, for the earlier weekly performances of the Śukravār kī bāl sahailī regularly lasted until the early hours of the morning, and often all night. There is a general sequencing of hymns in a contemporary performance but without the clear demarcation that structured the older ones.

The early part of the evening was devoted to bhakti hymns. These were directly addressed to the Jina as embodied and ritually present in the icon.[21] They included initial hymns that served as *maṅgal* (auspicious benediction) and *darśan* (ritual viewing of the icon).[22] Some hymns explicitly referred to and described Jina icons, and others enumerated the virtues (*guṇ*) of the Jina. Many of these hymns were characterized as *huzūrī*: hymns 'in the presence' of the Jina in which the devotee's supplicant status is clear. Related to the category of *huzūrī* are hymns characterized as *vinay* or *arz*, 'petitions', in which the devotee expresses his own inadequacies and asks the Jina for help. Using a variety of *rāga*s, a skilful leader of a singing group could orchestrate the emotions of the audience.[23] Some hymns were also appropriate to the season; in the season leading up to Holi, for example, many hymns would be in the seasonal style known as *phaguā*, but these hymns would never be sung at other times of the year.[24] In performances I attended, different members of the singing group took the lead for different hymns. In some cases, a particular singer was closely identified with a specific hymn. The singers chose hymns depending on the occasion and mood of the performers and audience, and often in response to audience requests. If the singing group had been invited to perform by a local congregation, members of that congregation who were known for their skills and/or enthusiasm for singing were asked to lead one or two hymns.

This part of the performance lasted from early evening until around midnight. Everyone then took a break for tea and a snack before returning to the singing. For the second part of the performance, a curtain was drawn across the doorway between the courtyard where the singers sat and the altar room in which the

Jina icon was enthroned. The earlier bhakti hymns were explicitly addressed to the Jina, to God as external to and mightier than the devotee. The second period of the night, however, as the singers sang from midnight until dawn, involved *adhyātma* hymns. In these, the singer exhorted the listener to understand that the perfected soul of the Jina is no different in its ultimate perfection and capabilities from the soul of each and every living being. The focus of the hymns is not outward upon the Jina as God different from the devotee, but rather inward upon the soul as identical to the Jina, and God as, therefore, inherent within the devotee. This theme was reinforced by the curtain drawn in front of the Jina icon.[25]

These hymns are also known as *updeśī*, 'instructional'. They emphasize that the material and social worlds are ephemeral and unreliable, and so one should cultivate a sense of inner dispassion and indifference. Many hymns emphasize the greatness of the guru, the teacher, who, in the Jain case, is ultimately the Jina himself, but also the true monk or *yogī* to whom the devotee can have more direct access.[26] Another theme is that since liberation can be attained only from a human existence, but such a birth is very difficult to attain, one should not waste this precious karmically-generated opportunity.[27] Finally, many hymns address the central theme of *adhyātma*: the fundamental difference, according to Jain cosmology, between the innately pure soul and the impure and binding material body. It is essential that a person comes to a knowledge of this difference, or what is known as *bhed-jñān* (also *bhed-vijñān*). This is expressed in a series of dualistic pairs. On the one hand is the soul (*ātmā*, *jīv*) and, on the other, is the body (*deh*), which is insentient matter (*dravya*, *pudgal*). The most dangerous form of matter is karma, which binds the soul to the seemingly endless round of birth and death (*saṁsār*). The soul is what is truly one's 'own' (*sva*, *nij*), while the body and all material and social reality is the 'other' (*par*). The body dies and all social relationships come to an end. The soul, however, is immortal. If one is ignorant, the soul will continue to be bound to body after body. A person thinks that he is his body; *adhyātma* teaches him that, in truth, he is only soul. If a person realizes and actualizes this, he is free.

Let me now turn to an analysis of ten Braj-bhasha hymns that were (and still are) sung in the Digambar community.[28] For the sake of unity, and in continuity with my 2003 article, all of them are by Dyānatrāy (known familiarly as Dyānat), who is the most popular of all the north Indian Digambar poets. As noted above, he lived in Agra and Delhi from 1676 to 1726.[29] The *oeuvres* of all five of the poets that I mentioned above, however, contain similar poems.

Bhakti Hymns

1. *bhāī āja ānanda haĩ yā nagarī (rāg paraj)*[30]

The initial hymn announces the birth of Ādinātha, the first Jina of this era. It describes the joy of his parents, King Nābhi and Queen Marudevī. The hymn also describes the women of the city singing the auspicious benediction (*maṅgal*), and so the singers and the rest of the audience can imaginatively project their own singing back in time to this joyous event. The performance of bhakti erases the temporal distance that normally separates the devotee and God.

Brother[31]
there is joy
in this city
today. (refrain)

Young women
their gait like elephants
their faces like the moon
sing the benediction. (1)

A son has come
to the home of King Nābhi.
Whoever was unfulfilled
now is fulfilled. (2)

Dyānat says
Marudevī's womb is fruitful.
The gods come
and serve her feet. (3)

bhāī āja ānanda haī yā nagarī; (ṭek)
gaja-gamanī śaśi-vadanī tarunī maṅgala gāvata haī sigarī;
nābhirāya ghara putra bhayo hai kiye haī ajācaka jācaka rī;
dyānata dhanya kūṅkha marudevī sura sevata jāke paga rī.

2. *jinavara mūrata terī śobhā kahiya na jāya*[32]

The second hymn is a *darśan* hymn in which the singer proclaims the inexpressible beauty of the icon of the Jina, as well as his own joy and bliss on seeing it. He explains the 'message' of the icon: the Jina seated in meditation demonstrates the virtues of peace and liberation. The perfection of the Jina icon is contrasted with Hindu icons and deities (here named as various forms of Indra), the worship of which only leads to further suffering (*dukh*) and rebirth. The final verse, in which Dyānat says that he worships, meditates upon and sings to the Jina icon, again allows the audience imaginatively to project themselves into the hymn itself.

Excellent Jina
your icon is so beautiful
I am speechless. (refrain)

I see your icon
and my hair stands on end
with joy.
My mind
overflows with bliss. (1)

Your peaceful form
shows the road to liberation
Your pose
shows how to meditate. (2)

The Indras of gods
the Indras of the underworld
the Indras of men—
they seem grand,
but your icon shows
they give only suffering. (3)

Dyānat
worships
meditates
& sings
with mind
speech
& body. (4)

jinavara mūrata terī śobhā kahiya na jāya; (ṭek)
roma roma lakhi haraṣa hota hai ānanda ura na samāya;
śāntarūpa śivarāha batāvai āsana dhyāna upāya;
inda phaninda narinda vibhau saba dīsata hai dukhadāya;
dyānata pūjai dhyāvai gāvai mana vaca kāya lagāya.

3. *aba mohi tāra lehu mahāvīra (rāg gorī)*[33]

The third hymn largely consists of a string of adjectives that describe the infinite virtues (*guṇ*) embodied by the Jina. In the translation, I have added 'you' to each of them in order to express the vocative power of the hymn more clearly. It starts with a direct request as the singer beseeches the Jina Mahāvīra to 'take me across', a standard Indic expression for being ferried across the ocean of rebirth. While, according to Jain theological doctrine, the Jina does not act directly within the world to assist the devotee, it is quite common to find hymns such as this in which the devotee assumes that the Jina is fully active in the world. In the conclusion to the hymn, however, Dyānat turns to a more orthodox understanding of the Jain religious path, as he says that what will save him will be to realize himself the Jina's virtues.

Now take me across, Mahāvīr. (refrain)
You are the beloved of Siddhārath[34]
You are venerated by the world
You uproot sin
You are firm.

You are wise
You are the meditator
You are the giver
You are the knower
Your speech is profound & deep

You are the cause of liberation
You destroy faults
You chop down anger
You are the hero. (1)

You are full of bliss
You are the form of equanimity
You grind up misfortune
You are the guide[35]
You have been celibate since childhood[36]
You are firm in the vows
You have right faith
You are the water that douses the flames of suffering. (2)

Your virtues are endless
You are the lord with no bounds
You are like the moon
    like camphor
    like snow
    like a diamond.
Dyānat says
if I can attain
a single one of your virtues
the affliction of birth will end. (3)

aba mohi tāra lehu mahāvīra; (ṭek)
siddhāratha-nandana jaga-vandana pāpa-nikandana dhīra;
jñānī dhyānī dānī jānī vānī gahara gaṁbhīra;
moṣa ke kārana doṣa-nivārana roṣa-vidārana vīra;
ānanda-pūrata samatā-sūrata cūrata āpada pīra;
bālajatī dṛḍhavratī samakitī dukha-dāvānala nīra;
guna ananta bhagavanta anta nahī̃ śaśi kapūra hima hīra;
dyānata ekahu guna hama pāvaī̃ dūra karaī̃ bhavabhīra.

4. *tuma prabhu kahiyata dīnadayāla*[37]

The fourth hymn also plays on the tension between the merciful activity of the Jina and his theoretical inaccessibility. We see here a Jain expression of a tension between God as near and God as far, and between God as interactive and accessible and God as remote and inaccessible, that is found in many religious traditions.[38] In the hymn's *ṭek* (refrain), Dyānat calls the Jina by an epithet common in South Asian religion: he is *dīn-dayāl*, the lord who shows mercy (*dayā*) upon the oppressed (*dīn*). Dyānat repeats this image in the hymn's final verse, when he describes the Jina as 'enormous in' (or 'full of') mercy (*kr̥pā-viśāl*) and asks the Jina to take him out of the suffering of the world. Elsewhere, he asks the Jina to save him from the root causes of karmic bondage, the twin problems of passion (*rāg*) and hatred (*doṣ*, *dveṣ*). In an image common to the *vinay* genre, Dyānat expresses his own imperfections: he keeps forgetting what he should remember, which is to focus on the Jina and his teachings. The fact that the Jina does not hold Dyānat's forgetfulness against him is further proof of his mercy. At the same time, Dyānat knows orthodox Jain theology. He says that the liberated Jina has gone from this world and now sits in meditation, and that it is the very nature of the superior, liberated Jina that, unlike inferior Hindu and Muslim deities, he does not give anything to his devotees.

This hymn also represents a Jain recasting of a familiar *alaṅkāra* in South Asian literature, the *nindā-stuti*, in which the poet ironically praises the deity through criticism of a perceived fault. A genre based on this figure of sense is especially well known in the devotional literature directed to Krishna.[39] In a Krishna poem, the poet criticizes Krishna for his waywardness, with the ultimate understanding that his contrary actions are an integral element of his divine play (*līlā*). Dyānatrāy gently rebukes the Jina for his aloofness. However, this is a defining characteristic of the liberated soul (and, therefore, the Jina), according to Jain theology, Dyānatrāy turns the criticism upon himself that in his spiritual ignorance, he wants the Jina to act in a way contrary to Jain theology.[40]

Lord
you are called
the mercy
of the oppressed. (refrain)
You've gone,
you sit in liberation,

while I wander
in the web of the world.

I recite your name faultlessly
with mind & voice
morning noon & night.
You give me nothing.
What, then, is my condition?

I may be bad
or good
but I am your devotee.
You know everything that I do.
I ask nothing of you—
just save me
from passion & hate. (2)

Forgive me if I've made a mistake,
for you are full of mercy.
Dyānat says
Lord
just for a moment
take me out of this. (3)

tuma prabhu kahiyata dīnadayāla; (ṭek)
āpana jāya mukata maĩ baiṭhe hama ju rulata jagajāla;
tumaro nāma japaĩ hama nīke mana vaca tīnaũ kāla;
tuma to hama ko kachū deta nahī̃ hamaro kauna havāla;
bure bhale hama bhagata tihāre jānata ho hama cāla;
aura kachū nahī̃ yaha cāhata haĩ rāga doṣa kaũ ṭāla;
hamasaũ cūka parī so bakaso tuma to kṛpāviśāla;
dyānata eka bāra prabhu jagataĩ hamako lehu nikāla.

5. *jinarāya ke pāya sadā śaranaṁ*[41]

Finally, in the bhakti section are two hymns that focus on another common devotional trope in South Asia: the salvific efficacy of the devotee's bowing to and taking refuge (*śaran/śaraṇ*) at the feet of the lord. The first hymn describes how the Jina's feet have sanctified the very ground they touch, and—using a common image that is also found in the first verse of the *Bhaktāmara Stotra*[42]—how the poet sees reflected in the Jina's toenails the jewels in the crowns of the deities who are bowing to them. In this *pad*, Dyānat ends every line with a Sanskritized flourish, using the Sanskrit accusative ending *-aṁ*. He also employs *tatsama* words and compounds like *sadā* (always), *bhav-jal* (ocean of birth) and *antar-pāp* (internal sins), all of which lend this *pad* a Sanskritized formality. In this context, many words can be perceived as parts of long Sanskritized compounds rather than as independent parts of a vernacular sentence with elided post-positions. This is permissible in early Hindi syntax. Here, however, he uses hardly any post-positions. Dyānat gets into this mood to such a degree that he includes even the *tadbhava* word *nikārana*, 'removing, remover', in a Sanskritic compound.

In the second hymn, Dyānat again takes refuge at the feet of the Jina and asks the Jina, whom he refers to as the 'foundation of mercy' (*karuṇādhār*), to carry him across and to remove the sufferings of birth and death.

Always take shelter
at the feet of the Jina King. (refrain)

They lift up the fallen
from the ocean of birth.
They remove the darkness
of the sins inside you. (1)

Any ground they've touched
is a shrine.
They shine
from the jewels
in the crowns
of the gods. (2)

Dyānat says
even death
flees from them.
When will I take the dust
from the feet of the Lord? (3)

jinarāya ke pāya sadā śaranaṁ; (ṭek)
bhava-jala-patita-nikārana-kārana antara-pāpa-timira-haranaṁ;
parasī bhūmi bhaī tīratha so deva-mukuṭa-mani-chavi-dharanaṁ;
dyānata prabhu-pada-raja kaba pāvai lāgata bhāgata hai maranaṁ.

6. *prabhu tuma carana śarana līnaũ*[43]

Lord, I take your feet as refuge.
Carry me across.
    You are the foundation of mercy. (refrain)

I wandered endlessly
from the seven hells
    to the nine heavens. (1)

The eight karmas
are my fierce foes
    they give me unequalled suffering. (2)

Dyānat says
this is my petition:
    take away birth & death. (3)

prabhu tuma carana śarana līnaũ mohi tāro karuṇādhāra;
sāta naraka taĩ nava grīvaka laũ rulyo anantī bāra;
āṭha karama vairī baṛe tina dīnõ duḥkha apāra;
dyānata kī yaha vīnatī mero janama marana niravāra.

Adhyātma Hymns

7. *aba hama ātama ko pahacānājī (rāg kāphī)*[44]

The first of the *adhyātma* hymns, in common with many of Dyānat's hymns in this genre, begins with the simple statement of his spiritual awakening. The use of the short but forceful adverb *ab*, 'now', gives the hymn an immediacy and directness. Dyānat asserts that *now* he has learned who he *really* is, for he has met and recognized his soul (*ātam*, *ātmā*). The verb here is a rich one, with resonances that the English 'to recognize' does not fully express.

The Hindi verb *pahcānnā* means that the person now recognizes, identifies, and understands something or someone in a way that he previously did not; he realizes something that has been hidden so far. It implies a level of intellectual discrimination between truth and appearance. The person not only knows the object made definite by the accusative post-position *ko*, he knows the object *well*.[45] I have translated this with the verb 'to meet' in an attempt to bring across that this is an existential encounter between Dyānat and his soul, and not just a matter of a new mental recognition. Dyānat then places this true self-recognition within Jain doctrine: that his own soul he now knows, is identical in its qualities to the liberated souls that reside in the realm of perfection (*siddha-kṣetra*) at the top of the universe. One of the defining characteristics of the soul is that it is pure consciousness (*cetan*), and so the wise man needs to distinguish the fundamental difference between soul and physical matter (*dravya*), which is 'other' (*par*) to his real self. It is this salvific knowledge that distinguishes between the wise man and a fool.

Now I've met my soul. (refrain)

Just as it shines
in the realm of perfection
so I know it inside. (1)

This body
& all other matter—
they are not mine.
My true nature
is consciousness. (2)

Dyānat says
he is wise
who knows this.
He who doesn't know
is insane. (3)

aba hama ātama ko pahacānā jī; (ṭek)
jaisā siddhakṣetra maī̃ rājata taisā ghaṭa mẽ jānā jī;
dehādika paradravya na mere merā cetana bānā jī;
dyānata jo jānai so syānā nahī̃ jānaī̃ so divānā jī.

8. *bhāī kauna dharama hama pālaī*[46]

The second *adhyātma* hymn is one in which Dyānat proclaims that he has found the true teacher (guru)—which, in his case, refers to the Jina. He indicates that Jainism is only one of many different religions (dharma) available in the world. Dyānat mentions Shaivism, Buddhism, the Vedas, Nyāya and Mīmāṁsā as alternative roads (*mārag*, *mārga*) and alternative faiths (*saradhā*, *śraddhā*), in addition to Jainism. He exhorts the listener to consider the options carefully but affirms that, in the end, the Jina is the true teacher and true lord, and, therefore, the Jina's teachings are the correct ones.

Brother,
which religion should I follow? (refrain)
One man says,
'Sing the lord of the family
in which you were born'.

There's the sect of Shiva,
there are Buddhists,
there are followers
of the Vedas and Nyāya.
There is the Mīmāṃsā sect,
there are Jains.
Each one says
'I am the best'.
So which faith should I follow? (1)

Listen to the teachings
where you find
the form of the supreme lord.
Those others ask many questions,
but don't say anything.
Why should I listen to them? (2)

Among all the faiths
the Jina explained the one road.
Dyānat says,
I have found the true guru.
My good fortune has arrived. (3)

bhāī kauna dharama hama pālaī;
eka kahaī jihi kula mẽ āye ṭhākura ko kula gā laī. (ṭek)
śivamata baudha su veda nayāyaka mīmāṁsaka aru jainā;
āpa sarāhaī ātama gāhaī kākī saradhā ainā. (1)
paramesura pai ho āyā ho tākī bāta sunījai;
pūchaī bahuta na bolaī koī baṛī phikara kyā kījai. (2)
jina saba mata ke mata sañcaya kari māraga eka batāyā;
dyānata so guru pūrā pāyā bhāga hamārā āyā. (3)

9. *anahada śabada sadā suna re*[47]

I have included the next *adhyātma* hymn because it shows how Dyānat and other Jain *adhyātma* poets freely borrowed from the larger, free-floating collection of images and metaphors available to any Hindi religious poet. In this case, Dyānat borrows an image well-known from *sant* poets of the 'unstruck sound' (*anahad śabad* [*śabd*]), as a metaphor for the essence of the universe. This is a cosmic sound that is spiritual, not physical, and so is not heard with the material ear. Dyānat extends the metaphor and compares the unstruck sound to the positive, life-giving buzzing of honey bees, in contrast to the negative buzzing of wood-boring bees, which he compares to karma.

Always listen
to the unstruck sound. (refrain)

It hums by itself
but others don't know it.
You don't need ears
to hear its melody. (1)

It thrums
like the buzzing
of bees—
set your mind inside it. (2)

Dyānat says
know you are liberated
    in this very life.
It's not the sound
of the borer of karma. (3)

anahada śabada sadā suna re;
āpahi gunai aura na jānai kāna binā suniye dhuna re;
bhramara guñja sama hota nirantara tā antaragata cita cuna re;
dyānata taba laũ jīvanamuktā lāgata nāhī̃ karama dhuna re.

10. *hama na kisī ke koī na hamārā (rāg rāmakalī)*[48]

In the final *adhyātma* hymn, Dyānat again declares that the material and social world—the body and the family—is the cause of suffering, not liberation. It is all something 'other' to his soul. In *jag kā byohārā*, he uses a phrase for the 'business of the world' that appeals instantly to the Jain merchants among his audience. He repeats another fundamental teaching of Jain *adhyātma* when he says that the distinction between good and bad in the Jain moral universe of karma—the distinction between merit (*punya/puṇya*) and demerit (*pāp*)—is tied to the world of suffering and rebirth (*saṁsār*). This again is basic Jain doctrine: whereas the distinction between good and bad karma is essential to Jain ethics, even good karma is still a form of karmic bondage and, therefore, not a cause of liberation. Dyānat concludes the hymn by affirming that all the judgements of the world are tied to its two fundamental faults, passion (*rāg*) and hatred (*doṣ*, *dveṣ*), whereas the soul is pure consciousness (*cetan*).

I belong to no one
    no one belongs to me.
The business of the world
    is all a lie. (refrain)
The whole family
    is tied to the body
but I know the body
    is something else.

Merit arises
    happiness increases
sin arises
    suffering grows.
Merit and sin
    are both the stuff of *saṁsār*.

I see all this
and I am the knower. (1)

I stand alone
in the three worlds
and the three times.[49]
But then I mix
with the world
and become stained.

Things seem to be firm
then are cut and torn.
There's neither joy
nor sorrow
for me
in all this. (2)

People like me
and think I'm a good man.
People dislike me
and think I am bad.
Neither like
nor dislike
belongs to me.
Dyānat says
I am just consciousness. (3)

hama na kisī ke koī na hamārā; jhūṭā hai jaga kā byohārā.
tana saṁbandhī saba paravārā; so tana hamane jānā nyārā.
punya udaya sukha kā baṛhavārā; pāpa udaya dukha hota apārā.
pāpa punya doū saṁsārā; maĩ saba dekhana jānanahārā.
maĩ tihũ jag tihũ kāla akelā; para saṁjoga bhayā bahu melā.
thiti pūrī kari khira khira jā̃hī̃; mere harṣa śoka kachu nāhī̃.
rāga bhāva taĩ sajjana mānaĩ; doṣa bhāva taĩ durjana jānaĩ.
rāga doṣa doū mama nāhī̃; dyānata maĩ cetanapada māhī̃.

God Outside, God Inside

Both the bhakti and *adhyātma* hymns involve the use of direct address on the part of the poet, but the person whom he addresses differs. Many bhakti hymns are addressed to the Jina as God, and the singer seeks the Jina's assistance. This is most evident in the *darśan* hymns but is prevalent in others as well. The devotee contrasts his own imperfections with the endless and perfect mercy of the Jina, and beseeches the Jina to save him from his own inevitable failings. The poem is a petition (*vinay*, *arz*). Even when the hymn addresses the devotee rather than God, it urges the devotee to focus attention on the Jina and his salvific powers rather than on the ephemeral, material affairs of the world. The devotee is dependent upon God.

In an *adhyātma* hymn, the poet addresses the spiritual seeker (I hesitate to call him a 'devotee' in this context). The poet urges the seeker to wake up to the truth of the world. Again, the singer recognizes his own inevitable failings; but rather than depend upon God to help him, he must look inwards and help himself. No one else can directly help him, although listening to the message of the guru (in proximate form as a human monk and in ultimate form as the Jina) will show him what he needs to do. The seeker is actually independent; to think he is dependent simply binds him further to karma. The poem is an instruction, a lesson (*updeś*).

In a bhakti hymn, God is external to the singer. God is the sacred Other. The Jina is perfect (*siddha*) and this perfection is visibly evident in the virtuous qualities (*guṇ*) that he embodies.[50] The only way to see God is through the senses, and therefore through the body. While the Jina is now disembodied and resides at the top of the universe in the land of the perfect (*siddhakṣetra*, *siddhaśilā*), his virtues are ritually and artistically inscribed in his icons which the devotee can see in the temple. Bhakti involves both the soul and the body.

In an *adhyātma* hymn, God is not something Other but the innate perfection of the person's own soul. What is Other is all the material stuff (*par-dravya*) of the cosmos, especially the subtle binding matter known as karma. This includes the body. The person should not focus externally on what is Other. Instead, he should focus inwardly on what is truly his own (*sva*, *nij*): the eternal and perfect soul. The senses are part of the material world, and so they do not allow one to see the soul. In *adhyātma*, the soul and body are opposed. True *darśan* is not the external sensory gaze upon an icon but the internal non-sensory direct perception of the soul. Even the senses must be renounced. The soul is simply pure consciousness (*cetan*). If Digambar bhakti entails the devotee developing the correct relationship with the Jina as God outside, *adhyātma* involves the person developing the correct relationship with his own soul as God inside.

This distinction is sung by the performers and heard by the rest of the audience. In the performances of the *sahailī*s in previous decades, it was also visually underscored by the relationship between the people and the Jina icon. During the bhakti hymns, everyone gazed reverently upon the Jina icon as the tangible symbol (and presence) of God outside. Then, during the *adhyātma* hymns, a curtain was drawn in front of the icon, visually instructing people that their gaze should not be directed outwards but inwards, on God inside.

NOTES

1. Publications related to this project are: J.E. Cort, 'Bhakti in the Early Jain Tradition: Understanding Devotional Religion in South Asia', *History of Religions*, vol. 42, 2002, pp. 59-86; J.E. Cort, 'Budhjan's Petition: Digambar Bhakti in Nineteenth-Century Jaipur', *Jaina Studies: Newsletter of the Centre of Jaina Studies*, vol. 4, 2009, pp. 39-42; J.E. Cort, 'Devotional Culture in Jainism: Mānatuṅga and His Bhaktāmara Stotra', in *Incompatible Visions: South Asian Religions in History and Culture: Essays in Honor of David M. Knipe*, ed. James Blumenthal, Madison: Center for South Asia, University of Wisconsin, 2005, pp. 93-115; J.E. Cort, 'Singing the Glory of Asceticism: Devotion of Asceticism in Jainism', *Journal of the American Academy of Religion*, vol. 70, 2002, pp. 719-42; J.E. Cort, 'A Spell Against Snakes and Other Calamities: The *Uvasaggaharaṁ Stotra* Attributed to Bhadrabāhu Svāmī', *Jinamañjari*, vol. 34, no. 2, 2006, pp. 34-43.
2. Funding for the 2007-8 research came from a Senior Short Term Fellowship from the American Institute of Indian Studies. Funding to attend the conference in Miercurea-Ciuc came from a grant from the Denison University Research Fund.
3. For examples of English translations of two of Banārsīdās's short *sajjhāy*-like texts, see Banarasidas, *Dhyanabattisi: 32 Steps to Self-Realisation*, tr. Jérôme Petit, Mumbai: Hindi Granth Karyalay, 2010; and J. Petit, 'Banārsīdās's Karmachattīsī: Thirty-six Stanzas on Karma', in *Svasti:*

Essays in Honour of Prof. Hampa Nagarajaiah, ed. Nalini Balbir, Bangalore: K.S. Muddappa Trust, 2010, pp. 231-42.

4. Cort, 'Singing the Glory of Asceticism', p. 733.
5. All five of these Digambar *stotras* are in Sanskrit, reinforcing a point I have made elsewhere (see n. 6) about the primacy of Sanskrit over Prakrit in Digambar culture, in contrast to the larger role played by Prakrit in the Śvetāmbar intellectual, literary and ritual culture. By way of contrast, different Śvetāmbar Mūrtipūjak lineages have valorized and regularly perform sets of nine or seven *stotras* (Navasmaraṇa, Saptasmaraṇa) that include *stotras* in both Sanskrit and Prakrit.
6. J.E. Cort, 'Making it Vernacular in Agra: The Practice of Translation by Seventeenth-century Digambar Jains', in *Tellings, not Texts: Singing, Storytelling and Performance*, ed. Francesca Orsini, Delhi: Oxford University Press, forthcoming.
7. This is a distinctly north Indian tradition. Research on Digambar bhakti in Dravidian languages, in particular Kannada, Tamil and Tulu, is a *desideratum* of Jain studies.
8. J.E. Cort, 'Dyānatrāy: An Eighteenth Century Digambara Mystical Poet', in *Essays in Jaina Philosophy and Religion*, ed. Piotr Balcerowicz, Delhi: Motilal Banarsidass, 2003, pp. 279-95.
9. An excellent recent discussion of the problems of the *saguṇ-nirguṇ* classification is J.S. Hawley, 'The Nirguṇ/Saguṇ Distinction', in *Three Bhakti Voices*, Delhi: Oxford University Press, 2005, pp. 70-86.
10. Cort, 'Bhakti in the Early Jain Tradition'.
11. J.E. Cort, 'Contemporary Jain Maṇḍala Rituals', in *Victorious Ones: Jain Images of Perfection*, ed. Phyllis Granoff, New York: Rubin Museum of Art, 2009, pp. 141-57.
12. W.C. Roof, 'Spiritual Seeking in the United States: Report on a Panel Study', *Archives de sciences socials des religions*, no. 109, 2000, pp. 49-66.
13. C. Vaudeville, 'Sant Mat: Santism as the Universal Path to Sanctity', in *The Sants: Studies in a Devotional Tradition of India*, ed. K. Schomer and W.H. McLeod, Berkeley and Delhi: Religious Studies Series and Motilal Banarsidass, 1987, p. 27.
14. The use of these hymnals, which is ubiquitous among both Digambars and Śvetāmbars in north India, is not found in south Indian Digambar temples except for important pan-Indian pilgrimage temples where one finds them—but only in Hindi. This is a fundamental regional difference in Digambar Jain ritual culture.
15. The suburbanization of Indian society and, therefore, Indian religion is another academic topic in urgent need of investigation.
16. Information comes from G. Bhāṅvsā, *Prācīn Jain Bhajan Saṅgrah*, Jaipur: author, 1956, as well as from interviews. The other important *sahailī* in Jaipur met on Sundays, and so was called the Prācīn sahelī ravivār (Sunday

Traditional Friends). It was founded in 1894. Information on it is found in another, smaller commemorative volume: G. Godhā, *Hīrak Jayantī Bhajanmālā*, Jaipur: Prācīn Sahelī Ravivār, 1968.

17. The connection between the *sahailī* and this temple is also mentioned by A. Nyāytīrth et al., eds., *Jaypur Digambar Jain Mandir Paricaya*, Jaipur: Śrī Digambar Jain Mandir Mahāsaṅgh, 1990, pp. 32-4. The temple, which was built in 1810, is very popular due to its miracle-working eleventh-century icon of Mahāvīra. It was one of the six temples in the Jaipur area that was associated with the *bhaṭṭārak* of Ajmer. The Śukravār kī bāl sahailī, however, had no specific sectarian affiliation, and performed regularly in both Bīspanth and Terāpanth temples. This lack of a strict sectarian affiliation of singing groups continues today, indicating the extent to which the Bīspanth-Terāpanth distinction in Jaipur is less a matter of strict 'sectarian' differentiation and more one of the ritual tradition followed in any given temple.

18. This temple, which was built in 1819, is affiliated with the Gumān Panth, a Jaipur-area Digambar sectarian orientation within the Terāpanth that emphasizes a very strict adherence to non-violence in its ritual practices and, hence, is also known as the *śuddh āmnāy* (pure tradition) of the Terāpanth (Nyāytīrth et al., eds., *Jaypur Digambar Jain Mandir Paricaya*, pp. 52-3). See my comment above that the Jaipur *sahailī*s are not organized along sectarian lines.

19. As far as I know, this is a male tradition with one exception. The Vīr mahilā saṅgh (Mahāvīra Women's Congregation) is an all-women group, founded in 1942. The founder was a pioneer Jain woman educator in Jaipur and most of the members of the group over the decades have either joined it when they were students or are themselves teachers. A brief biography of the founder, Mohanādevī Jain Nyāytīrth (1914-96), is included in a locally-produced book written by her son: T. Jain, *Bhaktāmar Bhāvāñjali*, Jaipur: Guruvāṇī Prakāśan, 1999, pp. ix-x.

20. I thank Ashok Gangval, leader of the Mahāvīr Saṅgīt Maṇḍal, for inviting me to join him for several performances in 2008. This group was founded in 1959.

21. While Jain ideology holds that the Jina is not present in the icon, an analysis of consecration and narrative texts, as well as hymns such as the ones in this paper, clearly shows that in ritual contexts the assumption has long been that the Jina, in fact, is present in the icon. See J.E. Cort, 'Installing Absence? The Consecration of a Jina Image', in *Presence: The Inherence of the Prototype within Images and Other Objects*, ed. R. Maniura and R. Shepherd, Aldershot: Ashgate, 2006, pp. 71-86.

22. See J.E. Cort, 'Situating Darśan: Seeing the Digambar Jina Icon in Eighteenth and Nineteenth Century North India', *International Journal of Hindu Studies*, vol. 16, 2012, pp. 1-56, for an analysis of the relevant *darśan* hymns.

23. See D.M. Wulff, 'Rādhā: Consort and Conqueror of Krishna', in *Devī: Goddesses of India*, ed. J.S. Hawley and D.M. Wulff, Berkeley: University of California Press, 1996, pp. 124-5, for an insightful discussion of the ways in which the performers of Bengali *padāvalī kīrtan* use the various musical and other performative means at their disposal to shape the emotional responses of the audience. While the desired emotional and spiritual responses are quite different in the two settings, the performative techniques are similar.
24. J.E. Cort, 'Three Eighteenth-century Holī Songs of Bhūdhardās', in *Professor Satya Ranjan Banerjee Felicitation Volume*, ed. J.R. Bhattacharyya, Kolkata: Sanskrit Sahitya Parishad, forthcoming.
25. In his oral response to this paper, Dan Gold commented that this two-part dynamic of a Jain bhakti performance is quite similar to that found in many Tantric rituals, in which the preliminary section involves the worship of an icon or other tangible, external object, and the culminating section involves the practitioner removing his gaze from the external material world and refocusing it internally, on his own spiritual essence. While this is indeed a common ritual pattern in South Asia, in the Jain case, it is not due to any Tantric influence, as much of Jain Tantra does not involve the same initiatory structure of Hindu and Buddhist Tantra. See Cort, 'Contemporary Jain Maṇḍala Rituals'. The Digambar ritual logic emerges directly from the foundational two-truth doctrine of Kundakunda, according to which the path to liberation involves going beyond the realm of relative truth (*vyavahāra naya*) in which things are only provisionally real, to the realm of ultimate truth (*niścaya naya*) in which one sees that only the soul is real. That much of Hindu and Buddhist Tantra also rests upon two-truths doctrines simply indicates another area of continuity among the religious traditions of South Asia.
26. I discuss the genre of hymns in praise of the true *yogī* in J.E. Cort, 'When Will I Meet such a Guru? Images of the Yogī in Digambar Hymns', paper presented at the 12th Jaina Studies Conference, School of Oriental and African Studies, University of London, 19 March 2010. It is important to remember that the Digambar hymns about the greatness of the true *yogī* were composed and sung in a period when the institution of the naked *muni* was extinct in north India. The living and oft-sung memory of the description of a true guru, however, helped lay the foundation for the revival of the *muni* tradition in the twentieth century. See Cort, 'Dyānatrāy', p. 283, n. 10, and M. Carrithers, 'Naked Ascetics in Southern Digambar Jainism', *Man (NS)*, vol. 24, 1989, pp. 219-35.
27. I discuss this trope in the context of Hindi hymns by Bhūdhardās and Daulatrām in Cort, 'The Cosmic Man', pp. 39-40.
28. While I have seen each of these hymns in various collections, the texts here are all from *Dyānat Bhajan Saurabh*, Mahavirji: Jainvidyā Saṅsthān, Digambar Jain Atiśay Kṣetra Śrīmahāvīrjī, 2003. This edition is accompanied

by Khari boli prose trots by T. Jain. This volume, in turn, is based upon the *pads* of Dyānatrāy that were included in *Jain Pad Saṅgrah*, vol. 4, Bombay: Jain Granth Ratnākar, 1909. Most of his *pads* were posthumously collected in 1727 in the *Dharm Vilās*, also known as the *Dyānat Vilās*, Bombay: Jain Granth Ratnākar, 1914. I have seen neither of these earlier publications. The anonymously edited collection *Dyānat Pad Saṅgrah*, Kolkata: Jinvāṇī Pracārak Kāryālay, n.d., contains only 90 *pads*, whereas *Dyānat Bhajan Saurabh* contains 328. As with almost all north Indian Digambar vernacular literature, no work has been done toward establishing a critical edition of Dyānat's writings.

29. Dyānatrāy's ancestors migrated to Agra from Lalpur. They were Agravāls of the Goyal *gotra*. In addition to *pads*, he composed the liturgies for many *pūjās* that are still performed daily by north Indian Digambars. See Cort, 'Dyānatrāy'.
30. *Dyānat Bhajan Saurabh*, no. 2, p. 2.
31. Dyānat frequently exhorts the listener, often in the very first word of the *pad*, by addressing him as 'brother' (*bhāī*), a stylistic device one associates with Kabīr.
32. *Dyānat Bhajan Saurabh*, no. 178, p. 208.
33. Ibid., no. 61, p. 64.
34. Siddhārath (Siddhārtha) is Mahāvīra's father.
35. Dyānat here uses the Persianate word *pīr*, indicating that he drew his spiritual vocabulary from the full range of traditions available to him in seventeenth- and eighteenth-century north India.
36. One of the disagreements between the Digambars and Śvetāmbars concerns the biography of Mahāvīra; the Digambars hold that he never married, and so was celibate from childhood (*bāl-brahmacārī*), while the Śvetāmbars believe that he married and fathered a daughter.
37. *Dyānat Bhajan Saurabh*, no. 185, p. 215.
38. See J.B. Carman, *Majesty and Meekness: A Comparative Study of Contrast and Harmony in the Concept of God*, Grand Rapids: William B. Eerdmans, 1994.
39. J.S. Hawley, *Krishna, the Butter Thief*, Princeton: Princeton University Press, 1983. I thank Jack Hawley for drawing my attention to the way Dyānatrāy reframes the *nindā-stuti*.
40. I should add that I have never heard a Jain refer to this as an example of *nindā-stuti*. The term *nindā* is a loaded one in Jain ethics, for the wise layperson is frequently advised to praise good behaviour (*sukr̥t anumodan*) and to censure bad behaviour (*duṣkr̥t nindā*); these mirror activities, in fact, are central to Jain karma theory. Nonetheless, we can see how Dyānatrāy has adopted a broader cultural genre here and employed it to specifically Jain uses.
41. *Dyānat Bhajan Saurabh*, no. 177, p. 207.

42. Cort, 'Devotional Culture in Jainism', p. 95. A version of this widespread South Asian trope is found in the opening verse of the Sanskrit *Devanāyakapañcāśat* of the fourteenth-century Śrīvaiṣṇava poet Vedānta Deśika. See S.P. Hopkins, *An Ornament for Jewels: Love Poems for the Lord of Gods by Vedāntadeśika*, New York: Oxford University Press, 2007, p. 47.
43. *Dyānat Bhajan Saurabh,* no. 202, p. 232.
44. Ibid., no. 71, p. 74.
45. One of the meanings of the word *pahcānnā* is 'to know well'. See R.S. McGregor, *The Oxford Hindi-English Dictionary*, Oxford: Oxford University Press, 1993, p. 616.
46. *Dyānat Bhajan Saurabh*, no. 125, p. 142.
47. Ibid., no. 73, p. 76.
48. Ibid., no. 271, p. 312.
49. A basic aspect of Jain cosmology is that each soul is distinct (*akelā*) from all other souls, in contrast to some Hindu theologies, such as Advaita Vedānta, that posit a fundamental connection among all souls. See Cort, 'The Cosmic Man', p. 41, for a verse in a hymn by Bhūdhardās that makes this same point.
50. According to Jain cosmology, the Jina is accompanied by thirty-four miraculous phenomena (*atiśay*), and embodies thirty-five virtuous qualities (*guṇ*) and 1008 auspicious characteristics (*lakṣaṇ*). See C. Krause, *Ancient Jaina Hymns*, Ujjain: Scindia Oriental Institute, 1952; rpt., *German Jaina Śrāvikā Dr. Charlotte Krause: Her Life and Literature*, compiled Hazarimull Banthia and Luitgard Soni, Varanasi: Pārśvanātha Vidyāpīṭha, 1999, pp. 313-464, especially pp. 335-7.

BIBLIOGRAPHY

Banarasidas, *Dhyanabattisi: 32 Steps to Self-Realisation*, tr. J. Petit, Mumbai: Hindi Granth Karyalay, 2010.

Bhāṅvsā, G., *Prācīn Jain Bhajan Saṅgrah*, Jaipur: Author, 1956.

Carman, J.B., *Majesty and Meekness: A Comparative Study of Contrast and Harmony in the Concept of God*, Grand Rapids: William B. Eerdmans, 1994.

Carrithers, M., 'Naked Ascetics in Southern Digambar Jainism', *Man (NS),* vol. 24, 1989, pp. 219-35.

Cort, J.E., 'Bhakti in the Early Jain Tradition: Understanding Devotional Religion in South Asia', *History of Religions,* vol. 42, 2002, pp. 59-86.

——, 'Budhjan's Petition: Digambar Bhakti in Nineteenth-Century Jaipur', *Jaina Studies: Newsletter of the Centre of Jaina Studies,* vol. 4, 2009, pp. 39-42.

——, 'Contemporary Jain Maṇḍala Rituals', in *Victorious Ones: Jain Images of Perfection*, ed. P. Granoff, New York: Rubin Museum of Art, 2009, pp. 141-57.

——, 'The Cosmic Man and the Human Condition', in *Victorious Ones: Jain Images of Perfection*, ed. P. Granoff, New York: Rubin Museum of Art, 2009.

——, 'Devotional Culture in Jainism: Mānatuṅga and His Bhaktāmara Stotra', in *Incompatible Visions: South Asian Religions in History and Culture: Essays in Honor of David M. Knipe*, ed. J. Blumenthal, Madison: Center for South Asia, University of Wisconsin, 2005, pp. 93-115.

——, 'Dyānatrāy: An Eighteenth Century Digambara Mystical Poet', in *Essays in Jaina Philosophy and Religion*, ed. P. Balcerowicz, Delhi: Motilal Banarsidass, 2003, pp. 279-95.

——, 'Installing Absence? The Consecration of a Jina Image', in *Presence: The Inherence of the Prototype Within Images and Other Objects*, ed. R. Maniura and R. Shepherd, Aldershot: Ashgate, 2006, pp. 71-86.

——, 'Making it Vernacular in Agra: The Practice of Translation by Seventeenth-century Digambar Jains', in *Tellings, not Texts: Singing, Story-telling and Performance*, ed. F. Orsini, Delhi: Oxford University Press, forthcoming.

——, 'Singing the Glory of Asceticism: Devotion of Asceticism in Jainism', *Journal of the American Academy of Religion,* vol. 70, 2002, pp. 719-42.

——, 'Situating Darśan: Seeing the Digambar Jina Icon in Eighteenth and Nineteenth Century North India', *International Journal of Hindu Studies*, vol. 16, 2012, pp. 1-56.

——, 'A Spell Against Snakes and Other Calamities: The *Uvasaggaharaṁ Stotra* Attributed to Bhadrabāhu Svāmī', *Jinamañjari,* vol. 34, no. 2, 2006, pp. 34-43.

——, 'Three Eighteenth-century Holī Songs of Bhūdhardās', in *Professor Satya Ranjan Banerjee Felicitation Volume*, ed. J.R. Bhattacharyya, Kolkata: Sanskrit Sahitya Parishad, forthcoming.

——, 'When Will I Meet Such a Guru? Images of the Yogī in Digambar Hymns', paper presented at the 12th Jaina Studies Conference, School of Oriental and African Studies, University of London, 19 March 2010.

Dyānatrāy, *Dyānat Bhajan Saurabh*. Mahavirji: Jainvidyā Saṅsthān, Digambar Jain Atiśay Kṣetra Śrīmahāvīrjī, 2003.

——, *Dyānat Pad Saṅgrah*, Kolkata: Jinvāṇī Pracārak Kāryālay, n.d.

——, *Dyānat Vilās*. Bombay: Jain Granth Ratnākar, 1914.

Godhā, G., *Hīrak Jayantī Bhajanmālā*, Jaipur: Prācīn Sahelī Ravivār, 1968.

Hawley, J.S., *Krishna, the Butter Thief*, Princeton: Princeton University Press, 1983.

——, 'The Nirguṇ/Saguṇ Distinction', in *Three Bhakti Voices*, Delhi: Oxford University Press, 2005, pp. 70-86.

Hopkins, S.P., *An Ornament for Jewels: Love Poems for the Lord of Gods by Vedāntadeśika*, New York: Oxford University Press, 2007.

Jain Pad Saṅgrah, vol. 4, Bombay: Jain Granth Ratnākar, 1909.

Jain, T., *Bhaktāmar Bhāvāñjali*, Jaipur: Guruvāṇī Prakāśan, 1999.

Krause, C., *Ancient Jaina Hymns*, Ujjain: Scindia Oriental Institute, 1952, Reprint, *German Jaina Śrāvikā Dr. Charlotte Krause: Her Life and Literature*, compiled Hazarimull Banthia and Luitgard Soni, Varanasi: Pārśvanātha Vidyāpīṭha, 1999, pp. 313-464.

McGregor, R.S., *The Oxford Hindi-English Dictionary*, Oxford: Oxford University Press, 1993.

Nyāytīrth, A., et al., eds., *Jaypur Digambar Jain Mandir Paricaya*, Jaipur: Śrī Digambar Jain Mandir Mahāsaṅgh, 1990.

Petit, J., 'Banārsīdās's Karmachattīsī: Thirty-six Stanzas on Karma', in *Svasti: Essays in Honour of Prof. Hampa Nagarajaiah*, ed. N. Balbir, Bangalore: K.S. Muddappa Trust, 2010, pp. 231-42.

Roof, W.C., 'Spiritual Seeking in the United States: Report on a Panel Study', pp. 49-66: *Archives de sciences socials des religions*, no. 109, 2000.

Vaudeville, C., 'Sant Mat: Santism as the Universal Path to Sanctity', in *The Sants: Studies in a Devotional Tradition of India*, ed. K. Schomer and W.H. McLeod, Berkeley and Delhi: Religious Studies Series and Motilal Banarsidass, 1987, pp. 21-40.

Wulff, D.M., 'Rādhā: Consort and Conqueror of Krishna', in *Devī: Goddesses of India*, ed. J.S. Hawley and D.M. Wulff, Berkeley: University of California Press, 1996, pp. 109-34.

CHAPTER 14

Kabīr's Prosody and a Metrical Reconstruction of his *Pads*

IMRE BANGHA

The fifteenth-century poet-saint, Kabīr, is one of the most outstanding authors of early Hindi literature. His poetry is also the most accessible to a modern Western audience, which made him the most widely translated Hindi poet. At the beginning of the twentieth century the Nobel laureate Rabindranath Tagore presented Kabīr to the world in English, the only poet (apart from himself) whom Tagore ever translated. While Westerners often perceive him as a mystic, in India Kabīr with his vigorous attacks on the hypocrisy in both religions has been viewed not only as a symbol of Hindu-Muslim unity but also, more recently, as one of the earliest representatives of the low-caste Dalit literature. His strong message of a higher devotional consciousness and his advocacy of a direct contact with an indescribable, *nirguṇ*, deity, expressed in powerful poetry with striking imagery, make him one of the most popular Indian poets both in India and abroad, whose appeal seems to have withstood the changing tastes of the past five centuries. In modern times Kabīr has been studied intensively, and one can fill a library with books dedicated to this iconic yet elusive figure.

Kabīr has also been a favourite at the Bhakti conferences. By its choice of theme, therefore, this paper is a tribute to those who have set-up the conference series. At the same time I am using a methodology—prosody as linked to textual criticism—that I find appropriate for a paper presented in Central Europe, where textual studies still hold strong positions. While all of us are aware that a study in our field today cannot be limited to the textual, yet when linked to the wider literary culture textual criticism is an indispensable method. This is especially true considering the lack of good critical editions of many early works in the languages of north India. It is textual criticism that can help us to unfold hitherto hidden layers of transmission of even the most widely researched poets.

In this paper I hope to show on the strength of one of the most popular poets of India that, when adapted to a modern multidisciplinary environment, textual criticism is still a much-needed discipline that can produce not only sound but also startingly original conclusions. I will make an attempt here to reconstruct earlier versions of some texts attributed to Kabīr. After tackling questions of prosody I will examine some peculiarities of transmission.

Neglect for Prosody

There is a commonly held belief that the uneducated weaver Kabīr was not particualrly conscious of his poetic metres and one should not expect metrically correct verses by him. Shyamsundar Das and Parasnath Tiwari, the editors of the two most influential *Kabīr-granthāvalī*s, did not pay much attention to Kabīr's poetic forms. In 1928 Shyamsundar Das presented a diplomatic edition of a manuscript which he thought dated from the early sixteenth century stating that he did not polish the text to present graceful poems abiding by the rules of prosody.

> I did not make any effort to polish them and prepare elegant and beautiful poems that are pure as regards the rules of prosody according to the method current these days.[1]

Parasnath Tiwari's scholarly edition of 1961, the most outstanding attempt to restore Kabīr's texts, gives a list of fifteen criteria for his restoration but, surprisingly, prosody is missing from them.[2] A prosodically consistent text was, however, produced by Ayodhyasimh Upadhyay 'Hariaudh' in his *Kabīr vacanāvalī*.[3]

The most detailed study of Kabīr's prosody can be found in a chapter of Gaurishankar Mishra 'Dvijendra': *Hindī sāhitya kā chandovivecan*, which counted 37 various metrical forms used in Kabīr's *pads*[4] based on the examination of the editions of Shyamsundar Das, 'Hariaudh' and Parasnath Tiwari. Unfortunately, 'Dvijendra' did not have access to an undoubtedly early textual tradition and his inclusion of corrupt later texts blurred his investigation.

The scene has altered when Winand Callewaert and his collaborators published all available early Kabīr-*pad*s in *The Millennium Kabīr Vāṇī*. The editors, just as Shyamsundar Das, presented the text of the manuscripts without any change. The early material introduced in this complex diplomatic edition can give a good guidance to Kabīr's prosody and in turn, the investigation of these songs can take us a step further back in time towards Kabīr.

Reconstruction

In contrast with the popular belief that an illiterate weaver cannot know prosody it can be argued that basic metrical knowledge was not the privilege of the literate classes in early modern times since the most commonly used metrical patterns can be felt after listening to a couple of poems in those metres. Moreover, if we assume that most poems in the early Kabīr corpus were produced among the weavers in Benares, we should also remember that weavers need a mathematical consciousness to be able to produce even the simplest pattern on their textiles, which far exceeds the requirements for the feel or calculation of a poetic metre.[5] In this paper I will argue that discrepancies in the Kabīr-poems as we have them today are due to the specificities of oral and written transmission and not to any lack of metrical command on the part of the composer or composers of the *pad*s.

I became intrigued by Kabīr's prosody while examining the metrical forms found in the famous the Fatehpur manuscript from 1582 published in a book format by G.N. Bahura and K. Bryant.

Here Kabīr's poems are presented in a form that only distantly resembles those of the *pad*s, under which label they figure later. The fourteen or fifteen poems attributed to Kabīr in this manuscript are more closely related to a poetic form already popular in the fifteenth century, namely *caupāī*. Although most of the Kabīr-poems in this Fatehpur manuscript have raga attributions they do not have a marked refrain, as most of Kabīr's *pad*s do in other collections. Taking into consideration syncopation and making minor emendations suggested by other early manuscripts, twelve out of its fifteen stanzas can be reconstructed as being written in one or another variety of *caupāī*, including *caupaī* and *caubolā*.

Let us see the first two lines of the first Fatehpur poem (F1, Millennium 329) as an example. (In the apparatus the siglum Dādū stands collectively for the shared reading of the Dādūpanthī manuscripts as published in *The Millennium Kabīr Vāṇī*.)

saravara[I] *taṭi haṁsinī tisāī* | *jugati binā hari jalu pīyo na jāī*[II] |
kuṁbha līye ṭhāḍhī panihārī[III] | *leja*[IV] *binu nīra kau*[V] *bharahi kaisai nārī* ||

At the edge of the lake
a thirsty *haṁs* bird:
But how, without the wherewithal,
can she drink Hari's water?
There stands the watercarrier.
She's brought her waterpot.
But the well has lost its rope:
how can she draw it up?

(Tr. J.S. Hawley)[6]

As can be seen the lines as they are do not show a strict metre. The four half-lines have 16(18), 19, 17(18) and 21 metric units.

We can observe that after discarding the explicatory possessive particle *kai*—as has already been done by a correcting hand in

[I] saravara] F[pc] Dādū; saravara kai] (unm) F[ac].
[II] na jāī] F[pc] Dādū; narjāī F[ac].
[III] panihārī] F[pc] Dādū; papanihārī] (dittography) F[ac].
[IV] leja] F[ac]; jala F[pc], guna Dādū.
[V] nīra kau] (unm.) F[ac]; nī[rā/ra kā] (unm.) Fa[pc], nīra Dādū.

the manuscript—the first half line is a complete *ardhālī* with 16 morae. The third half-line is also close to a complete *ardhālī* with 16 morae. We simply need to get rid of the dittography of the syllable *pa*—as has again been done by a correcting hand—and to make a more natural reading of the long *ī* of *līye* as a short syllable to arrive at 16 morae. This can either be considered a poetic or, more probably, an orthographic licence. The second half-line is more problematic with 19 morae. On the analogy of *līye* we may try to read a short *i* in the stressed first syllable of the word *pīyo*. But even then the line still has two extra morae. In this case we need to rely on another text critical tool, excision. The only word that the syntax would allow to excise is, surprisingly, *hari*. In this way, the line would be correct with 16 morae. It is true that the poem becomes a bit more enigmatic but its intensity increases with the removal of a word with didactic value.

Let us return to the last half line of our example. The scribes were confused by this desperately hypermetrical passage as can be seen from the corrections in the manuscript. The reading *nīra kau* was corrected into *nīrā* in the manuscript. Moreover, the Dādūpanthī tradition has simply *nīra* in this locus. But even then the half-line remains too long. One cannot give a definitive emendation of this passage although I can attempt the removal of the entire phrase *nīra kau* to arrive at a proper *caupāī* and to a grammatically more compact phrase. (Excised syllables are in square brackets, underlined letters indicate metrical shortening.)

> *saravara taṭi haṁsinī tisāī* | *jugati binā [hari] jalu pīyo na jāī* |
> *kumbha līye ṭhāḍhī panihārī* | *leja binu [nīra kau] bharahi kaisai nārī* ||

Let us stop for a moment at Ken Bryant's discovery of the role of stress in the *pad*s of Sūrdās.[7] Bryant demonstarted that the first syllable of each beat of four morae bears the stress. Apart from the optional breaking of two beats of four morae into a sequence of three beats of 3, 3 and 2 morae as accepted by Bryant, it seems that we can also break them into two beats, one of 2 and another of 6. Both lines can be divided into sequences of 4+2+6+4 | 3+3+2+4+4.

Most of the unmetrical lines in the manuscript are hypermetrical and can be emended by excision and by scanning the long syllables as short. There are, however, a few instances of hypometry. An example, the fourth line of F3 (Millennium 64), is quoted below,

aṣṭa mahāsidhi nava majhārī[I] | *kahi kabīra*[II] *hūdai dekhi bicārī* ||

The eight great accomplishments are within the nine.
Kabīr says, reflect and see (them?) in your heart.

It is again suggested by the 15+18 morae length that we should expect *ardhālīs* in both halves. If we overwrite the subsequent unmetrical transmission and, for example, take the word *hūdai* as *hṛdai* where the second syllable is read as short, then the second half becomes a correct *ardhālī*. The first half is more difficult with its obscure numerical enigma and there does not seem to be an easy way of lengthening any part. It is not difficult to translate this line but its meaning remains elusive as it must have been to most early readers of the manuscript. Here the readings of the Dādūpanthī manuscripts come to our help. The reading of these manuscripts gives a correct *caupāī* with a simple meaning: *aṭha sidhi nava nidhi nā̃va mājhārī* 'the eight accomplishments and the nine treasures are within the name'. What happened here was a corruption in the written textual transmission. The scribe's eye skipped from *nava* to the end of *nā̃va* omitting the words in between, *nidhi nā̃va*. A later scribe already felt that the line was hypometrical and tried to emend it by adding the well-known qualifying prefix *mahā-* to the word *sidhi*. This erroneous emendation shows the extent of how far scribes could feel the rhythm of the poems. The reconstructed version, therefore, is as follows:

aṭha sidhi[III] *nava nidhi nā̃va*[IV] *mājhārī* | *kahi kabīra hṛdai dekhi bicārī* ||

[I] majhārī] (unm.) F^{ac}; mani jhārī] F^{pc2}.
[II] kabīra] F^{pc}; bīra (unm.) F^{ac}.
[III] aṭha sidhi] Dādū; aṣṭa mahāsidhi (unm.) F.
[IV] nidhi nā̃va] Dādū; (omits) (eyeskip) F.

The eight accomplishments and the nine treasures are within the Name.
Kabīr says, reflect and see it in your heart.

This unmetrical reading shows that the Fatehpur manuscript is at least of a third generation written manuscript. The first generation had the reading that has been reconstructed above. The second generation had the reading that was the result of the eyeskip and the third generation is that of the false emendation that we have in the Fatehpur manuscript. Interestingly, the Dādūpanthī tradition in Rajasthan seems to be close to the first generation.

With a similar technique one can reconstruct, apart from the normally four-lined *caupāī*s, a longer *pad* (F10) in the *sār* metre (16+12 morae) and two others—again longer ones (F9, F15)—in a metre called *dohrā*, which is a variation on the *dohā*. These two songs are metrically eccentric but the most probable reconstruction is that their 13+12 morae lines have the two long syllables of the *dohrā* at the end instead of the long-short cadence of the *dohā* (13+11 morae).

The earliest manuscripts present most of Kabīr's songs as very close to another little-studied group of the Kabīr-corpus, the *ramainī*s consisting of a few *caupāī*-lines followed by a *dohā*. Indeed, the *caupāī*-based song is one of the most widely used metres in early Sant compositions. In continuity with earlier Apabhramsha works *caupāī* has a long history in Hindi as the most common metre of narratives. Sadhāru, Dāūd, Viṣṇudās and others used it in the fourteenth and fifteenth centuries.

If we extend our examination to the poetic forms used in the earliest documented collections of Kabīr's *pad*s as published by Callewaert we find that the *caupāī* along with the *sār* metre account for the overwhelming majority of the poems. Out of the first 500 poems of *The Millennium Kabīr Vāṇī* that are not exclusive to the *Guru Granth Sāhib* and are normally present in more than one manuscript, 238 can be reconstructed as composed in *caupāī*. The other popular metre is *sār* (185 poems). There are also 25 songs based on *dohā* and about one tenth of the poems (52) are in other—often corrupt or mixed—metres. As opposed to the songs of the Braj devotees that normally carry the same rhyme throughout a *pad*, Kabīr composed his *pad*s in couplets. Moreover, the Kabīr songs have a tendency of not having a shorter refrain. We can suspect that a reliance of a sort of 'pre-*pad*' performance technique accounts for this specificity of the Kabīr songs. It is probably this sort of performance that the Indo-Persian musical treatise, the *Chiśtiya Bihiśtiya*, mentions as the song genre *kabīrī* stating that Bairagis 'often used to come to Hazrat Makhdum (Shaikh Baha'uddin) to perform their verses and *kabīrī*s' and that Shaikh Baha'uddin himself composed *biśnupad* 'in every *raga*, some in imitation of Kabir, the weaver, and some of Surdas, the blind'.[8]

My next example is not from the Fatehpur manuscript but from the earliest *Pañcvāṇī* manuscript (1614) that served as the most important basis of the *Millennium Kabīr Vāṇī*.

iba tohi jāna na dehū̃ rā̃ma pyāre | jyū̃ bhāvai tyū̃ hohu hā̃māre ||
bahuta dinana ke bichūre hari pāe | bhāga bhaḍe ghari baiṭho āe ||
caraṇani lāgi karaū̃ bariyāī̃ | prema prīti rākhaū̃ urijhāī̃ ||
ita mani mandira rahau nita cokhai | kahai kabīra parau jini dhokhaī̃ || (W3, S3)

I won't let you go now, my dear Rama; be mine as it pleases you.
I acquired you, Hari, after being forsaken for long; it is my good fortune that you came and sat down in my house.
Let me fall at your feet with all my might (?); let me entangle you in my love.
Remain always genuinely (?) in the palace of my heart. Kabīr says, do not fall into delusion.

Here we have to discount for the early orthographic specificity of marking an *anusvāra* before the nasals. In this way the metre comes to 20 | 16; 18 | 16; 16 | 16; 17 | 16. The uneven *ardhālī*s can be emended by the scansion of naturally long syllables as short and by excision again. Interestingly, it is again the names of God in the first two lines that seem to be the easiest to excise. By removing the words *rāma* and *hari* from them, we arrive very close to proper *caupāī*s. Apart from this we need to read the *o* in *tohi* as short and perhaps take the *anusvāra* in the word *maṁdira* as a nasalization and thus keeping the metrical value of this word to three morae. The excision of *hari* can be confirmed by the readings of three other manuscripts (V, J and C in the *Millennium Kabīr Vāṇī*) that do not present this word either. Two of them (J and C), however, interpolate the word *rāma* in the next *ardhālī (bhāga baḍo ghari rāma baiṭhau āai).*

By comparing the Bījak with the Rajasthani and Sikh tradition Linda Hess observed:

> [Krishna names in the *Bījak* . . .] may have been added by singers as the material spread through the country. The virtual absence of the names from the *sākhī*s supports this theory: *sākhī*s are tight, terse, unlyrical, pleasingly aphoristic, therefore less amenable to 'creative' change than the loose *pad*.[9]

One can suspect that at this point we are able to put our finger on a specificity of transition from performance into written culture. If this poem was embedded into a performance probably accompanied by an exposition or sermon, then there was no need to give the clue within the poem. When it is detached from the explicatory surrounding, then the need arises to avoid obscurity. The process is similar to the findings of Christian Novetzke on the notebooks of Marathi Kirtankars that, with the passage of time, came to include the commentary into the songs.[10]

Let us now see an extreme example of metrical confusion. The following poem is presented in the oldest *Pañcvāṇī*:

> *kāhe kū̃ kījai pāṇḍe choti bicārā* |
> *chotihī taī upanā̃ saba saṁsārā* || *ṭek* ||
> *hamārai kaisaī lohū̃ pāṇḍe* | *tumhārai kaisaī dūdha* |
> *tuma kaise bāṁbhaṇa hama kaisai sūda* ||
> *choti choti karatā̃ tuma hī jāe* | *grabha vāsa kāhe kū̃ āe* ||
> *janamata chotī maratahī̃ choti* | *kahai kabīra hari ki nrimala joti* ||
>
> (W171, S126)

Why do you harbour touchability, O pandit?
Is it out of touchability that the whole world emerged? (refrain)
How do I have blood, O pandit? How do you have milk? How is it that you are a brahman and I am a shudra?

Were you born by caring for touchability and untouchability? Then why did you come from your mother's womb?
Touchability when you are born, touchability when you die. Kabīr says, God's light is stainless.

The metrical pattern is the apparently hopeless 22 | 19; 17+12 | 19; 18 | 15; 16;16. The last two lines, however, again suggest a *caupāī* metre as the basis. More precisely, the rhyming pattern of the last couplet suggests a *caupaī* with its long-short ending. If we excise the word *hī* or *tuma* from the third line, emend the two-morae *grabha* to the longer *garbha*, read the final syllable of the word *maratahī̃* as short and emend *kahai* to *kaha*, we arrive at metrically correct lines. But what do we do with the monster-like lines in the beginning? I suggest some trimming again. John Smith in his reconstruction of the *Vīsāḷdevrās* gave a list of forms most often demanding excision for a metrical reconstruction.[11] These include vocatives, personal pronouns and possessive pronouns. Excising these forms (*pāṇḍe*, *hamārai*, *pāṇḍe*, *tumhārai*, *tuma*, *hama*) from these lines we again arrive close to *caupāīs*. We may need to excise the postposition *kū̃* from the first half-line and the adjective *saba* from the second as well as read the final *ī* in *chotihī* short to get to the exact metre. The excision of the word *saba* is confirmed in the other manuscript of this poem.

kāhe [kū̃] kījai [pāṇḍe] choti bicārā | *chotih̲ī̲ taī upanā̃ [saba] saṁsārā* ||
[hamārai] kaisaī lohū̃ [pāṇḍe] | *[tumhārai] kaisaī dūdha* ||
[tuma] kaise bāṁbhaṇa [hama] kaisai sūda ||
choti choti karatā̃ tuma [hī] jāe | *garbha vāsa kāhe kū̃ āe* ||
janamata chotī maratah̲ī̲̃ choti | *kaha kabīra hari ki nrimala joti* ||

Why do you harbour touchability? Is it out of touchability that the world emerged?
How is blood? How is milk? How is a brahman? And how is a shudra?
Were you born by caring for touchability and untouchability? Then why did you come from your mother's womb?
Touchability when you are born, touchability when you die. Kabīr says, God's light is stainless.

The amplification in this poem can be the result of a similar explicatory process as in the case of the inclusion of the names of God in the stanzas examined above. This may be linked to the loss of an original environment, which included an oral exposition. Seeing the abundance of amplification in certain poems one is tempted to speculate that all explanatory amplification already took place in the phase of oral transmission. It is easy to imagine how one performer would include short unemphatic explanatory phrases into the lines and another would learn the song in the amplified form. Later this version would be committed to writing.

It can be observed that the metrical pattern of a song does not change easily since songs are normally transmitted in the same recognizable metrical form in almost all the manuscripts. Considering that the various Kabīr-repertoires do not go back to a written archetype, it can be stated that not even the most fluid oral transmission is able to change the metrical forms easily. In some cases, however, we can spot some metrical change. S164 (Millennium 212) is a composite *pad.* After its refrain, the first four couplets are in *dohā* and the last one in *sār*:

ai(ka) na bhūlā doi na bhūlā | *bhūlā saba saṁsārā* |
aika na bhūlā dāsa kabīrā | *jākai rā̃ma adhārā* ||

They did not forget one and did not forget two—but they forgot the whole world.
Only the servant Kabīr did not forget it, whose foundation is God.

This last line is present in the Rajasthani manuscripts with the only noteworthy metrical variation of shortening the last syllable in one of them and thus arriving at the *sarsī* metre (16 | 11). The text, however, shows more marked variants:

mālani bhūlā loga bhūlī | *bhūlo saba saṁsāra* |
eka na bhūlā kabīra paṇḍita | *jākai nā̃va adhāra* || (Raj102;1)

People forgot themselves in the deception of impurity (*mālinya*)—they forgot the whole world.
Only Kabīr, the pandit, did not forget it, whose foundation is the Name.

A variant close to this *sarsī* couplet may have served as a basis for the *Ādi Granth* version. In the *Ādi Granth*, however, the *sār* couplet was drastically changed and its metre became assimilated to that of the *dohā*s (although it still remained metrically incorrect),

> *mālini bhūlī jagu bhulānā hama bhulāne nāhi* |
> *kahu kabīra hama rāma rākhe kripā kari hari rāi* || (*AG* 479; 14)

> The world is crazy with the deception of impurity, but I am not crazy.
> Kabīr says, God protects me; be compassionate, Lord Hari.

Metres and Ragas

The division of the Kabīr-corpus into *pad*s, *sākhī*s and *ramainī*s is the most widely accepted one that goes back to the sixteenth century to the *Goindvāl Pothī*s. But if we look at Kabīr's prosody, we find that his *pad*s can be divided further into three major metres. Kabīr composed the overwhelming majority of his *pad*s in the *caupāī*, the *dohā* and the *sār* metres. The first two of these metrical forms account for the rest of his oeuvre, too: the *sākhī*s and the *ramainī*s. Indeed, the oldest *Pañcvāṇī* manuscript introduces Kabīr's *pad*s as *śrī rāmāyan*.[12] Is this a reference to the poetic form of combining *dohā*s and *caupāī*s?

Does the *caupāī-sār* metrical divide have any further relevance to the transmission of the *pad*s? It can be observed that scribes had a preference to write down poems that share the same metre next to each other. Consequently, we have long sequences of *caupāī* or *sār pad*s in the *Pañcvāṇī* manuscripts. Moreover, it seems that certain ragas had preferences for certain metres; for example 45 out of the 54 *pad*s in the *Rāmgiri* raga in the *Millennium Kabīr Vāṇī* were written in the *sār* metre, while 34 out of the 41 *pad*s in the *Bhairu* raga are based on the *caupāī*. In the latter case the scribes were aware of this connection and the non-*caupāī* songs only figure as eccentricities in one or two manuscripts, although the *caupāī*s of the same sequence are present in a large number of handwritten books. The connection between raga and metre is not restricted to the *caupāī* and *sār* metres. All seven songs in the *sarsī* metre (356, 357, 358, 365, 366, 367, 368) are in the same *Kedārau* raga.

A Glimpse into Performance History

A study of the poetic forms of the songs attributed to Kabīr can open up new perspectives not only towards the reconstruction of an ever earlier layer of the Kabīr-songs but also to the study of the dynamics of performance and textual transmission in north India in the sixteenth-seventeenth centuries.

Naturally, the reconstruction of a metrically correct poem does not mean that we have arrived at what Kabīr, or the pseudo-Kabīrs, composed. Sometimes it can be detected that a metrically correct line in the earliest manuscripts is already an accretion.[13] We can, however, say that a metrical reconstruction is possible in most of the cases and that the reconstructed poems do not simply take us a step closer to the earliest versions but also present more compact and poetically more beautiful compositions.

We can also detect something of the performance history of these *pad*s through an examination of metrical deviances. In India poems can be performed in at least three different ways: first, they can be recited (or read aloud) without any melody but with the metre clearly felt (*sasvar pāṭh*); alternatively, they can be sung to a melody set to the appropriate metre (*dhun*); and thirdly, they can be sung to a raga and a *tāla* (rhythm). There are several studies examining the performance of *pad*s in the sung raga context[14] prompted by the fact that in many manuscripts *pad*s are grouped according to their raga attribution. It has also been noted that *pad*s closely linked to musical traditions, such as dhrupad singing, may lack metrical structure, as is the case with the poetry of Svāmī Haridās.[15]

It may, however, be the case that the raga attribution is arbitrary and secondary to the poetic form and the frequent grouping together of *pad*s sharing the same metre would indicate this earlier organising force. Moreover, modern research tends to neglect the two other, more metrical ways of performance, which are more ubiquitous since they do not require much musical training.

Dohā and *caupāī* easily lend themselves to set melodies and this may have been the case in early modern times, too. In the recitation and singing to a set melody the metrical forms are clearly perceptible to anyone who is used to hearing poetry. *Tāla* and raga patterns are more complicated and also more flexible and are closely connected with the singing of *pad*s in metres such as *sār* or *sārinī*.[16] As this mode of performance requires training one can even suspect that it would be more characteristic of professional singers than of non-professionals. The relative lack of flexibility in recitation and singing to a set melody also suggests that transmission in this way did not allow as much change in the original metrical pattern as did singing in a raga. In the early manuscripts the metre is still perceptible whereas in the later Kabīr tradition it is not. This leads one to suspect that the early manuscripts were somewhat closer to a recited or set-melody performance, whereas with the process of time raga singing became more and more prominent. With the loss of feel for metre, recitation and singing to a set melody became less emphatic for the *pad*s. It may also have been the case that performance became more and more linked to professionally skilled singers. The written repertoires of these singers, the sources of the earliest Kabīr material (such as the Fatehpur manuscript, the *Pāñcvānī*s and the *Sarvāṅgī*s) already contain the changes effected by the performers.

Conclusion

In this paper I argued that the earliest Kabīr-poems as presented in manuscripts and published by Callewaert in *The Millennium Kabīr Vāṇī* have already undergone two phases of oral transmission. In the earliest phase they were metrically correct poems, probably recited or sung to a fixed melody and embedded into an environment where explanation was either not necessary or was provided along with their performance. This phase can be inferred from the fact that a systematic reconstruction of metrically correct poems is relatively easy and that the reconstructed poems devoid of explicative fillers are more compact, more ambivalent and more powerful. This phase in transmission can be called the poetic phase. In the next phase of oral transmission (what I would call the musical phase) these poems entered into singers' repertoires and spread over wide regions. Probably it was in this phase that they were set to raga and explanations of certain aspects were incorporated in them in the form of hypermetrical fillers.

The Rajasthani tradition, although present in relatively later manuscripts than the Punjabi recension, gives the metrically most consistent text. With the passage of time poems in various metrical forms were attached to the Kabīr-corpus but it is clear that although the poet was more aware of the metre than many of his modern listeners or readers would think, he was definitely not a virtuoso like later poets experimenting with a high number of metrical forms.

NOTES

1. *maĩne ājkal ko pracalit paripāṭī ke anusār kharād par caṛhākar suḍaul, sundar aur piṅgal ke niyamõ se śuddh banāne kā koī udyog nahī̃ kiyā.* S. Das, ed., *Kabīr-granthāvalī*, Kāśī: Nāgarīpracāriṇī Sabhā, 1928, Bhūmikā 6 (tr. I. Bangha).
2. P. Tivārī, ed., *Kabīr-granthāvalī*, Ilahābād: Rākā Prakāśan, 1989, pp. 222-57. See also M. Gupta, ed., *Kabīr-granthāvalī*, Agra: Prāmāṇik Prakāśan, 1969; rpt., 1996.
3. A.U. 'Hariaudh', ed., *Kabīr vacanāvalī*, 13th edn., Kāśī: Nāgarīpracāriṇī Sabhā, 1987.
4. G.M. 'Dvijendra', *Hindī sāhitya kā chandovivecan*, Patna: Bihār Hindī Granth Akādmī, 1975, pp. 168-96.
5. This was remarked by Cynthia Cort at the discussion of the paper at the conference.
6. J.S. Hawley, 'Kabir in his Oldest Dated Manuscript', in *Three Bhakti Voices*, New Delhi: Oxford University Press, 2005, p. 301.
7. K.E. Bryant, 'Three-three-two versus Four-by-four: Metrical Frames for the Padas of Surdas', in *Devotional Literature in South Asia: Current Research 1985-1988*, ed. R.S. McGregor, Cambridge: Cambridge University Press, 1992.
8. M.H. Sherani, 'Makh̲dūm Sahik̲h̲ Bahā'ud-dīn Barnāwī, part 3', *Oriental College Magazine*, August 1929, pp. 88, 87. (F. Orsini's translation in personal communication on 10 August 2010).
9. L. Hess, 'Three Kabir Collections', in *The Sants*, ed. K. Schomer and W.H. McLeọd, Delhi: Motilal Banarsidass, 1987, p. 140.
10. C. Novetzke, 'Note to Self: What Marathi Kirtankars' Notebooks Suggest about Literacy, Performance and the Travelling Performer in 17th Century Maharashtra' paper presented at the 'Tellings, Not Texts: Singing, Story-telling and Performance', seminar held at the School of Oriental and African Studies, University of London, 2009.

11. J. Smith, *The Vīsaḷadevarāsa: A Restoration of the Text*, Cambridge: Cambridge University Press, 1976, p. 13.
12. W.M. Callewaert, S. Sharma and D. Taillieu, *The Millennium Kabīr Vāṇī*, Delhi: Manohar, 2000, p. 115.
13. I. Bangha, 'Kabir Reconstructed', *Acta Orientalia Academiae Scientiarum Hungaricae*, vol. 63, no. 3, 2010, pp. 249-58.
14. See, for example, R. Snell, *The Eighty-four Hymns of Hita Harivaṁśa: An Edition of the Caurāsī Pada*, Delhi: Motilal Banarsidass and London: School of Oriental and African Studies, University of London, 1991; W.M. Callewaert and M. Lath, *The Hindī Padāvalī of Nāmdev: A Critical Edition of Nāmdev's Hindi Songs with Translation and Annotation*, Delhi: Motilal Banarsidass, 1989 and M. Lath, '*Bhajan* as Song: Towards an Oral Stemma of Nāmdev's Padas', in *Bhakti in Current Research 1979-1982*, ed. M.T. Horstmann, Berlin: Dietrich Reimer Verlag, 1983, pp. 225-35. Lath (pp. 226-7) even links the use of the *bhaṇitā* to the musical tradition.
15. L.L. Rosenstein, *The Devotional Poetry of Svāmī Haridās: A Study of Early Braj Bhāṣā Verse*, Groningen: Egbert Forsten, 1997, pp. 321-2. On the lack of a fixed metrical structure in the earliest sources about dhrupad see also pp. 61 and 313.
16. An illustration of how the *sār* metre can be applied to the *tīntāl* rhythm can be seen in R. Snell, *The Hindi Classical Tradition: A Braj Bhāṣā Reader*, London: School of Oriental and African Studies, 1991, pp. 24-5.

BIBLIOGRAPHY

'Dvijendra', G.M., *Hindī sāhitya kā chandovivecan*, Patna: Bihār Hindī Granth Akādmī, 1975.

'Hariaudh', A.U., ed., *Kabīr vacanāvalī*, 13th edn., Kāśī: Nāgarīpracāriṇī Sabhā, 1987.

Bahura, G.N., and K.E. Bryant, *The Padas of Sūrdās*, Jaipur: Sawai Mansingh II Museum, 1982.

Bangha, I., 'Kabir Reconstructed', *Acta Orientalia Academiae Scientiarum Hungaricae*, vol. 63, no. 3, 2010, pp. 249-58.

Bryant, K.E., 'Three-three-two versus Four-by-four: Metrical Frames for the Padas of Surdas', in *Devotional Literature in South Asia: Current Research 1985-1988*, ed. R.S. McGregor, Cambridge: Cambridge University Press 1992, pp. 209-24.

Callewaert, W.M., and M. Lath, *The Hindī Padāvalī of Nāmdev: A Critical Edition of Nāmdev's Hindi Songs with Translation and Annotation*, Delhi: Motilal Banarsidass, 1989.

Callewaert, W.M., S. Sharma and D. Taillieu, *The Millennium Kabīr Vāṇī*, Delhi: Manohar, 2000.

Das, S., ed., *Kabīr-granthāvalī*, Kāśī: Nāgarīpracāriṇī Sabhā, 1928.

Gupta, M., ed., *Kabīr-granthāvalī*, Agra: Prāmāṇik Prakāśan, 1969; rpt., 1996.

Hawley, J.S., 'Kabir in his Oldest Dated Manuscript', in *Three Bhakti Voices*, Delhi: Oxford University Press, 2005, pp. 279-304.

Hess, L., 'Three Kabir Collections', in *The Sants*, ed. K. Schomer and W.H. McLeod, Delhi: Motilal Banarsidass, 1987, pp. 111-41.

Lath, M., '*Bhajan* as Song: Towards an Oral Stemma of Nāmdev's Padas', in *Bhakti in Current Research 1979-1982*, ed. M. Thiel-Horstmann, Berlin: Dietrich Reimer Verlag, 1983, pp. 225-35.

Novetzke, C., 'Note to Self: What Marathi Kirtankars' Notebooks Suggest about Literacy, Performance and the Travelling Performer in 17th Century Maharashtra', paper presented at the 'Tellings, Not Texts: Singing, Story-telling and Performance', seminar held at the School of Oriental and African Studies, University of London, 2009.

Rosenstein, L.L., *The Devotional Poetry of Svāmī Haridās: A Study of Early Braj Bhāṣā Verse, Groningen Oriental Studies*, v 12, Groningen: Egbert Forsten, 1997.

Sherani, M.H., 'Makhdūm Śaikh Bahā'ud-dīn Barnāwī, part 3', *Oriental College Magazine,* August 1929, pp. 72-99.

Smith, J., *The Vīsaḷadevarāsa: A Restoration of the Text*, Cambridge: Cambridge University Press, 1976.

Snell, R., *The Eighty-four Hymns of Hita Harivaṁśa: An Edition of the Caurāsī Pada*, Delhi: Motilal Banarsidass and London: School of Oriental and African Studies, University of London, 1991.

——, *The Hindi Classical Tradition: A Braj Bhāṣā Reader,* SOAS South Asian Texts 2, London: School of Oriental and African Studies, 1991.

Tiwārī, P., ed., *Kabīr-granthāvalī*, Ilahābād: Rākā Prakāśan, 1989.

CHAPTER 15

The Language of Devotion: Transcending the Diversity of Linguistic Structures

INDIRA Y. JUNGHARE

Introduction

Language, religion and spirituality are integral parts of culture. Diasporic Indians bring their languages and religions into their new homelands. Most Indians are multilingual and practice some form of Hinduism. Diverse yet synthetic, Hinduism grants people of various languages and cultures access to temples of any deity or saint and participation in any liturgy. This paper analyses the devotional language of the Hindu-Muslim saint Shri Saibaba as practised in Minnesota. Out of the two saints of this name, Shirdi Saibaba and Sathya Saibaba, it is Saibaba from Shirdi, a town near Mumbai, whose devotion will be investigated.

This paper asks: What are the diasporic characteristics of Saibaba spirituality? What is the nature of worship? Are rituals or devotional songs more important? Which language is used for prayers or devotional songs? Through a linguistic analysis of the devotional language and its socio-cultural adaptations, I will analyse the characteristics of devotion to Saibaba.

Figure 15.1: Shirdi Saibaba

The Shirdi Saibaba Prayer Centre (Shri Sai Mandir)

History and Present Status

Minnesota's Indian devotees have always worshipped Saibaba. Members of the community volunteer to sponsor Saibaba's worship and satsang, 'religious gathering and partaking of food', every month. However, in 2002, when the Hindu Society of Minnesota built a two-million-dollar temple in Maplewood, devotees of Saibaba purchased their old temple and transformed it into a Saibaba mandir. Though the temple welcomes devotees of Sathya Saibaba, Shirdi's Saibaba is the main deity.

Figure 15.2: Shri Shirdi Saibaba Mandir, Minneapolis

Currently, the temple is run voluntarily; five persons help organize the daily and weekly worship, *satsang*, and the celebration of calendrical events. Occasionally, devotees of Sathya Saibaba also use the mandir for devotional songs and religious discourses. Additionally, the temple permits celebration of socio-cultural and religious festivals and *pūjā*, 'worship', including the Ganesh festival, Shri Satyanarayana worship, and blessing ceremonies for newlyweds and children's birthday celebrations. The diverse socio-cultural and spiritual needs of various communities are supported. Devotees volunteer in homeless shelters and donate generously to mainstream cultural activities.

The Structure of the Temple

The temple's two storeys include a main floor and a basement with kitchen. Photos of Baba's prominent devotees occupy one wall of the dining area. On the kitchen counter is a large photo of Saibaba with the sign: 'Food is God, do not waste it'.

Figure 15.3: The Main Image of Saibaba

The main room contains stacks of literature, mainly song-books used while performing *ārtī,* 'waving of a lamp around the face of Saibaba'. There is also a big marble altar and an image of Saibaba from Shirdi. To the right and left on the wall, the Marathi/Hindi words *śraddhā,* 'faith', and *sabūrī,* 'patience', are written in the Devanagari script. In front of the image is a big *pāḍukā,* a

Figure 15.4: Saibaba's Pādūkā (foot memorial)

marble 'foot memorial'; to the left of the *pādukā* are the *ārtī-dīp*, an 'oil lamp', and the *vibhūti*, 'sacred ashes'. To the right of the altar is a CD player for playing *ārtī* and devotional songs. The *prasād*, 'blessed food' (a mixture of almonds and raisins), fresh fruits and *tīrtha,* 'holy water or milk', are kept on a side-table and distributed to the devotees by Baba's attendant. A donation box sits on a small table. Facing the image on the wall hangs the scroll of Baba's Eleven Assurances such as: (1) 'No harm shall befall him who sets his foot on the soil of Shirdi'; (2) 'He who cometh to my *samādhi*, his sorrow and suffering shall cease.'

Next to the coat-room is the *chāvaḍi*, a room symbolic of Baba's meeting place for devotees. Following the ascetic tradition, Baba used to sit before a burning fire pit, the *dhūnī*, and provide advice and support to his disciples. Devotees offered coconuts and incense to the *dhūnī* (fire). After extinguishing the fire, Saibaba would distribute ashes (*vibhūti* or *ūdī*) as blessings. Devotees would eat a pinch and apply a pinch to the forehead. Though a fire-place serves as the *dhūnī*, it is not lit daily. However, *vibhūti* is kept in a bowl used for blessings in the main altar room. The *chāvaḍi* contains photos of Saibaba. On the small marble altar are a large photo of Baba, a small image and a silver *pādukā*. To the right is an idol of Saibaba. The important part of this room is the *dhūnī* as it represents Baba's saintly heritage or the guru tradition of guiding disciples before the fire-god. Most saints used to hold meetings with their disciples before the *dhūnī*.

Little is known about Saibaba's life. He was born Muslim, grew up speaking Marathi, and became an ascetic, a 'fakir'. The best-known event of his life is that on 15 October 1918, at the age of eighty, Baba performed *samādhi* (self-immolation). The Saibaba temple in Shirdi draws both Hindus and Muslims. Although Saibaba was an ascetic, i.e. detached from material possessions, his devotees in the Minnesota temple offer him a silver crown, colourful garlands, and gold chains.

Sai Spirituality

Minnesota's Saibaba devotees differ from those in India. Their diasporic culture represents Hindu tradition that is shaped in the American environment. Most people visit the Sai mandir twice a week at the most—on Thursday evening and Sunday noon. The worship is also less ritualistic. Most devotees do not bring garlands, flowers, turmeric, incense or sweets. Importantly, they are not allowed to perform any rituals but are permitted to participate in the collective performance of *ārtī*, which is led by one person. The absence of incense, fragrant flowers and food creates an atmosphere conductive for concentration on Saibaba.

Sai spirituality chooses the middle path. Though this spirituality precludes ritualism, the devotees worship collectively. The temple plays Saibaba's *ārtī*s and *bhajan*s, 'devotional songs'. Although the devotees may not understand the language of the prayers, they still try to mix words, feelings and thoughts with the sounds of music by putting complete faith in the sung words. Those who do not speak Marathi, the original language of the prayer, simply enjoy the music. Mostly Hindus attend, but about 2 per cent of those attending are Muslims. Saibaba primarily receives ritualistic worship; most Muslim devotees, not believing in idols, may not want to come to the temple. Saibaba worship also focuses on cleanliness; devotees wash their hands before prayers. Similarly, devotees are given napkins before they receive the *tīrtha* 'sacred and blessed water', customs that are absent in Indian worship.

The Nature of the Prayer Literature and its Language

I have collected the literature of prayers and devotional songs. These prayers and songs are transliterations of the Marathi originals. Saibaba had many well-educated devotees, and it is they who produced most of the Marathi literature used in the temple of Shirdi as well as in Minneapolis. As written language tends to evolve more slowly, the language of Saibaba-literature is somewhat closer to older forms of Marathi. The transliterated literature has characteristics that are greatly influenced by Telugu grammatical structure since most of the devotees speak Telugu.

The devotees speak various regional languages and dialects as well. As all of them sing and pray together, and since no priest has a monopoly on the recitation of prayers, the literary forms have been modified. English transliteration has led to the assimilation of the diverse original genres into four types of *ārtī*s: (1) *kākaḍ ārtī*: traditional *ārtī* offered to Saibaba at 9:15 a.m.; (2) *madhyānha ārtī*: traditional *ārtī* offered to Saibaba at noon; (3) *dhūp ārtī*: traditional *ārtī* offered to Saibaba at 6:00 p.m.; and (4) *śej ārtī*: traditional *ārtī* offered to Saibaba at 8:00 p.m. Sub-genres were made part of the *ārtī* literature without keeping the distinctions in form, i.e. without mentioning names of the sub-genres or numbering the couplets. Compare the temple handout transliteration with the transcription of the Marathi original below:

I. *Bhupāḷī* (morning song, *kākaḍ ārtī*)

Transcription and Translation	Temple handout: Transliteration
joḍuniyā kara caraṇī ṭhevilā māthā | (Folding my hands, I place my head at your feet)	*Jodunia kara charani thevila matha*
parisāvī vinantī mājhī sadgurunāthā ||1|| (Oh my True Guru, please listen to my request)	*Parisavi vinanti majhi Sadgurunatha*
aso-naso bhāva ālo tūjhiyā ṭhāyā | (I may not be very religious, but I came to you)	*Aso-naso bhav alo tujhiya thaya*
krupā driṣṭi pāhe majakaḍe sadgururāyā ||2|| (Oh my True Guru, please look at me with compassion)	*Kirpa drishti pahe majkade Sadgururaya*

Following is the transliteration of the second type of the *kākaḍ ārtī*, comprising eight lines generally called verses or stanzas—occurring in fours. This metrical composition to a specific melody is called *bhupāḷī*.

II. *Bhupāḷī*

Transcription and translation	Temple handout: Transliteration
uṭhā pāṇḍuraṅgā ātā prabhāta-samayo pātalā | (Oh God Panduranga, please wake up; it is morning)	*Utha Panduranga ata prabhata samayo patala*
vaiṣṇavāñcā meḷā garuḍapārī dāṭalā ||1|| (Devotees have gathered at the Garuda (front) gate)	*Vaishnawancha mela garuda pari datala* ||1||
garuḍa-pārā-pāsunīmahādvārā paryanta | (From the gate up to the sanctuary)	*Garuda para pasuni maha dwara paryanta*
suravarāñči māndī ubhī joḍūniyā hāta ||2|| (An assembly of divine devotees is waiting with folded hands)	*Suravaranchi mandi ubhi joduniya hatha* ||2||

Similarly, the third type of *bhupāḷī* consists of eighteen lines divided into two major sections along with the refrain, while the fourth type consists of twelve lines arranged in six couplets. All *bhupāḷī*s are in the genre of *ārtī*. As the original Marathi structure is not kept in transliteration, the diversity of melodies and styles is lost. See the examples below:

III. *Bhupāḷī*

Transcription and translation	Temple handout: Transliteration
uṭhā uṭhā śrī sāināthā gurū čaraṇa-kamala dāwa | (Oh Shri Guru Sainatha, please wake up; please show your lotus feet)	*Utha utha Shri Sainatha guru charana kamala dawa*
ādhi ***vyādhi*** *bhāvatāpa vārunī tārā jaḍavīvā* || *dhru*|| (Please protect our lives from sickness and disease, trouble and dangers)	*Aadhi* ***vyadi*** *bhawatapa varuni tara jadajiwa*

gelī tumhā soḍuniyā bhāva-tama-rajanī vilayā ǀ (The dark night ran away from you)	*Geli tumha soduniya bhawa tama rajani vilaya*
*pari hī **ajñānāsi** tumači bhulavi yogamāyā* ǀ (Just as your yogic power destroys ignorance)	*Pari hi **agnanasi** tumachi bhulawi yogamaya*

Sometimes, complex original structural forms have been reorganized into verses; for example, compare the transcription of the original fourth *Bhupāḷī* with its temple transliteration below. Also, phonological and phonetic structures of a number of words do not match, creating problems in meaning; for example, *vyādhī* and *ajñāna* above as well as *veḷā* and *goḷā* below are transliterated as *vyadi*, *agnan*, *vela*, and *gola*.

IV. *Bhupāḷī*

Transcription and translation	Temple handout: Transliteration
*uṭhā pānḍuraṅgā ātā darśana **dyā** sakaḷā* ǀ (Oh Panduranga, please wake up so everyone can share your presence)	*Utha Panduranga ata darshana **dhya** sakala*
*jhālā aruṇodaya saralī nidreči **veḷā*** ǀǀ1ǀǀ (The sun has risen; it is time to awake)	*Jhala arunodaya sarali nidrechi **vela***
*santa sādhū munī avaghe jhāletī **goḷā*** ǀ (Saints, holy men, and sages have all gathered)	*Santa sadhu muni avaghe jhaleti **gola***
soḍā śeje sukha ātā baghu dyā mukha-kamaḷā ǀǀ2ǀǀ (Please give up the comfort of sleep and permit us to see your lotus face)	*Soda sheje sukhe ata baghu **dhya** mukha-kamala*
jhāle mukta** dwara lābha jhālā **rokaḍā (Liberation! Immediate happiness!)	***Jale mukta** dwara labha jhala **rokada***
*viṣṇu dāsa nāmā ubhā gheuni **kākaḍā*** ǀǀ3ǀǀ (Holding the morning lamp, the servant of Vishnu is waiting)	*Vishnu dasa nama ubha gheuni **kakada***

There are problems in the perception of aspirated affricates in the temple transliteration. For example, *d* has been changed to *dh* in *dyā* but *jh* has lost aspiration in *jale* which can create ambiguities of meaning: *jhāle mukta*, 'became free', *vs* the uninterpretable *jale mukta*.

The *ārtī* genre also includes the religious song genre *abhaṅga* as exemplified below:

V. *Abhaṅga*

gheuniyā pañčāratī | *karū bābāñčī āratī* || *karū sāīñčī āratī* ||1||
(Let us perform the *ārtī* to Baba with five lamps. Let us perform the *ārtī* to Sai.)

uṭhā uṭhā ho bāndhava | *owāḷū hā ra mādhava* || *sāī ra mādhava* ||2||
(Wake up, oh brothers, wake up; let us honour the sage, the Sai-divine.)

karūnīyā sthira mana | *pāhū gambhīra he dhyāna* ||
(Let us calm our minds; let us see the profound yogi.)

sāīñče he dhyāna || *pāhū gambhīra he dhyāna* ||3||
(Let us see Sai yogi; let us see the wise yogi.)

Similarly, pamphlets and booklets which are compositions of specific genres of Marathi religious literature on Saibaba, such as *shrī sāī stotra* 'hymns of Sai praise'; *shrī sāī mahātmya*, 'greatness of Shri Saibaba', *shrī sāī dhyāna,* 'Shri Sai-Meditation', and *shrī Sāinātha-stavana mañjarī,* 'the holy flower in praise of Sai', are absent from the Minnesota temple. This means that the devotees of Saibaba of the Indian-American diasporic tradition have integrated the varied compositions and texts into the broad genre of *ārtī* literature.

Linguistic Analysis of the Structure of the *Ārtī* in Transliteration

Transliteration has further simplified the Marathi grammatical structures.

Phonetics/Phonology

Nasalization, vowel length and retroflexion are not indicated in the transliteration of the temple handouts. Occasionally, *anusvara,* the symbol for nasalization, is transliterated as '*n*', such as in the word *dasan*. As nasalization in Marathi is not phonemic, there is no problem in understanding the meanings of words. Similarly, length differences between *i* vs *ī* and *u* vs *ū* do not create problems of meaning. However, differences between *a* vs *ā* and the dental *t, th, d, dh, n, l* vs the retroflex *ṭ, ṭh, ḍ, ḍh, ṇ, ḷ* do create problems of meaning. The examples below will illustrate:

(i) Vowel length: *kāyā*, 'body', vs *kāya*, 'what?'
nāmā, 'the Marathi saint Nāmdeva', vs *nāma*, 'name'

(ii) Retroflexion: *kākaḍā*, 'large wick', vs *kākada*, 'crow-like'
bhupāḷī, 'hymns sung in the morning', vs *bhupālī*, 'girl's name'
kuṭhonī, 'from where?' vs *kuthoni*, 'to make strenuous efforts'

(iii) Deletion of vowels: *jagannātha* ⇒ *jagannāth*, 'Lord of the world'

(iv) Loss of aspiration: *mājhyā* ⇒ *mājyā*, 'mine', *mujhako* ⇒ *mujako*, 'to me'

(v) Use of aspirates for non-aspirates: *calā* vs *chalā* 'let us go'.

Morphological and Syntactic Problems

The *ārtī* focuses on the dialogue between the devotees and Saibaba. However, the wrong use of vowels, consonants and words impacts the emotional aspect of worship. An example is: *krupā karo mājhyā devā,* 'may you bless me, God', as opposed to *krupā kara mājhyā devā,* 'Bless me, God'. The first expression is polite while the second one sounds demanding.

Semantics

The grammatical problems mentioned above do not have significant impact on prayers and bhakti poetry for various reasons. First, the context corrects the misinterpretation of words and sentences. Second, though many devotees do not know Marathi, they simply enjoy the prayers and music. Third, and most important, intuitive knowledge of Hindu spirituality and the bhakti tradition revolves around the use of sound, root syllables, *mantras*, prayers and *ārtīs*. The meanings and functions of these lead to the devotees' perception and acceptance of the philosophies of non-dualism, dualism or qualified non-dualism, i.e. diverse relationships of the self with the Absolute. Devotees approach the deity through familial and intimate relationships, i.e. God as father, mother, guru, friend and loving companion. To understand the meaning of *ārtī* and its psychological and metaphysical implications, it is necessary to briefly review Indian theories of meaning.

Indian Theories of Meaning

From antiquity, Indians have analysed the origins of language, different forms of speech, relations between words and meaning, the relative permanence or impermanence of speech, and the development of speech into various dialects and languages. Indian etymologists conceived the fourfold classification of words, and the grammarians produced a scientific system of etymology and semantics that was also a remarkable philosophy of word and meaning.[1] Literature on word and meaning in Indian thought is so vast that it is beyond the scope of a short article to present a systematic account of Indian thought and draw a comparison with Western theories. The following discussion outlines important theories of word and meanings—language and thought.

Words, Propositions and Meanings

In Indian thought, there are two approaches to the study of the problem of meaning: *khaṇḍapakṣa* (morphology) and *akhaṇḍapakṣa* (syntax), which, according to Rajendra P. Srivastava, are comparable to Association theory and Gestalt theory in psychology.[2] According to *khaṇḍapakṣa*, or the analytical method, words are considered autonomous units of thought. Language studies are founded on words, and a sentence consists of linking words. The idea that words possess individual meanings is generally accepted in schools of Indian philosophy and, in the case of nouns, words are taken as names of things. Thus, the regular philosophical term for a thing, namely *padārtha* (*pada* and *artha*), is literally 'the meaning of a word'.[3] The Sanskrit term *nāmarūpa* (name and form), which stands for the word of things, also suggests that objects can be comprehended through names or visible shapes, and that names and shapes together constitute the essence of things. Buddhist thought[4] (both Mahayana and Hinayana) is a process philosophy that considers life as a process of constant flux (change or instability) and the self is non-substantive and evolutionary. The word *nāma* means 'perception, feeling, disposition and consciousness' while *rūpa* means form (body). The similarity between the nature of language and the nature of the individual self should be noted. As the self constantly changes and evolves, language also evolves. The five *skandhas* (aggregates) constitute the phenomenal world and the person, resulting in continued rebirth. The *skandhas* are characterized by *anitya* (constant change), *duḥkha* (suffering) and *anātman* (no soul).

Non-reality of Words

Even in ancient times, some schools emphasized the unreal (temporary) nature of words. According to Yāska, a Sanskrit grammarian who preceded Panini (fourth century BC), and the author of *Nirukta* (a technical treatise on etymology and the semantics of words), the statement as a whole is regularly present in the perspective of the hearer, and the fourfold classification of words into noun, verb, particles (post-positions and prefixes), adverbs and conjunctions does not hold up well.[5] Words are used for naming for reasons of simplicity and universal applicability. Other grammarians, such as Bhartṛhari and Vartakṣa, also believed that only the sentence is regularly present in the mind of the hearer.

Reality of Words and the Nature of Comprehension

Even among those who accept the reality of words, views differ regarding the nature of the verbal comprehension of a sentence. The two known views are: *abhihitānvayavāda* (logically connected, syntax) and *anvitābhidhānavāda* (morphemes simply linked to). *Abhihitānvayavāda,* followed by some Naiyāyikas, belonging to the school of logic (one of the six orthodox schools of Hindu philosophy), and the Bhaṭṭa school of mīmāṁsakas, holds that people first remember isolated word-meanings, and simultaneous collective memory gives the mutually connected meaning. Syntactically related word-meanings constitute the sentence-meaning. In sentences, words only perform the task of conveying isolated meanings. Syntactic relations are conveyed by word meanings, not by words.

Anvitābhidhānavāda, supported by the Prabhākara school of Mīmāṁsā, makes a further advance whereby words gradually convey the connected sentence-meaning. Individual words do not convey any meaning except in sentences and words must always be associated syntactically with injunctive verbs.[6] Sentences are units of speech though words can be considered units of language. These theories claimed that the necessary conditions for syntactic relations between words in a sentence are mutual expectancy, consistency and proximity. They also recognized the importance of context and intentions in determining the meanings of words.[7]

Primacy of the Sentence

According to Bhartṛhari, sentences are the essence of linguistic structures. They form a concept of 'wholeness', or a theory of mind and brain, describing the *gestalt effect.* Words have no independent reality and are only hints that help the listener arrive at a meaning. Many problems in linguistics are based upon the primary assumption that words are the counters of thought, but once that assumption is set aside and words are given their proper place in the language as unreal abstractions, the complexities of meaning disappear. Words have reality only at the pragmatic level. This philosophy explains why lost and mispronounced words in prayers and *ārtī*s do not matter much for devotees.

Importance of the Context

Ānandavardhana took cues from Bhartṛhari and developed the theory of *Vyañjana,* 'suggestion or allusion', whereby *artha,* 'meaning', included not only cognitive and logical meanings, but also emotional and socio-cultural connotations.[8] Logicians and philosophers may be satisfied with that portion of the total meaning of an utterance which is logical, precise and accurate, and which can be objectively studied, but poets and linguists cannot neglect vast areas of language that are imaginary or indescribable.

Word and Meaning: Relationship

As R.P. Srivastava points out, in India, all schools of thought have assumed a direct relationship between *śabda,* 'word', and *artha,* 'meaning', which corresponds to the relationship between the signifier/signal (*signifiant*) and signified/signification (*signifié*) of Saussure.[9] A sign for Saussure is twofold, made up of a concept (*signifié*) and an acoustic image (*signifiant*), both psychical entities. Without the concept, he says, the acoustic image would not be a sign.[10] According to Saussure's critics, C.K. Ogden and I.A. Richards, there is no direct relationship between the word and referent, and the relationship is only attributed.[11] Srivastava asserts that there is no contradiction between Saussure's philosophy and the Indian theory of the *śabda-artha* relation. A symbol is directly related only to the thought or meaning and not to the thing meant.

Bhartṛhari's Sphoṭa Theory: Philosophy of the Universal Essence

Bhartṛhari emphasizes that words are psychical entities which reveal themselves through articulate sounds. Indian thinkers recognized that words are something more than audible sounds uttered by speakers and heard by listeners. The concept of *sphoṭa* is something more than what is generally implied by the term linguistic sign, which is an imperceptible and eternal element in sounds and words, and a real vehicle of the idea that bursts and flashes on the mind when spoken.

The most important feature of Bhartṛhari's discussion about word, proposition and meaning is that his entire epistemological and semantic discussion is based on purely idealistic metaphysics, according to which the transcendental speech-essence (*śabda-tattva*) is the first principle of the universe. The *Vākyapadīya*, his monumental work on the philosophy of language, claims that the whole phenomenon of material existence is only the appearance (*vivarta*) of the speech principle, which is identical with the Ultimate Reality, Brahman: *śabdaṁ paraṁ brahman*. The entire world of things, whose individuality consists only of names and forms (*nāma* and *rūpa*), has its source in this speech-essence. Symbol and meaning are only two aspects of the same principle. In fact, it is the same speech-essence, which appears in the form of various ideas and their symbols—words and sentences—that constitutes the entire phenomenological world.

It is clear that (a) Bhartṛhari's concept of meaning is rooted in non-dualism; (b) the whole superstructure erected by Bhartṛhari assumes that words are indivisible units, and the plurality of linguistic forms, related as denoter and denoted, only has a provisional pragmatic validity.

Speech-essence, which is the Ultimate Reality and the essence of consciousness, has neither beginning nor end and is unchanging; but the phenomenal world appears as evolutionary, pluralistic and impermanent.

Concluding Remarks

The very nature of Saibaba's bhakti tradition is simple. There is no elaborate ritual or complex speculative metaphysics. This easy-going spirituality, combined with Saibaba's diverse and collective cultural and linguistic heritage—Islamic and Hindu as well as Marathi, Hindi, Urdu, Telugu, and others—is well suited for the Indian-American diasporic community, which also represents diversity of ethnicities. The multifaceted character of the diaspora has forced diverse Marathi literary genres on Saibaba to coalesce into one genre of *ārtī* of the linear form. Additionally, English transliteration has simplified the phonological, morphological and syntactic structures of *ārtī*s, which, at times, created semantic problems.

Problems of meaning, however, do not matter to devotees. As the language of spirituality primarily deals with the devotees' perception of reality, the transcendental nature of the language of Sai-bhakti can best be explained by Bhartṛhari's *sphoṭa* theory, which takes the utterance as a whole (gestalt) whose parts are not relevant. Words have no reality of their own; they are only hints that help listeners arrive at the meaning. What matters to devotees is speech-essence, sound, Absolute Reality.

Given George Lakoff's theory of epistemology,[12] knowledge is obtained through the language of metaphor. The language of Sai spirituality can be called the metaphorical language of love. The language of Sai-bhakti is a system of various dialects comprising linguistic (grammar and meaning), socio-linguistic (cultural), psycho-linguistic (mental perception), and meta-linguistic (the relationship of language to culture and society). Meta-linguistics goes beyond the meaning of words in the mind and takes into consideration not only what it is said but also how it is said. The function of the language of devotion is to help devotees transcend the world of suffering and reach the heavenly and mystical realms of divinity. Through loose linguistic structure, the language of bhakti frees devotees from oppression resulting from worldly duties, obligations, and demands. More importantly, the nature of the multifaceted diasporic community and their Western life-styles have contributed to simplifying Sai-bhakti and its language by means of acculturation.

NOTES

1. R.P. Srivastava, *Language, Meaning, and Religion*, Delhi: Ajanta Publications, 1990, p. 78. Srivastava's opinion receives support in P.C. Chakravarti, *Linguistic Speculations of the Hindus*, Calcutta: University of Calcutta, 1933, p. 5.

2. Srivastava, *Language, Meaning, and Religion*, p. 80.
3. Ibid.
4. R. Robinson and W. Johnson, *The Buddhist Religions: A Historical Introduction*, Belmont, CA: Wordsworth, 2005, p. 24.
5. Srivastava, *Language, Meaning, and Religion*, p. 81.
6. Ibid., p. 82.
7. Ibid.
8. R. Kunjunni, *Indian Theories of Meaning*, Madras: The Theosophical Publishing House, 1977, p. 10.
9. Srivastava, *Language, Meaning, and Religion,* p. 84.
10. F. Saussure, *Course in General Linguistics*, ed. C. Bally, A. Sechehaye and A. Riedlinger, tr. W. Baskin, Glasgow: Fontana/Collins, 1977, pp. 23-31.
11. C.K. Ogden and I.A. Richards, *The Meaning of Meaning*, Orlando, Florida: Harcourt Brace Jovanovich, 1989, p. 5 (note).
12. G. Lakoff and M. Johnson, *Metaphors We Live By*, Chicago: University of Chicago Press, 1980.

BIBLIOGRAPHY

Chakravarti, P.C., *The Linguistic Speculations of the Hindus*, Calcutta: University of Calcutta, 1933.

Kunjunni, R., *Indian Theories of Meaning*, Madras: The Theosophical Publishing House, 1977.

Lakoff, G. and M. Johnson, *Metaphors We Live By*, Chicago: University of Chicago Press, 1980.

Ogden, C.K. and I.A. Richards, *The Meaning of Meaning*, Orlando, Florida: Harcourt Brace Jovanovich, 1989.

Robinson, R. and W. Johnson, *The Buddhist Religions: A Historical Introduction*, Belmont, CA: Wordsworth, 2005.

Saussure, F., *Course in General Linguistics*, ed. C. Bally, A. Sechehaye and A. Riedlinger, tr. W. Baskin, Glasgow: Fontana/Collins, 1977.

Srivastava, R.P., *Language, Meaning, and Religion*, Delhi: Ajanta Publications, 1990.

CHAPTER 16

'Diamonds are a Girl's Best Friend'
The Female Body and Ornaments in Mīrābāī's *Padāvalī*

FLORENCE PASCHE GUIGNARD

Introduction

This title borrowed from a famous song associates femininity with ornaments, which are the main focus of our investigation on the representation of the female body in the poetic songs attributed to Mīrābāī, the sixteenth-century Rajput princess turned ascetic. Archaeological remains show that traditions of decorating the human body have existed all over the world since prehistoric times. Beauty care and aesthetic codifications are culturally and locally defined. In India (and elsewhere), ornaments have played a major role in the lives of women. While male practices of caring for the body and using ornaments also exist and Krishna-bhaktas, including Mīrābāī, often describe the splendour of Krishna (wearing the peacock crown, a yellow garment, earrings, a *tilak* on his brow, flower garlands, necklaces, etc.), our focus here will be exclusively on female ornamentation and representation of the body. The specificities of decorating practices as they appear reflected in the *Padāvalī* of Mīrābāī, considered a 'multiple tradition',[1] will be highlighted and contrasted with other textual testimonies, in the perspective of comparative study of religions, with special attention to gender issues. Moreover, as the method of cross-cultural comparison recommends, relevant contrastive examples from other cultures will also be summoned but limited to footnotes.

Ornaments and jewels can be understood as part of material culture or as metaphors. In several traditions, jewels and various ornaments are given as offerings and are conspicuous marks of social status and rank. Women receive them as gifts on special occasions. Very often, the dowry or bride-price consists of jewels, clothing and other feminine items. Ornaments and jewels represent wealth or symbolize something extremely precious. The word 'jewel' was frequently used in Buddhist and other Indian philosophical traditions.[2] In the titles of several works,[3] it also stands for spiritual value. Some myths and legends have diamonds or gold as their main theme.[4]

Before presenting Mīrābāī's specific use of the lexical field of ornaments, a preamble will briefly show how this topic is related to women in general in the Indian context. Despite the many local varieties in the shape, material and use of male and female ornaments, I consider that representations of these ornaments—in particular, in texts[5]—are stable enough through the time and space of the Indian subcontinent to attempt a selective but relevant comparative survey, starting with evidence about women and ornaments in the *Laws of Manu.*

Women and Ornaments in the *Laws of Manu*[6]

Several excerpts from the *Laws of Manu* mention ornaments in relation to women. Ornaments and negative behaviour are associated with women in *Manusmṛti* 9,17: 'The bed and the seat, jewellery, lust, anger, crookedness, a malicious nature, and bad conduct are what Manu assigned to women'. In the same chapter, a 'bad' spouse can be deprived of her 'jewellery and personal property' as punishment for showing disrespect (9,78). Ornaments appear as a commodity for woman in the same way as furniture (the bed and the seat).

Other regulations apply to the inheritance of ornaments in

Manusmṛti 9,200: 'The heirs should not share the jewellery worn by a woman during her husband's lifetime, for if they share them, they will fall'. An implicit distinction can be made between ornaments which have been worn and those which have not. In this sentence from Manu, the term 'ornaments' (*alaṅkāra*) means a set composed of several items (for example: earrings or ear pendants, forehead ornament, nose pin or nose ring, necklace(s), bracelets, bangles, anklets, finger or toe rings). In this context, the sharing of female ornaments between heirs can take place after the death of the woman or perhaps also after the death of her husband, if she is deprived of her ornaments as a widow. Why cannot ornaments previously worn by a woman be shared? From a material point of view, jewels are a commodity for stocking wealth. For the same commercial value, it is easier to carry and stock a precious stone or a bar of gold[7] than several tons of rice or other perishable goods. It is also easier to run away with a single precious stone in hand than with heavy bags of food. Ornaments were among the women's few personal possessions[8] which they could receive as gifts, even from an 'affectionate husband'. According to *Manusmṛti* 9,194-5:

> A woman's property is traditionally regarded as of six sorts: what was given in front of the (marriage) fire, on the bridal procession, or as a token of affection, and what she got from her brother, mother or father. In addition, any subsequent gift and whatever her affectionate husband might give her should become the property of her children when she dies, (even) during her husband's lifetime.

As the ornaments belonged to the same woman, they were probably matching and thus had more value as an ensemble than when divided into smaller lots for the heirs. Another hypothesis is the symbolic value of the worn jewels. As an ensemble, they were associated with the different body parts of the same woman. Dividing the set would be symbolically dismembering the female body.

Manusmṛti 3,55-62 also prescribes that,

> Fathers, brothers, husbands, and brothers-in-law who wish for great good fortune should revere these women and adorn them. The deities delight in places where women are revered, but where women are not revered

all rites are fruitless. Where the women of the family are miserable, the family is soon destroyed, but it always thrives where the women are not miserable. Homes that are cursed by women of the family who have not been treated with due reverence are completely destroyed, as if struck down by witchcraft. Therefore men who wish to prosper should always revere these women with ornaments, clothes, and food at celebrations and festivals.

There is unwavering fortune in a family where the husband is always satisfied by the wife, and the wife by the husband. If the wife is not radiant she does not stimulate the man; and because the man is unstimulated the making of children does not happen. If the woman is radiant the whole family is radiant, but if she is not radiant the whole family is not radiant.

In the *Manusmṛti*'s view, the welfare of the family directly depends on the happiness of the women of the household. Ornaments make women happy, beautiful and fertile. Beauty is linked here to sexual attraction and, hence, to fertility. Other laws regarding marriage also mention jewels. In two particular forms of the classical brahmanical marriage (*brahma* and *daiva* rites), it is specified that in the *kanyādāna* (gift of a daughter), the bride should be handed over 'decked with ornaments' (*Manusmṛti* 3,27-28). In contrast, if a girl chooses a husband for herself, she 'should not take with her the jewellery given to her by her father, mother, or brothers; if she took it away, she would be a thief' (*Manusmṛti* 9,92).

Other General Considerations about Ornaments and Women

Terms such as *bhūkhaṇ* (*ābhuṣaṇ,* 'ornaments'), *sāj* (*sajjā,* 'decoration, equipment'), *siṅgār* (*śṛṅgār*, 'dress, adornment, decoration, finery'), *rataṇ* (*ratna,* 'diamond'), *motī* ('pearl'), *soṇā* (*svarṇa*, 'gold'), etc., are used in Mīrābāī's *Padāvalī*, but there are no elaborate descriptions[9] of the jewellery items she uses. The term *alaṅkāra*, frequent in the *Manusmṛti*, is not used in Caturvedi's edition of the *Padāvalī.*[10] The practice of *solah siṅgār* follows specific cultural codes (see below), which were passed down orally and practically through generations, but never in the form of an exclusive canonical list. Ornamentation enhances the physical, visible beauty of women. It can also have a medical significance since specific stones and material are supposed to influence the well-being of their bearers. Sometimes they also work as charms against poison (*Manusmṛti* 9,218). In some cases, astrology determines which stones, gems, diamonds and precious metals (such as gold and silver) should be worn, when and on which part of the body in order to benefit from their qualities.

The poetic songs of Mīrābāī assume a female voice and are popularly ascribed to a female figure, but this does not imply that the composers of these songs were only women. That not all poems can be securely ascribed to a historical Mīrābāī has no importance here since our present interest lies in the representation of the female body and the use of the lexical field of ornaments in the *Padāvalī*. Whether men or women, the composers were familiar enough with the vocabulary and proper use of jewellery items. This familiarity with jewellery reflects the concerns of women and men who had some expertise with jewels. The poetic songs were handed down from generation to generation, just like the traditions and rituals of *solah siṅgār* and the other arts of adorning the female body. Fieldwork by anthropologist Parita Mukta has shown that the *pad*s attributed to Mīrābāī were also appropriated by castes of specialized craftsmen.[11] The crafters of ornaments as material objects were keen to sing about them and hear them in poetic songs. As stated by Bhatnagar *et aliae*, Mīrābāī's 'poetic reference to weaving and jewelry making is grounded in material realities. Rajasthan has long-standing and distinguished traditions dating back to medieval times of artisanal communities of weavers, gem cutters, and jewelry makers.'[12]

(Dis)order, Ornaments and Female Beauty

The results presented here are part of a wider research on the representation of female bodies in devotional and poetic contexts in a cross-cultural comparison. Many questions on the symbolic value of ornaments, which cannot be detailed here, arose from the study of the representation of female bodies and femininity in ancient Greece, and from the different meanings of the term *kosmos*: 'order', 'ornamentation' and 'universe'. Order is good and beautiful. Anything beautiful is in order and in its right place, and everything in order is beautiful. The idea of *kalos kagathos* (*kalos kai agathos*) meaning 'beautiful and good' is very important in the classical Greek context in which the three concepts of order, beauty and goodness are linked, as well as their opposites. Turning back to the medieval bhakti context, the relations between correct order, goodness and beauty are also significant.

In several texts relating to Krishna's sporting with the *gopīs*, disorder of the female ornaments is not necessarily considered negative. The motive of the 'inversion of ornaments' has two meanings in the Indian (Krishnaite or general *śṛṅgāra*) context. The first is *vibhrama* (confusion, error, agitation; it also expresses the move of 'whirling round'), which concerns the *gopīs* before meeting the beloved, as in the *Bhāgavata Purāṇa* (10,29,7) where the women 'were bedecking themselves with clothes and ornaments in a disorderly way'. When the lover approaches, 'the mind is overwhelmed and confused with the passion of love, the wrong or disorderly way of wearing clothes and ornaments is the characteristic of *Vibhrama* (confusion)'.[13] The other case of ornamental confusion takes place after the lovemaking (of the *gopīs* with Krishna or of lovers). Poetic texts in the vernacular languages of bhakti present this motive of *suratānt chavi* ('post-coital splendour' as translated by Snell[14]). After making love, the female lover quickly returns home and has no time to rearrange her dress and ornaments properly, or she is still under the spell of love and cannot focus her attention on her appearance. Thus, crumpled clothes and cosmetics or ornaments in the wrong place are the reminder of the love-night, as in *Bhāṣā-bhūṣaṇ* 51:

> Kohl is smeared on the lips, beloved, and betel-juice on the eyes,
> the impress of a pearl necklace is well apparent on your hard heart.[15]

Normally, kohl is for the eyes and betel juice is for the lips.

Whether before or after meeting the lover, the disorder caused by love is expressed in the mixed-up or displaced female ornaments. This disorder is a visible sign that 'something' has happened to the (female) body, physically or spiritually.[16] Both of these cases of confusion of ornaments are traditional motifs in which female ornaments have great significance and indicate the relation of the women concerned to the god. It is, hence, worth pointing out that such disorder or 'confusion of ornaments' is not a frequent motif in Mīrābāī's *Padāvalī.*[17]

Mīrābāī as Multiple Tradition and Direct Female Voice

For the purpose of studying the representation of the female body in one of the most famous devotional poets of northern India, I consider Mīrābāī as a multiple tradition ascribed to one female figure and expressed directly in the female voice. Contrary to Kabīr and Sūrdās who also used the poetic female voice, the composer here is assumed to have been a female figure. Thus, does this 'direct femininity' imply a greater use of typically feminine expressions or metaphors? Reference to female body practices such as using ornaments or renouncing them is a prominent aspect of Mīrā's poetry and has several meanings. The first aspect, already noted by Maurya, is that these constitute obstacles on the spiritual path:

> It is man who wants to see woman beautiful and he leaves no stone unturned to beautify her with ornaments, bangles, embroidered dress and praises to please and flatter. Mirabai was wise enough to understand the false docility of man, which makes woman not strong but weak. If we make a close scrutiny of her dialects and images which the poet employs in forms of suhag-sindoor, bangles, head-ornaments and beautiful dress material, we come to know that these things are a bondage, to self-realization.[18]

Maurya's statement is partially correct, but the poetess also uses the spiritual metaphors of adorning the female body in other specific and positive ways. In the following sections, a much broader picture of jewels and ornaments in the *Padāvalī* will be presented, with details as to the circumstances in which Mīrābāī refers to material objects of adornment, and of the ways in which these are applied to or removed from the female body.

Jewels and Female Ornaments in Mīrābāī's *Padāvalī*

Precious Metals and Stones as God or as Symbols of Wealth

In *pad* 24, Mīrā uses various metaphors to express the positive status of her devotional lifestyle, considered the greatest (lakes, ponds and rivers compared to the ocean, or bitter water compared to nectar, etc.). Diamonds (*hīrā*) are more precious than gold (*soṇa*) and silver (*rūpā*) in *pad* 24:

> Gold and silver are of no use to me,
> I am a dealer in diamonds.
> I am lucky indeed!
> I am connected with the Ratnākar.[19]

Whether one reads the untranslated word *ratnākar* as the similar-sounding *ratnakār* meaning 'jeweller'[20] or in its primary sense of 'mine' of jewels—as did Alston in his translation,[21] the meaning is the same: Mīrā has direct and abundant access to God. Her bhakti is trading in diamonds and this trade does not mean selling for profit but sharing. She gives away her jewels of bhakti without asking for a price to the audience of her songs, the community of *bhakta*s who know how to appreciate the spiritual value of her 'jewels'. Indeed, this exact value of jewels is known only by those who are very familiar with them: jewellers (*jauhara kī gata jauhara jāṇyā̃*; *pad* 70). Mīrā uses this metaphor to express that the value of bhakti and of Krishna's love is known only to those who practice bhakti and not to those without faith.

In some instances, God himself is the gold,

> Beloved, that which you sever I would not,
> having severed your love who can I connect with?
> if you are a tree I'm bird, if you are ocean I'm fish,
> if you are mountain I'm shadow, if you are moon I am chakora
> if you are pearl I am string, if you are gold I am suhaaga.
> Meera says god dweller of Braj you are my thakur [master], I your daasi [female slave].[22]

When considering God as gold, she substitutes 'lust for gold with the search for God'.[23] God is sought *instead* of ornaments,

Mother! Give me my Giridhar! Give me my Giridhar!
I desire no ornaments or dresses! (*bhūṣaṇa basana mohi nahī̃ bhāvẽ*)
I do not want even palaces![24]

When she finds God, she obtains wealth, as in the beginning of this *pad*,

I have obtained the wealth of diamonds that is Rama!
My good teacher gave me an invaluable thing and I have made it my own!
I have obtained the accumulated capital of several births
after searching in the entire universe!
The expenditure does not have to stop,
thieves will not rob,
Day by day the enjoyment increases![25]

The translator Subramanian uses a very 'capitalist' vocabulary to wealth in order to convey its meaning. The original language plays with alliterations of the words *Rām-ratan-dhan* (Ram-diamond-wealth). This jewel is priceless or invaluable (*a-molik*).

In *pad* 38, Mīrābāī compares herself to purified gold:

O King, I knew you had given me poison.
Just as gold burned in fire
Comes out glowing as a dozen suns,
I, too, emerged purified.

Mīrā refers to the persecutions she endures. She emerges purified, strengthened and refined, like pure gold, through the fire.[26]

Jewels as an Offering or Reward

Jewels and precious stones can be given as an offering or reward, like to the cuckoo (*pad* 84) whose beak will be plated with gold and who will serve as a head-ornament (or receive a crown?) if he announces the arrival of the Beloved:

I should have your beak plated with gold
And make you my honored crown.

This bird is of special significance with regard to beauty: the cuckoo is an ugly-looking bird (compared to the peacock), but it has a sweet voice. Like the frog, the cuckoo is heard but remains invisible. Visible beauty is of minor importance to saint singer: Mīrā's voice sings of Krishna and is more important than her physical appearance as a devotee.

In *pad* 187, as a reward for his humble offering and faith, Krishna transforms Sudāmā's broken hut into a palace studded with diamonds, pearls and rubies (*hirā*, *motī*, *lāl*). In *pad* 40, Mīrā receives a poisonous snake as a gift from the king who persecutes her. It is transformed into a necklace.

Rāṇā sent a basket containing a snake,
'Give it to Meṛtaṇī put it round her neck.'
Mīrā embraced it joyfully,
This indeed is my nine-string necklace.

In *pads* 39 and 41, the same snake becomes a *śālagrām*, a black stone symbol of Vishnu. Jewels (*ratan*) can also serve as an offering to the Beloved god, as in *pad* 150.

Jewels as Female Adornment

Mīrā uses ornaments to prepare herself in order to seduce her Beloved when she knows she will meet him. She also wears *ghuṅghar* (jingling anklets) when dancing for the god (in *pads* 17, 19, 31, 36 and 193). In *pad* 15, the mention of the bed alludes to sexual activity and the meeting which will take place soon. For this, Mīrā prepares the bed and herself (*siṅgār sajāvā̃*) in *pad* 15. The term *siṅgār* will be analysed in relation to *solah siṅgār* below. In *pad* 151, the preparation of the bed and the body are again associated. It is specified that the adornments (*sāj*) are worn *nakh-sikh* (from nail—in this case, toenail—to summit[27]), meaning 'from top to toe':

Come to my place Great Lord.
Having gathered the choicest buds
I have made for You the bed,
And adorned myself form toe to head.
I have been Your slave through several lives,
And You my Master indeed!
Mīrā's Lord is Hari, the Imperishable.
Come, grant me Your sight today.

In these lines, the word for 'Master', *sirtāj,* literally means 'head crown'. God is the head ornament of Mīrā. Being at the head of someone or on the head means to be master of it.

This adornment process, with which a parallel should be drawn with ritual equipment, has a special power to attract the lover, as in *pad* 201:

I groomed myself in attractive adornments,
My Beloved came running to me.

In these cases, jewels and ornaments (*siṅgār sāj*) work for the attractiveness of the female lover. She takes action in order to seduce and get what she wants: to be noticed by her Beloved, to seduce him, and to catch and retain him in order to unite with him. When the meeting is expected or planned, adorning the female body works as a preparatory ritual. A naked or natural body is not fit to be offered to the Beloved. It must be prepared, like the mind of the bhakta must be prepared to meet the Lord. This requires effort but is worth it because then the Lover will come. Poems where this type of female adornment is mentioned are not about *virah* (the pain of separation) but about the anticipation of meeting. Nevertheless, a necklace is referred to in a *virah pad* in which the tears of the abandoned, suffering woman are the pearls:

The one separated from her Lover,
is sitting in the pleasure palace,
stringing a necklace of pearls! (*motiyan kī laḍa*)
I have seen a similar, separated one stringing a necklace of tears!
(*aṇsuana mālā*)[28]

In *pad* 201, bangles are used as the symbol of the *suhāginī* (ever-auspicious married woman) who married no mortal man but Krishna himself, and who will never be abandoned or widowed. In *pad* 153, the allusion to the hair-parting symbolizes the rich status of the princess (time, special skill and pearls—which not just any woman can afford—are required) and also that of the married woman when this line is read in contrast with loose hair, that of the ascetic, not that of the married woman:

> Go to that land where the Beloved is attained,
> Go to that land.
> O Beloved,
> If You so say, I shall have my *sārī*, dyed red,
> If You so say, I shall wear ochre robe.
> If You say, I shall adorn the hair-parting with pearls.
> If You say, I shall leave them scattered loose.
> Mīrā's Lord is Girdhar Nāgar,
> Harken to the praises of the King, says she.

These allusions to Mīrā using ornaments can be read as 'jewels as spiritual metaphors' (see below). This active use of ornaments can now be contrasted with the rejection of ornaments and this type of wealth in other *pad*s.

Mīrābāī Renounces Ornaments and Criticizes Attraction for this Type of Wealth

In two situations, Mīrābāī becomes 'ugly'. Involuntarily, when she suffers the pain of *virah*, her body is deprived of beauty. She does not sleep and becomes emaciated. Endless crying makes her eyes red. She suffers sickness and her body becomes yellow (in *pad*s 72, 89, 117, 124 and 185 where she compares herself to a yellow leaf). In other circumstances, she is deprived of the special marks of her beauty as a princess. She renounces her preoccupation with cultural codes of beauty by shedding her ornaments in her path towards renunciation. Mīrābāī associates ornaments with other symbols of a wealthy lifestyle (fine clothing), or relates them to the female practice of adorning the body in order to seduce or to mark a high status in society. She opts out of this type of beautification of her body.

In *pad* 26, Mīrābāī denounces rubies, pearls, silks and special saris as *jūṭhā* (false, wrong), as lies:

False are these rubies and pearls,
False their glimmer and shimmer;
False are these ornaments; true is the Beloved's love.
False these silken clothes, and these *sārīs* from the south.
True are the rags of the Beloved
In which the body remains chaste.

In *pad* 32, Mīrā has taken decisive action. The verb of renunciation is *tyāg-*, 'to abandon':

I cast off all ornaments, and clothes, Rāṇā,
I gave up the bangles too.
I abandoned adorning
My eyes with lampblack,
My forehead with a dot,
And I abandoned tying my hair in a knot.
Mīrā's Lord is Girdhar Nāgar,
I have found a perfect groom.

Mīrā's renunciation is double. She stops being a *suhāginī*, a married woman (even though, in many other poems, she considers herself married to Krishna), and she stops being an elite Rajput princess. To be unadorned is to be dishonoured, as in the *Manusmṛti* (3,55), both adornment and honour go together. Asceticism is the opposite to both statuses, married and princely. In *pad* 32, however, Mīrā does not consider herself a widow, just as in the following *pad* 201:

Why choose a miserable bridegroom,
Whose life is bound to end!
O friend, I chose the Dark One for my bridegroom,
Thus my wedding bangles will be eternal.

Mīrā here alludes to the practice of a widow having her bangles removed or broken on the death of her husband. Other symbolic gestures like shaving her head strip the woman whose husband has died of her symbols and status of *suhāginī*. As a widow, she may not wear jewels either. It is unlikely that this rule was strictly enforced for all widows at all times and everywhere. In order to study the symbolism of female ornaments in the *Padāvalī*, representations of customs rather than actual practices are most valuable. Among such representations, which should in no case be considered as historical or anthropological accounts, the sati is in sharp contrast to the widow. When led to the pyre, the sati is bedecked with jewels and wears a wedding sari like a bride. Hagiographic accounts of Mīrā's life say that she refused to be a sati on the death of her earthly husband. Both figures co-exist in the *Padāvalī*: the eternal bride of Krishna and the ascetic devotee.

As she states in *pad* 34, cosmetics go along with ornaments:

I gave up the *kājal* and the *tīkī*
And chose the ochre robes.

This abandonment of decorating her body and wearing the clothes of a princess implies that she goes away from the king's palace and land. Mīrābāī chooses to become not just a female nun, but a wandering ascetic, travelling from place to place. For example, in *pad* 68, asceticism goes even further when renouncing jewels is associated with the shaving of hair, the ochre robe, and the travelling 'in four directions':

I have cast off jewels and ornaments,
Abandoned food and shaved off my hair.
For Your sake I have worn an ochre robe,
And looked for You in four directions.

Wandering asceticism is not compatible with jewels, ornaments, delicious food, a nice hairstyle and fine clothes. It was probably dangerous for a woman to wander alone without a male guardian to protect (and watch over) her. A lone female traveller must have attracted attention anyway, but a princess draped in full ornaments would have been spotted quickly as an easy prey for robbers and other malevolent persons.

Yogic Asceticism

Mīrā's asceticism can also tend to yogic practices expressed in the poems by the mention of several accessories. One can be an ascetic without being a yogi, but becoming a yogini implies some form of strict asceticism. In *pad*s 79-80, Mīrā expresses her transformation into a yogini. Her new ornament is the rosary worn around her neck, used as a necklace:

Rubies, pearls, I have cast off all,
And worn *yogi*'s rosary around the neck.

Several *pad*s can be interpreted as the transformation of Mīrā into a yogini. The mention of a yogini in this context might appear strange since Mīrā is not a devotee of Shiva but primarily of Krishna. However, reading the *Padāvalī* as expressing Krishna-bhakti alone her would be reducing the wide scope of Mīrā's poems. There are indeed 'multiple representations in the Mīrābāī tradition'[29] and the poems attributed to this figure should be read as expressing different sets of values that are, nevertheless, coherent. It is, therefore, possible to interpret, in a few *pad*s, Mīrā as a yogini or her lover as a wandering yogi. She alludes to her transformation into a female ascetic and, more precisely, into a female practitioner of yoga, a yogini (98, 117, 188). She also criticizes some yogic or devotional techniques such as the mechanical recitation of the name of Ram (158).

In other *pad*s, Mīrā also refers to the practice of smearing the body with ashes (46, 58, 94 and 188). In contrast, according to *solah siṅgār*, the woman should smear her body with turmeric or sandal oil after bathing. Mīrā tries the ashes associated with other yogic accessories in *pad* 188 in which she addresses her god as a yogi:

O *jogī*, I could not unravel Your mystery.
Assuming yoga posture I sat in a cave,
My mind absorbed in Hari,
Beads round the neck, *hājario* in hand,
Ashes smeared on the body.
Mīrā's Lord is Hari, the Indestructible,
I attained what I was predestined for.

The Metaphor of Spiritual Jewels in Mīrābāī's *Padāvalī*

Solah Siṅgār *as a Female Ritual*

In the following section, jewels used as metaphors will be surveyed in relation to the practice of *solah siṅgār*. This will be viewed here not only as a list but also as a female ritual whose meaning and practice should be understood before studying its metaphorical use. *Solah siṅgār* is usually interpreted as a series of cosmetics and ornaments applied to a female body in order to make it pleasant to a man, normally the bridegroom, if the ritual takes place in the context of wedding preparations.

Solah siṅgār means 'sixteen adornments'. The list of sixteen adornments is not fixed or canonical and may be different in each family. The number sixteen is symbolic of something perfect and accomplished. Sixteen also refer to the phases of the moon, which mirrors the menstrual cycle of the woman and a constructed biological femininity. *Solah siṅgār* may consist in cosmetic care, ornaments or specific characteristics of beauty which should be present in the woman or which can be provided for her: taking a scented bath, preparation of skin, styling of hair, vermilion, the use of flowers, henna on hands and feet, kohl on the eyes, make-up, *bindī* (dot on forehead), nose ring or nose pin, amulets, anklets, necklaces, earrings, bangles, bracelets, rings on the fingers and toes, red lines on the feet, waist-band in gold and *hathphul*, a sari, chewing betel, etc.[30]

Rarely is the female body totally 'natural'. It is not sufficient and beautiful enough in itself. In the traditional iconography of Krishna stealing the bathing *gopī*s' clothes, the *gopī*s are represented wearing jewels even though they stand naked in the river. Furthermore, in many traditions, the natural (biological) female body is considered impure and even dangerous (due to menstruations, childbirth). Putting ornaments on it is a way to civilize it and to make it fit to be enjoyed. Cosmetic care is not given and jewels are not worn, for instance, to promote the good health of woman (contrast with *yantra* and herbal medicine in *pad* 7). The main purpose of *solah siṅgār* is to charm a man and please him. In Mīrā's case, the 'man' is Krishna. The one who benefits from *solah siṅgār* is not the woman preparing herself but the man who will enjoy this woman adorned according to custom, whose body is in a way 'completed' by jewels and other ornaments. This enables her to attain a form of canonical beauty which she may lack 'naturally'. Indeed, these preparations are coded, even if several codes co-exist, and are also a form of art.

Solah siṅgār can be seen as a group practice. The help of at least one other person is necessary; for example, for applying complicated henna motifs or in order to set jewels, like the *ṭīkī*, in the right place. In the medieval Indian context, the 'helper', the person in close physical contact with the body to be prepared (that of the bride or of the lover), could only be a woman, who is either a servant or a family relative. However, some men also skilfully employed the lexical field of jewels and ornaments: jewellery-makers and craftsmen whose work was bought or appropriated by the ruling classes[31] or the people trading in them. As noted by Bhatnagar *et aliae*:

> Metaphors in North Indian dialect poetry are largely drawn from the labor processes that are a familiar and everyday part of the work-life of subaltern classes in medieval society. . . . These work processes are undervalued by elite classes. For the subaltern skilled or unskilled worker or craftsman, the work of weaving, tanning, pottery making, ferrying, and jewelry making is not measured in terms of its use or exchange value. Rather, work becomes the profound metaphor through which the subaltern worker perceives the world, nature, his or her relationship with other human beings, and God. Work is the central metaphor in dialect poetry.[32]

Mīrā refers to the goldsmith in *pad* 141 and she herself claims to trade in jewels in *pad* 24. Except for this particular group, the handling of female jewels and the preparation of *solah siṅgār* is left to women. This allows us to conclude that although the rite benefits a man, its performance relies on a woman, or rather a group of women. Through the mention of so many jewels, understood here as a reflection of Mīrā's spiritual *solah siṅgār*, a trace of 'female religiosity' can be detected. Choosing and wearing certain jewels on specific points of the body is a religious act, and all the more so since Mīrā addresses her devotion to a god which she considers her lover or her husband.

Virtuous Life as the Only Ornament

I suggest that Mīrā's adornment be read as a spiritual metaphor; for example, in *pad* 25, where the *tilak* and rosary, one a mark and one an accessory of devotion, are understood as 'auspicious bangles' and 'virtuous life' as the 'only ornament'. Such detachment is wisdom:

> *Tilak* and rosary are my auspicious bangles,
> And virtuous life is my only ornament.
> Other adornments don't please me,
> This is the wisdom I got from my *guru*.

In *pad*s 48 and 132, god himself is the 'adornment' of Mīrā's heart. The same term, *tāj* (crown, diadem or head-ornament), is used to refer to the cuckoo (84) or the god (151) being her head crown. Her heart and head can be adorned with the god.

Muja abalā ne moṭī nīrāṇṭa thaī—about *pad* 141

Pad 141 uses the metaphors of female jewellery and ornaments as spiritual sense. It refers to ornaments 'from head to toe'. Sukh Sampat Mehta gives a particular context for composing of this song: 'There is a childish story that narrates an incident by the offer of many valuables made by the Rana, Mīrā's brother-in-law, as an earnest for his marriage with her. Mīrā declined to accept either, but preserved the incident in the song. . . .'[33] Mehta considers this story to be 'childish' but it is a plausible context even if it would not fit into all the hagiographical stories on Mīrā's life. Mīrā is offered both ornaments and a marriage proposal by her brother-in-law (maybe after her earthly husband died, thus giving her the opportunity to escape widowhood). In this story, she declines both the marriage and the gifts. *Pad* 141 may, thus, be listing the gifts presented to her by the future groom, whoever he may be. It may indeed be a traditional set of gifts. If the ornaments of *pad* 141 are gifts given by the future husband, they can be interpreted as a visible 'marking' of the body of the bride: by wearing what is being given to her, she accepts that she will belong to the husband (and his family). By wearing them, she displays the wealth of her husband and, on particular occasions, she will also be displayed as wealth, even if the practice of purdah (seclusion of women) would make the general public display of women less likely to take place. As female infanticide was practised in this context, raising a girl could also be considered a luxury[34] and displaying her on selected occasions in special attire could be a sign of wealth and success. By the time they were married, women must have become used to being given ornaments as gifts and knew how to wear them properly when required. The Rajput elite also places value on female beauty. Bhatnagar et al. write: 'Alongside female infanticide and woman devaluation in medieval Rajasthan, there exists the religio-cultural tradition of supravaluation of female beauty and the fetishization of femininity through the marks that signify the married woman.'[35]

Wearing the ornaments of the *suhāg* is a way of marking the physical body (see below). For a married woman, ornaments are not signs of success, as they could be for a courtesan. By wearing them, the woman is displaying wealth, and she herself becomes an ornament and a living stand for the wealth of the family on display.

Many contexts for composing such a thematic song on female ornaments can be imagined. For example, it could be at the turning point in Mīrā's life, when she leaves the Rānā's palace and renounces her status as a princess in order to become a wandering ascetic and fully live her life of devotion. In this ascetic life, she will not need ornaments to mark her status as a Rajput lady.[36] In the refrain, the word *sācũ* (a derivation from *sac*, 'true') can be opposed to the *jhūṭhā* (false, lie) of *pad* 26. Here, the ornament (*ghareṇu*) is *śāmlo* (that is *Śyām*, the Dark One, Krishna) himself. In this simple life, superfluous adornments have no place and do not impress the other members of devotional communities.

It is worth quoting the full translation of *pad* 141:

O friend, my trust is complete.
Śyām is my true ornament.
I will have earrings made of Biṭṭhal, the groom,
Hari for a necklace is already mine.
Caturbhuj is the rosary, my mind dwells on Him;

He is my auspicious bangles,
Why go to the goldsmith's house.
My anklets are made of Jagjīvan,
Kṛṣṇajī is the ornaments of my feet and legs.
Toerings and anklets are made of Rāmnārāyaṇ, [*sic*]
The Inner Controller is my big toering.
I shall have a casket composed of Puruṣottama
And a lock by the name Trīkama. [*sic*]
I shall have the key of Karuṇānand.
Wherein I shall lock all my jewels
(That are Krishna Himself).
I am sitting adorned in my in-laws' house,
Without even a blouse.
Mīrā says: O Lord, Girdhar Nāgar,
I find solace at the feet of Hari.

Right from the beginning, in the *ṭek*, Mīrā presents herself as a woman, using the Sanskrit-derived term *a-balā*, 'without force'. Faith will supply the strength that her physical body may lack. Pieces of jewellery and ornaments are applied to the whole body, like in a *nakh-śikh* description, in the same way as the body of a warrior is covered in armour. The warrior exercises strength and military power. He is a figure of force whereas Mīrā is 'without-force'. Despite her lack of physical strength, she has strong faith. Taking further the analogy of the warrior, this *pad* can be read as Mīrā donning her bhakti equipment in the form of female ornaments, just as a warrior would wear different pieces of his armour. It covers her whole body, from head to toe. In the description, it seems that Mīrā begins with the upper body to finish with the feet. However, this is not completely consistent. The body parts mentioned are in this order: ears, neck or chest, wrists, ankles, feet, legs, toes, big toe, possibly the waist (if *peṭ* means *kamarband*, a belt[37]), and chest or breasts.

This *pad* should be read as a spiritual *solah siṅgār* even if Mīrā does not exactly mention sixteen items of ornamentation. The only explicit reference to *solah siṅgār*, the sixteen ornaments, in Mīrā's *Padāvalī* is in *pad* 193:

Wear anklets of good conduct,

And dance the dance of contentment.
Bedecked in sixteen ornaments, with a crest-jewel of gold,
Love only the Dark One, be indifferent to all others.

The spiritual *solah siṅgār* is worn in the 'realm beyond going' where Mīrā (or her soul, or the other *bhakta*s whom she addresses in this *pad*) dances the 'dance of contentment' wearing 'anklets of good conduct'.

Devoted Souls, Marked Bodies

Devotees mark their bodies with specific items such as special clothing, a *mālā* (rosary or necklace, garland) or a *tulsī mālā.*[38] It is not possible to link each one of the jewellery items of Mīrā in *pad* 141 to a specific ritual accessory. Moreover, in the *pad* 141, she mentions both the *mālā* (ritual prayer accessory) and other jewels. Both registers coexist: devotional and ornamental. The *mālā* could be worn as a decorative ornament but the reverse is not true: ornamental jewels cannot be used as practical devotional accessories. There is, however, some symmetry in the way these accessories are positioned on the body. For instance, the *ṭīkī* is on the forehead and so is the *ṭīkā* or *tilak*. The *mālā* is worn around the neck and so is the *hār* (necklace). *Mehendi* designs are traditionally part of the *solah siṅgār*. The only allusion to designs being drawn on the skin is of *yantra*s having a medical purpose (*pad* 7). Some yogis smear ashes on their body. According to Entwistle, devotees draw the signs of Vishnu (disc, conch) on their skin. For some of the traditional ornaments of the *solah siṅgār*, like the *bajullā* (ornament worn on the upper arm), there are no parallels, unless the practice of branding the skin is taken into account. According to Entwistle, this practice did exist but was rather rare, even though it was recommended in certain texts:

> Marks of Vishnu's attributes are occasionally seen drawn or stampled with *candana* on the chest and arms, but only a few ascetic followers . . . take the trouble to brand themselves. When they do so clarified butter is smeared on the arm before the mark is made with a silver brand.
>
> The concept of branding, however, survived even among sects which have never practiced it.[39]

Branding the skin is an irreversible and permanent practice, contrary to other forms of marking which use vegetable or mineral products (henna, ink, *kājal*) to draw motifs lasting for a few days or weeks only, at the time of a ritual or festival. Even though branding was considered extreme by most *sampradāya*s and was not a widespread practice, it should be pointed out that it is also a visible sign and marking of the body.

A more common and easy practice is the drawing of a *tilak* on the forehead. This shares some aspects with the cosmetics of *solah siṅgār*. The *tilak* is a drawing, which may be elaborate, made of special substances and specific colours just like make-up. Saffron and rice, and red powder or sandalwood are used.[40] Mineral and vegetable materials are preferred but animal products like cow urine (*rocana*) can also be found. In *pad*s 2, 3 and 12, Krishna wears the *tilak* and Mīrā emphasizes the description of his beauty. In *pad* 25, the *tilak* and rosary replace the 'auspicious bangles', and 'virtuous life' is now her 'only ornament'. In *pad* 158, Mīrā criticizes the hypocrisy of applying *tilak* after washing the forehead but 'without cleansing the dirt from the heart'. In Shashiprabha's word index to the *Padāvalī*, *tilak* is defined as *ṭīkā*.[41] This term is not referenced but *ṭīkī* (in *pad*s 32 and 34) is, in turn defined as *ṭīkā* and as *bindī*.[42] In Mīrā's poetry, these terms overlap, thus allowing a new meaning of female ornaments not only as a beautifying device but also as a female practice and symbol of visible devotion.

Mīrā's ornaments give her a specific devotional identity, marking her body as wholly offered to God. A married woman wearing specific marks on her body like red vermilion powder (*sindūr*) in the parting of her hair and specific items of jewellery (like bangles in *pad* 201) expresses not only her auspicious status as a married woman, a *suhāginī*, but also her belonging to a man that she should consider as her lord and god as well (*patidev*), if she is a devoted wife (*pativratā*). In some areas and in specific groups, widows were forbidden to wear jewellery; hence wearing jewels was equated with the married state. In the same way, devotees of specific *sampradāya*s wear distinctive accessories (*mālā* beads and *tulsī mālā*) and mark their body with a *tilak* of sandalwood or with permanent marks by branding their skin (principally on the arms). Thus, their status as devotee and their belonging to a specific tradition can easily be identified visually. This idea, originally formulated by Young,[43] can also be applied in the bhakti context. When she mentions her use of ornaments, Mīrā combines both. She is the married woman or the lover when she adorns herself in preparation for meeting her Beloved. Alternatively, she is the ascetic devotee when she shuns these ornaments and renounces them (and the wealthy lifestyle associated with them). Of course, Mīrā 'makes a distinction between the fetishized married Rajput woman and women's pleasure in self-adornment'.[44] When she uses the metaphor of the spiritual *solah siṅgār*, she combines both self-adorning and the ascetic bhakti path because ornaments bestow her with a specific devotional identity, thus marking her body for Krishna. The spiritual jewels mark her as belonging to Krishna in the same way as the *tilak* marks the devotee's belonging to a specific *sampradāya.*

Conclusion

The specificity of Mīrā's use of female ornaments in her poetry emerges when the *Padāvalī* is contrasted with other texts dealing with female ornaments. The most important elements of this investigation in the Indian context will now be summed up. Several excerpts of the *Manusmṛti* convey the idea that giving ornaments to women makes them happy. Women must be adorned and honoured by their male relatives. Ornaments make them beautiful and, hence, sexually attractive for their husband and, by implication, fertile. Their beautification indirectly ensures the prosperity of the household. Ornaments are thus associated with positive aspects of women (fertility, happiness of the household). However, elsewhere, the *Manusmṛti* also associates ornaments with negative female behaviour. Several regulations on dowry, marriage, widowhood and inheritance specifically mention jewels and ornaments.

It would be relevant to extend our investigation on female ornamentation to other examples in the Sikh tradition, and to the bhakti and *sant* poetry of medieval India. This could confirm the general statements gleaned from an overview of a few representative texts of early modern India. For instance, in the *Guru Granth Sāhib*,[45] *solah siṅgār* applied to the woman is enjoyed both by herself and by the man. In a more traditional way reflected in this text, it is used for the primary purpose of adorning a female body so that a man will enjoy it. But all this pleasure does not give happiness. This beauty and sensual enjoyment is not sufficient spiritually, even if it is not explicitly condemned and rejected. Only the Name of God gives happiness and the 'body is miserable' (*deh dukhālī*) without it. In some of her *pad*s Mīrā is much more critical of ornaments than is the *Guru Granth Sāhib*. In verses by Sūrdās[46] and Kabīr, ornaments are traditionally associated with women and, in particular, with Māyā,[47] as personified in a beautiful and deceitful female body. Beautifying this body is useless and futile if love is not true, in the following verses of Kabīr:

> She alone can comprehend
> if her love for Him is true and deep
> but if not so
> futile will be all her make up (*kājar*).
>
> If you cannot win the love of the Lord
> what if you can lord over your neighbour?
> What is the good of dressing your hair
> and donning your feet with jingling jewellery?
> What is the value of all your make up
> with kajar to your eyelids
> and vermilion to your forehead
> and all the efforts to deck yourself
> if you are not loyal in your love?
> It is all a self deception
> and does not touch the Lord at all.
> Says Kabir—if you surrender
> your body, mind and heart to the Lord
> and remain loyal in love to Him,
> sans make up and ornaments
> you will win His favour
> in whatever state you be![48]

This is a negative aspect of the use of ornaments on a female body, which is seductive and leading the devotee astray.

While women and wealth are generally considered obstacles on the path of devotion in many bhakti traditions, Mīrābāī's *Padāvalī* relates to women's practical skills of preparing and decorating the body, and turns them into a positive spiritual experience. Preparing the body is a ritual before meeting the Lover God. It puts the female figure in good spirits and in a suitable state of mind for the encounter. It also works as seduction but in a way different from that of the Māyā of Sūrdās and Kabīr. While a non-human female entity (Māyā) tries to seduce devotees with her ornamented body, Mīrā is ready to seduce a male god like a lover or a husband. The seductive power of the ornamented woman acknowledged by Mīrābāī is turned into a positive devotional use. Bhakti can contain *bhukti* (enjoyment) in the pleasure taken by the lover in anticipation of the union and the desire to give god a sensual enjoyable offering. This offering is the body of Mīrābāī herself, whether her true physical body through ritual practices (such as performing dance and music for Krishna or prostrating and touching his feet) or through the metaphorical use of preparing her 'soul' for meeting god and maybe, thus, accessing *mukti* (release, deliverance).[49]

Mīrābāī uses ornaments and the beautification of the body in *pads* where she considers herself the lover or wife of Krishna. The opposite of the beautification of the body in anticipation of a union is found in the *virah pads* where she insists on describing the bodily damages of the *virah* pain. Nevertheless, in other *pads* attributed to Mīrābāī, she voluntarily adopts renunciation and advises the de-beautification or de-feminization of the body. She gives up ornaments symbolizing both her wealth and status (as a Rajput princess), and her femininity. Renunciation may also lead her to enter the ascetic path, sometimes as a yogini, in which case the yogic accessories (garland, rosary beads, ashes) take the place of traditional beauty care and ornaments. In some other *pads*, however, the Mīrābāī tradition manages to reconcile both the adoption and rejection of ornaments by referring to them as spiritual metaphors. When entering the ascetic path, ornaments are substituted by other elements such as the good deeds and behaviour of the devotee (the anklets of good conduct, the crown of contentment) or the God himself (who is gold or ornaments). The imagery of female ornaments is converted into a spiritual set of devotional values or attitudes. Mīrābāī's poetry is original for its perspectives on the female body and its juxtaposition of these two views: the adoption and the rejection of ornaments.

NOTES

1. 'Multiple tradition' is a term that stands for the great diversity of voices and traditions reflected in the *Padāvalī*. Mīrābāī is not considered here as a single historical character or composer but as an emblematic figure to whom the poetic songs of the *Padāvalī* were ascribed by various traditions. See, for instance, N.M. Martin Kershaw, *Dyed in the Color of Her Lord: Multiple Representations in the Mirabai Tradition*, Berkeley: Graduate Theological Union, 1995.
2. The expressions 'three jewels' or 'three treasures' are examples of this.
3. Several Buddhist works could also be quoted. An example from early Hindi is the *Bhāṣā-bhūṣaṇ* of Jasvant Siṁh. In Sanskrit, *Vādaratnāvalī* is the 'jewel-necklace of argument' of Viṣṇudāsācārya, or the *Viveka-cūḍāmaṇi* is translated as 'Crest-jewel of wisdom' of Śaṅkarācārya.
4. In the Indian context, many legends exist about the Koh-i-noor diamond. In the Greek context, the necklace (originally goddess Harmonia's wedding necklace made by the God Hephaestus) is enough to corrupt a woman (Eriphyle) and decide the fate of a war.
5. Archaeology and the study of material culture could help complete the picture of female body ornamentation in medieval India but I chose to concentrate on bhakti poetry, used here as 'textual' evidence, although I acknowledge its predominantly oral character.
6. Translations are from *Laws of Manu*, tr. W. Doniger O'Flaherty and B.K. Smith, London-New York: Penguin Books, 1991.
7. For considerations on gold's 'universal exchangeability' according to Marx, see R. Bhatnagar, R. Dube and R. Dube, 'Meera's Medieval Lyric Poetry in Postcolonial India: The Rhetorics of Women's Writing in Dialect as a Secular Practice of Subaltern Coauthorship and Dissent', *Boundary 2*, vol. 31, no. 3, 2004, p. 29.
8. As a comparison, in the classical Greek context, the dowry given along with a bride (money, ornaments made of jewels, and precious stones or metals) would stay with her and, should she move out of her husband's home, her dowry would move out, too.

9. The *Aṣṭayām* (eight watches) by the male poet Dev (1673-1745) is an example of an elaborate description of a woman's preparation to meet her lover with details on cosmetic care, jewels, ornaments and special garments. Dev describes the woman in the third person (R. Snell, *The Hindi Classical Tradition: A Braj Bhāṣā Reader*, London: School of Oriental and African Studies, 1991, pp. 166-71). By contrast, Mīrābāī uses the first person (*maĩ*) in her poems, saying what she is doing with the ornaments and accessories.
10. *Mīrābāī kī Padāvalī*, ed. Paraśurām Caturvedī, Allahabad: Hindī Sāhitya Sammelan, 1989.
11. P. Mukta, *Upholding the Common Life: The Community of Mirabai*, Delhi: Oxford University Press, 1994.
12. Bhatnagar, Dube and Dube, 'Meera's Medieval Lyric Poetry', p. 28.
13. *The Bhāgavata Purāṇa*, ed. G.V. Tagare, Delhi: Motilal Banarsidass, 1978, p. 1434.
14. Snell, *The Hindi Classical Tradition*, p. 139.
15. Ibid., p. 157.
16. As a comparison, in one of the Greek comic plays by Menander (*Epitrepontes*, 485ff.), the tearing of hair and the 'filmy and lovely cloak' that is ruined and torn to rags are the symbols of violent rape and not of love-making. In this context, disorder is considered negative.
17. This motive never appears in the 202 *pad*s of Caturvedi's edition and it is never presented as a characteristic or central motive of this poetry. However, it is possible that examples of the confusion of ornaments can be found in other editions that I have not consulted.
18. R.S. Maurya, 'Feminism: A Core-Concept', in *New Lights on Indian Women Novelists in English*, ed. A.N. Prasad, Delhi: Sarup & Sons, 2006, p. 30.
19. If not specified otherwise, all English translations of the Padāvalī are taken from K. Kumar, *Mīrā: The Emancipated Soul*, Delhi: Harman, 2004. In the quotations, I follow her specific use of diacritics and italics. The numbering of the *pad*s follows Caturvedi's edition.
20. This possibility that has been pointed out to me by Prof. Peter Schreiner.
21. A.J. Alston, *The Devotional Poems of Mīrābāi*, Delhi: Motilal Banarsidass, 1980, p. 43.
22. Jafri, *Prem Vani* 107, as quoted in Bhatnagar, Dube and Dube, 'Meera's Medieval Lyric Poetry', p. 26. Bhatnagar and her co-authors provide an interpretation of this song together with a reflection on the fetishization of women in Rajput society. Subramanian translates the last line as: 'You are the pearl! I am the string! You are gold! I am the cleansing powder!' because he reads *suhāgā* (instead of *suhāg*) as meaning 'borax added to gold', a substance which can be used as a detergent (V.K. Subramanian, *Mystic Songs of Meera*, Delhi: Abhinav Publications, 2005, pp. 110-11, no. 46). *Suhāg* generally means the happy state of a woman when her husband is alive.

23. Bhatnagar, Dube and Dube, 'Meera's Medieval Lyric Poetry', p. 30.
24. Subramanian, *Mystic Songs of Meera*, pp. 62-3, no. 22: *De mā̃ girdhārī, mohi de mā̃ girdhārī.*
25. Ibid., pp. 38-9, no. 10: *Pāyojī maĩne rāma ratana dhana pāyo.*
26. For a comparison with gold and fire in the Christian context, see 1 Peter 1:7 in the *Bible*.
27. *Nakh-śikh* is also a descriptive technique in poetry 'according to which the poet provides a systematic statement of the beauty of the figure he is describing' (J.S. Hawley, *Sur Das: Poet, Singer, Saint*, New Delhi: Oxford University Press, 1984, p. 78). In *pad* 171, Radha and Krishna's beauty is described with this technique but in a less elaborate way than examples found in Sūrdās' poetry.
28. Subramanian, *Mystic Songs of Meera*, pp. 50-1, no. 16: *Maĩ virahina baiṭhī jāgū̃ jagata saba sove ālī.*
29. See N.M. Martin-Kershaw, 'Dyed in the Color of Her Lord: Multiple Representations in the Mirabai Tradition', Berkeley: Graduate Theological Union, 1995.
30. An example of the list can be found in Kumar, *Mīrā: The Emancipated Soul*, pp. 123-4.
31. Bhatnagar, Dube, and Dube, 'Meera's Medieval Lyric Poetry', p. 28.
32. Ibid.
33. S.S. Mehta, *A Monograph on Mirabai, the Saint of Mewad*, Bombay, 1900, p. 87.
34. For comments on the value of a daughter's life in this context, see Bhatnagar, Dube and Dube, 'Meera's Medieval Lyric Poetry', pp. 29-30.
35. Ibid., p. 30.
36. As another cross-cultural comparison, Saint Francis of Assisi is also said to have left all his clothing in front of his father and the bishop. Few cases of Indian female saints renouncing garments for the sake of religious practice are known, as noted by Bhatnagar *et aliae*: 'A number of female saints in the pan-Indian tradition, such as Mahadevi in the South, and Lala Ded in Kashmir, have, unlike Meera, left home naked, disavowing the body and the psychosocial restrictions placed on the female body', Ibid.
37. The translation of this line is difficult. If we take *peṭ* as meaning *peṭī*, a sort of box, this may be a jewellery box in which the woman keeps her precious ornaments when not wearing them. Caturvedi suggests that *peṭ* means a belt.
38. A.W. Entwistle, *Vaiṣṇava Tilakas: Sectarian Marks Worn by Worshippers of Viṣṇu*, 2nd edn., Vrindavan: Vrindavan Research Institute, 2003.
39. Ibid., p. 37.
40. Kumar, *Mīrā: The Emancipated Soul*, p. 124.
41. Śaśiprabhā, *Mīrā̃ koś*, Allahabad: Smṛti Prakāśan, 1974, p. 78.
42. Ibid., p. 66.

43. K.K. Young, 'Om, the Vedas, and the Status of Women', in *Jewels of Authority: Women and Textual Tradition in Hindu India*, ed. L.L. Patton, Oxford-New York: Oxford University Press, 2002, pp. 84-121.
44. Bhatnagar, Dube and Dube, 'Meera's Medieval Lyric Poetry', p. 30.
45. Examples can be found in the *Guru Granth Sāhib* in *Phunahe mahalā* 5,3 (p. 1361), or in *Gauḍī mahalā* 1,1-4 (p. 225).
46. An example in Sūrdās is *pad* 44 in N. Vājpeyī, ed. *Sūrsāgar*, 2 vols., Vārāṇasī: Nāgarīpracāriṇī Sabhā, 1950-52.
47. For a thorough analysis of the concept of Māyā as evil in bhakti and, particularly, in Kabīr's work, refer to D.P. Saklani, 'Maya as Evil—From Classical Hindu Thought to Bhakti Saints and Kabīr: A Historical Exploration', in *Probing the Depths of Evil and Good: Multireligious Views and Case Studies*, ed. J.D. Gort, H. Jansen and H.M. Vroom, Amsterdam-New York: Rodopi, 2007, pp. 41-56.
48. Translation by G.N. Das, *Love Songs of Kabir*, Delhi: Abhinav Publications, 2003, pp. 80-1, no. 39 (*nisi din khelata kahi sakhiyana saṅga*), and p. 98, no 53 (*jau paī piyake mana nāhi bhāyai*).
49. For a comparative investigation of the Gauḍīya Vaishnava *Bhakti-rasāmṛta-sindhu* and the spiritual exercises of Ignatius de Loyola, see M. Voss Roberts, 'Neither Bhukti nor Mukti: The New Sensorium in Devotional Practice', *Practical Matters*, vol. 1, no. 1, 2009, pp. 1-18. V. Roberts explored the tensions between *bhukti* and *mukti* in these traditions.

BIBLIOGRAPHY

Alston, A.J., *The Devotional Poems of Mīrābāi*, Delhi: Motilal Banarsidass, 1980.

The Bhāgavata Purāṇa, ed. G.V. Tagare, Delhi: Motilal Banarsidass, 1978.

Bhatnagar, R., R. Dube and R. Dube, 'Meera's Medieval Lyric Poetry in Postcolonial India: The Rhetorics of Women's Writing in Dialect as a Secular Practice of Subaltern Coauthorship and Dissent', *Boundary 2*, vol. 31, no. 3, 2004, pp. 1-46.

Das, G.N., *Love Songs of Kabir*, Delhi: Abhinav Publications, 2003.

Entwistle, A.W., *Vaiṣṇava Tilakas: Sectarian Marks Worn by Worshippers of Viṣṇu*, 2nd edn., Vrindavan: Vrindavan Research Institute, 2003.

Hawley, J.S., *Sur Das: Poet, Singer, Saint*, Delhi: Oxford University Press, 1984.

Kumar, K., *Mīrā: The Emancipated Soul*, Delhi: Harman, 2004.

Laws of Manu, tr. W. Doniger O'Flaherty and B.K. Smith, London-New York: Penguin Books, 1991.

Martin-Kershaw, N.M., *Dyed in the Color of Her Lord: Multiple Representations in the Mirabai Tradition*, Berkeley: Graduate Theological Union, 1995.

Maurya, R.S., 'Feminism: A Core-Concept', in *New Lights on Indian Women Novelists in English*, ed. A.N. Prasad, Delhi: Sarup & Sons, 2006, pp. 11-21.

Mehta, S.S., *A Monograph on Mirabai, the Saint of Mewad, Dorab J. Saklatwalla Memorial Series*, 1, Bombay, 1990.

Mīrābāī kī Padāvalī, ed. P. Caturvedi, Allahabad: Hindī Sāhitya Sammelan, 1989.

Mukta, P., *Upholding the Common Life: The Community of Mirabai*, Delhi: Oxford University Press, 1994.

Saklani, D.P., 'Maya as Evil—From Classical Hindu Thought to Bhakti Saints and Kabīr: A Historical Exploration', in *Probing the Depths of Evil and Good: Multireligious Views and Case Studies*, ed. J.D. Gort, H. Jansen and H.M. Vroom, Amsterdam-New York: Rodopi, 2007, pp. 41-56.

Śaśiprabhā, *Mīrā̃ koś*. Allahabad: Smṛti Prakāśan, 1974.

Snell, R., *The Hindi Classical Tradition: A Braj Bhāṣā Reader, SOAS South Asian Texts*, 2, London: School of Oriental and African Studies, 1991.

Subramanian, V.K., *Mystic Songs of Meera*, Delhi: Abhinav Publications, 2005.

Vājpeyī, N., ed., *Sūrsāgar* 2 vols., Vārāṇasī: Nāgarīpracāriṇī Sabhā, 1950-2.

Voss Roberts, M., 'Neither Bhukti nor Mukti: The New Sensorium in Devotional Practice', *Practical Matters*, vol. 1, no. 1, 2009, pp. 1-18.

Young, K.K., 'Om, the Vedas, and the Status of Women', in *Jewels of Authority: Women and Textual Tradition in Hindu India*, ed. L.L. Patton, Oxford-New York: Oxford University Press, 2002, pp. 84-121.

CHAPTER 17

Mātrā in Bhakti Poetry and Perso-Arabic Metres

HIROKO NAGASAKI

Hindi poets during the period that is generally known today as *Bhaktikāl*[1] composed poems in literary vernaculars such as Brajbhasha, Avadhi and Maithili. Apart from a few instances of syllabic (*vārṇik*) metres, most verses, as a legacy of Sanskrit, employed moraic (*mātrik*) metres. During the early *Bhaktikāl*, there was no difference between the prosody of Hindu and Muslim poets. Later, however, with the emergence of classical Urdu, Perso-Arabic metres entered the Indo-Aryan field.[2]

This paper first compares the *mātrik* prosody of Hindi, using Sanskritic rules and Apabhramsha forms, with the handling of Perso-Arabic metres in Urdu. Based on this survey, I will point out that some popular forms of the *mātrik chand* can also be scanned as Perso-Arabic metre. Finally, I will focus on the significance of north Indian Bhakti literature as a common stage after which the two literary styles began to split.[3]

Traditional Prosody in New Indo-Aryan: The Hindi *mātrik chand*

Metres used in Brajbhasha and Avadhi can be distributed into two major categories, the syllabic *vārṇik chand*s and the moraic *mātrik chands*.[4] While some forms of *mātrik chand* are traceable to the *Prākṛta Paiṅgalaṁ*, a survey of Prakrit and Apabhramsha metrical forms composed in the fourteenth century, many are peculiar to Hindi. The *mātrik chand* is based on the counting of morae (*mātrā*s) that are units of syllabic weight or, in modern terminology, syllabic length. Heavy/long syllables, either containing long vowels or diphthongs or followed by consonant clusters, counts as having two *mātrā*s. A light/short syllable, which is not followed by a consonant cluster, has one *mātrā*. The inherent vowel 'a', which is silent in Modern Standard Hindi, is usually pronounced in scanning and has a value of one mora.

Some syllables can be counted as having either one or two *mātrā*s; for example, a syllable followed by conjunct consonants whose second member is the semivowel 'y' or 'r'. The diphthongs 'e' and 'o', and sometimes any long vowel, can be counted as short if the metre requires it. Due to the uncertainties of early Hindi orthography, an *anusvāra* can be considered a sign for nasalization and thus not creating a cluster.

Perso-Arabic Metres in Urdu

Classical Urdu borrowed not only the Persian writing system and adjusted it to the peculiarities of Indo-Aryan but also the Persian metrical world, which in turn originated in Arabic. This is also a moraic system with some further peculiarities.[5] In the Perso-Arabic writing system of Urdu, the short vowels *a*, *i* and *u* are not written, but metre distinguishes the *mutaḥarrik* 'moving' (CV) characters, which have a vowel, from the *sākin* 'silent' (C) characters, which do not have a vowel. Light syllables are of the shape CV. There are two types of heavy syllables, CVC and CVV.

The conjunction of two *sākin* (C) letters, a consonant following a long vowel or a diphthong which is also treated as consonant character *sākin* (C), is regarded as a *mutaḥarrik* that accompanies the short *a* and counts as one syllable (CV). Let us consider an example *nām* 'name' CVCCV. The character *alif*, which represents the long *ā*, and *m* are *sākin* (C) letters, but *m* is treated as *ma mutaḥarrik* (CV). In the conjunction of three *sākin* (C) letters, the first is treated as *sākin* (C), the second as *mutaḥarrik* (CV) and the third is dropped, as in the word *rāst* 'straight' CVCCV.

There are eight types of feet,[6] which derive from the feet of Arabic metre and their variations. The combinations of these eight foot types create twelve verse types, which are the same as in Arabic metre. But in Perso-Arabic metre of Urdu, *munṣariḥ*, *muẓāreʿ*, *muqtaẓab*, *mujtaṯh*, *k̲h̲afīf* and *sarī*, are not used for actual composition. We can find only their variation instead.[7]

Similarities and Differences between *mātrik chand* and Perso-Arabic Moraic Metres

If we assume that the syllabic value of CVV is equal to that of CVC, we find, interestingly, that the ways of counting morae by *mātrik chand* and by Perso-Arabic metre are essentially the same.

In *mātrik chand*, the inherent *a* is taken into account in scanning a prosodic line, whereas, in Persian metre, it is not counted. However, in both cases, the number of *mātrā*s is the same in *mātrik chand*, the word *ba-da-na* 'body' has three syllables of one mora each and, in Perso-Arabic metre, it is counted as *ba-dan*, two syllables with 1+2 = 3 morae. Conjunct consonants are treated differently in *mātrik chand* and Perso-Arabic metres. For example, in *mātrik chand*, the word *duśmana* 'enemy' is CVCCVCV –⏑⏑ *vs* Perso-Arabic metre: *duś-man* CVC-CVC – –. In both cases, the number of the moras is the same.

In Urdu, aspirated stops are written as consonants followed by the consonant character *he*.[8] In Perso-Arabic metre, all characters have a syllabic value in principle but, in this case, *he* is not counted as such. Therefore, in both the *mātrik chand* and the Perso-Arabic metre, the aspiration is treated as the same. For example, *mātrik chand*: *gha-ra* 'house' CV-CV⏑⏑ *vs* Perso-Arabic metre: *g*(*h*)*ar* CVC –.

Alif, *ye* and *vāo*, added to indicate long vowels at the end of Indo-Aryan words or to show diphthongs 'ai' and 'au' can be ignored in metrical scansion. These end up the same as in *mātrik chand* explained above.

Nūn ghunna that indicates nasalization and *nūn* that represents a nasal consonant can be ignored in mora counting. This is the same as in *mātrik chand*.

The character *ye* in certain Indo-Aryan words is not counted in Perso-Arabic metre, for example, *pyār* 'love' CVVC –⌣. In *mātrik chand* as well, if the second consonant of conjunct consonants of a perfect form is *y*, the preceding syllable with a short vowel is not counted as having two *mātrā*s, as in *karyau* 'did' ⌣–.

Besides these similarities, differences between the *mātrik chand* and the Perso-Arabic metre should also be mentioned. A remarkable one consists in the alignment of the word boundary with metrical sections inside a line. In *mātrik chand*, the *pāda* 'sectional boundary' usually coincides with the word break. Yet it is okay for a word to cross the sectional boundary in Perso-Arabic metre because it is not made for New Indo-Aryan originally, and a word break does not necessarily coincide with a sectional boundary.

Moreover, by way of word-*sandhi*, *alif* and *vāo* at the beginning of a word can be connected with the final sound of the preceding word. For example, the conjunction *aur* can be connected with the consonant of the previous word and omitted. The *r* of *aur* is metrically treated as *mutaḥarrik* (CV).

1. p(h)ū-l au-r/CVV-CV CVC-CV
2. p(h)ū-lau-r/CVV-CVC-CV
3. p(h)ū-lu-r/CVV-CV-CV

Of these three kinds of *sandhi*, the third one is not known in Hindi.

Although Perso-Arabic metre is regulated by character, as stated above, many exceptional rules are applied to adjust the characters to the original pronunciation. Therefore, compared to the *mātrik chand*, the Perso-Arabic metre of Urdu is more complex.

The Stage Prior to the Split

Before discussing how the adoption of the Perso-Arabic metre occurred and how the two metrical systems developed separately, the prosody of time before the split will be surveyed briefly.

Maulānā Dāūd in the fourteenth century, allegedly the first Sufi poet of Hindi, composed the Avadhi romance, *Candāyan,* in *caupāī* and *dohā* metres. But Dāūd's *dohā*s do not always follow the rule of 13+11 morae as later *dohā*s do.[9]

bhalẽ lora tumha āehu ihavā̃, rākhehu cinta hamāra |
⏑ – –⏑ ⏑⏑ –⏑⏑ ⏑⏑–, –⏑⏑ –⏑ ⏑ – ⏑ | 16+11 *mātrā*s
jo kachu ahai hamāraĩ, so phina jāna tumhāra ||[10]
– ⏑ ⏑ ⏑ – ⏑ – – , – ⏑⏑ – ⏑ ⏑ – ⏑ || 12+11 *mātrā*s

It was good that you came here. My worry has been settled.
Whatever I have, think of it as yours.

The stanzas of the sixteenth-century Sufi poets, Qutuban, Mañjhan and Jāysī, are made up of a certain number of *caupāī* hemistichs (*ardhālī*s) followed by a *dohā*. An *ardhālī* is half of a given metrical unit that is a verse of a couplet and two verses of a quatrain, etc. While there are relatively few irregularities in the *caupāī*s of these poets with respect to the rules of *mātrik chand* as we know them, it is not necessarily the case with their *dohā*s. According to Vasudev Sharaṇ Agraval, the editor of the Jhansi Sahitya Sadan edition of the *Padmāvat*, many odd *pāda*s of *dohā* in the manuscripts of Jāysī have 16 *mātrā*s instead of 13. Sufi poets from Dāūd to Jāysī have the same tendency of using hypermetric *dohā*s. In Mataprasad Gupta's edition of the *Padmāvat*,[11] there are several *dohā*s whose odd *pāda*s have 16 *mātrā*s, but in the edition of the Nāgarī Pracāriṇī Sabhā by Ramchandra Shukla, these hypermetric *dohā pāda*s are normalized to 13 *mātrā*s.[12]

This style of the Sufi poets' stanzas, which consist of several *ardhālī*s of *caupāī* followed by one *dohā*, was apparently adopted by Tulsīdās. His typical stanza in the *Rāmacaritmānas* is eight *ardhālī*s preceding a *dohā*. Agraval argues that the normalization of hypermetrical *dohā*s was done in the period earlier to the adoption of Jāysī's style by Tulsīdās and that is why the latter did not compose hypermetric *dohā*s. But in Mataprasad Gupta's edition of the *Rāmacaritmānas*, there are some hypermetric or hypometric *dohā*s, while in Vishvanath Prasad Mishra's edition, these too are emended to regular *dohā*s. Mataprasad Gupta did not lay much emphasis on metrical correctness in his editing, but if we regard his edition as reflecting earlier manuscripts which are closer in time to the original, then it means that Tulsī considered the optional shortening of long vowels as poetic licence. Vishvanath Prasad Mishra used special signs to make these shortenings of 'e' and 'o' clear in his edition.

Perso-Arabic metres in Urdu appeared much later than the *mātrik chand*, even among Muslim poets. The earliest examples of such metres are found in fifteenth- or sixteenth-century Dakkinī poetry. Kabīr, Jāysī and other poets who represent the early literature of Midland New Indo-Aryan languages used *mātrik chand*, as non-Muslim poets did.[13] In this stage, the difference in religion was not reflected in the literary style and language. Tulsīdās and Sūrdās also used a certain amount of Perso-Arabic vocabulary. As poets of the same region, they obviously had much in common. Both Jāysī and Tulsīdās were Avadhi poets, so they composed poems in a similar style and language, although they belonged to different religions and literary genres: Rāma bhakti literature *versus* Sufi love epics. Yet I would like to claim that poets who did not get formal poetic training in *mātrik chand* did not follow the conventions of metre, possibly because they were less bound by literary traditions.

Similarities of the *mātrik chand* and Perso-Arabic Metrical Forms as Pointed out by Jagannāth Prasād 'Bhānu'

The *Kāvya Prabhākara* (1893) and the *Chandaḥ Prabhākara* (1909) written by Jagannāth Prasād 'Bhānu' are among the most comprehensive works on Hindi poetics. Bhānu divided metres into three divisions as in Sanskrit and arranged them by the number of *mātrā*s. The three divisions are *samavr̥tta* 'equal metre', in which each *pāda* contains the same number of *mātrā*s, *ardhasama* 'half-equal metre', in which odd and even *pāda*s contain equal *mātrā*s, and *viṣama prakaraṇa* 'unequal metre', in which each *pāda* contains a different number of *mātrā*s. He gave the definition of every metre in *dohā* and quoted examples from Bhakti literature. Interestingly, he mentions four forms of *mātrik* *chand*: *sumerū, digpāla, gītikā* and *harigītikā*, which are similar to Perso-Arabic metres. The *mātrik chand* and the Perso-Arabic metre have essentially different structures, so it is unlikely that they happened to share the same metrical form by chance.

The following is an example of *harigītikā* composed by Tulsīdās. According to the definition, each line of *harigītikā* has 16 + 12 = 28 *mātrā*s. The 5th, 12th, 19th, and 26th *mātrā*s are short. The end rhyme is ⏑–.

pada kamala dhoi caṛhāi nāva na nātha utarāī cahaũ |
⏑⏑ ⏑⏑⏑ –⏑ ⏑– ⏑ – ⏑ ⏑, – ⏑ ⏑⏑– – ⏑ –
mohi rāma rāuri āna dasaratha sapatha saba sācī kahaũ ||
⏑⏑ –⏑ –⏑⏑ –⏑ ⏑⏑⏑⏑, ⏑⏑⏑ ⏑⏑ – – ⏑–
baru tīra mārahũ lakhanu pai jaba lagi na pāya pakhārihaũ |
⏑⏑ –⏑ –⏑ ⏑ ⏑⏑⏑ – ⏑ ⏑, ⏑ ⏑ ⏑ –⏑ ⏑–⏑–
taba lagi na tulasīdāsa nātha kṛpāla pāru utārihaũ ||
⏑⏑ ⏑⏑ ⏑ ⏑⏑– –⏑ –⏑ ⏑,–⏑ –⏑ ⏑–⏑– (*Rāmcaritmānas* 2.100)

After washing your lotus feet, I will take you on board but I will not accept any toll. I tell you the truth, O Rāma, swearing by yourself and Daśaratha,
Lakṣmaṇa may shoot me with his arrow, but I will not take you across, gracious lord of Tulasī Dāsa, until I have bathed your feet!
(Tr. by F.S. Growse)

Bhānu thinks that *harigītikā* has a structure similar to the following example of Perso-Arabic metre. This is his example quoted from the *Kāvya Prabhākara*[14]:

vo jo | *ham*|*mẽ tum*|*mẽ qa*|*rā*|*r* t^h*ā*| *tumhẽ* | *yā*|*d ho*| *ke na*| *yā*|*d ho*|[15]
mutafā ʻilun mutafā ʻilun mutafā ʻilun mutafā ʻilun
⏑ ⏑ – ⏑ – | ⏑ ⏑ – ⏑ – | ⏑ ⏑ – ⏑ –| ⏑ ⏑ – ⏑ –|

Do you remember or not the promise between you and me?

This Urdu verse has 28 *mātrā*s, and like *harigītikā*, the 5th, 12th, 19th and 26th *mātrā*s are light syllables. Three other examples which are mentioned by Bhānu seem to follow the rule of *mātrik chand*. Table 17.1 summarizes the close similarities between *mātrik chand* and Perso-Arabic metre in the following four metrical forms.

TABLE 17.1

	mātrik chand	Perso-Arabic	metre	Number of morae
sumerū	12+7 = 19 or 10+9 = 19 The 1st, 8th and 15th *mātrās* are⌣. The end rhyme ⌣ - - is preferred.	mafā'īlun, mafā'īlun, fa'ūlun	⌣ - - -, ⌣ - - -, ⌣ - -	7+7+5 = 19
digpāla	12+12 = 24 The 5th and 17th *mātrās* are ⌣.	maf'ūl, fā'ilātun, maf'ūl, fā'ilātun	- - ⌣, - ⌣ - - , - - ⌣, - ⌣ - -	(5+7)+(5+7) = 24
gītikā	14+12 = 26 The 3rd, 10th, 17th and 24th *mātrās* are ⌣. The end rhyme is ⌣ -.	fā'ilātun×3+ fā'ilun	- ⌣ - -, - ⌣ - - , - ⌣ - -, - ⌣ -	(7+7)+(7+5) = 26
harigītikā	16+12 = 28 The 5th, 12th, 19th and 26th *mātrās* are ⌣. The end rhyme is ⌣ -.	mutafā'ilun×4	⌣ ⌣ - ⌣ -, ⌣ ⌣ - ⌣ -, ⌣ ⌣ - ⌣ -, ⌣ ⌣ - ⌣ -	(7+7)+(7+7) = 28

In these four cases, the total number of morae, the internal rhyme and the external rhyme are the same in *mātrik chand* and Perso-Arabic metre, except that the divisional boundaries of *sumerū* and *harīgitikā* are different.

The Bhakti Period: The Shared Literary Stage of Muslim and Non-Muslim Poets

As stated above, it is clear that the same metrical forms can be explained by *mātrik* as well as by Perso-Arabic prosody. The Perso-Arabic metre which is applied to Urdu makes some exceptions to the rule in order to count the exact syllabic weight of New Indo-Aryan. Therefore, the way of counting metrical weight in Urdu Perso-Arabic metre and Hindi *mātrik chand* is not different from each other.

It is highly probable that poets found that almost the same metrical forms can be composed either by *mātrik chand* or by

Perso-Arabic metre, and so they composed verses in metres popular at the time. Indeed, besides the four metrical forms mentioned above, many metrical forms of *mātrik chand* can be defined by Perso-Arabic metre as well. Take the *dohā*, for example, one of the most popular metres during the Bhakti period. According to the definition of Perso-Arabic metre, many variations of *dohā* are found to be canonical such as:

(1) fe'lun - - fe'lun - - fā'ilun - ⌣ -, fā'i - ⌣ fa'ūlun ⌣ - - fā'i - ⌣. 13+11
(2) fe'lun - - fe'lun - - fe'lun - - fa'-, fe'lun - - fe'lun - - fā'i - ⌣. 14+11
(3) fe'l - ⌣ fa'ūlun ⌣ - - fe'lun - - fa ⌣, fe'lun - - fa'ūlun ⌣ - - fa' -. 13+11
(4) fe'lun - - fe'lun - - fe'l - ⌣ fa' -, fā'i -⌣ fa'ūlun ⌣ - - fā'i - ⌣. 13+11
(5) fe'lun - - fe'lun - - fe'l - ⌣ fa' -, fe'lun - - fe'lun - - fā'i - ⌣. 13+11 etc.

These are quite similar to the definition of *dohā* in *mātrik chand* but even in these cases, there are lines which contain 25 *mātrā*s, as in the second example. This fact leads us to the assumption that Urdu poets learned *dohā* by ear and tried to compose similar verses. As a consequence, the *dohā*s by early Sufi poets contain many irregularities from the viewpoint of *mātrik chand*.

When we consider the background underlying the hypermetric *dohā*s in the works of Sufi poets, the importance of recitational performance should also be noted. As still partly the case nowadays, verses were composed for recitation and not for publication. According to Shivnandan Prasad, the author of a comparative study of *mātrik chand*, hypermetrical *dohā*s never contain more than 16 *mātrā*s in a *pāda*, because these verses were sung in *tāla chand* musical metre. One line of a *dohā* is divided into four musical bars, each bar containing 8 moras. It means that an odd *pāda* is filled up anyway to make two bars, i.e. 8 + 8 = 16 moras, whether it has 13, 14 or 15 moras. The same holds true for an even *pāda*, which typically contains 11 moras. On the other hand, if a *pāda* has more than 16 *mātrā*s, it would be difficult to sing. What later poetical tradition considers aberrance from the rules of prosody as in those hypermetrical *dohā*s, did not count as such to the Sufi poets or singers, as long as the *pāda*s of such *dohā*s did not exceed 16 *mātrā*s and could be sung in a similar way to more 'academic', traditionally-based *mātrik chand.*[16]

Non-Muslim poets kept using indigenous Indian metres while the tradition of Muslim poets incorporated Perso-Arabic prosody, which was probably foreign to the linguistic rhythm of Indo-Aryan languages, even though Persian and Indo-Aryan both belong to the Indo-Iranian group and naturally have much in common. Such discrepancy of language and metre might be one of the factors that led to literary differences between Hindi and Urdu. It may look as if their rhythmic preferences would differ from each other, but I would like to point out that this is not really the case. The poems of the Bhakti period by non-Muslim and Muslim (including Sufi) poets do not show any essential difference. Poets of those days had an influence on each other regardless of their religious affiliation because they lived in the same regions such as Avadh or Braj and composed in the same language such as Avadhi or Brajbhasha. Tulsīdās especially seems to have borrowed metrical styles from Muslim poets. Besides the above-mentioned influence of the Sufi love epics which consist of eight *ardhālī*s followed by a *dohā*, it is said that the *barvai* (a couplet with 12 + 7 *mātrā*s in each line, ending in ⏑ - ⏑.) used by Abdurrahīm 'Khānkhānā' (1556-1627) inspired Tulsīdās to compose his *Barvai Rāmāyaṇa.*[17] Shivnandan Prasad states that *barvai* is a late metrical form.[18] Traditionally, it is believed that *barvai* derives its name from the *birva* sapling. There is a legend that a servant of Abdurrahīm 'Khānkhānā' took leave for his own marriage. He was late in going back and was afraid he would be reproached. His wife wrote down a verse and told him to give it to the Rahīm as an excuse:

prīti rīti kau birvā calehu lagāya.
sīcana kā sudhi lījai murajhi na jāya.[19]

By the custom of love, a sapling was planted.
Do remember to water it so that it does not wither away.

Rahīm was impressed by this metre and started to compose poems on the taxonomy of heroines, *nāyikā-bhed*, in the very same metre.

Rahīm has traditionally been regarded as the godfather of *barvai*, but before him it was called *dhruvā* or *nandadohā*. Some scholars consider it a variation of the *dohā* because the 12-*mātrā* odd *pāda*s of *upadohā* or *dohrā*, which is a hypometric variation of *dohā*, are followed by 7 *mātrā*s. The above-mentioned legend also tells us that Rahīm borrowed this metrical form, which had already existed, to compose his work.[20]

From an early period, Hindu and Sufi poets influenced each other, or rather worked from a shared literary heritage, which included shared metrical forms. The adoption of Perso-Arabic prosody by Muslim poets was a later phenomenon.

NOTES

1. The term originates from R. Shukla, *Hindī sāhitya kā itihās*, Allahabad: Indian Press, 1929. Shukla defined the Bhakti period as the period between the early fourteenth and mid-seventeenth centuries, more precisely between Vikram Saṁvat 1375 and 1700.
2. Modern Sindhi and Punjabi poets compose poetry in Perso-Arabic metre such as *ghazal*, but they traditionally preferred the vernacular metre. On Sindhi verse, see A. Datta and M. Lal, *Encyclopaedia of Indian Literature*, vol. 2, Delhi: Sahitya Akademi, 1988, p. 1248. In Punjabi Sufi verse, see L.R. Krishna, *Pañjābī Ṣūfī Poets: A.D. 1460-1900*, Karachi: Indus Publications, 1938; rpt. 1977, pp. xxiii-xxv.
3. Professor Takamitsu Matsumura, Professor So Yamane and Professor Suhail Abbas Khan gave me valuable comments on Urdu and Punjabi metre. I am deeply grateful to them.
4. In addition to the above two, the musical metre *tāl chand*, applied to *pad* verses usually dedicated to Krishna, is also mentioned in treatises on Hindi prosody such as M.S. Mahesh, *The Historical Development of Medieval Hindi Prosody: Rāmānanda-Keśava, 1400-1600 A.D.*, Bhagalpur: Bhagalpur University, 1964, pp. 18-23, 63-7 and S. Prasad, *Mātrik chandõ kā vikās*, Patna: Bihār-Rāṣṭrabhāṣā-Pariṣad, 1964, pp. 141-52. This metre, however, is a variation on the *mātrik chand*.
5. The rules of Perso-Arabic metre cited in this paper are based on M. A.-A.-R. Barker, S. Abdus Salam and M.A. Siddiqi, eds., *A Reader of Classical Urdu Poetry*, 3 vols., New York: Spoken Language Services, 1977.

6. Eight types of foot; fa-'ū-lun (⏑– –), fā-'i-lun (– ⏑ –), ma-fā-'ī-lun (⏑ – – –), fā-'i-lā-tun (– ⏑ – –), mus-taf-'i-lun (– – ⏑ –), maf-'ū-lā-tu (– – – ⏑), mu-fā-'i-la-tun (⏑–⏑⏑–), mu-ta-fā-'i-lun (⏑ ⏑ – ⏑ –).
7. (1) *hazaj*: ma-fā-'ī-lun (⏑ – – –)×4
   (2) *rajaz*: mus-taf-'i-lun (– – ⏑ –) ×4
   (3) *ramal*: fā-'i-lā-tun (– ⏑ – –) ×4
   (4) *munṣariḥ*: (mus-taf-'i-lun (– – ⏑ –) + maf-'ū-lā-tu (– – – ⏑))×2
   (5) *muẓare'*: (ma-fā-'ī-lun (⏑ – – –) fā-'i-lā-tun (– ⏑ – –))×2
   (6) *muqtaẓab*: (maf-'ū-lā-tu (– – – ⏑) + mus-taf-'i-lun (– – ⏑ –)) ×2
   (7) *mujtaṣ*: (mus-taf-'i-lun (– – ⏑ –)+fā-'i-lā-tun (– ⏑ – –))×2
   (8) *sarī'*: mus-taf-'i-lun+ mus-taf-'i-lun+ maf-'ū-lā-tu (– – – ⏑)
   (9) *k̲h̲afīf*: fā-'i-lā-tun (– ⏑ – –)+ mus-taf-'i-lun (– – ⏑ –)+ fā-'i-lā-tun (– ⏑ – –)
   (10) *mutaqārib*: fa'ū-lun (⏑ – –)×4
   (11) *mutadārik*: fā-'i-lun (– ⏑ –)×4
   (12) *kāmil*: muta-fā-'i-lun (⏑ ⏑ – ⏑ –)×4

   The *munṣariḥ* and *sarī* have never been used for Urdu poems, perhaps because Urdu words do not end in CV like the end of maf'ūlātu (– – – ⏑). On the other hand, there is no restriction like that for *muẓāre'*, *muqtaẓab*, *mujtaṣ* and *k̲h̲afīf*, so these metrical forms might not have been favoured.
8. As the aspiration of Urdu is written with the character *he*, Urdu speakers have nowadays obtained different pronunciation from that of Hindi speakers. Urdu speakers tend to pronounce *h* as an independent segment while Hindi speakers pronounce it as an aspiration. In view of the fact that *mātrik chand* and Perso-Arabic metres treat aspirated stops as single consonants, it can be said that different pronunciation had not occurred at the time when Perso-Arabic prosody was adapted to Urdu.
9. Naseem A. Hines argues that Indo-Sufi poets simply adopted from Apabhraṁśa the practice of composing in the poetic unit *kaḍavaka*, which consists of several *yamaka* lines and ends in a *dhattā* (*sic*). However, the rules are not rigidly adhered to by early Indo-Sufi poets. Later, the metrical system became standardized and Tulsīdās followed the rules of Svayambhu. N.A. Hines, *Maulana Daud's Cāndāyan: A Critical Study*, Delhi: Manohar, 2009, pp. 92-8.
10. V. Prasad, ed., *Candāyan*, Agra: Kanhaiyālāl Munśīlāl Hindī tathā Bhāṣāvijñān Vidyāpīṭh, Āgrā Viśvavidyālaya, 1962, p. 39.
11. M.P. Gupta, ed., *Padmāvat*, Allahabad: Bhāratī Bhaṇḍār, 1963.
12. V.S. Agraval, ed., *Padmāvat*, Jhansi: Sāhitya-Sadan, 2000, pp. 12-13. For an approach from an assumption that hypermetric verses resulted from interpolations in the course of transmission, see Imre Bangha's article in this volume.
13. Academic surveys such as A. Schimmel, *Classical Urdu Literature from the Beginning to Iqbāl*, Wiesbaden: Otto Harrassowitz, 1975, do not include these poets of Urdu literature but comprehensive histories such as J. Jalibi,

Tārīkh-i adab-i urdū vol. 1, Delhi: Educational Publishing House, 1977, treat them as early Urdu poets.

14. Jaganāth Prasād 'Bhānu', *Kāvya prabhākara*, Kāśī: Nāgarī Pracāriṇī Sabhā, 1971, revised edn., p. 26.
15. Bhānu did not mention the author but the poet of this verse is Momin.
16. In the works of Kabīr, there are many hypermetric metres, as in the works of Sufi poets. In another paper in this volume, Imre Bangha shows how he can reconstruct metrically correct verses. His approach helps us to consider how oral transmission changed texts and metres.
17. Maheshwari Sinha Mahesh, *The Historical Development of Medieval Hindi Prosody: Rāmānanda-Keśava, 1400-1600 A.D.*, p. 126. But, Rupert Snell claims that *barvai* of Tulsīdās has more flexibilities than that of Rahīm, so he thinks that Tulsīdās did not rigidly borrow the style of Rahīm. R. Snell, 'Barvai' Metre in Tulsīdās and Rahīm', in *Studies in South Asian Devotional Literature*, ed. A.W. Entwistle and Françoise Mallison, Delhi: Manohar, 1994, pp. 373-405.
18. Prasad, *Mātrik chandõ kā vikās*, p. 399.
19. This famous *barvai* is quoted in V. Mishra and G. Rajnish, *Rahīm granthāvalī*, Delhi: Vāṇī Prakāshan, 1999, p. 12. Strangely the *barvai* 53 by Yaśodānandana (eighteenth century) is exactly the same as this *barvai*. Kiśorī Lāl, who edited the edition *Yaśodānandana Racnāvalī*, claims that this *barvai* was actually composed by Yaśodānandana and Rahīm's episode should not be taken at its face value, even though Kiśorī Lāl accepted that Rahīm was the godfather of *barvai*. According to his claim, the question how this *barvai* is connected to the legend of Rahīm arises. But in any case, the evidence of the existence of material precursors of barvai confirms that Rahīm adopted this metrical rhythm from some source that already existed. See K. Lal, *Yaśodānandana Racnāvalī*, Indore: Manasvī Prakāśan.
20. The influence of Rahīm on Tulsīdās derives from the *Mūlgosāī̃ Carit* which tells us that Rahīm sent a *barvai* couplet to Tulsī. M. Gupta, *Tulsīdās: ek samālocanātmak adhyayan*, Allahabad: Allahabad University, 1965, p. 53.

BIBLIOGRAPHY

Agraval, V.S., ed., *Padmāvata*, Jhāṁsī: Sāhitya-Sadan, 2000.

Barker, M.A.-A.-R., S. Abdus Salam and M.A. Siddiqi, eds., *A Reader of Classical Urdu Poetry*, 3 vols, New York: Spoken Language Services, 1977.

'Bhanu', J.P., *Chandaḥ prabhākara*, Bilāsapur: Jagannāth Press, 1939.

———, *Kāvya prabhākara*, rev. edn., Kāśī: Nāgarī Pracāriṇī Sabhā, 1971.

Datta, A. et al., eds., *Encyclopaedia of Indian Literature*, vol. 2, Delhi: Sahitya Akademi, 1988.

Growse, F.S., *The Rāmāyaṇa of Tulasīdāsa*, Cawnpore: E. Samuel, 1891, rpt., Delhi: Motilal Banarsidass, 1978.

Gupta, M., ed., *Tulasī granthāvalī*, vol. 1, Allahabad: Hindustānī Ekedemī, 1949.

——, ed., *Padmāvata,* Allahabad: Bhāratī Bhaṇḍār, 1963.

——, *Tulsīdās: ek samālocanātmak adhyayan*, Allahabad: Allahabad University, 1965.

Hines, N.A., *Maulana Daud's Cāndāyan: A Critical Study*, Delhi: Manohar, 2009.

Ja'far, S. and G.C. Jain, *Tārīkh-i adab-i urdū 1700 tak*, Delhi: Qaumī Kaunsil barā'e Furogh-i Urdū Zabān, 1998.

Jalibi, J., *Tārīkh-i adab-i urdū*, vol. 1, Delhi: Educational Publishing House, 1977.

Krishna, L.R., *Pañjābī Ṣūfī Poets: A.D. 1460-1900*, London, Bombay, New York: Oxford University Press, 1938, rpt., Karachi: Indus Publications, 1977.

Lal, K., *Yaśodānandana Racanāvalī*, Indore: Manasvī Prakāśan, 2003.

Mahesh, M.S., *The Historical Development of Medieval Hindi Prosody: Rāmānanda-Keśava, 1400-1600 A.D.*, Bhagalpur: Bhagalpur University, 1964.

Mishra, V.P., ed. *Rāmcaritmānas*, Benares: Kāśīrāj, 1962.

Mishra, V., ed., *Rahīm Granthāvalī*, Delhi: Vāṇī Prakāśan, 1985.

Orsini, F., *Before the Divide: Hindi and Urdu Literary Culture,* Delhi: Orient Blackswan, 2010.

Prasad, S., *Mātrik chandõ kā vikās*, Patna: Bihār-Rāṣṭrabhāṣā-Pariṣad, 1964.

Prasad, V., ed., *Candāyan*, Agra: Kanhaiyālāl Munśīlāl Hindī tathā Bhāṣāvijñān Vidyāpīṭh, Āgrā Viśvavidyālaya, 1962.

Schimmel, A., *Classical Urdu Literature from the Beginning to Iqbāl*, Wiesbaden: Otto Harrassowitz, 1975.

Shukla, R., *Hindī sāhitya kā itihās*, Allahabad: Indian Press, 1929.

——, ed., *Jāyasī-granthāvalī: arthāt, Padamāvata, Akharāvaṭa, aura Ākhirī kalāma*, Kāśī: Nāgarīpracāriṇīsabhā, 1949.

Snell, R., '"Barvai" Metre in Tulsīdās and Rahīm' in Alan W. Entwistle and F. Mallison (eds.), *Studies in South Asian Devotional Literature*, Delhi: Manohar, 1994, pp. 373-405.

CHAPTER 18

Śṛṅkhlā: A System of Musico-Religious Performance of the *Samāj-gāyan* in Braj

TAKAKO TANAKA

Purpose and Approach

As an ethno-musicologist, I have worked on bhakti music for many years. The subject of this article is more the process of my work than the results that I found through it. It is impossible to reach a full understanding of bhakti without considering its musical aspects. Bhakti, from its very beginning, has been associated with the singing of the *āḷvār*s in south India and has been closely linked to music till the present. From a musicological point of view, I wonder how *bhakti saṅgīt* differs from other kinds of Indian music. Does it have a distinct peculiarity? In what way are Indian musical factors integrated into bhakti?

It was about a quarter of a century ago that I first heard a *bhajan* of Mīrābāī in Tokyo. It was sung by Dr. L.N. Tewari at the end of a vocal recital of Indian classical music. At that time I was a graduate student majoring in ethno-musicology, and studying Indian classical music. I asked the singer what a *bhajan* was. He explained to me 'Bhajan means a devotional song for Hindu Gods'. His answer was far from satisfactory. In 1983, I received a two-year scholarship from the Indian government to learn music in Lucknow and Delhi. I continued to ask people that I met in

India what a *bhajan* was and how I could hear it. I tried to go to as many places as possible to listen to *bhajan*s and record them on cassette tapes.

I carried out further field research of a few weeks each in 1986 with Prof. Teiji Sakata and other scholars, and alone in 1996. In this way, by 1996, including the recordings made together with Prof. Sakata, I had made almost 380 tape recordings of different kinds of music, about half of which were related to *bhakti saṅgīt*.

Data and information about each recording was integrated into a database: not only the extraneous information of the recordings—dates, time of day, occasion or event, the city and exact place, names and other features of the singers, musical instruments used—but also the essential data of musical characteristics—the full musical structure of performances (notated using the alphabet and special signs invented by myself); whatever I noticed about scale, rhythm, tempo, pitch, singing form and singing structure; the relationship between the melody and the text and so on. I had great difficulty in writing down the texts after listening and to avoid this problem, I tried, whenever possible, to ask the singers themselves to write down the text, or to get printed copies of them. In many cases, however, it was impossible; some of them were illiterate, others did not have the time, or I was not allowed to ask them.

I sometimes feel jealous of scholars of literature who study written materials. My study depends mostly on oral performances and the sound itself, when only the moment of the song provides material for me. I think this is the biggest point concerning the difference of approach between my study and other studies in this volume. I do not care whether the sung text is grammatically wrong, or different from the 'vulgate' texts or 'original' manuscripts.

The purpose of my study is to find the relationship between the religious and the musicological aspects of *bhakti saṅgīt* as a performed genre of music today. In other words, I aim to study musical phenomena in their scale, rhythm and so on.

Studying *bhakti saṅgīt* as Music

Bhakti music has long been the subject of musicological study. The work of Stephen M. Slawek on the *kirtan* with ample notations of his recordings—some overlapping with mine—is worthy of special mention.[1] The scholar of Hindi, Rupert Snell, presented an analysis of metres in a musical performance in *The Eighty-four Hymns of Hita Harivaṃśa.*[2] His work inspired me to write on the metre and rhythm in a Kabir *bhajan*. Selina Thielemann, a brilliant musicologist and classical singer of *dhrupad*, has worked on the many types of *bhakti saṅgīt*, including the *samāj* tradition of the Braj area, and has written many books.[3] She mostly analyses *bhakti saṅgīt* on the basis of the classical tradition and theory of Indian music, and I think the method is effective for most of her objects of study. My approach, however, is not diachronic since I am basically interested in finding actual musical characteristics through the analysis of my recordings of performances facilitated by the documentation on each performance and performer. As publications in Japanese are inaccessible to most bhakti scholars, I give here a brief survey of what I have written and published during my study.

My first article concerning *bhakti saṅgīt* was from a pilgrimage in Braj with Prof. Sakata and other scholars in 1986.[4] I found that the pilgrims sang various types of bhakti songs according to religious situations. My research on the difference between Islamic Sufi music and Hindu *bhakti saṅgīt* also resulted in some articles[5] where I analysed the music construction of the *qawwālī* performance and songs during the rituals called *mahfil-e sama'* and the relationship between religious ideas and music. Linked to this research, I edited a laser disc of *qawwālī* performances filmed in Ajmer and Delhi.[6] *Samāj gāyan*, a two-volume CD with a commentary recorded at the Haridās Sevā Sansthān in Vrindaban, was published in 1992.[7] A Japanese article on it followed in 1993.[8] In 1998, I submitted a dissertation[9] to the Tokyo National University of Arts, which was published ten years later in 2008.[10] The book is written in Japanese and is divided into three parts. The first part, 'The Structure of Samāj-gāyan Music', is a musical analysis of the various types of *bhakti saṅgīt*—including *samāj-gāyan* performances. Here, I also point out some special characteristics found exclusively in *samāj-gāyan*.

The second part 'The Land of Samāj-gāyan: History of Thought and Singing in Hinduism', deals with the spiritual and historical background of the various traditions of *bhakti saṅgīt*. In its six chapters, I discuss why and how *bhakta*s are supposed to sing for gods according to their spiritual and historical backgrounds.

In the last part, 'The Musico-Religious Structure of Samāj-gāyan', I analyse the relationship between the musical factors discussed in the first part and the spiritual and historical background treated in the second part. I arrive at the conclusion that each performance of *Samāj-gāyan* is constructed of numerous small units of music, which are combined by the singers just like 'a chain' consisting of small pieces. I call this *śṛṅkhlā*, 'chain'. While a previous English paper of mine[11] mainly focused on a chapter of the third part, the present article relies on the findings of the analysis of singing forms discussed in a chapter of the first part of the Japanese book.

General Characteristics of *Bhakti saṅgīt*

Text, Music and Emotion

How can *bhakti saṅgīt* be distinguished from other Indian musical genres? Figure 18.1[12] shows an example of the traditional taxonomy of Indian vocal music by R.B. Qureshi. Qureshi made her table with the intention of showing the taxonomy of Islamic vocal music, so it is natural that we cannot find any inclusion of *bhakti saṅgīt* here. Yet Qureshi's distribution of music into *pakkā gānā* or *śāstrīy saṅgīt*, '*rāga* music', *gānā*, 'song', and *paṛhnā*, 'chant', is a pragmatic one. Is melody or are words more important in music? The same question arises with regard to our Japanese traditional vocal music. Indian music is divided into *rāga-pradhān* (*rāga*-primary) and *śabda-pradhān* (word-primary) categories. *Rāga*-primary means 'music-primary', while the second category

INDIC MUSIC

NORTHERN (*Hindustani*)		SOUTHERN (*Karnataka*)
RAGA MUSIC (*pakkā gānā bajānā*)	SONG (*gānā*)	CHANT (*paṛhnā*)
Music primary	**Words** primarv	**Words** primary
Verbal delivery may or may not be present	Verbal delivery always present	Musical delivery may or may not be present
Instrumental accompaniment included	Instrumental accompaniment included	Instrumental accompaniment excluded
Form extended cyclic	Form strophic or cyclic	Form strophic

	LIGHT CLASSICAL (*halkā*)	POPULAR (*filmī bāzārī*)	FOLK (*lok gīt*)	SECULAR	RELIGIOUS
				tarannum	*nātkhwānī*
dhurpad	*ghumrī*		*shādī kā gānā*		*sozkhwānī*
khayāl	*dādrā*	*filmī ghazal*	*lorī*		*marsiyā-khwānī*
tarānā	*ghazal*	*filmī qawwālī*	(etc.)		
asthāyī	*ṭappā*	*filmī gīt*			
	qawwālī				

Figure 18.1: Qureshi's taxonomy of Indian vocal music

is concerned with verbal delivery, strophic or cyclic form, and the existence of instrumental accompaniment.

Under which criteria should *bhakti saṅgīt* be located? It is clear that the idea of *raga* cannot be primary in bhakti vocal music, although we sometimes hear ritual singing at Hindu temples such as the Vallabhite *kirtan* in Braj sung in the *dhrupad* style, which would be considered *rāg-pradhān* music. Some *bhajan*s are also sung at the end of classical concerts, as I have heard in Tokyo. I collected *bhajan*s regarded as songs and others as chanting. Consequently, *bhakti saṅgīt* cannot be located collectively in one category of music. Devotees define *bhakti saṅgīt* not by its musical characteristics but by the spiritual content of the text or the contexts of the performances. A bhakta explained to me that *bhakti saṅgīt* was *bhāv-pradhān* 'emotion-primary' music.[13]

Forms of *Bhakti saṅgīt*

Ways of Singing Bhajans and Kirtans

Against a spiritual background, Hindu devotees sing songs in different styles, languages and repertoires for the gods, which are collectively called *bhakti saṅgīt*. Even if we confine ourselves to the Braj area, a variety of *bhakti saṅgīt* traditions can be observed, including *bhajan*s, *kirtan*s, *ārtī*s, *viṣṇupada*s and *samāj-gāyan*. Each tradition has its own context and characteristics as music.

Generally speaking, in terms of musical form, most *bhajan*s are sung by a solo singer in a strophic form structured by the refrain (*tek* or *dhruva*) with or without instrumental accompaniment. Figure 18.2 shows a sample of the full notation of a *bhajan* performance of sample [1048] in two ways; the upper notation is in the Indic way using letters and the one below is written in the staff notation of Western music.

The Kabīr *bhajan Bīta gaye dina* was taught to me through several lessons by a professional singer of classical music in 1983 in Lucknow. He sang by heart, but I found the similar text in M.K. Gandhi's *Āśram-bhajanāvalī*,[14] which I transliterated in Figure 18.3, underlining words that were sung differently from the text. The *bhajan* has seven lines in the *caupāī* metre containing 16 *mātrā*s in each line. The first line [d] is the refrain (*dhruva* abbreviated in the text as *dhru*) followed by three couplets [1-1] [1-2], [2-1][2-2] and [3-1][3-2]. An analysis of the performance indicates that this *bhajan* operates with four melodic units ([1]-[4]).

Figure 18.4 shows how the textual units are linked to the melodic units in performance. Each textual unit is combined with a certain melodic unit. In this way, after the refrain [d] with melodic unit [1] is repeated twice, each couplet has either melodic units [2][3] or [4][3]. This shows the interdependence of the text's metrical structure and the musical structure of the song.

*Bhajan*s are relatively simple to sing and anyone who has a repertoire of them can sing freely according to his/her capacity and knowledge of the text and music. In performances of *bhajan*s, singers are often heard to sing in *rāga*s different from those written in the printed text. There are also many cases when the singing manner of a certain *rāga* by bhaktas differs very much from when the same *rāga* is sung by a classical vocalist. In this sample [1048], the *rāga* actually sung is regarded as *rāg bihāg*, while it is written as *rāg bhairavī* in the text.

Music sample [1048]

Upper line indicates melody.
Lower line indicates texts.

[1] – <– G> <– M><P Sh>| N <– D> <P m> P |<P G> <– G> <M P> <– M> | G R S – |
[d] – – bī – – ta ga ye – – di – na – – – -bha ja na – bi nā – re –

[2] – <– G> <–M> <P N> | Sh <N N> Sh – |Sh <– N> <– D> <– P> |<D N> Sh N – |
[1-1] – – bā – – la a va – (a)s thā . . – – – khe – la – gā vā . – – yo –

[3] – <N N> N Sh | N D <P m> P | – <– G> <M P> <– M >| G R S – |
[1-2] – ja – ba ja vā nī ta – ba – – mā – na – gha nā – re –
[2-2] – a ja hū na ga ī ma – na – – kī – tṛ – (i) s nā – re –
[3-2] – pā – ra u ta ra ga – ye – – sa (a)n ta – ja nā – re –

[4] – <– G> <– M> <P N>|Sh N Sh Sh |– <– P> <N Sh> <– Rh>|Gh Rh Sh – |
[2-1] – – lā – – he ke kā – ra na – – mū – la – gā vā – yo –
[3-1] – – ka – ha ta ka bī – ra – – – su no bhā – ī sā – dho –

Figure 18.2: Full notation of a *bhajan* performance in two ways

A *kirtan* is generally sung by one lead singer accompanied by others antiphonally, that is, in 'call-and-response' style. Figure 18.5 shows the three types of melodic units (A, B, C) of a sample

bīta gaye dina bhajana binā re	ǀdhru oǀ	[d]
bāla-avasthā khela gãvāyo,		[1-1]
jaba javā*nī* taba māna ghanā re	ǀ1ǀ	[1-2]
lāhe ke kārana mūla gãvāyo,		[2-1]
ajahũ na gaī manakī tṛsnā re	ǀ2ǀ	[2-2]
kahata kabīra suno *bhāī* sādho,		[3-1]
pāra utara ga*ye* santa janā re	ǀ3ǀ	[3-2]

Figure 18.3: Transliteration of the bhajan *Bīta gaye dina*

Musical units:	1	1		
Textual units:	[d]	[d]		
	2	3	1	1
	[1-1]	[1-2]	[d]	[d]
	4	3	1	1
	[2-1]	[2-2]	[d]	[d]
	4	3	1	1
	[3-1]	[3-2]	[d]	[d]

Figure 18.4: Combination of the textual and musical units in the full performance of Music sample [1048]

recorded at Krishna Janma Bhūmi in Mathura in 1984, using staff notation. The lyric is the common *Mahāmantra*—a combination of only three words *hare*, *Krishna* and *Rama*. The *akhaṇḍ kīrtan* (non-stopped *kirtan*) goes on for long time with many repetitions of the same spiritual words, changing the choice of melody as follows:

Figure 18.5: Melodic units in a *kirtan* performance

Leader: A → Others: A → Leader: A → Others: A ...→
Leader: B → Others: B → Leader: B → Others: B ...→
Leader: C → Others: C → Leader: C → Others: C ...→
Leader: A → Others: A → Leader: A → Others: A ...→

In a *kirtan*, any bhakta may join in a group and show full devotion, continuing for hours as long as he or she wants to stay praising the gods.

The *Samāj-gāyan* and its Singing Structure

The following discussion of the singing structure of the *samāj-gāyan*, as compared to those of the *bhajan* and *kirtan*, will be limited to its special characteristics. The *samāj-gāyan* tradition can be seen today in several temples belonging to the Haridās, N̄imbārka, Rādhāvallabh and Caitanya *sampradāyas*. *Samāj-gāyan* at the

Gauḍīya Rādhāraman Temple in Vrindaban has been studied by Selina Tielemann.[15] My study relies mainly on observations at other temples in Vrindaban such as the Śrī Gadādhar Bhaṭṭ Gosvāmī Pīṭh and the Śrī Madan Mohan jī kā Mandir (hereafter called Bhaṭṭ jī kā Mandir) belonging to the Caitanya *sampradāya*, and the Haridās Sevā Sansthān of the Haridās *sampradāya*. *Samāj-gāyan* is an indispensable part of the ritual *samāj*, strictly held according to the divine calendar of Krishna and his *līlā*s. Hence, the devotees as singers believe that they are not supposed to practice it at other times as music.

As has been mentioned, *samāj-gāyan* is basically sung antiphonally between two groups: a senior singer (the *mukhiyā*) and the less-experienced *jhelā*s. Figure 18.6 shows the same *pad* sung on different occasions in the *samāj-gāyan* at Bhaṭṭ jī (Upper Sample [1419]) and Haridās Sevā Sansthān (Lower Sample [1421]). The musical expression was completely different on each occasion. The number of textual units is the same, fifteen units in total (from [1-1] to [4-4]), but the way of dividing each line into units according to the melodic units differed. Some words (that are underlined) were added to the text and left unsung as compared to those of the same *pad* in the *Śṛṅgār ras sāgar: śrī rādhāvallabh jī kau varśotsav*,[16] or repeated.

Figure 18.7 shows the whole structure of the performances in the same way that was used in analysing the *bhajan* performance. The whole performance of music Sample [1421] took eighteen minutes to complete and Sample [1419] took eight minutes. The indicator M shows that the text was sung by the *mukhiyā*, J by the *jhelā*, and MJ was sung by both. What is revealed is a highly complex structure of performance in terms of both the musical and textual points of view. The number of melodic units is almost ten in both samples.

Another noteworthy characteristic of *samāj-gāyan* is that not only the *tāla*, 'rhythmic cycle', but also the tempo changes many times during one continuous performance, as is shown especially in Sample [1421]. The letter V indicates that it is to be sung 'in slow tempo' and D 'in fast tempo'.

Thus, the singing structure of each repertoire in *samāj-gāyan* is

Printed Text [SRS 1:373]

श्री स्वामी हरिदास जी महाराज कृत–सुनि धुनि मुरली वन बाजै हरि रास रच्यौ। कुँज कुँज द्रुम बेली प्रफुलित मंडल कंचन मणिनु खच्यौ ॥ १ ॥ निर्त्तत जुगल किशोर जुवति जन मन मिलि राग केदारौ मच्यौ। श्री हरिदास के स्वामी स्यामा कुँज विहारी नीकैं आजु प्यारो लाल नच्यौ ॥ २ ॥ २१ ॥

Units of Text[1421]

suni dhuni mura-: lī vana vājai hari: śrī hari rāsa racyau |
[1-1] [1-2] [1-3]

kuñja kuñja druma : velī praphulita : maṇḍala kañcana : maṇinu khacyau || 1 ||
[2-1] [2-2] [2-3] [2-4]

nirttata jugala ki-: śora juvati jana : mana mili rāga ke-: dārau macyau |
[3-1] [3-2] [3-3] [3-4]

(śrī)* haridāsa ke svāmī syāmā : kuñja bihārī : nīkain āju pyāro : lāla nacyau || 2 ||
[4-1] [4-2] [4-3] [4-4]

Units of Text[1419]

suni dhuni muralī vana : vājai e hari: rāsa racyau |
[1-1] [1-2] [1-3]

kuñja kuñja druma : velī praphulita : maṇḍala kañcana : maṇinu khacyau || 1 ||
[2-1] [2-2] [2-3] [2-4]

nirttata jugala ki-: śora juvati e jana : mana mili rāga ke-: dārau macyau śrī |
[3-1] [3-2] [3-3] [3-4]

(śrī) haridāsa ke svāmī syāmā : kuñja bihārī śrī : nīkaiṃ āju pyāro : lāla nacyau || 2 ||
[4-1] [4-2] [4-3] [4-4]

Figure 18.6: Printed text, its transliteration and division of the *pad* sung in *samāj-gāyan* performance

complex with systematic, but asymmetrical, calls-and-responses.[17] Furthermore, every *samāj-gāyan* performance usually consists of several *pads* sung differently and each occasion of *samāj* has its own repertoire for any part of the liturgical year. Although the repertoire of a year is huge and people may sing from handwritten or printed texts, neither the structure of singing the texts, nor any of the musical instructions necessary to realize the literal texts

Sample[1421]

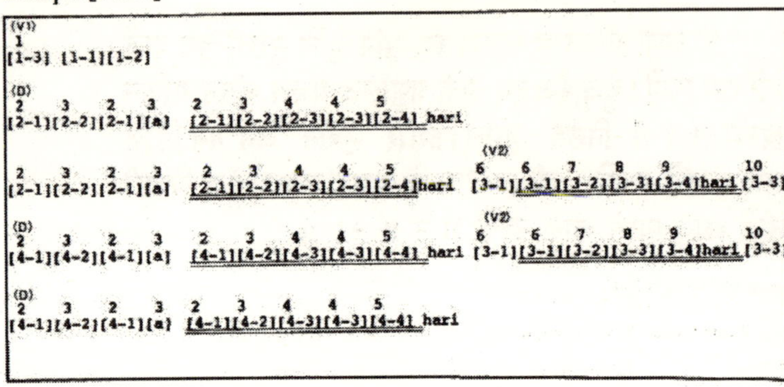

Sample[1419]

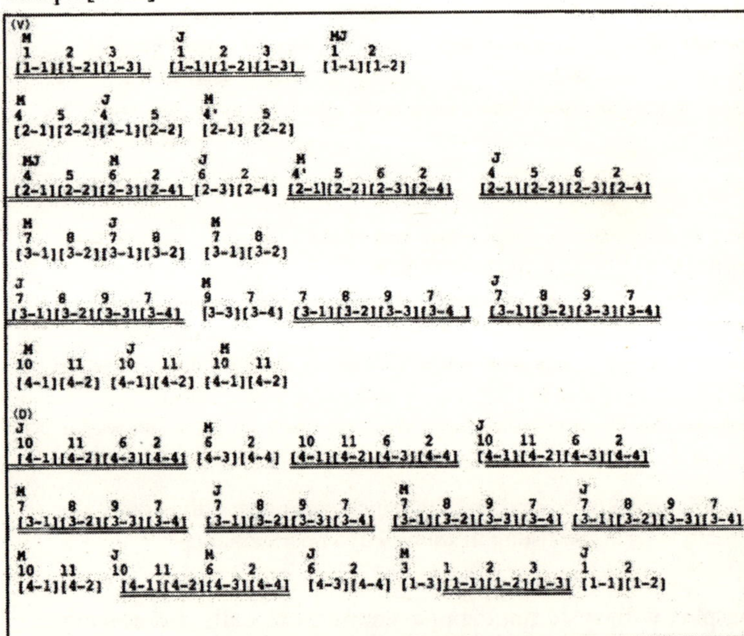

Figure 18.7: Full notation of the combinations of textual and musical units in the *samāj-gāyan* performances of Sample [1421] and Sample [1419].

into a music performance, have ever been written down. Singers are supposed to learn these by heart as practising devotees taking part in the rituals, which is also expected from them as bhaktas in the spiritual context.

Śṛṅkhlā: The Chain-like Structure in *Samāj-gāyan*

The asymmetrical call-and-response style requires the bhaktas' heightened attention because the *mukhiyā* is always responsible for remembering and choosing suitable units of text with the music, and the *jhelā*s must always be sensitive to what the *mukhiyā* sings and respond immediately to it. There is no score, no notation, no composer, no conductor, no teacher, nor any chance of practising the whole performance except in ritual *samāj*; only bhaktas sitting for hours together in ritual *samāj*, overwhelmed with bhakti for their lord.

The special character of a *samāj-gāyan* lies in the fact that the *mukhiyā* and the less-experienced *jhelā*s are supposed to link the numerous musical and textual parts originating from their spiritual leaders with the power of bhakti for Krishna in a highly complex manner. As a result, they compress the performance of a *mahotsav,* 'seasonal ritual', into a few hours, recreating and experiencing Krishna's *līlā*s in their own style.

This interlinked singing, borrowing a word from the title of the *Haridāsī* anthology, *Samāj śṛṅkhlā*,[18] can be called the *śṛṅkhlā* system. This system makes the *samāj-gāyan* tradition unique for the *sampradāya*s of Krishna devotees in Braj. The word *śṛṅkhlā* literally means 'chain', that is, 'a series of links or rings connected or fitted into one another' and this definition provides a fitting image for the structure of *samāj-gāyan.* Even though the use of the word *śṛṅkhlā* by Bhaṭṭ jī performers is seen only in its textual and liturgical aspect, the singing form consists of a series of connected musical and textual units, reminding one of the musical aspect of *śṛṅkhlā*s. The chain-like structure in both musical and textual terms can be seen as a sequence of lines and stanzas with slow and fast sections, a main singer (*mukhiyā*) and secondary singers (*jhelā*s), but, on a higher level, it is also a sequence of verses corresponding to the sequence of Krishna's *līlā*. *Śṛṅkhlā* denotes all combinations of the texts, as I have discussed in detail in my latest article.[19]

Thus, *Samāj gāyan* is an example of the various ways in which musical structures are integrated into and maintain the rich tradition of the performance of bhakti.

NOTES

1. S.M. Slawek, 'Kirtan: A Study of the Sonic Manifestations of the Divine in the Popular Hindu Culture of Banaras', Ph.D. dissertation, University of Illinois, 1986 and S.M. Slawek, 'Popular Kirtan in Benares: Some "Great" Aspects of a Little Tradition', *Ethnomusicology*, vol. 32, no. 2, 1988, pp. 249-64.
2. R. Snell, *The Eighty-four Hymns of Hita Harivaṁśa: An Edition of the Caurāsī Pada*, Delhi: Motilal Banarsidass and London: School of Oriental and African Studies, University of London, 1991.
3. S. Thielemann, *Musical Traditions of Vaiṣṇava Temples in Vraja: A Comparative Study of Samāja and the Dhrupada Tradition of North Indian Classical Music*, Delhi: Sagar, Associated Book Centre, 2001; S. Thielemann, *Singing the Praises Divine: Music in the Hindu Tradition*, Delhi: APH Publishers, 2000; S. Thielemann, 'Devotional Poetry in Performance: Samājagāyana at the Temple of Śrī Rādhāraman in Vrindaban', in *The Banyan Tree: Essays on Early Literature in New Indo-Aryan Languages*, ed. Mariola Offredi, Delhi: Manohar, 2000, pp. 559-74.
4. T. Sakata et al., 'Chijou no Tenkai o Aruku Hitobito (Pilgrims Aspiring for Unity with Krishna, the Hindu Deity of Justice and Love)', *Journal of Asian and African Studies*, vol. 37, 1989, pp. 69-121.
5. Among others, T. Tanaka, 'Kawwārī: Minami Asia no Sūfī no Uta (Qawwālī: Songs of Sufis in South Asia), *Girei to Ongaku (Rituals and Music)*, vol. 1, 1986, pp. 57-90, pp. 120-3.
6. Ibid., The original filming was done in 1985.
7. T. Tanaka, *Indo Haridāsu no Tera ni Hibiku Kurisyuna Sanka: Samāju-gāyan* (*Devotional Songs for Krishna at a Haridās Temple: Samāj-gāyan*), Tokyo: 1992 . The original recordings were carried out in 1984.
8. T. Tanaka, 'Kita Indo ni Okeru Hindū Kyouto no Girei to Ongaku no Jissai (Practices of Hindu Rituals and Music in North India)', *Journal of the Association for the Study of Indian Music*, vols. 2-3, 1993, pp. 106-235; in Japanese with summary in English.
9. T. Tanaka, 'Hindū Kyouto no Shūdan Kayou Samāji-gāyan Kenkyū: Kami to Hito tono Rensa Kouzou (A Study of Samāj-gāyan; Congregational

Singing of the Hindus: The Chain-like System Connecting People with God)', dissertation, 1998 (unpublished).

10. T. Tanaka, *Hindu Kyouto no Shudan Kayou: Kami to Hito tono Rensa Kouzou (Congregational Singing of the Hindus: The Chain-like System Connecting People with God)*, Kyoto: Sekai Shisousha Pvt., 2008.
11. T. Tanaka, 'The Samāj-gāyan Tradition: Transmitting a Musico-Religious System in North India', in *Music and Society in South Asia: Perspectives from Japan*, Osaka: National Museum of Ethnology, 2008.
12. R.B. Qureshi, *Sufi Music of India and Pakistan: Sound, Context and Meaning in Qawwālī*, Cambridge: Cambridge University Press, 1986, p. 47.
13. Interview with Nirmani Bhatt Gosvami on 6 September 1996.
14. K. Kālelkar, ed., *Āśram-bhajanāvali*, Ahamadābād: Navajīvan Mudraṇālay, 1950, p. 104.
15. Thielemann, 'Devotional Poetry in Performance', pp. 559-74.
16. Tulsīdās Bābā, ed., *Śṛṅgār ras sāgar: Śrī rādhāvallabh jī kau varśotsav*, 4 vols, Vrindaban: Tulsīdās Bābā, 1956-62. This is an anthology of about 3,000 *pads*, used primarily within the Rādhāvallabha *sampradāya*, but also at the Madanmohan Temple (Bhaṭṭ jī kā mandir) of the Caitanya *sampradāya.*
17. The 'call-and-response style' is one of the most popular singing forms and recognized as the form sung by one leading singer and the chorus group alternately, and widely seen in the world in the workers' song, gospel music and so on,
18. Śrī Svāmī Haridās Sevā Sansthān, *Samāj śṛṅkhlā*, Vrindaban, 1981.
19. Tanaka, 'The Samāj-gāyan Tradition', 2008, p. 99.

BIBLIOGRAPHY

Kālelkar, Kākā, ed., *Āśram-bhajanāvali*, Ahamadābād: Navajīvan Mudraṇālay, 1950.

Qureshi, R.B., *Sufi Music of India and Pakistan: Sound, Context and Meaning in Qawwālī*, Cambridge: Cambridge University Press, 1986.

Sakata, T., M. Fukunaga, T. Hashimoto and T. Tanaka, 'Chijou no Tenkai o Aruku Hitobito (Pilgrims Aspiring for Unity with Krishna, the Hindu Deity of Justice and Love)', *Journal of Asian and African Studies,* vol. 37, 1989, pp. 69-121.

Slawek, S.M., 'Kirtan: A Study of the Sonic Manifestations of the Divine in the Popular Hindu Culture of Banaras', Ph.D. dissertation, University of Illinois, 1986.

——, 'Popular Kirtan in Benares: Some "Great" Aspects of a Little Tradition', *Ethnomusicology,* vol. 32, no. 2, 1988, pp. 249-64.

Snell, R., *The Eighty-four Hymns of Hita Harivaṁśa: An Edition of the Caurāsī Pada*, Delhi: Motilal Banarsidass and London: School of Oriental and African Studies, University of London, 1991.

Śrī Svāmī Haridās Sevā Sansthān, *Samāj śṛṅkhlā*, Vrindaban, 1981.

Tanaka, T., 'Hindū Kyouto no Shūdan Kayou Samāji-gāyan Kenkyū: Kami to Hito tono Rensa Kouzou (A Study of Samāj-Gāyan; Congregational Singing of the Hindus: The Chain-like System Connecting People with God)', dissertation, 1998 (unpublished).

——, *Hindu Kyouto no Shudan Kayou: Kami to Hito tono Rensa Kouzou (Congregational Singing of the Hindus: The Chain-like System Connecting People with God)*, Kyoto: Sekai Shisousha, 2008.

——, *Indo Haridāsu no Tera ni Hibiku Kurisyuna Sanka: Samāju-gāyan (Devotional Songs for Krishna at a Haridās Temple: Samāj-gāyan)*, Tokyo: JVC Corporation, 1992.

——, 'Kawwārī: Minami Asia no Sūfī no Uta (Qawwālī: Songs of Sufis in South Asia)', *Girei to Ongaku (Rituals and Music),* vol. 1, 1986, pp. 57-90.

——, 'Kita Indo ni Okeru Hinduukyouto no Girei to Ongaku no Jissai (Practices of Hindu Rituals and Music in North India)', *Journal of the Association for the Study of Indian Music,* vols. 2-3, 1993, pp. 106-235.

——, 'The Samāj-gāyan Tradition: Transmitting a Musico-Religious System in North India', in *Music and Society in South Asia: Perspectives from Japan, Senri Ethnological Studies*, 71, Osaka: National Museum of Ethnology, 2008, pp. 87-101.

Thielemann, S., 'Devotional Poetry in Performance: Samājagāyana at the Temple of Śrī Rādhāraman in Vrindaban', in *The Banyan Tree: Essays on Early Literature in New Indo-Aryan Languages*, ed. M. Offredi, Delhi: Manohar, 2000, pp. 559-74.

——, *Musical Traditions of Vaiṣṇava Temples in Vraja: A Comparative Study of Samāja and the Dhrupada Tradition of North Indian Classical Music*, Delhi: Sagar, Associated Book Centre, 2001.

——, *Singing the Praises Divine: Music in the Hindu Tradition*, Delhi: APH Publishers, 2000.

Tulsīdās Bābā, ed., *Śṛṅgār ras sāgar: Śrī rādhāvallabh jī kau varśotsav*, 4 vols, Vrindaban: Tulsīdās Bābā, 1956-62.

APPENDIX

Corrections in *The Millennium Kabīr Vāṇī*

WINAND CALLEWAERT

Working on the *Dictionary of Bhakti*[1] gave me an opportunity to consider and reconsider every single word in the *pad*-edition of Kabīr[2] that was part of the database. This produced a few corrections in the reading of the manuscripts, especially in the separation of words. The result of this careful study and a fresh comparison with the manuscripts is given in the list of corrections below.

(1) Mistakes in the Counting of the ** *pad*s and the * *pad*s.

On p. 75, in the section 'Seven Repertoires' the first line with 20 *pad*s (2, 3, 31 . . .) was wrongly marked as having ** (it should be *). Similarly, on p. 77, in the section 'Five Repertoires', the eighth line with 26 *pad*s (18, 22, 28 . . .) was wrongly marked as having ** (it should be *). These corrections should also be made in the Alphabetical First-line Index (pp. 65-73).

(2) The Text on p. 75

The text on p. 75 should read as follows:

Depending on the occurrence of a *pad* in a number of repertoires,

I have marked *pad*s as 'more or less popular around 1550', that is, one generation after the death of Kabīr.

48 *pad*s have three ***, suggesting a high probability of the *pad* belonging to a very early core because it is found in each of the repertoires and regions:

[1] the *Ādi-granth* and/or *Mohan Pothī*
[2] at least one *Pañc-vāṇī* manuscript (S, A, V)
[3] at least one *Sarvāṅgī* (Gop and/or Raj)
[4] C and/or J

51 *pad*s have two ** because the *pad* is found in the *Ādi-granth* and/or in the *Mohan Pothī,* and in at least 2 of [2] [3] [4].

141 *pad*s have one * because the *pad* is found only in Rajasthan (*Pañc-vāṇī* S, A, V; and/or *Sarvāṅgī*, Gop and/or Raj; and/or C, J) and not in Punjab (*Ādi-granth* and/or *Mohan Pothī).*

(3) Corrections in the Text Edition (pp. 115-629)

p. 118, *pad* 4 (S4, A4, V4)

1 षट दल कवल निवासिया । चंहुंकूं फेरि मिलाइ ।

should be

षट दल कवल निवासिया । चंहुं कूं फेरि मिलाइ ।

p. 121, *pad* 5 (S5, A5, V5, J90, C4)

4 साधे सिधि अैसी पाइऐ । क्यंबा होइ महोई ।

should be

साधे सिधि अैसी पाइऐ । क्यंबा होइ म होई ।

p. 135, *pad* 17 (S13)

2b सहंस अनेक छतीसौं धागा । निहिचै नाकै पोवै ।।

should be

सहंस अनेक छती सौं धागा । निहिचै नाकै पोवै ।।

p. 135, *pad* 17 (A15)

2b छसै सहंस इकीसौं धागा । निहचै नाकै पोवे ।।

should be

छ सै सहंस इकीसौं धागा । निहचै नाकै पोवे ।।

p. 136, *pad* 18 (S14)

3 यहु रस पीवै को गूंगां गंहिला । जाकी कोई न बूझै सीर रे ।

should be

यहु रस पीवै को गूंगां गंहिला । जाकी कोई न बूझै सार रे ।

p. 144, *pad* 26 (S21)

3b करि परिपंचं मुकट बधि या । किलि मिलि सबै मिटाई हो रांम ।

should be

करि परिपंचं मुकट बधि या । किलि किलि सबै मिटाई हो रांम ।

p. 151, *pad* 33 भौ जलि **should be read as** भौजलि

p. 163, *pad* 45 (S37)

a अब मेरी रांम कहैगी बलईया । जा मंण मरंण दोउ डर गईया ।। टेक।।

should be

अब मेरी रांम कहैगी बलईया । जामंण मरंण दोउ डर गईया ।। टेक।।

p. 163, *pad* 45 (A47)

a अव मेरी रांम कहैगी वलइया । जो मंन मरन दोऊ डर गइया ।। टेक।।

should be

अव मेरी रांम कहैगी वलइया । जोमंण मरन दोऊ डर गइया ।। टेक।।

pp. 173-4, *pad* 53 (all manuscripts): 1a वदौरे भाई should be वदौ रे भाई
(all manuscripts): 1a जौर should be जौ र

p. 176, *pad* 55 (A59)

3 तांमस विसमल भरम किं दूरी । पंचूं भषि ज्यौं होइ सवूरी ।

should be

तांमस विसमल भरम किंदूरी । पंचूं भषि ज्यौं होइ सवूरी ।

(V49)

3 बिसमिलि तांमस भरंम कं दूरी । पंचू भषि ले ज्यूं होइ सबूरी ।

should be

बिसमिलि तांमस भरंम कंदूरी । पंचू भषि ले ज्यूं होइ सबूरी ।

(Gop55;5)

3 बिसमिल तांमस भरम कूं दूरी । पंच भूषि ज्यूं होइ सबूरी ।

should be

बिसमिल तांमस भरम कूंदूरी । पंच भूषि ज्यूं होइ सबूरी ।

p. 179, *pad* 60 (S48)

4 इहि बनि बाजै मदन भेरि रे । वुहि बेनि बाजहि तूरा रे ।

should be

इहि बनि बाजै मदन भेरि रे । वुहि बंनि बाजहि तूरा रे ।

p. 205, *pad* 85

3 कहि कबीर को कोनहि राषे । रांम रसाइन जिन जिन चाषे ।

should be

कहि कबीर को को नहि राषे । रांम रसाइन जिन जिन चाषे ।

p. 208, *pad* 89 (all manuscripts): 4 देस माल वो should be read as देस मालवो

p. 211, *pad* 92 (all manuscripts): 3 पीवत म्रद न लाग should be read as पीवत म्रदन लाग

p. 219, *pad* 101 (all manuscripts)

3 कहै कबीर नट नाटि कथा के । मंदला कौंण बजावै ।

should be

कहै कबीर नट नाटिक थाके । मंदला कौंण बजावै ।

p. 225, *pad* 108 (S83)

1 किसकी ममा चचा को किसका । किसका पुगंरा जोई ।

should be

किसकी ममा चचा को किसका । किसका पुंगरा जोई ।

p. 227, *pad* 110 (all manuscripts): 0 घर घर वात should be read as घर घरवात

p. 233, *pad* 115 (S89; V86; Gop; Raj)

2b पुंजी बितडि बंदिलै दैहै । तब कहैं कौंन कै छूटै ।

should be

पुंजी बितडि बंदि लै दैहै । तब कहैं कौंन कै छूटै ।

p. 237, *pad* 120 (all manuscripts)

1 धूप दाझ तां छांहि तकाई । मति तरवरि सचु पांउं ।

should be

धूप दाझतां छांहि तकाई । मति तरवरि सचु पांउं ।

p. 264, *pad* 148 (all manuscripts)

है हरिजन स्यूं जगत स्यूं लरत है । फुनिगा कैसैं गरर भषत है ।। टेक

should be

है हरि जन स्यूं जगत स्यूं लरत है । फुनिगा कैसैं गरर भषत है ।। टेक

p. 265, *pad* 149 (all manuscripts)

1 आपन देही चरवा पांनी । ताहि नीदहि जाहि गंगां आंनीं ।

should be

आप न देही चरवा पांनी । ताहि नीदहि जाहि गंगां आंनीं ।

p. 266, *pad* 150 (S121)

2 अंधे कूपक दीयौ बताई । तरकि परै परि हरि न पत्याई ।

should be

अंधे कूप क दीयौ बताई । तरकि परै परि हरि न पत्याई ।

p. 270, *pad* 155 (S125; A134)

3 दूजा बणिज नही कछू बाषर । राम नाम तत दोउ आषर ।

should be

दूजा बणिजन ही कछू बाषर । राम नाम तत दोउ आषर ।

p. 275, *pad* 164 (all manuscripts)

0 संतौ सुरतैं नाद उतारै ।

should be

संतौ सुर तैं नाद उतारै ।

p. 283, *pad* 176 (all manuscripts)

4 बिनर जांनि प्रणवों परसोतंम । कहि कबीर रंगि राता ।

should be

बिन र जांनि प्रणवों परसोतंम । कहि कबीर रंगि राता ।

p. 289, *pad* 181 (all manuscripts)

6 ऐकनि गंध बासनां प्रगट । घट तैं रहै अकेला ।

should be

ऐक निर्गंध बासनां प्रगट । घट तैं रहै अकेला ।

p. 292, *pad* 184 (all manuscripts)

2 बिनहीं तालां ताल बजावै। बिन मंदिर पटताला ।

should be

बिनहीं तालां ताल बजावै। बिन मंदिर पट ताला ।

p. 295, *pad* 186 (all manuscripts;
see also Pītāmbaradatta Baḍathvāla, गोरख बानी, pad 17.4)

3 काटत बेली कूंपल मेल्ही । सींचत डांकु मिलांणीं ।

should be

काटत बेली कूंपल मेल्ही । सींचतडां कुमिलांणीं ।

p. 305, *pad* 195

2b कूकडौ मीनकी स्यूं लरै । झलपांणी दौरै ।
3 सुरही चूषै बाछातरि । बाछी दूध उतारै ।

should be

कूकडौ मीनकी स्यूं लरै । झल पांणी दौरै ।
सुरही चूषै बाछ़ा तरि । बाछी दूध उतारै ।

p. 312, *pad* 202 (also A178; V164)

1b नाद सरूप बरंण नहीं जाकै । घटि घटि रह्या समाई ।

should be

ना दस रूप बरं नहीं जाकै । घटि घटि रह्या समाई ।

p. 336, *pad* 223 (all manuscripts)

1b जंगल मैंहि के जंगम मारे । तूंर फिरैं अपरोगी ।

should be

जंगल मैंहि के जंगम मारे । तूं र फिरैं अपरोगी ।

p. 350, *pad* 241 (S189; A201)

4 भरी छाबरी मन बैकुंठा । सांई से तीरंगा ।

should be

भरी छाबरी मन बैकुंठा । सांई सेती रंगा ।

(V183; Gop)

4 भरी छाबड़ी मंन बैकूंठां । सांई सौं रहियौ रंगा ।

should be

भरी छाबड़ी मंन बैकूंठां । सांई सौंर हियौ रंगा ।

p. 352, *pad* 243 (all manuscripts)

1b कबहूं न सोवै काज सवारै । पांणं तिहारी माती

should be

कबहूं न सोवै काज सवारै । पांणंतिहारी माती ।

p. 358, *pad* 250

माला जपतां मन झूठौ मन । है कतर नीर हत छिपांयें । टेक ।

should be

माला जपतां मन झूठौ मन । है कतरनी रहत छिपांयें । टेक ।

p. 363, *pad* 256 (all manuscripts)

1 चारि षूंटी दोइ चमर षलाई । सहजि रहटवा दीया चलाई ।

should be

चारि षूंटी दोइ चमरष लाई । सहजि रहटवा दीया चलाई ।

p. 364, *pad* 258 (all manuscripts)

2 बाप साव कौ करत लरइया । माया सद मतिवारी ।

should be

बाप सावकौ करत लरइया । माया सद मतिवारी ।

p. 371, *pad* 266 (all manuscripts)

1 नांहूं ब्याही नांहूं कवारी । पूत जणौ द्यौंहारी ।

should be

नां हूं ब्याही नां हूं कवारी । पूत जणौ द्यौंहारी ।

p. 373, *pad* 268 (all manuscripts)

2b आये चोर तुरंग म ले गयें । मौरी राषत मुग्ध फिरै ।

should be

आये चोर तुरंगम ले गयें । मौरी राषत मुग्ध फिरै ।

p. 394, *pad* 286 (all manuscripts)

4b कबीर पनह षुदाइ की । रह दिगर दावानेस ।

should be

कबीर पनह षुदाइ की । रह दिगर दावा नेस ।

p. 395, *pad* 288 (all manuscripts)

1 यहु संसार हाट करि जांनौं । सब को बनिज न अया ।

should be

यहु संसार हाट करि जांनौं । सब को बनिजन अया ।

p. 401, *pad* 297 (all manuscripts)

नकटी कौ ठंण गंणबा डांडूं । कणैं सपूतै काटी तूं ।। टेक ।।

should be

नकटी कौ ठंणगंण बाडां डूं । कणैं सपूतै काटी तूं ।। टेक ।।

p. 426, *pad* 321 (all manuscripts)

1 कर गहि ऐक बिनांणी । ता भीतरि पंच प्रांणी ।

should be

करगहि ऐक बिनांणी । ता भीतरि पंच प्रांणी ।

2b जा तैं पासै छसैं तांणीं । तौ सुष स्यूं रहै परांणी ।

should be

जा तैं पा सै छ सैं तांणीं । तौ सुष स्यूं रहै परांणी ।

(A282 and following manuscripts)

3b तणि वुंणि मुरि तव कीन्हां । तव रांमराइ पूरा दीन्हां ।

should be

तणि वुंणि मुरितव कीन्हां । तव रांमराइ पूरा दीन्हां ।

p. 458, *pad* 354 (all manuscripts)

1b सोवत हीर जगाइयै । जागत भये उदास ।

should be

1b सोवत ही र जगाइयै । जागत भये उदास ।

p. 473, *pad* 367 (all manuscripts)

1b मरहठ लग सबलोक सगौ रे । हंस अकेलौ जाइ ।

should be

मरहठ लग सब लोक सगौ रे । हंस अकेलौ जाइ ।

p. 478, *pad* 371 (S289)

3 या जोगिया की जुगति सुजाणैं । सो सतगुर का चेला ।

should be

या जोगिया की जुगति सु जांणैं । सो सतगुर का चेला ।

(V324)

1 जोरत कटक जु घेरत सब गढ । करत बझेली झेला ।

should be

जोरत कटक जु घेरत सब गढ । करत ब झेली झेला ।

p. 495, *pad* 388 (all manuscripts)

4 अबरण बरंण स्यांम नही पीत। हां हू जाइ न गावै गीत।

should be

अबरण बरंण स्यांम नही पीत। हांहू जाइ न गावै गीत।

p. 499, *pad* 390 (all manuscripts)

1 सो सुलतांन जु दोइ सुरतांनै । बाहरि जीता भीतरि आंणै ।

should be

सो सुलतांन जु दोइ सुर तांनै । बाहरि जीता भीतरि आंणै ।

pp. 506, *pad* 397 (all manuscripts)

6b सहं सबाह के हरे परांन । दरजोधन घाल्यौ षैं मांन ।

should be

सहं सबाह के हरे परांन । दरजोधन घाल्यौ षैंमांन ।

p. 510, *pad* 400

1 माइ बाप कीनें ककुनंकांनी । सुसरहि मरि भरावे पांनी ।

should be

माइ बाप की नेंकु नं कांनी । सुसरहि मरि भरावे पांनी ।

p. 526, *pad* 415 (all manuscripts)

2 पारधी पणौ जे साधै कोई । अध षाधा सा राषै सोई ।

should be

पारधीपणौ जे साधै कोई । अध षाधा सा राषै सोई ।

pp. 557, *pad* 450 (all manuscripts)

3 कबीर बिचारि इहै डर डरिए । कहैं का होइ हांनैं मारिए ।

should be

कबीर बिचारि इहै डर डरिए । कहैं का हो इहां नैं मारिए ।

p. 558, *pad* 451 (all manuscripts; see below p. 574, *pad* 467)

3b कहै कबीर कुसमल हरै । मांहि लौ अंग पषालि रे ।।

should be

कहै कबीर कुसमल हरै । मांहि लौ अंग पषालि रे ।।

p. 562, *pad* 456 (all manuscripts)

2b तींनि जगाती करत रारि । चले हैं बंनिजू वा बंनिज झारि ।

should be

तींनि जगाती करत रारि । चले हैं बंनिजूवा बंनिज झारि ।

p. 574, *pad* 467 (see above p. 558, *pad* 451)

3b कहै कबीर कुसमल हरै । माहि लौ अंग पषालि रे ।।

should be

कहै कबीर कुसमल हरै । माहिलौ अंग पषालि रे ।।

p. 585, *pad* 480 (all manuscripts)

b जतंन करत पतंन है जैहै । भावै जांणिम जांणी ।। टेक ।।

should be

जतंन करत पतंन है जैहै । भावै जांणि म जांणी ।। टेक ।।

p. 586, *pad* 481 (all manuscripts)

1 अनदिन ग्यांन कथै घरियार । धूवां धौरह रहै संसार ।।

should be

अनदिन ग्यांन कथै घरियार । धूवां धौरहर है संसार ।।

p. 587, *pad* 483

1 उन देसि जइ बौरे बाबू । देषि बारे लोक किंनं किन षैबू ।

should be

उन देसि जइबौ रे बाबू । देषिबा रे लोक किंनं किन षैबू ।

4 जल बिन हंसनि सहि बिन रबू । कबीरै कौ स्वामी पाइ परिकै मनैंबू ।

should be

जल बिन हंस निसहि बिन रबू । कबीरै कौ स्वामी पाइ परिकै मनैंबू ।

pp. 595, *pad* 490 (all manuscripts)

बिरहीजंन कौ बालहौ सव सुष आनंद कंदौ रे ।। टेक ।।

should be

बिरही जंन कौ बालहौ सव सुष आनंद कंदौ रे ।। टेक ।।

p. 598, *pad* 494

1b अनहद सबद की गुरी बाजे । ता जोगी मन धीजै ।

should be

अनहद सबद कीगुरी बाजै । ता जोगी मन धीजै ।

4b कहै कबीर रमिता सूंरमणां । देही बादि न षोई ।
should be

कहै कबीर रमिता सूं रमणां । देही बादि न षोई ।

(4) First-line Index (pp. 27-64)

In the First-line Index of the *Millennium Kabīr Vāṇī* (pp. 27-64) I give on the right side, in bold, the numbering of the *pad*s in my edition, and to its immediate left the number in the edition of Mātā Prasād Gupta (*pad*s 1-384 on pp. 140-383), numbered by me consecutively. In the Gupta edition, however, the *pad*s are numbered within the *rāg*-section in which they are given in the manuscripts, starting each time with 1, and the consecutive, totalling number is only found at the end of each *rāg* section. This makes it very difficult to find in the Gupta edition the corresponding *pada* of my edition.

In order to facilitate research I give below (column 1) the consecutive numbers with which I numbered the *pad*s in the Gupta edition, and in column 2 the numbering within each *rāg*-section of the Gupta edition. It is to the consecutive numbers in column 1 that I refer when I refer to the Gupta edition in the First-line Index (pp. 27-64). In order to find the *pada* in the Gupta edition, one has to consult column 2.

Consecutive numbering	*rāg*-wise numbering in Gupta, (1969; repr. 1996)	Consecutive numbering	*rāg*-wise numbering in Gupta, (1969; repr. 1996)
	p. 140, गौड़ी	158	8
1	1	159	9
till	till	160	10
150	150	161	11
	p. 232, रामकली	162	12
151	1	163	13
152	2	164	14
153	3	165	15
154	4	166	16
155	5	167	17
156	6	168	18
157	7	169	19

170	20
171	21
172	22
173	23
	p. 250, रामकली
174	24
175	25
176	26
177	27
178	28
179	29
180	30
181	31
182	32
183	33
184	34
185	35
186	36
187	37
188	38
189	39
190	40
191	41
192	42
193	43
194	44
195	45
196	36
	p. 268, आसावरी
197	1
198	2
199	3
200	4
201	5
202	6
203	7
204	8
205	9
206	10
207	11
208	12
209	13
210	14
211	15
212	16
213	17
214	18
215	19
216	20
217	21
218	22
219	23
220	24
221	25
222	26
223	27
224	28
225	29
226	30
227	31
228	32
229	33
230	34
231	35
232	36
233	37
234	38
235	39
236	40
237	41
238	42
239	43
240	44
241	45
242	46
243	47
244	48
245	49
246	50
247	51
248	52
249	53
	p. 302, आसावरी
250	54
	p. 303, सोरठि
251	1
252	2
253	3

254	4	295	9
255	5	296	10
256	6	297	11
257	7	298	12
258	8	299	13
259	9	300	14
260	10	301	15
261	11	302	16
262	12	303	17
263	13	304	18
264	14	305	19
265	15	306	20
266	16		p. 336, मारू
267	17	307	1
268	18	308	2
269	19	309	3
270	20		p. 338, टोड़ी
271	21	310	1
272	22	311	2
273	23		p. 339, भैरूं
274	24	312	1
	p. 317, सोरठि	313	2
275	25	314	3
276	26	315	4
277	27	316	5
278	28		p. 343, भैरूं
279	29	317	6
280	30	318	7
281	31	319	8
282	32	320	9
283	33	321	10
284	34	322	11
285	35	323	12
286	36	324	13
	p. 325, केदारौ	325	14
287	1	326	15
288	2	327	16
289	3	328	17
290	4	329	18
291	5	330	19
292	6	331	20
293	7	332	21
	p. 325, केदारौ	333	22
294	8	334	23

335	24
336	25
337	26
338	27
339	28
340	29
341	30
342	31
343	32
344	33
345	34
346	35
347	36
	p. 360, बिलावल
348	1
349	2
350	3
351	4
352	5
353	6
354	7
355	8
356	9
357	10
	p. 367, ललित
358	1
359	2
360	3

	p. 369, बसंत
361	1
362	2
363	3
364	4
365	5
366	6
367	7
368	8
369	9
370	10
371	11
	p. 376, मालीगौड़ा
372	1
373	2
374	3
	p. 378, कल्याण
375	1
	p. 378, सारंग
376	1
	p. 379, मल्हार
377	1
378	2
	p. 380, धनाश्री
379	1
380	2
381	3
382	4
383	5
384	6

NOTES

1. W.M. Callewaert (with the assistance of S. Sharma), *Dictionary of Bhakti: North-Indian Bhakti Texts into Kharī Bolī Hindī and English*, 3 vols, Delhi: D.K. Printworld, 2009. A digital version is under preparation.
2. Ibid. (with the assistance of S. Sharma and D. Taillieu), *The Millennium Kabīr Vāṇī: A Collection of Pads*, Delhi: Manohar, 2000.

Index of Names and Works